Psychic and *Paranormal Phenomena* in *The Bible*

———————

The *True* Story

by

Ted Martin
Minister-At-Large[tm]

Copyright © 1997 by Ted Martin

published by

psychicspace.com*pany*

"the inner dimensions"

Psychic and Paranormal Phenomena
in The Bible

The *True* Story

Copyright © 1997 by Ted Martin

Library of Congress Catalog Card Number: 96-95063

ISBN: 0-9654413-0-X (hardback)
ISBN: 0-9654413-1-8 (paperback)

Published by

psychicspace.company
7051 Hwy 70 S #145
Nashville, TN 37221
615-662-4987 or 888-psi-is-it / fax: 615-646-9152

http://www.psychicspace.com
publisher@psychicspace.com

"the inner dimensions"

Ted Martin is available for lectures, workshops, and consultation. Please contact publisher.

Disclaimer: Author has made responsible efforts to accurately render Biblical passages. Any errors or misinterpretations are solely the providence of the author and are hereby humbly apologized for.

Acknowledgments

Thank you, God, for choosing me as one of your wordgicians, and for the passions of this questing trade!

To my mother, Shirley Marian Ciuba, who caught me to believe that paranormal phenomena like angels, messages, Gods, visions, and synchronicities are normal. To steady, prudent, intelligent, providing Ted – Theodore John Ciuba – my Dad, who gave us the gift of a natural transition during the final months of this manuscript.

To my children: Alysha Beth Ciuba, Miranda Angel Estrada, Ted² – Theodore Martin Ciuba II, and one I would wish so, Abril Denison-Rueda. *My love for you is eternal!*

To the spiritual teachers who have coaxed my awareness beyond conventionally promulgated box-thinking: my grandmother, Dee Cutting, living in L.A., who was my first true metaphysical master this lifetime, Merlin, Saint-Germain, the Rosicrucian Order, the Great White Brotherhood, Unity, and Religious Science. Among them, firewalkers Tolly Burkan, Peggy Dylan, and Michael McDermott.

To the women who shared my life, my dreams, and my hopes for this day: K. Judy Melgoza-Ciuba, who for great years gave me what makes this book possible, her love and encouraging support; Debbie Webb, true friend, whose unquestioning belief bolstered me through the months and the years and the minutiaes of weariness and passion that roller-coaster through such a long-term project; Sharon Modena, blessed mother of our children, for raising them and giving me the freedom to engage the life of adventure, scholasticism, and writing; Karen Dorroll, stunning ladie, the one who selected the book's final title; Clarice Reavis, for her unbridled love of me and the project, who with honor gave her sensitive reading and critiquing of the manuscript and suggested promotional copy.

To the men who have inspired me most, from childhood to today, King Arthur, Sir Lancelot, and Sir Percival. As a writer, Shakespeare; as a proactive person, ever-crafty Odysseus.

To Dr Arvilla Taylor, who respected my brutally raw talent at twenty-one. Ron Hawthorne, uncle and writing buddy, *Here's to you!* To the giants in my life, men like Ted Nicholas, Michael Enlow, Ken Roberts, and Larry Williams, all who started out determinedly with a dream, wobbly credit cards, and persistent effort, for helping me believe that I could do it too.

Students, friends, and associates throughout the years, angels, guides, and mentors, you are too numerous to mention, but I thank you, extending to you also,

All Blessings!

Ted Martin, Minister-at-Large
20 March 1997

Dedication

"I Will Love One Woman Only"

Though we dispersed a thousand years ago,
I was one of the blessed select
Pledging my honour and my life
To Arthur and the Table Round.

And so meaningful was it
That yet today I enshrine these standards
Imposed by that inspired King
And his high ideals - beacons both of a New Age.

And though I'm not free to share the contents
Of that solemn oath we sware,
Know that a part of it pertains to womankind....
And seeing you, portions of the oath return:

"And I will love one woman only, and serve her,
For years, if necessary, to win her love;
Ever the same, won or delayed,
From youth to age I dedicate my days."

Ted Martin

Psychic and *Paranormal Phenomena* *in* The Bible

The *True* Story

Table Of Contents

Psychic and Paranormal Phenomena in The Bible
The *True* Story

Your Adventure Through Psychicspace Starts Here

V ast truths lie concealed in plain view.
The same parable plain to the pure of heart puzzles the profane. Alas, it is not *hearing* that delivers the promise. Most do not understand, being previously committed to unexamined positions. Though they surely possess the capacity, they have long since diminished access to it.

Jesus, however, reveals the deeper meaning in his stories to his apostles, because they earnestly seek spiritual understanding.

> *"To* you *it has been given to know the secrets of the kingdom of God."*
> (Lk. 8.10)

The gospels proclaim that these individuals do come to *perceive.*

We are like the apostles. And on this special psychicspace tour we get the insider's picture of the psychic dimension of life and spirituality. With our earnest desire we open to the truth, even if it comes slowly. We want to correct a myriad of misunderstandings concerning the psychic gifts. You can learn to hear the message and the truth. Even more, you can learn to feel in your soul, in the elevated realms of spiritual dominion. You have indicated your willingness by purchasing your ticket today.

We will stop at some psychicsites and visit for a while. We will do some research and linger while certain psychic insights feather into our being. At other psychicsites we will just have the need or opportunity to do the equivalent of a touch-and-go, happy all the while, integrating every experience into our developing awareness of psychicspace. As your grateful guide for this tour, I'll do everything my inspiration and my craft empower me to do.

God Communicates With Us Through The Psychic Gifts

Most Christians hold that the Bible is the revealed word of God. Most spiritually discerning individuals hold the document, in spite of its multitudinous inaccuracies, as an inspired piece. Only the ignorant ridicule it.

The Bible contains thousands of revelations. The psychic channel, of course, is *the* channel for messages from God. Indeed, we see that the psychic arts are practiced extensively by the divine and divinely inspired characters and writers of our waybook, this compilation called the Bible, and that they are beneficial and natural.

Among a multitude of other Biblical characters, Joseph is psychic, Samuel is psychic, David keeps Gad on retainer as a psychic, Isaiah is psychic, Ezekiel is psychic, Daniel is psychic, Peter is psychic, John is psychic. And, yes, Jesus is psychic. And when he appears today, whether in the stigmata on a fanatic's body or to someone's inner sight, it is a psychic event.

It is *because* of the marvels associated with their psychic abilities that we accord these individuals the status we do, *not in spite of it!* Isn't that a marvel? Psi facility is a sign of spiritual development.

It's also interesting to note that the *entire Bible* is a *channeled document.* No one has ever made the claim that God came to Earth and with his own stylus scribed characters on documents of rolled papyrus... He works from beyond the material realm. This one consideration alone proves the point that God works through the psychic channels.

Always I have known, instinctively, intuitively, that telepathy, clairvoyance, prophecy, divination, and magic are Godly gifts. I needed no justification in *my* heart. But neither did I have a logical argument for those who challenged me. Reading the Bible with an understanding heart has changed that.

We turn 180^0. Far from being the negative or evil realm some people believe it to be – the psychic dimension is the very channel established and used by God to communicate with humanity! The psychic arts are therefore, the *essence of Divinity* to us incarnates.

The Bible establishes that mediums, divination, clairvoyance, esp, telepathy, and magic are real abilities. The Bible does not condemn psychic skills. In bluntest contradiction to that thesis, the Bible shows that psychic skills are a natural concomitant to the spiritual life. Not the masses, who like to be led, but a representative number – normal people, surely – all through the Bible demonstrate them. It's a small jump to make to then recognize that, since the Bible is speaking to us, all people have and can use psychic abilities.

God Is Speaking Through These Scriptures

Our humble efforts compass but a sensitive rational reading appertaining to the paranormal in the Bible. We are not out to prove the Bible is or is not "true," any more than we would attempt to prove any treasured collection of fairy tales, myths, or stories revered by a culture is true. We are not here to feel good judging and second guessing the editorial motives of church patriarchs of antique eras. We accept the premise of the millions who hold the Bible so esteemed – God is the author. None can argue that he is the main character.

Interestingly enough, however, you don't need to subscribe to the principle of Divine authorship to get the benefit either the Bible or this present work offers. You don't need to be a "believer" to benefit. It matters little whether you believe the Bible is the only "Word of God" or not. It matters little whether you believe in *this God,* or even whether you believe in God at all.

Whether it is the *only* inspired word is preposterous. Those with right eyes see God's word even in the very stones and grassy glades. And I won't tell you what a comparative religions student would think of the Bible, whether as a document or philosophy it is any more or any less inspired than any of the variety of other sacred writings. I can't tell you what an interstellar visionary would say about it, either. For our purposes, these are considerations which we choose not to engage.

The Bible is a grand storybook. This is *psi-fi*. Front to back it's riddled with discrepancies and inaccuracies. Wouldn't you find it hard to believe God is making errors of significance? "Truthfulness" is a relative term. Every thing from the arching theme of the story to the tiny artifact communicates something. The details of the stories are chosen as symbols, signs, and theme developers. The truth is embodied, not in the facts, but in the stories, images, dialogues, commands, and discourses. Every one is a store house, a treasure trove, a thick round tower – guarded by the dragons of misconception, fear, training, and ignorance. My literary friends call it *faction*. Neither wholly fact, nor wholly fiction, it is incident crafted to intent.

Those who recognize this are in a position to receive the authentic value therein. An understanding heart, is the "open sesame," the mystical key, to celebrating with the riches that are here.

Embedded in this supposition is the obvious fact that God is God, the omnipresent being, alive at every moment, simultaneously, *still* speaking to us, not about a dead past, but in the ever-living present. Would you expect anything less from the Divine?

The Bible is written for us, humanity. Not for our forbears alone. True, the stories, poetry, and prophecies all are embedded in particular historical situations. That's the way life is lived. The Bible is a literary rendering of the spiritual development of a select people. Not a fact book. Though its setting is the ancient Middle East, its location is everywhere, its time, always.

Will you agree that life did not stop 1900 years ago? Will you agree that humans did not stop loving one another 1900 years ago? Then shouldn't we recognize that spiritual revelation and the psychic-spiritual life did not stop suddenly 1900 years ago, either?

Authored from the heart of God, designed with the specific intent to inform, guide, and persuade us on spiritual matters, the stories of the Bible speak with mythic significance. The boundaries of the material world do not confine the Spirit and the soul. Spirit touches all points in the nonlocal though the local, the timeless through the timebound. This can be simple. Even as we read today, for instance, a living Jesus *is* teaching. Isn't he?

God *still* speaks directly to us. There are people today who are undergoing similar experiences and revealing similar and progressive insights as the patriarchs, the prophets, Jesus, the apostles, and the disciples. With the increased attending to such works as this, with the developing spirituality within large segments of the world's populace, there is more of this happening today than ever before. You are among this blessed group.

God is not dead.

The Psychic Gifts

We can benefit from a non-exhaustive definition of the terms we use throughout this book. Most of this should sound familiar to you.

When we identify and discuss different gifts we are but discussing various ways the One Universal Reality expresses. There is a mystical unity among the differing manifestations of particular phenomena.

Webster, the Cognitive Sciences Lab, Rhine, Rosicrucian Order AMORC, the Association for Research and Enlightenment, *et al.* helped with the following definitions:

Anomalous Cognition (AC): a form of information transfer in which all known sensorial stimuli are absent. Access to information from events outside the range of the senses. *ESP.* The sixth sense.

Anomalous Mental Phenomena (AMP): a general term that includes AC and AP. Also known as *PSI.*

Anomalous Perturbation (AP): a form of interaction with matter in which all known physical mechanisms are absent. This phenomenon is also known psychokinesis (PK). Magic.

astrology: the science and art of discerning the meaning to humans and human affairs of the position or movement of celestial phenomena, mainly the stars and planets.

channeling: the most widely practiced psychic arts in the Bible stories. The entire Bible is a channeled document. All of the prophets channeled their messages.

Channeling is receiving a message from one being or force and transmitting it to another. The prophets receive impressions from God and convert them into words for the people of their time. They transmit God's message, much as a radio today might channel some electromagnetic impressions in the atmosphere into organized sound audible at a specific location.

clairvoyance: knowledge of a distant time or location acquired through extrasensory perception. Can involve the present, the past, or the future – that is, simulcognition, .retrocognition, or precognition.

divination: involves using some physical plane device or occurrence to discern God's will. Because the items are consecrated to God, God does the choosing and indicating. There are a multitude of divination instances in the Bible. During the various Biblical stories God uses stones, lots, arrows, and animal livers to reveal his will.

Today people more commonly consult the Tarot, the I-Ching, the message in a random page from the Bible, and the like. Though specific magical artifacts differ from time to time and culture to culture, the practice is essentially the same.

ESP. see *extrasensory perception.*

extrasensory perception (ESP): the ability to acquire information without using the known senses. Real-life experiences that appear to involve ESP are commonly termed psychic experiences. *Anomalous cognition.* See also clairvoyance, precognition, retrocognition, telepathy, the sixth sense.

ESP is an acronym, a term made from the first letters of the words *extra-sensory perception. Extra* means "above," "beyond," or "super."

ESP, proper, deals with the receptive arm of psychic phenomena. Its very name says so. ESP is distinguished from PK, the active or outgoing arm.

On another level, ESP actually embraces all psychic phenomena. The term seems to shapeshift into *extra-sensory phenomena.* In this sense each of the psychic gifts are particular manifestations of ESP. They each have their own characteristics and qualities.

healing: another of the psychic gifts. The kind of healing that occurs in the Bible – and occurs among spiritually awakened people forever – is accomplished through prayer and the transfer of energies.

Jesus does much of his healing by the laying on of hands. Yet he tells the apostles at one point that certain healing can only be accomplished by prayer: *"This kind can not be driven out by anything but prayer"* (Mk. 9.29). Clearly, there is a hierarchy of power in psychic activity/healing.

This subject is by itself so large that it merits a separate book. On our current adventure we only cursorily visit healing and the healing principles.

hypnosis: state wherein one is particularly suggestible. May exhibit signs of trance behavior or may appear to act with total waking awareness.

intuition: art or process of coming to direct knowledge or certainty without rational processing.

magic: causing events to occur by the use of mental-spiritual directives. Psychokinesis (PK) *is* magic. When Elijah commands the lightning, he performs magic. By the utilization of his mental directives, he commands fire.

mystical: 1) having a spiritual meaning, existence, reality, or comparable value that is neither apparent to the senses nor obvious to the intelligence. 2) of, resulting from, or manifesting an individual's direct or intimate knowledge of a communion with God.

paranormal: not scientifically explainable within the classical model of reality; beyond normal; supernatural.

parapsychology: the science that lies *beside* or *beyond* psychology -- studies paranormal experiences and capabilities.

PK: see *psychokinesis.*

precognition: knowledge of the future gained through esp.

psi: taken together, all of the ESP and PK phenomena. Anomalous mental phenomena. Communication and movement occurring beyond the normal confines of the physical senses. Represented by the Greek letter psi, Ψ.

psyche: the vital principle of corporeal matter that is a distinct mental or spiritual entity that is co-extensive with but independent of body or soma, soul, and self.

psychic: 1) of, arising in, or relating to the psyche. 2) not physical or organic. 3) a person sensitive to nonphysical or supernatural forces and influences. 4) one who receives or practices any of the *paranormal* arts and sciences; one who, either intentionally or spontaneously, experiences any form of the psi phenomena of ESP and PK.

psychical: of or pertaining to things of the realm of psi.

psychokinesis (PK): less common than ESP, is the direct influence of the human mind on the environment. Mind over matter. Anomalous perturbation (AP). Magic.

reincarnation: the phenomenon in which the human being who dies is born again as a human. Reincarnationists hold that we move through a train of embodiments acquiring more sublime truths or spiritual functions, much as we progress through grades in the school system.

This also is one of the family of psychic phenomena in the Bible. It is a subject of sufficient magnitude that we treat of it in another book.

retrocognition: knowledge of the past gained through esp.

sixth sense: extrasensory perception, clairvoyance.

spiritual: of, relating to, or consisting of spirit; of the nature of spirit rather than material.

synchronicity: an "amazing coincidence" that is not coincidental. By objective reckoning, there is no visible connection between two independent events, however, there are organic correlations operating at/from the spiritual level.

telepathy: discerning the thoughts, feelings, intentions of other people through esp.

teleportation: moving (portation) over a distance (tele). It involves being or getting somewhere without using the conventional modes of travel, which during Biblical times were primarily walking and assing.

Psychic phenomena are subjective, right-brain phenomena, of the spiritual realm.

"As We Prepare..."

All will have a good time. While we're still near home port, we ought to discuss a few preliminary matters. One big issue that usually comes up early in any discussion of psychic phenomena with "believers" concerns the direct Biblical proscriptions against the psychic arts. We will see the true story on that one. We must likewise address Jesus, a distinct, even Godly, case. He demands special considerations.

We will also consider a number of other things, including the question as to why there even exists this misunderstanding and mislabeling of psychic phenomena. We will chat a little about the *art* aspect of evoking psi phenomena, the testament factor, and the gender of God, among other things.

What About The Biblical Prohibitions Against The Psychic Arts?

Every sincere reader will want to know how to reconcile the apparent Biblical injunctions against divination and the psychic arts. I frequently encounter militant misunderstandings of the Biblical proscriptions. Those who object usually misquote a passage to prove their point, but even when they get the literal statement (translated and edited) correct they are still rendering it wrongly. The real need calls for discernment. Looking more closely, we will see that we can't just egregiously condemn the psychic arts entire.

Deuteronomy, the "Book of the Law," inveighs against prophets, psychics, dreamers, miracle workers, and diviners. Most of the "evil" you have heard against the psychic arts has its roots and its supposed Biblical support therein. But when we examine the passages of this book, its message, and its author, we find it's not war against practitioners of the psychic arts – of which the followers of Yahweh make a great and influential number – but against those who would persuade his people to worship God under a *different form*.

Yes, God says that the psychics, channelers, and dreamers "shall be put to death" (Dt. 13.5). But he says a lot of other things, too. This is also the chapter in which God, reconsidering his earlier demands for utter destruction of the peoples that live on the land the Jews are taking, says that if the inhabitants of a city are peaceable and unable or undisposed to make war with you... Perfect! – *You'll need slaves!*

> "These peaceful peoples you shall enslave to your will, your profit, and your leisure!" (Dt. 20.10-11)

God also changes his mind about what to do with the populace of resisting towns. The new rules are that now, instead of utter destruction, they only need kill the males. They can keep the attractive and serviceable females for their favors (Dt. 20.14).

Further, females of the tribe are forbidden in this chapter from wearing any men's clothing... *Levi*'s included. Woman who do are an abomination... And you surely know the consequences of that feeling of righteous hatred in God's heart.

And any woman who is not a virgin on her wedding night shall be cast onto her father's front porch and there the men of the city shall stone the bitch to death (Dt. 22.20-21). Do you believe this?

And no child born out of wedlock shall ever be allowed to enter the Temple or church. Vile pollution! Nor shall any child's child of any child's child of any child's child of any child's child of any child's child of any child's child even to the tenth generation – approximately 300 years – that has any trace of this person's blood in them be allowed to enter the worship of God. Hm-m-m.

Also, when it's time to go number two, you have to do it outside. First, you take your stick, that you always keep with your weapons, dig a hole, drop it in, and "turn back and cover up your excrement" (Dt. 23.13). Do you know anybody who still does it outside? Do you know anybody who believes you *should*?

In the midst of such drivel Moses says,

> "There shall not be found among you any one ... who practices divination, a soothsayer, or an augur, or a sorcerer, or a charmer, or a medium, or a wizard, or a necromancer. For whoever does these things is an abomination to the Lord; and because of these abominable practices the Lord your God is driving them out before you. For these other peoples give heed to soothsayers and to diviners; but as for you, the Lord your God has not allowed you so to do." (Dt. 18.10-14)

Can we take him at his word here? It's been forty years since his heyday. Who knows what a man is thinking when he's 120 years old? His prohibitions and concerns seem way off base to us today. We can't believe a God would inspire us to steal a land at the red edge of bloodshed and booty or to actually *kill* a young bride on her wedding night.

Perhaps Moses goes overboard. Perhaps he gets petty and cranky in his final days. It's a common enough ending. *Bless him.*

But he continues. After himself, Moses says, there shall come another. This chosen one shall be a child who channels. God says through Moses,

> "I will put my words in his mouth, and he shall speak to people all that I command him." (Dt. 18.18)

First, in the very act of channeling through his instrument, God condemns channeling. Then he promises the very thing he seems to condemn, another, after Moses, like Moses, who will serve as the mouthpiece of Divinity. So? We can only fall into error by being too obtuse to understand the connection and the sense in which God is speaking his prohibitions and punishments. We may indeed have the truth laid bare before our eyes, yet lack comprehension.

Here's the way it is. He sets it up, identifying the psychic:

> "If a channeler appears among you, or a clairvoyant, and gives you a sign or a wonder, and the sign or wonder which he tells you comes to pass..." (Dt. 13.1-2)

Then he moves to the crux of the matter:

> "And if he says 'Let us go after other Gods, and let us serve them...'" (Dt. 13.2)

Herein is the crime. It's not dreams, divination, sorcery. It's an issue of Godforms. Moses does not want the people worshiping God under any form but the one his ethnocentric positioning leads him to believe is the *only* one.

Remember, the Jewish big push for millennia now has been to retain a firm racial identity – with or without a homeland. *Anything* that would encourage cultural assimilation *out-of-the-fold* is anathema. It's not the psychic arts themselves – of which Moses is an adept, a soothsayer, a diviner, and a sorcerer – that are bad. Moses but singles out one identified use of the arts to which he objects.

To say that Moses is condemning the psychic arts in general, and not just a misuse of them, would make as much sense as to argue that a physician who disapproves of the illegal drug traffic is opposed to drugs.

How do the blood-stained, slobbering pulpit preachers so misconstrue the passage, trying to convince you otherwise?

A Rose By Any Name Smells As Sweet

There is no static universal language. Words and meanings are in ceaseless fluctuation, much like some dynamic electrical charge blowing from the poles of the earth. We frequently use different words for the same thing.

We can drive a car, an auto, a vehicle, a four-door, a convertible, or wheels. I've heard people refer to their big loosely enduring cars as a *whale* or a *bus.* Whatever the word, the meaning is the same. What English speakers call a tree, Spanish speakers call un *arbol*. A different name does not make it a different thing. A rose by any name smells as sweet.

Now let's cast this in a modern light. Many of the Biblical prophet-characters are advisors to kings and statesmen, as well as to ordinary people. Today we seldom use the word *prophet*, to refer to a person who utters inspired truths, even though they are doing identically the same thing. Not the substance, not the action, but the *words* have changed.

This evolution of terms has been occurring time immemorial. There are even clear Biblical precedents for this:

> In days gone by in Israel, when a man wished to consult God, he would say, 'Let us go to the seer.' For what is nowadays called a *prophet* used to be called a *seer*. (1 Sam. 9.9)

And, what is nowadays called a *psychic* used to be called a *prophet*. Names and terms always change. The underlying reality is the same. Seer, prophet, channeler, soothsayer, psychic – all the same. Magician, miracle worker, sorcerer, wizard – all the same.

Another instance. Many of the prophets are speaking the words of God or some other figure. They often speak the words of an angel, who in turn is speaking the words of God. This occurs with Moses and John, among others. This they called *prophecy*. We seldom use the term; today, the identical practice is called *channeling*. Calling it prophecy rather than channeling does not change the essential nature of it. Nor does calling it channeling rather than prophecy.

Using different terms can lead us into the trap that Jesus calls us on, having eyes, but not the sight; possessed of ears, devoid of hearing.

We need the archeologist's mind to see the similar in the different. "Judge not by appearances." The Catholics, for instance, call it ritual when they do it, and magic when others do it. But what ever name you give to it, the essence of magic is directing phenomena by the use of thought and words. The magical incantations their priests chant over their altars call the Christ spirit into the receptive bread and wine, transforming them into the actual mystical body and blood of the Christ.

Calling it a miracle rather than magic does not change the essential nature of it. Calling it mystical rather than magical does not change the essential nature of it. Saying it is a tradition instituted by Christ does not change the essential nature of it.

Tremendous things follow from this recognition.

Why Psi?

We take the lens to psychic phenomena simply because it is our desire at this moment.

Surely the psychic domain of the Bible's wisdom is not all there is to it. No claims are made to blow anything out of proportion. In examining this domain closely we are like the scientist who takes the sun's rays through a prism and then focuses on examining in profound depth the indigo light. Right at the outset, we see, the sun's light is not what it appears to be. The Bible and the light manifest as a synergy, but it's possible to separate the major components making the whole and consider them separately.

The scientist is not discounting the value of the other rays of the spectrum. What the scientist does, while not an everyday occurrence for ordinary people with run-of-the day concerns, can easily be accomplished by anyone. Neither are we discounting the value of the other realms of wisdom, grace, God, and insight in the Bible nor making any special claims to special talents and abilities that everyone can't activate.

Because psi is *exciting*, that's why.

Why Do We Call Them *Psychic "Arts"*?

When we call them *psychic arts* we do so in recognition of the fact that the consistent evocable enjoyment of these phenomena becomes accessible through an individual's conscious exercise of both *innate* and *acquired faculties*. Conscious direction of psi is accomplished by opening and using both the heart and the head, intuition and the intellect.

Once we recognize the gift, we may apply ourselves to improve the flow and effectiveness of it, just as an artist, once she's felt the initial stirrings of the sculptor's urge, might enroll in classes and dedicate her time in the development of her art.

This is ever the way of art.

How Much Psychic Activity In The Bible!

From its first to its final pages the Bible, as a mystical document, is filled with psychic occurrences. Yet even while psychic phenomena is the subject of this present work, we cannot list all its occurrences. It would be pointless. It would be repetitious. There are many more events – the listing and explanation of which, were they written, would fill so many books the Library at Paris could not hold them all. This work is not meant to be a psychic concordance or index.

Yet, while not exhaustive, it certainly is thorough. The selections teach much about the psychic arts. In that thoroughness it is also suggestive. Once your perception is awakened, read the Bible yourself. You will discover countless other psychic incidents and psychic insights. And as joyously, you will see the psychic drama playing about you in your life.

The Testament Factor

Psychic activity occurs in the Bible from its first pages to its last. We will cover these two terminals and points between.

There may actually be more psi activity recorded in the Old Testament than in the New Testament. "Stop right there!" I occasionally hear, "we don't use the Old Testament anymore!" The implication is that anything coming from the Old Testament is automatically invalid. This objection is easy to answer. Don't churches actively promulgate the *Ten Commandments*? They are in *Exodus*, the *second* book of the Old Testament, and among the *oldest*. Come to think of it, how many Christian churches have you ever seen that do not subscribe to and use the *entire* book, Old Testament and New Testament integrated together?! Also, remember that for some of our brethren, the Old Testament *is* the Bible!

However, there are a couple of things to consider along these lines. First, though there are more incidents of psi in the Old Testament than in the New, any imputed disparity is offweighed by the fact that Jesus performs the most perfected psi of all. Jesus is the flower of perfection of the development of the psychic arts. Then there are the apostles and the disciples....

Further, in the time of Jesus, Paul, and the apostles, if dramas of psi are not so frequently *individually* storied it is because psi is so taken for granted. They are frequently lumped together as the practices of Jesus and a large number of apostles or disciples as "signs and wonders" (Acts 2.43; Acts 4.30; Rom. 15.19; Heb. 2.4, etc.). In the New Testament prophecy is a matter of common course – as is healing.

The difference is a function of the purpose and structure of the two great divisions of the Bible. The Old Testament concentrates on teaching by stories and illustrations. The New Testament concentrates on teaching by principles as well. These are different and valid ways to reach the heart and mind of spiritual seekers. Living the corroboration of the two is beneficial, embedded in the timelessness of the mythic present.

Biblical Sources

The Bible is my source for this book. Not to mention what I studied during the years of my development, during the research and writing of this book I engaged various Bibles. I studied conventional interpretations as well as non-conventional interpretations. I recommend this for the sincere Biblical student. It will really open up your eyes.

I must admit, however, that all of my Biblical sources are rather recent English translations. We all know how much can get lost or recast in a translation. Even the "source" documents we have in Hebrew, Aramaic, Greek, and Latin are not originals. They are just closer to the source. Even only in English – *Read them, you will see!* – the same passage in different versions can seem to say something vastly different. You will see how much difference an editorial slant affects what is written.

Congruent with my mission, I wanted a Biblical source that would be readily available to everyone and that, in itself, didn't provoke too much controversy. After all, Biblical psi can be controversial enough. Therefore I chose to use several of the currently most widely subscribed to versions. The *Revised Standard Version* has been my primary source. The highly readable *New English Bible* has been my secondary font.

Because of its pivotal position as the first sanctioned English translation in the Euro-American religious tradition, I frequently consulted the original 1611 printing of the *King James Version*. However, because its archaic and poetic structure makes it difficult for the average reader, the actual material taken from it is limited. I also pull a small number of quotes from *The Living Bible, The New International Version*, and the *American Standard Version*. Finally, as a literary-Biblical scholar, I've done some minor crafting of my own, generally to change the tense.

If, when you run to your Bible to authenticate a reading, what you see does not match exactly what you see quoted in this book, recognize that our sources are manifold. Look beyond the Bible you happen to use most commonly. Also, look to read the spirit of the passage, rather than solely the words.

All of these Bibles and more, plus a wide array of other spiritual/metaphysical books and gifts, are available through **psychicspace.com***pany.* You can log on at **http://www.psychicspace.com**, or, if you prefer, call, write, or fax requesting *free* information on the Bibles we offer you.

Disclaimer: This book makes extensive use of Biblical quotations and citations. I've made sincere efforts to accurately identify the source and to properly render each quoted passage. Any errors, omissions, or misinterpretations are my own, and are hereby humbly apologized for.

Enough Errors Analysis

One lament I consistently hear from those who are aware of the transmissional gaps, errors, translations, and editorial adjustments in the Bible, is that it's such a shame we don't have the Bible in its pristine purity. What of it? First of all, it didn't happen that way. The history of the construction of the Bible, which is available information to all who seek it, indicates that there never was a pristine version, anyway. Second, and by far the more crucial consideration is, *look at how much we do still have! So much* spiritual good still shines through!

The Divine Creative Loving Intelligence knew better than to charge the folly of humanity, governments and churches, to pass these Truths along, so he inscribes his very Spirit inside these poetic and prophetic verses. This literature, diffused widely enough already to escape the clutches of
religious bigotry and political intolerance, enshrines the message of Divinity.

The Special Case: Jesus As A Metaphor

Jesus, by any standard, is unique. Probably the majority of people who encounter this book consider him God. Not just *a* God, but *God.* Now, is this a special case? *Yes* or *yes?!!*

Just by virtue of being a God, like all the other Gods throughout the history of the different cultures, Jesus possesses superhuman attributes. Different Gods have different powers. For instance, not counting the ascension, when he is already dead and therefore ethereal anyway, Jesus never flies. Yet Mercury possesses a super skill of flying. Goddess of the Parthenon, Athena, needs no flight. She just magically appears in different places, stepping from the veil of the Spirit realms.

So, since Jesus is taken as a God, we can hardly hold the things he does as attainable by mere mortals. Or can we?

Jesus is arguably the most highly developed human alive, the one who expresses the spiritual-psychic gifts in their fullest flower. Jesus is the compassionate teacher, a man who understands humanity and Divinity; a man who teaches, guides, and motivates us. But Jesus, other than by development, taken at his own words, is no different than us. Jesus never claims any special powers or relationships for himself that he doesn't also attribute to us. Jesus freely admits,

"It is not I, but the Father within who does the works." (Jn. 14.10)
Jesus is the one who reminds us that we ourselves are Gods:

"Ye are Gods." (Jn. 10.34)
Jesus is the one, recall, who says to us reiteratively,

"Everything that I'm doing... *you* can do, too. Hey, even *greater* things than *these*!" (Jn. 14.12)

Jesus is the one who awakens our awareness that we are *one in the identical Divinity* with him (Jn. 17.20-26). With the awareness of our Divinity, such as Jesus possesses, we can begin in small ways to approach the house which Jesus, going on ahead, opens for us.

If Jesus claims no special position over and beyond that which he freely invites us to recognize for ourselves, then what can he be? A God? *The* God? He never says so, nor do his actions indicate such. A teacher? He *is* a teacher, aware.

Jesus' purpose on Earth, encompassing compassionate love and healing to all whom his day touches, is to demonstrate the higher life, thereby teaching its existence and the pathway there.

Undoubtably, the most visible trait of Jesus' ministry is healing. The stories are so multitudinous and so widely circulating that we don't need to repeat them here. But he does more. Jesus demonstrates his magical abilities in other ways also – *Get ready!* We'll enjoy visiting a number of his stupendous psychicsites!

He teaches that we, like him, can activate our psychic abilities. He specifically practices telepathy, mental healing, clairvoyance, channeling, and magic, all of which we visit in the appropriately denominated chapters. But he does more...

He also teaches those possessed of higher sensitivities, for he seeks to commission workers in the harvest. For those in this category he reveals his high consciousness by teaching the power of prayer, belief, forgiveness, and love.

He teaches by parable, a story form in which the characters and events in the story represent others. There is meaning beyond the surface. He speaks to the human condition, explaining, demonstrating, and guiding us to accept and express the Divinity we are.

In the same way, Jesus writes a story with the actions of his life. Jesus knows he is on display, and that what he does is the final arbiter of what he says. If he doesn't walk his talk, his talk is meaningless. As in his parables, so in his life. Though every message and act is contexted in a specific historical event, he teaches with multiple levels of depth, holocosmically, both to the specific event and to all of eternity. Humanity has a connection to the Divine that it can access.

A Hard Teaching

The Western masses have been so greatly influenced by the priesthood and protestant hierarchy that they feel it's a great risk to even consider things beyond their current doctrine. The programming has worked splendidly; they themselves don't want to look any more deeply than they are instructed and allowed!

This ties in with the psychic arts. Most people's expectations regarding psychic phenomena are not rooted in reality but on prejudicial beliefs – even if acquired through perceived authority. A form of hypnosis. Under the spell, it makes perfect sense.

Nothing is said in this entire book that is not revealed directly from the Bible. The characters, principles, and practices are for us to learn from and fashion into our lives.

The interesting thing, and Jesus keeps referring to it also, is that even though the truth is openly revealed, it remains hidden, as it has done all these years. In full view and declaration the mysteries hold themselves concealed. The unworthy, base, and profane have eyes and cannot see, have ears yet cannot hear.

As an institution, organized religion has warred against the psychic arts. Most of its leaders are uninspired, having themselves been taught with misunderstanding and misrepresentation. This is pitiable, but, at least they have good motives. These leaders and their sheep are the ones the inspired medieval poet, Dante, speaks to when he writes:

> "You dull your own perception with false imaginings and do not grasp what would be clear but for your preconceptions." (*Paradiso* 1.88-90)

The psychic gifts are common, good, and innate to the human condition, both to seek as a living spiritual being, and for select ones to perform as psychics.

The inspired have always known this.

Today the educated do not debate the *existence* of psi. Across the globe, in the parapsychological think tanks they've long since quit testing to *establish* that ESP and PK exist, or to document verifiable occurrences of these phenomena. What they are working to discover is *how the process occurs.* That is, what are the mechanisms, mediums, and methods that facilitate the occurrence of one of the manifestations of ESP or PK?

The frontiers of the Renaissance today are in the domain of consciousness. The purpose of this research, of course, is practical, not metaphysical. That is, once the processes are discerned, we will then apply the psychic life to the further advancement of humanity.

The Bible, in an inspired format, holds all the scientists are looking for. Just as the`cutting edge of scientific conception now approaches the message of the Bible, their continuing research will but explicate the truth the Bible now encodes in dramatic presentation. They, too, are opening the door to conscious stimulation of the psychic experience.

Some of the more prominent organizations conducting this research include:

- ▸ Amsterdam University
- ▸ Association for Research & Enlightenment (ARE)
- ▸ Cambridge University
- ▸ Centre for Parapsychological Studies
- ▸ Cognitive Sciences Laboratory
- ▸ Consciousness Research Laboratory
- ▸ Institute of Noetic Sciences
- ▸ Koestler Parapsychology Unit
- ▸ Princeton Engineering Anomalies Research (PEAR)
- ▸ Rhine Research Center Institute For Parapsychology
- ▸ Rosicrucian Order, AMORC
- ▸ Scientific & Medical Network
- ▸ Society for Psychical Research

Contact information is included in the Resources.

To find loads of great information on psi and on these organizations follow these   and   other   psychical   links   on   our   website   at

http://www.psychicspace.com. If you are so inclined, you can even participate in ongoing psi research.

Is It God... Or Is It The Channel's Personality?

Yes. It is.

We accept, as does tradition, that it is God speaking through the channelers and diviners. We accept without question all the ESP events that relate to God recorded in the Bible. Yet you surely must see the channel's personality. Do you believe God is racist? Do you believe that God encourages slavery? Do you believe God encourages you to satisfy your sexual urges with the tinsel of whores, prostitutes, an battle-won booty? Without a lot of arcane abstruse convoluted obfuscation, we simply can come to no other conclusion than that the Spirit – or God – is manifest through and colored by the personality of the individual channel's unique personality, situation, nationality, race, and times. The entire drama of the Bible takes place in the present tense in the concerns of a small race of people. And when it spreads, at the end, it is only in the Mediterranean border nations.

Even today, when we go to a psychic, we are encountering the same thing. This idea upsets some... How many Biblical psychics see spacecraft and alien beings? Yet isn't this common today? This idea of cultural-temporal relativity upsets most querents, as well as a number of psychics. Yet, what richer evidence do we have than the inspired performance of Divinity, the Bible?

The Gender Of God

Many people still hold rigid ideas that God is a *man*. The subject of the gender of God is a subject worthy of an entirely different book.

Someone else will do that work. I'm not going to fight it. Though there are some hints and codes of a God of difference, especially in the early chapters of Genesis, the clear Biblical preference is for a God of masculine gender. For our purposes, it works.

Fuzzy Boundaries

I usually avoid reflecting on the writing process, preferring instead to let the work speak for itself. Nevertheless, today I want to briefly relate some particular challenges I encountered in writing this book.

First, there is a broad readership base to this book – some of us are ministers and/or Biblical scholars, while others of us have never read an entire page of the Bible, much less understood what we read. Many of us have received all our Biblical knowledge from the distorted mouths of primitive preachers, televangelists, and the popular press. As we discuss instances of the different phenomena, our strategy to address this divergence is to tell *enough* of each contexting story so that even Biblical "illiterates" will have sufficient background to grasp the richness of the point we're making. With the new psychic spin we illuminate in the stories, it is hoped that Bibliophiles, likewise, will find the excitement they need.

Here is another struggling point. Many, if not most, of the Biblical psi events simultaneously demonstrate several different phenomena and concepts. The ways of psi are incredibly rich! The nonexclusive categories of psi have at best fuzzy boundaries with leaky margins. For instance, *esp* is a butterfly term, that leaves us, even while discussing it, discussing some of its manifestations such as intuition and clairvoyance. Yet clairvoyance itself can occur through channeling, divination, dreams, or astrology. What else should we expect from such a uniquely Divine subject?

Here is where understanding the HoloCosmic basis of reality – *The whole in every part; in every part the whole* – simplifies the understanding of psi multiplicity. All the assorted identifiable gifts are actually the same gift, psi, manifesting in diverse forms.

You often experience the individually appearing gifts of channeling and divination together, as with Samuel and Saul for instance, for instance, because they travel like the left hand and the right hand of the body. The body aggregate is psi. Any part of it can be labeled with its own individuality. But it is the body and has no life apart from the body.

It wasn't easy on me and my scholasticism, but fortunately the work resisted my efforts toward linear orderliness. Yes, the book still ended up with some order in chapters that discuss these different gifts, but it's done with sufficient openness to honor the interpenetrating essence the Spirit Itself infuses into these gifts.

The whole story comes together as the composite of each motion of psi. This feature is at once one of our greatest consternations and outlandish joys in a deep reading of this present work. We don't get the whole scope on a specific story, angle, consideration, or psychic event, until we enrich our conceptions by the reading of them all. It's the panoramic interdependent dancing unity of the whole – the layout of the stage, the leap of rhapsody, the glitter of angels, the messages they proclaim – that rushes beyond itself to its ultimate effect.

Adventures In Truth

Just making the efforts to conceptualize an understanding of the truths in this book, opens you to being that fertile soil that produces the thirty, sixty, one-hundredfold increase Jesus illumines (Mt. 13.8). Your prayerful attention by itself impels the reconstructive process in your mind. If you earnestly consume this book, your life will be forever altered. You have joined company with beings holding hands in their upward migration. This is alchemy. You yourself will be the living experience through which you demonstrate one of the theses of this book, that the psychic gifts are natural and can manifest through any person.

The SupbraConscious *Is* The HoloCosm

We are current residents in eternity, right now, right here. The distance between now and eternity – in space or in time – is nil.

Eternal reality is at once a living, responding, all-pervasive organism. Every part of the multidimensional reality – including all levels of Spirit and materiality and all moments simultaneously of the past, present, and future – is part of this one vast organic system.

We term this Universal Being the *HoloCosm*. In this Universal Being, all is the one. The one is all. The all is distributed through all its parts. Thus each part *is* the all. Not *all* of the all, but *all*. This is the Universal Essence, God, the HoloCosm,
In whom we live and move and have our being. (Acts 17.28)
The very spirit which establishes the subconscious mechanisms of our bodies to operate as they do, all across nature, is the Great Being. Post-Freudians recognize the effect of the subconscious on our behaviors. Not only do we develop our traits, inclinations, and decisions from our subconscious programming, but – entirely without our awareness or conscious participation, we pump blood, breathe, assimilate oxygen, convert oxygen to nutrition, digest food, eliminate wastes, and the like. Our lives are outplayed according to the engrams routed in our subconscious. We recognize the subconscious mind of that Great Spiritual Being as the *SuperConscious*. It is contrasted from the relative subconscious of its manifestations. We are that essence.

The expression of life is dual. We are spiritual beings having a material experience. We are affected on both sides, the Divine and the mundial.

With the specific intent of connecting with this simultaneity, and this channel of working, I coined the term *SupbraConscious* mind. It contains both the *sup-r* of the SuperConscious, and the *su-b* of the subconscious. These two minds are actually one and the same, as the droplet is the ocean. They are both the ocean. The droplet is the ocean. The ocean is the droplet. No matter where in the ocean the droplet is, or which one it is, it is the same thing in the same place, the ocean. The SupbraConscious *is* the HoloCosm, the one universal energy simultaneously at once everything, connected, being all things.

Standing on the shore of specificity, it can appear there is no connection between water in different seas. With a higher vision, however, it's easy to recognize they are but segmented appearances of the one vast ocean. We are connected in the SupbraConscious Mind, the living feeling Cosmic Universal. We cannot not be connected.

Psi: How It Works

Psi is the connective, communicative medium of Spirit. We are all connected in consciousness and spirit. Channeling, divination, and indeed, all psychic phenomena, work directly because all is one.

Psi works simply because the Universe is structured that way. It is a spiritual universe *en toto*. The material facets of the universe are not separated from the grand spiritual organism or structure. Psi works because everything is an integral component in the continuum of reality that emanates from supraliminal levels of the vibratory essence of the Universe. The interdependent reality is seamless and absolute. What affects one, affects the whole; what is part of the whole is affected when the whole is affected. The whole is in every part; in every part is the whole. The whole *is* every part, every part *is* the whole.

Just as a radio frequency can be tuned into by anyone who has a receiver, whether they be favored or disfavored, saved or unsaved, black or red, psi is available to all. It is hardwired into the human being, in this spiritual universe.

"It's Ready For You!"

In this book you'll see many instances of the psychic arts in motion. Psi manifests in the lives of slaves and inmates as well as emperors, to the erudite as well as the dense. Psi comes more often, surely, to those who practice priestcraft, but also occasionally to those who do not. The psi phenomena manifest to and through those who embrace the current faith principles outlined in the times of the Bible and those who don't, those who, by insider's standards, are rank outsiders. They come to the spiritual, those attuned to higher things – as you might expect – as well as to the political, those living a life of the ultimate crassness and materiality.

No one has a lock on the inner life, the realm of the spiritual and the psychic. The psychic sense comes simply with the gift of humanity.

At various times, nearly every human being has had some manifestation of esp. Whether they sensed a loved one in trouble, knew who was calling on them, or received some other intuitive insight in an impression, vision, or a dream, they've had it. The professional psychics are just better at it; they've made it their art and their profession to consistently and reliably access the psychic realm and the gifts it offers.

Right where you are, as you move forward in spiritual development, with an interest in psi phenomena, it's in motion. *"Only believe..."* and it appears.

When The Student Is Ready The Teacher Appears

It's an ancient truism among those who pursue the esoteric sciences: "The mysteries guard themselves." It's okay to speak them openly, because the masses can neither see nor hear. It is a matter of consciousness. And, when we're speaking of things of the Divine, it is a matter of *higher* consciousness.

Jesus talks of the blindness people encounter when they look in the usual ways, with their human conceptions and expectations:

> "The kingdom of God is not coming with signs to be observed; nor will they say, 'Lo, here it is!' or 'There!' for behold, the kingdom of God is in your midst." (Lk. 17.20-21)

He unveils the omni-existent Heaven as existing implicate within the outer reality the Pharisees are lost inside of. Of course, they don't understand. But while Jesus baffles the stupid, he enlightens those who breath the sensitive heart.

All this communication with the Infinite is unseeable through the common windows of the human sense abilities, but vitally real and visible in its effects. Some misguided people make the mistake, and feel rigidly justified in their position, that because they can't *see* it it doesn't exist. But they are looking wrongly. They look like the person searching for a radio wave with a flashlight. With the correct tools and technology, however, we can see into the vast deeps of interstellar space reading radio waves.

In the same way, we miss the psychic-spiritual dimensions of life we could enjoy. When we turn to the technologies and tools of divination, for instance, we see that they just make the content or intent of the Divine conversation *visible.* They transform the message into a medium perceivable to the normal levels of the human senses.

Those who are ready, receive more:

"Privately to his own disciples he explains everything." (Mk. 4.34)
To the initiate group he makes clear ever so much more!

We, with expanding consciousness in these times, gathered in Spirit, are blessed members of the initiate group. We are here to learn, and this is the reason you are receiving this deeper instruction. It is given to you to understand... And to act differently.

Connecting With This Mind

The process of connecting with this mind is surprisingly simple. We discuss it in some detail in an upcoming book. It's just not surprisingly easy.

Simply put, we connect with this mind by attuning to it through meditation. It is, allways. Our opportunity is to dissipate the anxiety the world throws before us and to connect with the rhythm that moves the ages. There is no conflict between the eternal and the temporal. The eternal manifests in and through the temporal. The temporal is the stage on which the implicate eternal projects.

All levels co-exist simultaneously, in the same moment and place. They all exist, all the time, but what we *experience* is a function of where our consciousness resides. There is no distance between you and the spiritual domain. At your core, you are *pure spirit*. Yet, at the level where your awareness tunes in, you experience life. It has everything to do with where your heart is. If you don't claim it, you don't own it. In the practiced act of awareness we make attunement.

By frequent periods of re-mindedness, you move into a general recognition and acceptance of the fact that there is no disjunction between the apparently different realities of the spiritual and material aspects of creation. They are but faces of the one.

You can recognize the connected, heard in Jesus when he says,
"I and the Father are One." (Jn. 10.30)
And the power follows in train.

Good News For Psychics

Good news for psychics! Most of the psi events in the Bible demonstrate a sanctification of the psychic arts. Psi is a legitimate and needed profession – there is a service to be done for others. People have various needs to "inquire of the Lord."

Clearly, some are more attuned to the gift than others. But beyond that, when we accept the sight we also accept the charge to help others. As the parable of the talents teaches, if we do not use our gift, even what we have is taken from us, whereas, if we use the gift, we foster its increase. Preferring to remain blessed, we must share with others.

God Wants Us To Seek Psychics

The psychic arts are just as the name implies. Like any art, as for instance music or the palette, not everyone has equal abilities, interests, inclinations, or time to pursue them. If your interests lean more toward seeking out those with psychic abilities rather than developing your own, the Bible encourages this, also.

For instance, Rebekah wants to know about the destiny of the offspring yet in her womb. She receives the word from a psychic.

Pharaoh, his nation, the entire world, and the Hebrew people particularly are blessed because Pharaoh seriously seeks an able psychic, finding Joseph in his own prison.

In his early days Saul seeks out a seer and is blessed. The seer, unbeknowst to Saul, has already received psychic foreknowledge that Saul is coming, and in those messages has received specific instructions to bless him. Saul, finding the psychic, is anointed the *first* king of Israel.

David seeks out and receives numerous blessings from different psychics and diviners. He wins numerous battles for his people following the advice of his psychic advisors. He keeps Gad and Nathan on commission as his seers/prophets.

Nebuchadnezzar is given a vision of the end of times, but only comes to an understanding of its blessings when he finds the one psychic who can not only relate his dream, which he has forgotten, but can also interpret it. Daniel satisfies the monarch and saves the lives of a number of people.

These stories and more are discussed in this book.

Yes, the seers, psychics, and diviners have many gifts to give us. Explicit in the document called the Bible, God tells us to seek the psychic.

Tell It Like It Is

All practicing psychics must consider what to tell their clients. You'll hear some saying they never tell their clients anything bad. They pretend they are shielding the querent. But, hold on! This "something bad" may be exactly the thing that God, whom you have ventured to channel, wants said. Are you going to counter God?

Consider a couple of ready instances. One time Isaiah, unsought by the king, goes to visit the sick Hezekiah. He tells him this is no ordinary sickness, that he's certainly going to die. Jonah causes a stir around Nineveh shouting to the people,

"Yet forty days, and Nineveh shall be overthrown!" (Jon. 3.4)

Evil words, both. Yet these psychics are speaking the word as they are commanded.

Here's another crinkle. They utter the curses, but as things turn out, they are both entirely wrong! Hezekiah does not die, but recovers so rapidly that within three days he is out of bed and giving thanks in the Temple. Nineveh is not enslaved by a conquering potentate. The city of grace continues its high position in commerce and the arts. *Is the reputation and livelihood of these psychics at stake?*

But if the evil psychic impressions these men broadcast to their targets are wrong, and they are definitely channeling as God commands, which is the only supportable conclusion from the passage, then what's going on here? Indeed, something significant does occur. Isaiah channels, and Hezekiah is saved. Jonah channels, and Nineveh is spared.

Perhaps God understands the psychology of the king and the city well enough to know that the only way he can accomplish his true purpose – turning them to his way – is through the *takeaway close*. The man and the city may not have "gotten it" if these psychics had simply delivered a message to the like of, "You better do what you know you should! You need to meditate and pray more."

But under the threat of destruction Hezekiah takes refuge in his soul. He prays. He's been a good man, and he's done many good deeds. He's just forgotten lately, being so occupied with political problems. God is moved and, instead, adds fifteen years to his life, plus gives him the military and political autonomy he's been struggling for. Under the threat of destruction Nineveh, potentate to peon, prays and offers sacrifice. Having drifted off course, they right themselves at once. God continues to bless the bountiful city.

The command is clear. As a person of God who has taken the starred cloak of the psychic, you must speak when commanded. This is what you vowed to do. Don't second-guess God. To do other than bless whom God blesses and curse whom God curses is evil. And evil always recoils on its perpetrator.

Psychic, Beware!

This brings us to a few more dangers of the gift. There are hungry rocks all through the channel. If you are not assiduously on course and fortunate, they will take you down. Certainly God wants and needs us to communicate his message, malefic or benign. But *you must speak when commanded* also means you must *not* speak when *not* commanded.

The issue involves consequences. Consequences in God's plan, in the lives of clients, and personal consequences to *you*, the psychic.

Psi is an impressive thing. Jesus himself employs it to woo the crowds. However, you have to be aware that once you start sharing messages from the dimensions beyond the curtain of the mortal eye, you are trafficking with the Gods. The stakes are high. Suddenly, your responsibility is greater.

You have accepted the charge to share the message as you are given it to share. You see what happens to Jonah when he tries to evade the threatening task of cursing Nineveh. Can you chance that you will be saved from drowning, only to end up facing the slower death worked over by the intestinal fluids of a whale, only to miraculously end up thrown out in the vomit of a whale? Even then, Jonah capitulates and transmits the message he is charged to broadcast.

Here's one jutting out of the water. If you have hung out the psychic shingle, placing yourself in a position where you are forced or rewarded to perform, you may find yourself producing without inspiration. Psychic contact depends on a lot of subtle conditions. If you have a reputation, a station, prestige, or perhaps a paycheck to uphold, you may end up as laughable and regrettable as the 400 psychics around Ahab:

"Oh, Yes, King! Go up! You shall win this war." (1Kg. 22.6)
Obsequious yes men, every one of them, fawning for favor.

And one of the lot, Zedekiah, son of Chenaanah, is forever scribed in ludicrous infamy. He makes fantastic iron horns and stomps and charges like the bull of Israel, and snorts:

"With these you shall push the Syrians into oblivion!" (1Kg. 22.11)
The battle is disastrous for the Hebrews, fatal for the king. Do you think this is what Zedekiah wanted?

Psi itself, especially in its interdependent dance with the soul ensconced in the animal form, goes through periods of high and low performance. God does not always have something to say to you, but more to the point, you are not always in the proper place or state to sense truly what it is he does say. Combine biorhythms with Cosmic rhythms with the different trends and cycles of racial development and the anxieties of the particular affairs of the day and what do you have? Instant and consistent inspiration? It's doubtful. One of the impressive things regarding psi in the Bible is how seldom in a lifetime it may visit even the favored.

It visits Joseph but a handful of times over twenty years. Solomon only has two recorded psychic trips. Even the output of a Jeremiah or an Ezekiel is limited when considered over the span of a lifetime. The visionary John of Revelation only leaves records of one psi event, in the closing days of his life.

Consider the consequences. There are very good reasons to honor your abilities – even if developed through loving study – as gifts, never going professional with them. If you do, *"Psychic, beware!"*

The Paradigm Shift

These are times of tremendous spiritual craving.

We are all involved in this awakening... It's a networking world – and blessings transmit from person to person at the grassroots level. They do not come from the polished marble of the Caesars. Person-to-person, one person at a time, share your enthusiasm. Talk passionately about these vital ideas.

This is the least you can do. If you contact us we can fill you in on other ways you can spread the psychic word. We offer both home study and group activities. We have other books, manuals, courses, workshops, and tours on the psychic arts available, as well as audio and video tapes. Our organization also offers lectures, seminars, and workshops for your church, community, or organization. Contact us at **http://www.psychicspace.com** or at the publisher's address for free details. Spread the word.

As more and more of us get it, it gets easier for others. There is a natural law demonstrated in the "100th monkey" effect. After the great war scientists were studying the behavior of monkeys on a chain of South Sea islands. To encourage them to expose themselves to observation, rather than remaining hidden in the foliant wilds, the government flew daily sweet potato drops along the beaches.

It worked perfectly. The scientists were able to observe the things they came to study. However, they got a bonus. The potatoes were not without their chagrins. Just imagine! The sand that caked on the potatoes was unfriendly to the monkey's mouths, digestion, and general enjoyment. But, one youthful monkey washed her potato in the surf. Hmmm. After a passage of some months, those nearest her, her brothers and sisters, her mother, and her uncles and aunts and their families also washed their potatoes. And they enjoyed them far more.

But that's still just a tiny group in a civilization of hundreds of thousands. As more months rolled by, more and more of their friends and members of their community began washing their potatoes and enjoying them more. Still not a general phenomenon.

And at some point in this slow progress of enlightenment, a critical mass was reached. Scientists said it was the 100th monkey – while admitting the *exact* number wasn't the issue. Sudden and complete, a transformation occurred. Overnight, every monkey on every island of the chain washed their potatoes and enjoyed them more.

Evolution takes a giant leaps in an instant – assimilating into the living psycho-genetic behaviors of an entire race!

We can lift the world by our efforts. Our positive efforts do bear fruit. This is one of the multi-meanings Jesus codes into his statement,

"And I, if I be lifted up, draw all men unto me." (Jn. 12.32)

Here is our unique human grace. We can lift the world by our *conscious* efforts. You, in fact, have the duty to move in accord with the divine unfolding plan. *You* are on the cutting edge, responsible for evolution. Encourage the compelling spirit in your heart.

Your part can be so simple... Encourage others to get this book and to study it with an open heart. Therein flowers your blessing, as while you positively impact the human condition, in a loop of loving reward, you simultaneously are impacted by a progressively positive world. Do what you are led to do.

Look! We're arriving! The domain of ESP looms directly ahead!

Chapter 1

ESP As
Clairvoyance, Intuition, And Telepathy

———··•··———

A ll psychic phenomena is a form of esp. However, in this, the first excursion of our psychicspace tour, we visit the sites related to esp in its more commonly perceived manifestations of clairvoyance, intuition, and telepathy. And we promptly encounter the issue of nonexclusive categories.

ESP

ESP is an acronym for *extra-sensory perception*, a term coined by Dr Rhine during his psychic research days at Duke University. Though we don't favor the term in this book, the phenomena of esp have recently been labeled anew as *anomalous cognition*. It speaks to identically the same phenomena. The process, event, or phenomena of coming to knowledge of a person, thing, event, condition, or circumstance by means of a method that transcends the commonly known five senses of sight, sound, hearing, taste, and touch. Many of us call this the *sixth sense*.

ESP should be the first stop on our tour through psychicspace. ESP, while a general term, is also understood in specific applications. In its broadest application, it refers to any experience that has a paranormal aspect. The Cognitive Sciences Lab, in efforts to think more clearly about the subject, labels this topmost and most inclusive tier *anomalous mental phenomena*.

Getting more specific, and more accurate, the phenomena of esp are dual. There is an easy break regarding the passive, receptive arts and the active, outgoing arts. It is almost tongue in cheek to say passive, because it may take a lot of effort to get into that effortless spot. It is like the ballerina pirouetting in grace. Sometimes it comes so strongly it reaches you anywhere anyway. But those who choose the life of phenomenal things soon learn they occur as the flower of a disciplined heart. A message, impression, guidance, instruction, feeling, or the like, enters through a receptive modality.

At this level ESP is clearly distinguished from *PK*. ESP, or the arts of anomalous perception, of *knowing* without the senses, is the receptive arm of anomalous mental phenomena. PK, otherwise known as *anomalous perturbation*, is the arm which commands and gets results. In other words, we call it *magic*. It simply means causing by mental power, command, affirmation, or knowledge, phenomena in the "normal" world to occur. ESP, though it concerns the real world, is considered to stay in the paranormal world. Thus, when a man sees in your aura that you have had five husbands, other than knowing or seeing something, he's not really doing anything that directly causes an effect in the world. However, when a man calls fireballs from hell and they come, he's *doing* something that moves *from* the paranormal dimensions *into* the real world. Elijah kills 102 police officers inside of an hour with metaphysical magic, a pretty real world effect.

Discussing clairvoyance, intuition, and telepathy first, as related channels of the esp phenomenon at work, will give us insights and lenses of perception that will enable us to more greatly enjoy our visits to the other prominent arts of esp – channeling, dreaming, and divining.

Clairvoyance

The esp packet of information may come as a precognition, retrocognition, or simulcognition. That is, the subject of the paranormal occurrence may concern thoughts, actions, events, or conditions of the future, the past, or the present.

This function of distance, in relation to either time, place, or both time and place earns esp the term "far-seeing." Though it may involve impressions and intuitions, rather than visual images, it is clairvoyance.

It is knowing what cannot be known through the normal five human senses. When people speak of the fascinating *sixth sense*, they are generally talking about a form of clairvoyance.

Intuition

In popular parlance, when esp is spoken of as an identifiable specific gift, it is often what we call intuition. Intuition is a good instance of what we're speaking of when we say the gift can be enhanced by its usage. As we discuss in the Introduction, intuition involves coming to direct knowledge or certainty of something without normal sensory input or without logical reasoning or inferring according to the "normal" left-brain models, knowing by a *feeling*.

The intuitive gift of esp can come wrapped in the mantle of a dream. It also manifests straight as an intuition, coming solely from the Divine without the cover of another method, as when God speaks to Samuel in the day.

The Bible vindicates intuition in many places. A sampling of these incidents takes us to visit the suddenly inspired young soldier, Gideon; the characters of the early realm of kingship in Israel, Samuel, Saul, and David; as well as Jesus and his industrious apostle, Philip, and his possessed disciple, Paul.

Telepathy

The Bible contains many instances of telepathy, demonstrating, at least for believers, the validity of its occurrence, and, for Biblical and psychic students, insight on exactly what telepathy is and what it accomplishes as well as how it is accomplished.

We visit a limited sampling of the phenomenon of telepathy to illuminate some of our points. First we stop at several incidents from the early chronicles of the Jewish spiritual life and practice, and then we look at several instances of telepathy in the life of scripture's flower, Jesus.

Telepathy is a specific manifestation of the psychic arts which, in accord with the law of duality, has two arms. First, and most commonly, it concerns knowing or "reading" the thoughts of other people. This is its receptive arm. Its active arm, which can be classed as PK or magic, involves *projecting* a thought or image into the mind of another. The target may or may not be able to discern its origins, not thinking, not believing, not conceptualizing that the thoughts they are thinking may not be their own.

The Bible Is Yours

Seekers interested in developing your own psychic abilities, the Bible is a treasure trove!

Not all people who read and subscribe to the Bible do so mindlessly. Many seekers of the Higher Life make an important distinction – in this culture at this present time – between the "religious" approach taught by self-serving organized religions, and the "spiritual" approach, a wholistic approach that sees through the surface text to God underneath – the same God every culture on Earth has worshiped according to its nature, under many forms.

Wherever you are, perhaps believing because you have been taught you *must*, subjected with threats of mighty damnation if you do not also believe exactly the correct way, or searching the words you recognize as sacred and inspired for psychi-spiritual fulfillment and development, the Bible is yours. It is written for you – from God to your soul. See what it says.

****

Clairvoyance, Intuition, And Telepathy

Enjoy yourself and learn as we adventure through a number of the decidedly exciting psychicsites of Biblical action in the nonexclusive domains of clairvoyance, intuition, and telepathy.

One Man's Colossal Massive Commitment To An Intuition

Truly, as the story tells it, *Noah* is the reigning father of humanity. Adam comes first, but then humanity is narrowed a second time to the loins of a single man. Genesis tells the story that God wants to change the course of human evolution. Some of Jesus' brothers have been having sex with the fair humans, and as a result these Godly offspring are living hundreds of years (Gen. 6.5). Noah himself is 500 years old before he fathers his first child (Gen. 5.32). Things have not turned out the way God wants.

But, with the small seed of a good and righteous specimen, a very early incident of genetic engineering, God can repopulate the world. The millions and millions of animals are just innocent victims in the flood; God really only wants to kill the people. So he provides for the animals' continuance, too.

God selects Noah to prepare a vessel – the "ark" – to carry himself, his family, and mated couples of all the living creatures on Earth. The vast multitudes of humanity are destroyed in the giant flood that follows. At this juncture there is only the family of Noah. All humanity owes its existence to Noah.

A Testament

The psychic side of the story of Noah bears testament not only to clairvoyance, but most notably to the impact clairvoyance can have in human affairs. Look at the consequences and results!

What is more meaningful than occupying the pivotal position of the continuance of the entire human species? And he does the deed. What if he had just moaned about recurring nightmares, lacking the sensitivity and drive to follow up on these divine visitations? Do you think for a moment the psychologists would have supported him in his grand delusion?

What an impact a clairvoyant impression can have! It is so strong and definite that Noah commits to and executes the apparently fruitless *massive* task of building an oceangoing ship in the middle of the desert, in the middle of life with its ongoing concerns. It takes SO MUCH effort, planning, preparation, resources, perspiration, and dereliction of other duties and social functions. Noah and his family actually *reorient* their lives, not according to societal norms – which at best laugh at Noah, at worst taunt him and his actions – but according to inner guidance.

"It Is *You!*"

Gideon. For the three hundred years between Moses and the monarchy, Israel is ruled by judges. At one point in this era Israel finds itself leaderless and under rout by the troops of Midian. Several years earlier Israel had fled to the hill country, and have been living clandestinely in dens and caves, disguising their activities, while the Midianites, their camels, and their herds lay waste to the fertile valley land.

Gideon, fated to be one of those leader-judges, is hiding, beating out harvest wheat in the wine press, when an angel appears at his side. At this point in his budding manhood he becomes an active participant in the psychic arts, receiving much guidance for himself and his nation. The angel speaks with prescience,

"The Lord is with you, mighty man of valor." (Jg. 6.12)

Gideon entertains a doubt... He says,

"If the Lord *is* with us, then why is all this bad stuff happening? And the people say he's done such tremendous things for us before." (Jg. 6.13)

Watch closely. There is an angel on the scene. Now the Lord *himself* turns directly to Gideon and speaks,

"Go in this might of yours, and deliver Israel from the hand of Midian. Do not *I* send you?" (Jg. 6.14)

In this psychic event the mystical transformation of a messenger into the ultimate sender, *God,* is a shapeshift of grand proportions. The experience swoops to a grandly deeper level.

The whole experience is overwhelming – both the mystical visitors and their messages of destiny. Gideon requests a *sign.*

He runs to his tent and cooks some meats and broths. When he gets back, the intensity of the mystic moment having dissipated during his withdrawal into Earthly involvement in meat and the fixings, God has undergone anther mystical transformation. He has resubordinated into the angel.

The angel consumes the food in a flash of fire, disappearing in the selfsame act. Gideon's intuitive flash occurs in that metaphysical moment. He "*perceives,*" or finally *accepts* what has occurred. The impact of this paranormal series positively alters Gideon's self-conception. From this point on, accepting his commission and the strength conferred with it, Gideon drives through a string of successes. This selfsame night is not too soon; he organizes a party of bandits and starts his career of conquest, contribution, and prestige.

"There's A Psychic In The City"

When *Samuel* grows older, though he retains his spiritual position, he hands the reins of the nation to his two sons, Joel and Abijah, making them judges, the final judges in Israel's pictured history. Like most politicians, they misuse their offices, squandering off the choicest of the kingdom's wealth. But these politicians are particularly overt about it, so it causes unrest amongst the citizenry. So they approach Samuel, whom they still revere, to remove his sons and to appoint them a *king*, like the nations surrounding them have. The citizenry must be placated.

After some sessions of intuitive psychic communications, Samuel acquiesces. God intends to use the occasion for a lesson. Samuel is to prepare both the people and the future king for their positions in the changed state of affairs. As a priest and psychic, Samuel is also to anoint the chosen one. First he is to warn the people that a king will be even worse, pressing their sons into his own vain battles, spiriting their blooming daughters to his harem, and exacting heavy taxes from the best of their produce. But they do not listen. They've already got it in their hearts that they want a king. God, using the esp channel of intuition, gives Samuel instructions.

It seems that some ass belonging to Saul's father have wandered from the flocks. In what should have been a routine maintenance mission, Saul is out days looking for ass. Finally he says to his companion that they should return home, or else his father will start worrying – not about his ass anymore, but about him. The servant, however, mentions that he has heard that a powerful psychic practices in a city not too far down the road:

> "Hold on. There's a psychic in this city. He is *good* – all that he says comes true. Let's go there; maybe he can tell us about the journey on which we have set out." (1Sam. 9.6)

Meanwhile, Samuel, a man of frequent meditation, has been receiving clairvoyant intuitions that Saul is on his way. God whispers in his psychic ears,

> "Tomorrow about this time I will send to you a man from the land of Benjamin, and you shall anoint him to be prince over my people Israel." (1Sam. 9.16)

Samuel's esp continues working in this episode. The next day, at the moment Samuel lays eyes on Saul, God's voice speaks:

> "Here is the man of whom I spoke to you! He it is who shall rule over my people." (1Sam. 9.17)

Saul, however, is not so closely in tune with the Infinite, and does not know who Samuel is when he sees him. He even asks Samuel for directions to the "seer's house." Samuel identifies himself as the seer he seeks, and invites him to attend the services and meal he is about to offer. He then invites Saul to spend the night as his guest, promising to give him the reading he seeks on the morrow. He then – quite possibly to "hook" Saul, certainly because it is part of his technique as a practicing psychic – gives Saul some psychically gathered intelligence. Saul *has not* yet shared his concerns with the seer, yet the seer says to him casually, in the midst of conversation on other things,

> "As for your asses that were lost three days ago, do not set your mind on them, for they have been found." (1Sam. 9.20)

Thus Samuel effects a simple demonstration of telepathy, reading the thoughts and concerns of Saul, and clairvoyance, knowing the condition of the ass he's been looking for. He also reveals enough of Saul's future dominion – like the psychic sisters before MacBeth – to start him seriously wondering.

Secret Seditious Ceremony

David. Samuel chooses and anoints Saul. But Saul has a mind of his own, so Samuel gets upset with him. So God visits Samuel with clairvoyant guidance to go to Bethlehem to anoint a new king. Interestingly, God designs a subterfuge for Samuel to use to get past the current king, Saul, who would view his purpose an act of treason. God tells him to mislead Saul and the governmental forces by carrying along a heifer and claiming to be going to sacrifice. The authorities consider religious observances of little consequence to the affairs of state, so, taken in by his dissimulation, they let him, on a matter threatening national security, pass.

God is with him when he arrives. Being psychically guided to do so, Samuel invites Jesse and his sons to sacrifice, consecrating them to the Lord in the ceremony he stages. Samuel sees the handsome, strong twenty-two year old son of Jesse, Eliab, and assumes that he has got to be the one God wants. He is the perfected specimen of young man's virility and grace. But God appears to Samuel in an intuitive flash with the message that Jesus later repeats when he admonishes, "Judge not by appearances" (Jn. 7.24):

> "Do not look on his appearance or on the height of his stature, because I have rejected him; for the Lord sees not as man sees; man looks on the outward appearance, but the Lord looks on the heart." (1Sam. 16.7)

An interesting story with plenty of dramatic tension follows. The next six prize sons of Jesse pass before Samuel's gaze, yet Samuel never receives the positive intuitions that *the* one is in front of him. Only then does Samuel discover, upon inquiry, that the youngest son, out tending the sheep, is not present. No one thought him of any consequence. Samuel sends for the youth.

Immediately as David enters his presence, the Lord rises in Samuel's heart and moves him to anoint the youth king. As he does, the Spirit of the Lord enters into David and never departs from him. Less fortunately, at the same moment, the Spirit leaves Saul, leaving him grumpy and recalcitrant. He finishes his days out in enmity with himself and all who surround him. A new age begins, overlapping an old age dying.

Of Psychic Verities

This psychicsite holds a number of distinctions we can benefit from. Every one of these involves major considerations on the part of the budding psychic student. Psi manifests primarily on a "need to know" basis. This is one major reason why the normal person experiences so few truly psi occurrences. A corollary of that principle is that when you do need to know, you do. Then we see what happens when it's your number.

On A "Need To Know" Basis. The passage reads that God gives Samuel the clairvoyant impression to go to Bethlehem to anoint the king from among the sons of Jesse. However, Samuel receives no instruction on who this person is. He only receives word that he is to go, that he is to go to Bethlehem, and that he is to select the king from among Jesse's sons. This is often how esp/intuition works: one step at a time – or, as the military might say, you are given information only on a "need to know" basis. Frequently God reveals only enough to lead you to the right time/place so the next step can occur or be revealed. It is only *after* Samuel arrives in Bethlehem, at the party at Jesse's, that he receives further transmissions that guide his actions.

It is a good lesson in trust, but it's also the real beauty of it all! You don't have to have all the facts and answers before you set out on the spiritual path. *You don't need them.*

"Is He The One?" When we are expecting an answer or a sign, we have a tendency to jump in our eagerness at everything that approaches. We see here the difference, however, when the right one comes along. Samuel, looking upon Eliab, figures he surely must be the one. God's thinking, however reveals to him that this is not the man. Tentativeness is a sign.

Yet look how certain Samuel is when he does encounter the chosen one. As soon as he sees David with ruddy cheeks and beautiful eyes, the voice of God sounds off inside him saying,

"Arise, anoint him; for this is he." (1Sam. 16.12)

David is the one. David, root of the royal line that leads straight to Jesus. An accompanying feeling of certainty characterizes esp phenomena. There is no shade of doubt when the correct option presents itself to Samuel.

"It Will Find You..." David is oblivious to Samuel's designs on him. Yet, in the space of a few moments David rises from the lowest occupation, a tender of sheep, to the highest, king of a nation. Simply put, it is David's time. When it is your time, the Universe conspires to attach you. Whether you consciously know it is approaching or not. Note the distinction. David does not go and seek the honor, rather, it comes looking for him.

And The Training Begins. When Higher Consciousness lifts you up, you likely have more training to do. Even though you are anointed with the throne, you do not necessarily wield the scepter until you develop yourself to the power. David spends years honing his martial disciplines, living the while as a Robin Hood leading his outlaw band in the wilds of South Israel.

Ahijah With The King's Wife

Wife of Jeroboam. *Ahijah* has a relationship of some duration with Jeroboam. It is Ahijah whose clairvoyance reveals to him the circumstances surrounding Ahijah's *future* rise to power. Even while King Solomon is still alive, Ahijah plays out the psychic drama before the future king by removing his cloak and tearing it into twelve pieces to illustrate God's intention to split the unity of the tribes under Solomon, giving ten of those tribes to the very hand of Jeroboam. As the psychic foresees, Jeroboam later becomes the first king of Israel.

However, though Jeroboam's rise to power is of God's design, Jeroboam does not stay faithful to the fiats of the Lord. For political expediency, he decentralizes the worship services. Up to this time the chief temple at Jerusalem has been the *sole* anointed house of God. Since the rebellion, however, Jerusalem, the old capital, is occupied by the enemy tribe of Judah. How can Israel enter Judah? Jeroboam establishes "high places," regional temples where people can go to worship.

As time goes on, Jeroboam receives several psychic missives telling him of his sins, including the visit of an unnamed psychic-magician who freezes his arm into an outstretched, immovable position. He reverses the spell before he leaves, fortunately. But Jeroboam knows he is in ill favor with the powerful mystics of the Jehovahan persuasion.

Because of this, when his son, Abijah, falls seriously ill, and Jeroboam needs the vision of a psychic, he is unable to go himself. So he sends his wife to inquire of Ahijah. He also has her disguise herself, going as a normal high class lady, not as the wife of the king of Israel.

She hastens to Ahijah's sanctum under this pretense. Yet Ahijah receives telepathic intelligence that she is coming. He takes immediate advantage of his position to display his paranormal insight. As he hears her cross the portal, he speaks, first identifying her, next unmasking her disguise, and then reading the thoughts in her heart, thoughts of the kingdom and her son:

> "Come in, wife of Jeroboam. Why do you pretend to be another? For I am charged with heavy tidings for you." (1Kg. 14.6)

When she gets settled before him, he gives her the reading she came for. Again, she never has to say anything. Ahijah is reading her mind. He knows why she is before him, and he speaks to these concerns.

Once Ahijah settles into Alpha, God himself comes through, speaking directly to the woman. After reciting the reason he is upset with Jeroboam, he pronounces a mighty hex upon the king, saying,

> "Behold, I will bring evil upon the house of Jeroboam, and will cut off from Jeroboam every male, slave or citizen, in Israel, and will utterly consume the house of Jeroboam, as a man burns up dung until it is all gone. Any one belonging to Jeroboam who dies in the city the dogs shall eat; and any one who dies in the open country the birds of the air shall eat." (1Kg. 14.10-11)

As Ahijah comes back to his own consciousness, freed from possession by the Spirit, he tells the lady to go on home. Yet unasked, he answers the direct concern she came for:

> "When your feet enter the city, the child shall die." (1Kg. 14.12)

How would you feel if God reviled and fated you with such a heinous curse?

It comes to pass. Her son dies as she steps on the threshold of her house. Some time later, Judah successfully overcomes Israel, killing Jeroboam, and leaving him to the beaks of prey scouring the battlefield. Two years later, Basha, Judean military officer, extinguishes the line of Jeroboam, killing his final son, King Nadab. It is finished. Forever. He kills Nadab and "all the house of Jeroboam; leaving not one male breathing" (1Kg. 15.28-29). The dogs eat them.

It is a heavy curse to be God damned.

Psychic Police Intelligence

Elisha. Here's an interesting one! It is not uncommon, though generally played down, for police to use psychics to solve crimes. In this episode we visit the first recorded case of psychic intelligence I know about.

Naaman, of "washed seven times in the Jordan" fame, is cured of his leprosy. He offers generous gifts to Elisha for healing him, but Elisha refuses them all. Elisha's sole purpose is to make a statement. He sends the grateful Naaman on his way.

But Elisha's servant, Gehazi, is stirred by the emotions of greed. He's seen the gold of the rich man, Naaman. He chases after him and says a new need has arisen, that his master has changed his mind, and *will* now accept a gift.

Naaman gives Gehazi what he requests. Gehazi blesses him Godspeed and returns to the monastery, slipping in unseen by the garden gate. Then he appears before his master.

Already knowing, Elisha questions Gehazi about what he has done. Gehazi, knowing there is no way he could know, fabricates a story. No "objective way" he could know, that is. As the *New Oxford Annotated Bible* annotates the passage, Elisha catches the culprit by extrasensory perception:

> "Did I not go with you in spirit when the man turned from his chariot to meet you?" (2Kg. 5.26)

He's caught him, he saw it all through clairvoyance.

"What You Say In Your Bedchamber"

Samuel. The *king of Syria* is warring with Israel, but strategy for strategy he is frustrated. Such fortune, the king knows, could only happen if Israel knows his plans. There must be a leak..

So the king of Syria gathers his advisors, officers, and servants and roars before them. But they are silent. He accuses them, saying at least *one* of them knows who the leak is. He appeals to their loyalty for that man to come forward. Finally a small servant does come forth. It is not one of the king's men, he says, but one with telepathic abilities who is foiling him:

> "It is none other than Elisha, a psychic in Israel, who tells the king of Israel what you say in your bedchamber." (2Kg. 6.12)

It is Elisha feeding information to the king of Israel. Elisha tells him where Syria is heading and what they are planning to do. As the Bible sums up:

> Thus he used to warn him, so that he saved himself a number of times. (2Kg. 6.10)

The king of Syria is powerless to defeat a man who reads his thoughts. Another case of the sight used for political and military purposes. Effective.

Of course, you see why the military complex is so intensely interested in the psychic and the paranormal. What an advantage it confers!

Far-Seeing: In Parallel Time

Nathaniel. In his thirtieth year *Jesus* experiences his great awakening. The mystical experience is a magnificently magnified event in which, at the moment of his baptism, the hand of God enters Earth so that many of those in attendance even *see* God, in the form of a dove, descend and land on Jesus. Then they hear him rumble.

Mad in this experience, Jesus is driven to the wilds of Galilee. There he makes sense of the experience – boy, does he! Upon his return from his lengthy vision quest, he turns to immediate, urgent, and unceasing activity. In fact, one of his motto lines becomes:

> "We must work the works of him who sent me, while it is day; night comes, when no one can work." (Jn. 9.4)

Though the different gospels disagree in the details – mere surface stuff – what is certain is that Jesus immediately sets about selecting companions. In a matter of days he has the intimate cadre that will support him and reflect his teachings throughout his brief but fruitful career. These are the same that remain and work after he is gone.

The stories of the selection of the apostles are reflective of a spiritually inspired approach to life. To our purposes in this book, the story surrounding Nathaniel's initiation bears significant interest. It being of a mystical nature, it is not surprising to find that John, and only the sensitive John whom Jesus loves, records it.

On Jesus' first day in Galilee he finds Philip. Philip, turned on in a deep spiritual experience with this man, in turn brings Nathaniel to meet Jesus. As they are approaching, Jesus says,

> "Behold, an Israelite indeed, in whom is no guile!" (Jn. 1.47)

Jesus demonstrates his gift of psychic receptivity here, reading Nathaniel's aura. Nathaniel, of a more cautious and suspicious orientation to life, not having fully made the transition into the spiritual life, challenges Jesus with, "How do you know me?!" (Jn. 1.48).

Jesus' reply evinces his natural use of clairvoyance and telepathy. As it often does to people, it impresses Nathaniel. Jesus answers his challenge, providing other information – the fig tree scene – that he could know no other way than through the sight, in the words,

> "Before Philip called you, when you were under the fig tree, I saw you." (Jn. 1.48)

This perfect demonstration of clairvoyance is the incident that gives validity to Jesus' demonstration of telepathy. After all, if this man has the ability of *far-seeing*, then the telepathy he demonstrates, though it speaks of an item of an abstract nature, guilelessness, can be accepted for what it is. Nathaniel at that moment becomes a believer.

Simulcognition

Note that this clairvoyant impression relates to a present-time occurring event. In a simulcognitive event Jesus sees Nathaniel moving under the fig tree at the actual time it is happening. This timing of the psychically seen event contrasts with the more common precognitive dimension of esp, seeing something in the future, such as Peter's upcoming denial of Jesus *before* the cock crows.

Jesus Hits On A Lady At The Well

The story of *Jesus* at the well with the Samaritan lady contains a superb instance of Jesus demonstrating the telepathic arts. Jesus is waiting at the well when a Samaritan lady approaches to draw water. Racism is prevalent, so when Jesus speaks to her, she, being an "untouchable," questions why he would talk to her.

Thus they initiate a conversation that Jesus shortly turns to metaphysical subjects. After some exchanges about the nature of God and the teachings that he offers, she is still resisting. Finally he says to her, "Go, call your husband, and come here" (Jn. 4.16). "I have no husband," she replies.

Then Jesus provides her with intelligence that he could have gathered no other way than through the psychic channels of telepathy and clairvoyance:

"You are right in saying, `I have no husband.' Even the man whom you now do have is not *your* husband. This you said truly." (Jn. 4.17-18)

Like Nathaniel, and like so many others at the point of an undeniable psychic demonstration, she *believes*. She runs back to her people gushing with enthusiasm over the man with psychic abilities. And because of her many come to see and to believe in Jesus.

Jesus' reading does have a purpose.

Getting Ass

Occurrences with psychic components occur more rapidly as *Jesus* approaches his final hour. During this period he is more in tune with the Infinite, more in the power – by development, yes, but more so by the psychic attunement attendant the climax of his mission on Earth.

Jesus enters Jerusalem preparing for the celebrations surrounding the Passover. With a little advance PR, Jesus makes plans to enter the city to popular acclaim. This will really provoke the conventional elite. He enters in triumph – at least to his followers. Institutionalized religion has it in for him, and when they visit him, it is not to receive instruction or grace in his presence, but to trip him in his words and find sufficient cause to effect the final solution.

The instructions Jesus gives his disciples, instructions relating to securing his ride, an ass, using no money, show evidence of Jesus' use of both clairvoyance and telepathy. Again, it is not surprising that multiple gifts show up simultaneously. They frequently manifest in packages. Yet, looking analytically at the demonstration, we can break it down into different dimensions for discussion's purposes.

Approaching Jerusalem, at the suburb of Bethany, Jesus sends a couple of the disciples in to pick up the ass he wants. His clairvoyance allows his to send his disciples in, telling them,

"Go into the village opposite, where on entering you will find a colt tied, on which no one has ever yet sat; untie it and bring it here." (Lk. 19.30)

Then, seeing the scene in the thoughts and hearts of the ass's owners, he tells the men that if anyone asks why they are untying the colt, they are to simply reply,

"The Lord has need of it." (Lk. 19.31)

The Code That Unlocks The Secret
Which, of course, they have occasion to do. If we're not careful, we can read right over the code that unlocks the secret of this event as a psychic demonstration rather than a mere coincidence. Jesus identifies the owner's approach as coming during the specific time they are *untying* the colt – not taking it, not approaching it, not walking in slow motion away. Luke records the event as occurring at that specific moment. *Listen, you fortunate one with ears!*

The Destruction Of The Temple
On Tuesday, April 10th, before the fateful Friday when *Jesus* is executed on the cross, all three synoptic gospels record him prophesying the destruction of the Supreme Grand Temple in Jerusalem. The remarkable uniformity among their accounts indicates that both the writers and God, who inspires their writing decisions and editorializing, invest high importance to this psychic event. It helps prove Jesus is indeed the one he says he is.

The incident runs the entire chapter in Matthew 24, Mark 13, and Luke 21. During these days, Jesus is going every morning to teach in the Temple. On this particular day, having made pointed efforts to affront the political and religious hierarchy, who, admittedly, are plotting against him, Jesus moves to leave the Temple. When he does, some of the disciples point ecstatically to the noble buildings and the exalted stones embedded in the architecture of the complex. Unimpressed, Jesus utters the fate of the Temple:

Matthew
> "You see all these, do you not? Truly, I say to you, there will not be left here one stone upon another, that will not be thrown down." (Mt. 24.2)

Mark
> "Do you see these great buildings? There will not be left here one stone upon another, that will not be thrown down." (Mk. 13.2)

Luke
> "As for these things which you see, the days will come when there shall not be left here one stone upon another that will not be thrown down." (Lk. 21.6)

As it turns out, this is a *major event* in Jewish history, ranking right with the Egyptian deliverance. Esp in action; Jesus *knows.*

The Final Meal
Jesus demonstrates his clairvoyance several times in the stories surrounding the Last Supper. When it comes time to consider where they will celebrate the Passover – the very day of thanksgiving, none too soon, thank you – Jesus sends Peter and John into town to prepare the feast for the group. He gives them instructions according to the clairvoyant impressions he has received. He tells them when they enter the city a man carrying a jar of water will greet them, and that they are to follow him. When they follow the man, an employee-slave, to his master's house, they are to tell the homeowner the "teacher" wants to know where his guest room is, so that he may celebrate Passover there.

As he foresees:

"When the hour comes, he sits down at table, and the apostles with him."
(Lk. 22.14)

Peter's Cock

Peter. Jesus also makes advantage of his consuming-important final evening on Earth with another clairvoyant demonstration. After supping and singing a bit, the group walks out to the Mount of Olives, one of Jesus' favored meditation spots. Jesus is sweating blood now, and he is giving what he senses are his final focused words to his apostles. Jesus tells Peter, his handpicked successor, he has prayed for him that he may have the strength to endure the upcoming rigors of the spiritual path. Jesus, with his superior mystical abilities, has kept them insulated from harm. He won't be there to protect them anymore.

Peter, certain of his commitment, but unaware of the imminence of the event he speaks of, affirms,

"Lord, I am ready to go with you to prison and to death." (Lk. 22.23)
Jesus, with love, not judgment in his voice, replies with what his precognitive insight reveals;

"I tell you, Peter, the cock will not crow three times this day, until you three times deny that you know me." (Mk. 14.30)
It happens as Jesus in his prescience calls it. In the instant of fulfillment Peter recognizes his error, and turns to look into the understanding captive eyes of Jesus.

Philip And The Royal Eunuch

Philip, one of the companions of Jesus while he was living, receives an impression by extra sensory perception that he should travel down a particular desert road. Philip is not aware of the reasons behind this paranormal urging, but encouraged by an unnamed angel, he moves on it.

Thereon he sees a high-positioned government functionary reading, of all things, *Isaiah*. He is the Secretary of the Treasury for Candice, Queen of Ethiopia.

This is intuition:
The Spirit says to Philip,
"Go up and join this chariot." (Acts 8.29)
He does as he is instructed.

Philip, aware of how abstruse Isaiah can be – after all, he does speak in a mystic tongue – asks the man if he understands what he is reading. "Alas!" the man sighs, "I need help." Not surprisingly, Philip understands the passage he is reading, Isaiah 53.7-8, as relating to his recently departed hero/companion, Jesus. So he shares the good news of Jesus with this receptive man.

Good comes of it. Traveling along, they encounter a river with water so that the inspired dignitary cries out,

"See, here is water! What is to prevent my being baptized?" (Acts 8.36)
Nothing. Another soul is won.

Who Sees The Vision And The Voice?

Few people who would care enough to read a book such as this haven't heard about *Paul*'s conversion to the cause of Christ. The SuperConsciousness that is God enters forcibly into Paul's awareness. The Bible plays panorama in this extrasensory event. It's so powerful that even those riding with Paul recognize something other than madness has got him. Though they see nothing, they *hear* everything. It's so paranormal it makes the hairs on their hands and the backs of their necks stand up.

It happens while Saul,
a righteous, learned attorney, spurs madly on a mission against the Christian practitioners. He is heading toward Damascus, with evil in his power, but,

As he nears Damascus, suddenly a light from Heaven flashes around him. He falls to the ground and hears a voice thundering,

"Saul, Saul, why do you persecute me?"

"Who are you, Lord?" Saul asks.

"I am Jesus, whom you are persecuting," he replies. "Now get up and go into the city, and you will be told what you must do."

The men traveling with Saul are transfixed – hearing the sound, but not seeing anyone. (Acts 9.3-8)

After a while they help the unsteady Saul to his feet and shake him off, but he cannot see anything. So one of their number escorts the shaken man on foot into Damascus.

With a slight alteration of his current name, he assumes *Paul*, a man changed to his dying day.

Change Your Thinking, Change Your Life

As does every incident, this episode teaches some particular truths. It illuminates the absolute effects in one's life and the greater reality that can come about simply from a change in thinking. The man has personal experience behind the line he later pens,

Be ye transformed by the renewing of your mind. (Rom. 12.2)

We take on the character and destiny of those we pledge our dreams to. Look how rapidly it happens! Saul addresses the Spirit as "Lord" on the spot. After the three days of darkness, Saul arises in the power of Spiritual Truth. Paul's genius, passion, and drive to adventure, now harnessed to the capacities of the Christ, earn him a stellar role in the drama of the Christ.

Saul's story demonstrates the mystic maxim, "Change your thinking, change your life."

The Beseeching Man Of Macedonia

Luke. The Apostles. Acts relates the missionary efforts of *Paul* and some of his cohorts. At one point they've been through the regions of Phrygia and Galatia, feeling uninspired to preach there. They then journey to Mysia and, restless and wanting to preach now, attempt to enter the city of Bithynia, but are blocked from doing so. So they go down to Alexandria, but the spirit does not move their hearts nor open opportunities before them there, either.

It is here that Paul is visited by a Macedonian man, haloed in the mists of a dream, standing earnestly before him beseeching him to come to Macedonia and help them. The writer of Acts, Luke the physician, likewise the author of the Gospel of Luke, says simply,

And when he had seen the vision, immediately we sought to go on into Macedonia, concluding that God had called us to preach the gospel to them. (Acts 16.10)

They go.

Of Psychic Verities

As short as our stay at this psychicspot is, we can still note some significant mystical principles.

The Interpretation Is Clear. The interpretation of Paul's dream is clear and unquestioned by the men. They are to go to Macedonia and teach. This is characteristic of esp. The insight, hunch, and direction it provides arrives as a certainty. Paul and his followers do not investigate the number of churches, denominations, and disciples currently there, a rational enough approach. They don't evaluate their possibilities of profit before they go. They perceive the psychic import of the message, recognizing that Spirit is directing them to a community that needs their help. They simply receive the message and go. Powerful.

The Don't Zone. Closed doors deliver much of the guidance esp-intuition offers. Paul and his companions have been wandering the area of Greece, unable to find their right place. They try Phrygia and Galatia, but their intuition, once they get there, "forbids them to speak" (Acts 16.6). So they wander on – holy men in search of a needful pulpit. Their sixth awareness won't let them enter the several cities they journey to.

A "no" is an answer. A "not this place" or "not this man" is an answer. What makes it exasperating for the human animal is that we want more certainty. We like to know what *to do.* Nevertheless, the Spirit keeps them moving on until it positions them where it wants them. Then it provides the compelling opportunities for them to talk. The direction provided in esp comes in its own perfect spiritual timing, not the timing desired or guessed at by man – yet, following intuition every step of the way, synchronicity brings it all to pass in time for all things.

From Dawn To Dusk

Esp informs the Bible from its dawning to its dusking pages. In this chapter we've explored the dimensions of esp particularly through clairvoyance, intuition, and telepathy, enjoying our visits to some engaging psychicsites in Biblical literature.

From early in the Bible's lore we encounter Noah, second father of humanity, undertaking his massive project guided solely by the whisperings in his heart. Things don't look that threatening at the time he begins gathering the materials to build his ark. Later we visit Samuel seeing Saul's thoughts and Ahijah reading the heart of Jeroboam's wife. Near the storybook's end Jesus uses telepathic demonstrations to impress candidates and turn them into proselytizers.

As we read, study, and realize the truth of what occurs in these situations, it is good to reflect on our unspoken premises in this book, significant premises, as well, of the Bible itself. The psychi-spiritual life and its manifestations are not only for a chosen people, focused solely in a narrow slip of time – they are for you. What we learn to see, we open to demonstrate in our own spiritual adventures. *Your* spiritual adventures.

Chapter 2

Channeling: Revealing The Word

———···••··———

he sees what others do not see,
hears what others do not hear,
feels what others cannot feel...
and lets us see it,
hear it, feel it
in his poetry, his lessons,
and the dramas of his life.
(ted martin)

hanneling is the quintessential psychic art, the most commonly recorded psi
event in the Bible.
   It seems expressions of esp fluctuate through periods of more or less
prominence. Divination, for instance, enjoys tides of high usage, but it also has its
ebbs. While channeling follows that wave, it never seems to dip to the same degree
as the others. It is more consistently popular.

In channeling, a human individual delivers information received – visibly,
audibly, or kinesthetically – through a psi connection. The phenomenon imparts
information, insight, powers, and abilities to the instrument that he or she would
certainly not otherwise possess. The channel makes visible the unvisible,
transmuting the Universal Energy into poetry, story, explication, drama, art,
admonishment, business, and/or politics.

The prophets are metaphysical transformer stations, receiving high voltage
impressions from God and converting them into messages suitable for the people
of their time and locale – and beyond.

We find another suitable analogy in radio transmissions, since they also appear
to be immaterial. A radio receiver makes the message moving in the ethers
understandable. All the while the message is surely there, whether there is an
instrument available to pick it up or not. First the radio receives the message. But
the average human doesn't understand electricity very well, so the receiver must
then decode/recode it. It changes its form from one type of energy waves into
energy waves perceivable to humans as human speech and communication. It
particularizes the message to a specific place, before specific individuals.

Carrying this analogy further, we see another parallel in the relative power of
the source and the receiver. The channeler receives messages from the All-

Pervading Energy, but the message is much broader than the single application. It has massively more expanse than the particularization. Anyone, for instance, even millions of individuals simultaneously, can tune in to the same radio frequency, receive the same transmission, receive the same message, and never diminish the power of the Energy at all. In the same way, messages from the divine energy field are meant to provide light to many persons, including succeeding generations of humanity.

Additionally, the typical channel serves as a two-way radio, a receiver and a transmitter, also carrying humanity's praise and petition to the Spirit. God is the base station, the channeler is the field unit. As channelers, we receive the message and share it with the individuals who happen to be surrounding our particular situation in the panoply of eternity. Field units talk back, sending reports, thanking the base for the support, direction, and adventures of the day, seeking clarification and further direction as necessary.

Truly, the channel, that human receiver-transmitter tuned to the frequency of Divinity, is a marvelous instrument.

It is a gift available to all. Paul exhorts you to "earnestly desire the spiritual gifts, especially that you may prophesy" (1Cor. 14.1). Praising the channelers in their midst, those who speak for the benefit of others, he concludes his discourse with, "I *want* you to channel" (1Cor. 14.5).

Awake!

Variations On A Theme

When we picture channeling, we usually see a medium dropping into trance. An individual wafts away the self-conscious dimensions of their person and allows an entity to speak through his or her body, speaking words using his or her mouth. This specialty is well represented.

The voice also speaks through the pen and the actions, severally or jointly, of any affected individual. Massively obvious, we know the entire scriptural writing we've codified as the Bible is all channeled material. This subject demands no treatment amongst believers. Written under the finger of numerous individuals, *Alpha* to *Omega*, beginning to end, the Bible is a channeled document. No one has put forth any claims of God's direct penmanship.

We also visit several psychicsites of channeling as acting. We also see channeling as architecture, in King Solomon's case. And though there is a separate chapter devoted to the topic, we also make a brief stop on this wing of the tour to visit channeling through the medium of divination, a specialty of its own.

Most incidents of Spirit possession occur to a lone individual, even when he or she is in the company of others, as with Elisha before the kings and Ezekiel before the elders. In the story of Pentecost, however, the Spirit enters the hearts of each of the individuals praying, chanting, and healing together. This is the famous drama of the tongues of fire, and the excesses the spirit drives them to.

The authors of many of the prophetic occurrences are the channelers themselves, who title their books with their own names. Multi-talented Moses is the notable exception in naming; tradition avers he writes the first five books, together called the *Pentateuch*, none of which bears his name. The notable exception to writing is Jesus. You know, of course, that Jesus does not write a word. The stories are written *about* him *sixty years after he passes on*. This just shows how the Cosmic Spirit provides for its own – it is not intended that Jesus' words be lost.

The subject can concern *anything*. And though the message is always contexted in the themes of the times, the work of the channelers possesses the timeless quality we recognize in things Biblical. Even today we are enriched with the influence of Biblical channeling.

Channeling Channels

As quickly as we thoughtfully encounter channeling, we discover several distinctions we may not have noted while we were only casually curious or outright non-believers in the phenomenon. There are four points that we visit today. The first of these distinctions concerns the state of the channel when the message comes, sleeping or waking. The second point involves the form these messages come in, visions, auditions, or sensations/intuitions. Third, we note that the divine messenger may actually be God himself or an angelic intermediary... or some medley of them both. Finally, the channeled message may be entered into and delivered in real time or it may be received and recorded for rebroadcasting later.

Waking Trance Or Sleeping Vision?

The message may come to the channel under both of the two basic states of the human organism, waking and sleeping. It may come in a dream or it may come in the ephemeral feeling state of waking Alpha, the period of relaxed objective brain activity, when the subconscious autonomic is ascendant.

Joseph of Genesis, Pharaoh, and Nebuchadnezzar all dream their messages of magnificent import during the subconscious movement of the night. Daniel's vision of the night comes as a dream. Joseph of Jesus receives direct guidance in a series of four dreams that come to him packaged in the space of Jesus' infancy.

During nonordinary cracks in the broad of day, angels and Gods appear to Abraham, Moses, Balaam, and Habakkuk. The *alpha* state – kin to paranormal sleepfulness.

In Visions, Auditions, And Feelings

You'll note, as we stop in on the different channelers, some talk more about *hearing* the voice or words of the Spirit, which they are sharing with us. Others speak more about *seeing* magical scenes and dramas that the Lord has prepared for them to see and to share.

In fact, one may *be* the other. Isaiah, just one who identifies the synphenomenal manifestation of the message, starts off his second message conflating the two separately appearing phenomena by identifying the *word* which he *hears*, simultaneously as the *vision* which he *sees*. He writes:

> The *word* which Isaiah the son of Amoz *saw* concerning Judah and Jerusalem. (Is. 2.1)

Sight and sound, seeing and hearing, are often juxtaposed in the Bible.

Further, these individuals may just be objectifying in the common visual or auditory sense what they are receiving as private metaphysical sensations from the Spirit. They clothe the impressions in local color. As Joseph Conrad, the Polish seafaring novelist says, the mind "gives a local habitation and a name" to what the heart feels.

That this takes place below the level of conscious awareness does not change the phenomenon. Certainly, the very function of the channel is to render divine things in terms the senses can connect with.

The Executive Position: God Or An Angelic Intermediary?

On our visit we will see that often the channeler identifies God as the speaker. Thus Zephaniah, as one instance, begins his discourse with,

> The word of the Lord which came to me:
> "I will utterly sweep away everything
> from the face of the Earth,"
> says the Lord. (Zeph. 1.1-2)

Zephaniah is sharing the message of God.

Sometimes the messenger is identified as an angel, as for instance the angel in the rockway before Balaam and his ass.

But it's not always so simple. It is sometimes difficult to distinguish between what appears as an angelic intermediary and God himself. The Lord visits Abraham one desert day. Abraham feels God's presence before him, and looks up to three mysterious visitors. The men ask for his wife, Sarah; and *God* speaks to her. It is an angel in Moses' burning bush; yet *God* speaks.

And John, in masterful strokes of illusion, announces his work and its inspiration as the revelation of Jesus the Christ... which God gave to Jesus, who gave it to the angel, who gives it to himself. Near the conclusion of his mystic psychosis, the grateful John falls at the feet of the angel who brings the message. But the angel will not accept worship, calling himself a companion to John and his kind. Yet he says the words of eternal life,

> "I am the Alpha and the Omega, the first and the last, the beginning and the end." (Rev. 22.13)

Sometimes it is God speaking; sometimes it is Jesus speaking; sometimes it is the angel speaking; sometimes it is John speaking. You have it here on good accord, each of these individuals is the God Spirit personified.

Real Time or Rebroadcasting?

Here is another distinction. Even while the message is channeled from a higher entity or force, it may be coming through live, in real time, or it may be coming through by rebroadcasting.

We find a good analogy in two very common instruments of our present society, the telephone or the recorder-player. When the channel functions as a telephone, the speaking entity is present in real time. The message is being heard by the recipients as it is spoken. God is interactive in the situation. The channeling is shared live, with the channeler acting as equipment. Thus when Elisha floats into the imaginal realms before the kings, God enters his body, assumes his vocal apparatus, and speaks.

When the channel functions as a recorder-player, he or she receives the message of God, records it, interprets it, and prepares it. The message is then shared as a playback performance. Thus Ezekiel works out his staging in advance to communicate a particular theme or message of God, and goes out specifically to render an effective and moving performance.

Channeling: For Weal Or For Ill?

Certain persons have decried "channeling" as a tool of the devil. Though for the most part they are well-intentioned, you don't have to get sucked into that dark abyss of ignorance, fear, and delusion.

Nevertheless, we acknowledge the charge that channeling can be used to an unwholesome purpose. But that does not build a case against the phenomenon of channeling. Channeling is simply a tool of communication, an access medium between the co-existing physical and spiritual domains. Beneficial spirits also are channeled.

Anything can be used for evil or for good. The striking match that lights the candles at the high services of Solomon's Temple is abused by the king's forces routing out the citizenry of an occupied land. Both the high mass in Italy and the black mass in Transylvania celebrate the divine-human transliteration through the red vitality of blood. The same nectar that gives wings to an artist's inspiration steels the thug slugging one down before he enters to rob the convenience store. Even his gun can be used to sustain human life, rather than spill it in the oppressive city streets. All this paints the inevitable conclusion: good or evil lies not in the instrument or phenomenon, but in the character of the wielder.

With skills dedicated to the Spirit, a great good is done. There is a long and revered tradition of channeling. Nehemiah says, "God warns his people by His Spirit through His prophets" (Neh. 9.30). King David, that worldly sensitive, thinks it important enough that he says in the last words of his songwriting career – and his life – "The Spirit of the Lord speaks by me, his word is upon my tongue" (2Sam. 23.2). John confirms, in Revelation, "The testimony of Jesus is the spirit of prophecy" (Rev. 19.10). In fact, channeling is so common in the spiritual tradition that we even have a book called the *Chronicles of the Seers.* Though it does not make the editorial cut into the Bible, Paul refers to it in 2Chr. 33.19.

God "speaks" through channels... He has never spoken but by channels... Never as himself... And God has much to say.. From Genesis to Revelation this entity channeling, God says, is Himself:

> They channel *me.*
> It is *I* speaking to the psychics;
> It is *I* who give vision upon vision;
> *I* ringing in their voice and their acts,
> *I* in the images of their poetry, drama, story, and song. (Hos. 12.10)

The Gift: Kiss Or Curse?

This is a seldom considered face of the phenomenon of channeling, though we are familiar with this concept in relation to eccentric or excessive artists. The channeler is changed by the charge of the Spirit flowing through.

Spirit flows through the channel according to the channel's own gifts, inclinations, experience, and character. This is exactly the reason the Force chooses the particular channel, because his or her predisposing qualities can best communicate the message. The Spirit chooses the channel through which to express, finding it suitable as it exists, simultaneously also positively transforming the channel. Channeling puts the channel into hyper-drive. It accentuates their outrageousness.

Ezekiel is dismissed as a mad man, a teller of allegories and riddles. Daniel and Micaiah are threatened politically, told they must render the proper message. Hosea hears the voice of God telling him it's alright – in fact a good thing – to sleep with the babes he's been salivating over.

The apostles begin their independent careers channeling. Prior to this time they are obscured in the shadow of the Master. The High Voltage inrush from a direct connection with the Ultimate Energy source causes massive changes. They suddenly display powers and abilities they would not otherwise unleash. Onlookers think they are drunk, though it is the middle of the day. "Many wonders and signs are done by the men" (Acts 2.43).

The sudden dramatic change in productivity, opportunity, infamy, and power that attends Cosmic illumination wreaks tidal waves through a person's affairs and public appearance.

Some don't think this so good... but why don't you ask the affected?

****

Channeling As We Know It

Buckle your belts! As we tour the channeling phenomenon we will see many prominent psychics channeling, from Moses to John, from *Genesis* to *Revelation*. We will pass a bank of minor channelers working, noting just how common it is in sacred literature. We will see the message of God coming direct to a medium from God, and we'll see it coming through angels. We will see the message coming in visions and we'll hear it coming direct in words. We will see channeling expressed through its own most common channel, the words of poetry, song, and discourse. We will see it as well expressed in art, architecture, and drama.

Buckle your belts, we're off!

Alien Visitors

The story of aliens visiting with *Abraham* and *Sarah* involves the query we played with earlier in this chapter. Is it God? Is it an angel? Only the discerning know for sure.

Abraham has the promise of God... From him will spring the chosen people. But, at an advanced age, with a equally old and unsteady wife in Sarah, he still has no child.

Abraham is dozing in the heat of the summer, sitting in the breezy doorway of his tent. Suddenly the Lord materializes before him.

Then, the passage continues,

> He lifts up his eyes, rubs them, but behold, *three* men are now standing in front of him. (Gen. 18.2)

God has now metamorphosed into three men. I'd be surprised, too, wouldn't you? God is now this trinity.

At Abraham's petitions, the strangers agree to stay for a meal. In the days before commercial eating establishments, this is expected courtesy. He calls his servants to hastily prepare a hearty meal for the men.

After the meal they kick back, take a drink and a smoke, and share their mystic message with Abraham:

> They say to him,
> "Where is Sarah your wife?"
> And he says,
> "She is in the tent." (Gen. 18.9)

In the very next words *God* is cited as the speaker,

> The *Lord* says,
> "I will surely return to you in the spring, and Sarah your wife shall have a son." (Gen. 18.10)

Sarah overhears their conversation and laughs at the preposterous idea. She hasn't had good sex in years. God challenges her, and tells her that she *will* have a child, "in the spring" (Gen. 18.14). Then, the prescience delivered, the speaker lowers its energy levels and transforms again into the three men. They set out from there.

Talk about channeling! These men are so much identified with God that their words and identity are repeatedly addressed as God. They are individuations of the Cosmic Force.

"Two Nations Are In Your Womb"

Rebekah. Finally, at forty, Isaac has his wife. The story is touching, how she, not knowing Isaac at all, accepts him, sets out for him, and meets and marries him.

But – complications! They pass the next twenty years without getting child. Rebekah is barren. Not to worry, though – this is a story. Isaac prays to God for her, and in response, God grants his prayer. She becomes pregnant. And when she gets several months into her pregnancy she must know. The child is continuously kicking and turning and moving within her. Since they did not have the same level of medical technology back then, no doctor can help her. She goes instead, to someone who can discern by metaphysical means what the issue is. She goes to "inquire of the Lord" (Gen. 25.23), and, the Bible tells us, not the psychic, but, the *Lord* – speaking through the psychic – answers her:

"Two nations are in your womb,

and two peoples, born of you, shall be divided;

the one shall be stronger than the other,

the elder shall serve the younger." (Gen. 25.23)

No wonder she's burdened! The reader tells her she has twins inside her struggling, as they will all their lives, for dominion one over the other.

When her days are fulfilled, as the psychic sees, she has twins. Esau, the firstborn, becomes the father of Edom, while Jacob, who changes his name to Israel after a dream wherein he wrestles with the devil all night, becomes the father of the twelve tribes of Israel.

Patronize The Psychics

The Bible's positive regard for psi makes it clear psi is a legitimate and needed profession. There is a service to be done for others – people have many needs to "inquire of the Lord." We all have different talents. Those who are psychic are naturally the ones the person with a question or concern will seek out.

This story of Rebekah and the children still in her womb, brings the consideration of psi as a profession to the fore. Answers are sought by a querent, that is a questioner. Rebekah has a concern in her heart and she seeks out a man able to see the unseen – present and future – and tell her what God's will and way is. Thus is the phrase repeated numerous times in the Bible, to "inquire of the Lord."

The mother of both the Judeo-Christian and Moslem worlds, Rebekah, seeks mystic answers. The Lord answers her in prescient poetic language.

The reassurance is beneficial. The reading is correct.

If, as some would have you believe, the exercise of psi is somehow wrong or evil, it is doubtful God would give this portentous and correct reading regarding the destiny of such a large portion of humanity to their sole mother.

Angel In The Burning Bush

When *Moses* kills a policeman, he takes a dive far from his status as the grandson of Pharaoh. Blood shows. He is an alien in the land. Now the clever criminal, he runs to Midian. There he takes a job tending sheep. And he marries the farmer's daughter. Forty years pass uneventfully – then Moses sees something!:

> The angel of the Lord appears to him in a flame of fire out of the midst of a bush. (Ex. 3.2)

We have an angel here. *Watch the shift* – recognizing he has Moses' attention, God calls to him out of the bush. (Ex. 3.4)

God, not an angel, announces himself, saying,

> "I am the God of your father, the God of Abraham, the God of Isaac, and the God of Jacob." (Ex. 3.6)

Clearly, we have God here. The angel and God are conflated in Moses' mystical visitor.

What follows then is a dialogue in which God tells him what he shall do and how he shall do it. He shall go to Pharaoh and secure the release of his people. He shall accomplish this mission with whatever means are necessary.

Backed and directed by God, Moses is assured his efforts will be successful.

Moses remains in close contact with God throughout the remainder of his career and his life. Moses is the human instrument through whom God acts on the stage of human history at this moment.

The Ten Commandments

Moses is in power. He wrests the nation from the clutches of Egypt with a magic unparalleled in either the ancient or the modern worlds. Then it's time to manage the nation suddenly nomadic. Early in this period Moses brings forth the ten commandments. The story, as *Exodus* 19-20 tells it, has God talking with Moses, giving him the channeled messages he is to relate to the people he leads.

After Moses enters the sacred mountain, the first words of God, quoted by Moses, are instructions to channel:

> "Thus you shall say to the house of Jacob, and tell the people of Israel..." (Ex. 19.3)

This is the beginning of a series of messages that Moses receives over the course of the next three ritual days. Moses gets high, gets an inspiration, and shares it with the people as the very word of God. They listen to him and affirm,

> "All that the Lord has spoken we will do." (Ex. 19.8)

This sentence tacitly says that the people accept and believe the words Moses speaks as the very words of God. They recognize Moses as a channel, a vehicle through whom the intended message flows.

Moses also channels upstream, carrying the people's messages back to God, as we find in Exodus 19.8 that "Moses reports the words of the people to the Lord." Thus Moses serves as a channel in both directions, from God to humanity and from humanity to God.

In chapter 20 God gives Moses the ten commandments atop Mt. Sinai. But the people are down below, not even touching the mountain's base. They are not capable of meeting God directly, as is the illuminati Moses. God speaks to Moses in dark clouds, accompanied with his celestial train of lightning, thunder, fire, and the sound of trumpets. Moses understands. And he takes the message to the streets.

Most people don't know it, but there is a lot more rigamarole that Moses lays on the people. (Most people haven't read the Bible.) In fact, God lays down rules and regulations for the Israelites the full length of the next three chapters, chapters 21, 22, and 23. And Moses writes all the words of the Lord (Ex. 24.4). And there is much, much more. Written or spoken, the channeled message of Infinity. And it is here today.

Channeling As An Artist

Bezalel. After God meets with Moses and gives him the statutes, ordinances, and the covenant, he directs him, with the people of Israel, to build him a mobile home. In Exodus chapters 26-30 God gives very explicit instructions for the construction of his elegant holy tent. It's a good read. Such a grand project requires exceptional artists and artisans. Not to worry, however, this is God.

The Lord tells Moses he has filled certain of the men – in fact, "all able-bodied men" (Ex. 31.6) – with the requisite ability. (Here is an early form of the draft.) However, there is one God has anointed above all others. All others serve his artistic insight and ability. God tells Moses,

> "I have called Bezalel by name, and I have filled him with the Spirit of God, with ability and intelligence, with knowledge and all craftsmanship, to devise artistic designs, to work in gold, silver, and bronze, in cutting stones for setting, and in carving wood, for work in every craft." (Ex. 31.2-5)

Here God elevates art and architecture to the same status as words and other inspired action. True, channeling God through words and writing is more common, and, perhaps in former days, reached more people, yet God here consecrates art in the service of the divine as a channeling phenomenon also. Like the scribed words of Moses, art leaves an artifact.

Further, as always, every great person has an army of subordinates and contract persons handling the details. It is here that God assures Moses that other worthy artists and artisans will willingly enlist in the grand service and extensive project Moses is to coordinate:

> "And behold, I have appointed with him Oholiab, and I have given to all able-bodied men ability that they may make all that I have commanded you: the tent of meeting, and the ark of the testimony, and the mercy seat

that is thereon, and all the furnishings of the tent, the table and its utensils, and the pure lampstand with all its utensils, and the altar of incense, and the altar of burnt offering with all its utensils, and the laver and its base, and the finely worked garments, the holy garments for Aaron the priest and the garments of his sons, for their service as priests, and the anointing oil and the fragrant incense for the holy place. According to all that I have commanded you they shall do." (Ex. 31.6-11)

It makes sense God would direct the building and the ornamentation of his temple, doesn't it? The designers, artists, and craftsman channel the Divine.

"I Must Speak Only That Which The Lord Speaks"

The story of *Balaam* particularly demonstrates the multidimensional nature of the psychic arts. In the passages describing Balaam's adventure it seems that divination and channeling are the same phenomenon. They may be different, however, in which case the validity for them each seems co-equal. We will check out the treatment of them, and how the treatment they receive indicates their equality.

During the Egyptian exodus, Balak, king of Moab, is faced with this great horde of people entering his land. He has seen what the Jewish army has done to other peoples, their possessions, and their lands, so he seeks the assistance of the psychic, Balaam, because, as he says to him,

"He whom you bless is blessed, and he whom you curse is cursed." (Num. 22.6)

Here we get an insider's view of the channeling phenomenon. Clearly, we see the channeling event. God *comes* to the call of a man, even a "heathen" and an "outsider." Of equally great significance to our present conversation, we actually see him channeling that message. Remember, channeling a message is simply taking a message received via psychic, emotional, mental, visionary, auditory, or kinesthetic channels and repackaging/transmitting it. Here we see the psychic receiving the message, direct from God. In his meditation,

God comes to Balaam and says,

"You shall not go with them; you shall not curse the people, for they are blessed." (Num. 22.12)

His next course of action is simple. Upon awakening, he sends the messengers on their way,

"For the Lord has refused to let me go with you." (Num. 22.13)

In this statement, we see the channeling consummated, the message delivered. But look at what's happened to it during transmission. Absolutely, the message is there. But it is filtered. Balaam does not say anything about the people being blessed; instead he softens the message. Instead of having any direct content beneficial to the king's enemies, it is truncated to a statement that Balaam is not allowed to go.

Also note this. God *speaks* directly to Balaam. God has identifiable words. However, Balaam does not deliver the exact words of God, as Isaiah, Jeremiah, and a host of other practicing channelers frequently do. Balaam gives a *summary*. Not that there is anything essentially wrong with giving a summary of a message. It is simply good and valid that we querents into the psychic arts note this point. There are many questions.

Again, Balak sends a commission of princes and nobles, more numerous and more high ranking. Through them the king tells him, in effect, "name your price" (Num. 22.16-17). Balaam does not rule out the profitable proposition. After all, the priestcraft *is* his profession. But he will not be driven solely by money:

> "Though Balak were to give me his house full of silver and gold, I could not go beyond the command of the Lord my God, to do less or more." (Num. 22.18)

He asks them to tarry this night, too, while,

> "I see what God wants me to do." (Num. 22.19)

Would that Israel's own were so moved by rectitude.

God tells him he can go, but, like Jesus instructing his chosen centuries down the timeline, tells him not to prepare in advance. He is to say such as he is inspired to say in the moment:

> "Go with the men; but only the word which I bid you, that shall you speak." (Num. 22.35)

Still no commitment – neither to curse nor to bless.

When he arrives, King Balak really excoriates him. How could this small-time psychic not come and partake of the glory of the king? You need to recognize just how significant Balaam's original refusal was to this level of a man. Would you decline an invitation from the president of the United States? Would you tell her *no*?

Again, Balaam indicates that he will speak only the word of the Lord, only what God channels through him:

> "Well, I've come to you now, but I, of myself, have no power to speak anything. I am but a channeler. I will speak. But it is what the Lord speaks that I will say." (Num. 22.38)

Either way, of course, he'll get the money. Sure enough, when the time comes, the transmission is a blessing on the Israelis, not a curse.

Stubbornly, Balak pays him to prepare an even more elaborate nighttime ritual communion with the Lord.

The reading does not change. So Balak pays for some more. God has spoken. The reading does not change.

Balaam's final oracle, the beautiful blessings on the Israelites – and curses on the Moabites – are preserved for you in the poetic song of *Numbers* 24.5-9. The "Spirit takes possession of him" (Num. 24.2), and he starts,

> "The oracle of Balaam the son of Beor,
> The oracle of the man whose eye is opened,

The oracle of him who hears the words of God,
Who sees the vision of the Almighty." (Num. 24.2-4)

Psychic Considerations

There are a couple of interesting points we do well to note in this psychicstop. Morning is always a good time to attune to Cosmic forces, because of the freshness in the face of the world. Nighttime, however, has some advantages of its own. We also come face-to-face with one of the reasons God talks to us through the psychic channels, to warn us that we may avoid some proposed or projected course that would bring evil consequences into our lives. Would you listen?

In The Hours Of The Night. We see that Balaam's preferred time of communing with the Universe is during the hours of night. This has traditionally been a time of prime mystical activity, because there is less interference with outside sources of "noise."

Something you have no doubt experienced before attests to this. Have you ever noticed how, in the hours of the night you can receive distant radio stations which you can never receive in the day? There is less electromagnetic interference. Psychic impressions, though subtle, are waves nevertheless, and are affected by the same things. In fact, because they are so subtle, they can easily be drowned-out during the coarser day. The night time offers quiet to attune to the refined impressions of Spirit.

Now you know why mystics work the night.

"I Told You So-o-o." Why would you pay for the services of a psychic and then ignore the advice if it doesn't match what you wanted to hear? Balak has seen what will come of what he proposes – Balaam has told him. Surely Balak is given the opportunity to alter events by implementing a different course of action, but he does not. What can you do for someone who won't listen? Events transpire as foretold, to Balak's misfortune.

"Samuel! Samuel!"

Samuel is dedicated to the service of the Lord even before he is born, even before he is conceived. His mother, poor, pitiful, barren Hannah, utters a soulful vow after years of fruitlessness. Her husband's other *fruitful* wives lord it over her. She prays to God that if he will see fit to bless her with a male child, "then I shall give him to you all the days of his life" (1Sam. 1.11). She gratefully gives the boy to the service of God as soon as he is weaned. Like Arthur with Merlin.

Samuel, some years later as a young boy, is ministering in the monastery to Eli during a time when "word of the Lord is seldom heard, and no visions are granted" (1Sam. 3.1). He gets a wake-up call from God. Three times God rouses him, calling "Samuel! Samuel!" (1Sam. 3.4, 6, 8). But Samuel doesn't get it; he keeps rising and waking up Eli, his teacher. Finally, on this third time, Eli does. He tells the lad to go lie down again,

"And *this* time, if you hear the voice, *reply* to the Lord." (1Sam. 3.9)

Are you surprised that the Lord comes and calls as before?

God brings Samuel news about the upcoming destruction of the house of Eli. And it comes to pass. When the oracled battle takes place, two things happen. First, the Israelites lose the ark of the covenant, the very presence of God, to the Philistines, and, second, Eli's sons die in battle. Old Eli, upon hearing of the losses, falls backwards from his seat, breaks his neck, and dies.

From this point on, throughout a long career which includes anointing the first two kings of Israel, Samuel is a true and faithful channeler of God:

As Samuel grows up, the Lord is with him, and none of his words go unfulfilled. From Dan to Beersheba, all Israel recognizes that Samuel is a channel of the Lord. (1Sam. 3.19-21)

Even In The Political Machine

Samuel. Saul. Most people view government as the antithesis of anything Godly. While that may be true in the normal sense, Samuel, priest and psychic by profession, is the chosen instrument who anoints God's first two kings to rule his people. Saul first. David second. That's Godly government.

Patriated in their homeland, the Jewish people get restless and demand a king. "Everyone *else* has a king!" they whine. Samuel, being chief judge at the time, discusses the issue with God, who indicates that, though He might rather not, to appease them and maintain dominion, he will give them a king.

On the sudden, some days later, he tells Samuel that the next day he will send the man who is to be king. The instant Samuel sees the tall, good-looking Saul the next day, he knows.

In The Doing

The day following, when he anoints Saul king in a secret ceremony, by *doing* the words of God, Samuel is channeling the Lord. He is *doing* the Lord's message. This, instead of the more normal form of *saying* the Lord's message, which is, of course, its own kind of doing.

The Anointing Of David

David. One day *Samuel* remembers how unfriendly the Amalekites were when the Jews were subduing their native lands. It's time for payback. Samuel instructs Saul to mobilize his army and,

"Go, and smite Amalek, and utterly destroy all that they have; do not spare them, but kill both man and woman, infant and suckling, ox and sheep, camel and ass." (1Sam. 15.3)

It is a massively successful campaign. They kill masses of them, utterly destroying every man, woman, and child of Amalekite blood but one, Agag, king of the Amalekites. They also spare,

> The best of the sheep and of the oxen and of the fatlings, and the lambs, and all that is good, and do not utterly destroy them; all that is despised and worthless they utterly destroy. (1Sam. 15.9)

This is the crime: they do not kill *every* living thing and artifact of the populace; they covet the valuable spoil God has decreed for destruction.

This turn of events causes God to repent of having made Saul king. God wants this race erased from Earth. Samuel later consummates the genocide by himself hewing the king into bloody pieces. This arm of the Amalekite irritant is gone, according as the Lord commanded, but not because of Saul's fidelity, but Samuel's.

And the faithful channel delivers a new message to Saul:

> "Because you have rejected the word of the Lord, he has also rejected you from being king." (1Sam. 15.23)

None of Saul's importunities for leniency bear fruit. The stage is set for David. One day the Lord prompts Samuel:

> "Fill your horn with oil, and go; I am sending you to Jesse the Bethlehemite, for I have provided for myself a king among his sons." (1Sam. 16.1)

After numerous candidates, all of whom Samuel rejects, not receiving the definitive nod of God, finally the overlooked David arrives. The instant Samuel sees the ruddy, handsome youngster, God whispers the command:

> "Arise, anoint him; *he* is the one." (1Sam. 16.12)

Samuel rises and anoints the lad king by divine right.

This is serious, because Saul is not dead. He is still on the throne. It is some service, some adventures, some battles, some years later that David ascends to the actual throne. However, his psychic awareness and the grace God bestows to him are preparing him every moment for the moment of the big acceptance.

Channel In The Doing

Samuel, following the impelling of the inner voice, acts as the message dictates. Thus Samuel, again with this king, channels God in the *doing* or executing of the act God intends. Samuel channels, *performing* the word of the Lord. Cosmic illumination expresses itself through the medium of the chosen channel for the chosen purpose.

Channeling A Channeler

Medium At Endor. Samuel. Saul needs some advice. He's frantic before the massed army of the Philistines he must fight on the morrow. He's tried, but none of the psychics of Israel can help him, God is not answering his inquiries,

> ...not by dreams, by divination, nor by channeling. (1Sam. 28.6)

But Saul knows Samuel has answers. So, cloaked by the night, he visits the sensitive sister at Endor. Through her potent psychic spells and abilities, she establishes a connection with the UnderWorld. Samuel answers the call.

It is possible that she just bewitches Saul, with her accoutrements and behaviors of the occult – the night, the candles, the incense, her bells, the rhythm of her moves, her powerful prayer of invocation – and causes him to have the delusion that Samuel is before him and he is sharing a conversation with him. But an open reading of the passage cannot carry the weight of that premise.

Samuel curses Saul. Saul dies the *next* day.

Of Psychic Verities

You'll find a fuller telling of this incredible story in chapter 6, when we visit the potpourri of necromancy. Even as little as we see today, however, this passage has many things to tell.

But To Understand! Again, let's give the Bible the credit it is due as a pool of the truths of life. Accepting it as the channeled work of God, we seek to *understand* the Bible, not to bend it to our own biases. We seek to be among the few with ears that hear, eyes that see, and hearts that understand.

A Psychic Phone Call. In the HoloCosm, it does not seem impossible at all. The medium puts in a psychic telephone call to Samuel, so to speak, and he answers. Except this phone is a holo-videophone, transmitting not only his voice, not only a picture, but his very presence, too. Never leaving the Nether realms of his habitation, Samuel appears before Saul in the present time and space. The words he speaks to Saul are spoken by Samuel and no other. The channeler is not, as we have often seen, receiving the message and then rebroadcasting it. The channeler in this case, with her superior psychic abilities, opens the channel for Samuel, and he comes through in real time. It is a real time curse. That it works this Biblical story clearly demonstrates.

The Psychic Channels. Note the apparent equivalence the Bible portrays between the separate psychic inquiry channels. Dreams, divination, channeling, oracles, necromancy are but different facets of discerning the Divine will. Through these atemporal arts, the able practitioner establishes a connection with the Divinity of the Spiritual God.

All the psychic arts are used to the same end. The Divine speaks. We might consider the likeness of the different channels as compared to a communication we might want to make with a friend. The message will go through whatever channel or medium we choose. For instance, we might pick up the phone and call our friend. Or we might write a letter, and send it as email or as postal mail. Or we might tell a friend to relay our message to her. Or we might make the journey to her presence, and tell her face-to-face.

In all cases, the message is basically identical. Only the vehicle of transmission and connection differs. In the same way, the diverse psychic arts are but differing devices of the Divine's expression.

"O, But God Does Answer!" Sometimes God does not appear to answer when sought. That *is* an answer. Now it still needs to be interpreted and understood, but it *is* an answer. You tell me... What is the meaning of no connection in the querent's consciousness? Saul is careening out of balance at the time he is seeking the Lord. In regards to this fact, is no answer the proper answer? Does God refusing to speak to Saul say anything? If so, what?

The operating counterpoint here is best noted by the words of Jesus,
"Seek, and you shall find." (Mt. 7.7)
Saul keeps looking; he finds. He finds a sensitive of a higher power to make the contact with the psycho-spiritual realms. And finally God answers.

"Don't Ask If You Don't Want To Know." The truly anointed channeler reveres his or her commitment to the craft. A part of that commitment is to speak what is revealed. There must be a reason God gives Samuel to see what he does. Should Samuel then second-guess *God?* *Could* Samuel, foreseeing Saul's death, give any other news? Should the disturbed Samuel dissimulate?

Poor Saul. He finds, alright. And Samuel pronounces the curse of death on him with one day's fuse!

Querent, careful! You may not like what you hear... Don't ask if you don't want to know!

Oh, But She Is An Insider! God is above parochial favoritism. It just doesn't happen. That's a bias of times and peoples which God more allows than encourages. As we see with Balaam, and we see again with this sensitive sister, no, you don't have to be an "insider" – someone professing the currently politically correct God or Gods – to establish true and actual contact with the spiritual realms. You don't have to have the blood, the God(s), or the belief systems of the self-appointed superior peoples. God, being the father-mother of all creation – even to its *billions of galaxies*, even the father-mother of *every human* – gives to all the full measure of his bounty.

Illustrating just this fact in a powerful way, none of the psychics in the fold are able to give Saul the assistance he seeks. A king has resources. He keeps looking. He consults this lady, who in fact is the psychic with the greatest power and ability. She does what they cannot. And not only does she channel, but she channels a channeler who himself gives Saul what he seeks.

This story clearly demonstrates that channeling works.

A House Not Built Of Hands

Nathan. David has control of the kingdom, having subdued all external threat and quelled all internal opposition. In his leisure he gets to thinking. He realizes he lives in a pampered house built with the elegant cedars of Lebanon, but that God still lives in the tent Moses built for him hundreds of years ago. He is struck with a profound project: *I shall build God a Temple!!!*

He shares his thoughts with one of the psychics he regularly counsels with, Nathan. Nathan approves, telling him,

"Go and do all that is in your heart; for the Lord is with you." (2Sam. 7.3)

David is blessed; the Lord has favored his ways. So, quite naturally, Nathan infers that if David wants to build a temple to the Lord, it is right. But, it turns out, that is Nathan's own advice. The words that trail the heels of his statement indicate how he discerns otherwise:

But that same night the word of the Lord comes to Nathan." (2Sam. 7.4)

God has selected Nathan as his channel, to carry his words to King David. Nathan receives a message for rebroadcasting:

"Go and tell my servant David:
  'Thus says the Lord:
      "Would you build me a house to dwell in? I have not dwelt in a
      house since the day I brought up the people of Israel from Egypt to
      this day, but I have been like a nomad, a tent for my dwelling. In all
      places where I have moved with all the people of Israel, did I ever
      speak a word saying, 'Why have you not built me a house of
      cedar?'"'" (2Sam. 7.5-7)

In other words, God says, "Hey, I haven't complained! I *like* it in my tent! Come to think of it," God seems to think next, "You *want* a house... You'll *have* a house!" – chuckling under his breath, "*My* way!" Always one with a clever word sense, in an utter twist of the roles of the actor and the acted for, God promises to build David a house, bending *house* to its metaphoric meaning of *lineage*. God is still talking to Nathan, giving him, at this point, the exact words he is to say to David,

      "When your days are done and you go to the grave, your very own son,
      king by divine right, shall build a house for my name. I declare that I will
      make of *you* a house; I will establish the throne of your kingdom for
      ever." (2Sam. 7.11-13)

David will not build a temple. Solomon will build the physical temple. God will build the royal house with a name that runs through David, forever favored. There is only so much a mortal may do.

David, world leader that he is, accepts the psychic's message. He acts according to the part apportioned him. The building of the Temple unfolds in mythic proportions, completed royally by David's son, Solomon. David's temple role is another. He plans the temple, he amasses riches, materials, and supplies. But it falls to Solomon to actually accomplish the building of it. David's privilege in destiny is to simultaneously be and to lead ultimately to the "house not built of hands." *Sangreal.*

Indeed, the prescient words of Nathan are fulfilled. It is from the royal house of David that Jesus is born. The spiritual transformation of David is complete.

"Choose Your Evil"

David. Gad channels God at a point several years later than Nathan. It has been a peaceable few years, but there is still administration. A nation does not run itself. As part of the process of tightening control, David orders a census. God does not like this.

The logical thing to stir repentance and obedience is a harsh punishment, and God has a lalapalooza in store for David. He visits Gad, "David's seer" (2Sam. 24.11), and instructs him to go see David and offer him a choice of three evils: 1) a famine of three years duration, 2) military aggression against him for three months, or 3) a pestilence of three days in the land. David says he'll take hand of the Lord over the hand of man, any day. His choice is only *not* door number two. God kills 70,000 men in the three days of the plague. Too bad about the trauma on their wives, daughters, and infant sons. And David has to adjust the census figures hurriedly.

What Government Really Is

In this channeling incident God offers David a hand in how things will play out.

God shows David what government really is. God treats David exactly as David intends to treat the people. Hem them in and give them choices. All choices of the ruler's design, mind you, but choices. Pick your poison.

Channeling As Acting

The scene between the able captain, *Jeroboam*, and *Ahijah*, the wizard-seer is another Biblical scene right out of *MacBeth*. Of course, when we say this, we understand that it is actually the other way around. The Biblical writers didn't get their inspiration from Shakespeare, rather he got inspiration from them. He knew it well. He was, after all, editor on the King James project.

David has gone to sleep with his fathers, and Solomon is at the helm of state. Solomon builds the Temple. However, after the unifying and ennobling national effort of building the Temple is completed, things get lax in the land. God gets mad and decides to get even. He will punish Solomon. God then raises up both external and internal enemies.

In fact, the man who eventually takes ten twelfths of the throne, is not a family member at all, but a commander in Solomon's forces. He is the Captain of the Labor in the province of Joseph, a mighty position he handles superbly. A man on the rise.

At this time when Jeroboam is brimming in power and confidence, a weird brother appears before him on the road. Like the sisters of the cauldron, Ahijah utters strange words promising the throne and all it represents, lands, power, money, and prestige.

After Ahijah sets things up with his dramatic presentation, he opens and channels God in real time. Spirits from the unseen assume his body and vocal apparatus. The two of them in the open country, Ahijah takes his new flowing garment off, methodically tears it lengthwise into twelve strips, and lays them out before Jeroboam. He looks up at him, attentive all the while in this mystery, then says, "Take ten... Any ten." After Jeroboam's chosen, the entity that has Ahijah resumes:

"For thus says the Lord,
'Behold, I am about to tear the kingdom from the hand of Solomon, and give you ten of the tribes. All this I will give to you. Though I will have Solomon keep Judah, homeland of my heart and my worship, I will take you, and you shall reign over all that your soul desires, and you shall be king over Israel.'" (1Kg. 11.31-37)

Why do you say I *will be king? Can it be so? What shall I do? Wait! Come back! Tell me more!...*

Just like MacBeth. Prescient promises of power he cannot hope to achieve drive him on.

Here is the beginning of the divided kingdom of Israel and Judah. It begins as an idea and intention in the mind of God. God notifies his players, setting things up like a master chess player. He inspires and motivates the key players to cooperate with him. It manifests in reality.

Psychic Advisor To The Throne
Shemaiah. Understandably, King Rehoboam, Solomon's successor-son, isn't happy about having the massive portion of his inheritance, ten of the landed tribes, sheared from his hand. So he prepares for war. He has already assembled the military machine necessary to invade and take back the reprobate Israel, and is accomplishing the final strategizing and training when,

The word of God comes to Shemaiah, the man of God. (1Kg. 12.22)

Shemaiah receives the script which he is to rebroadcast to Solomon and the assembled troops, which he does:

"Thus says the Lord,
'You shall not go up or fight against your kinsmen, the people of Israel. Return every man to his home, for this thing is from me.'" (1Kg. 12.24)

It Is Accomplished Through A Channeled Message
Notice, again, how often the characters in the Bible act on the channeled word. They *believe* it is God speaking through the psychic. They believe the psychic speaks the actual and true words of God. And they then *act* on that belief in what,

should you really believe, is the logical fulfillment of the inspirations and instructions received:

They hearken to the word of the Lord, and go back home. (1Kg. 12.24)

Would that we all could do so well. Does this change the drama of history? If they had invaded and subjugated the breakaways, such as the United States North did the Confederate South, would there have been no divided kingdom in the chronicles of history? Would it have remained one nation united under God? Who can say? But surely – looking at it through the Biblical believer's lenses – it is easy to see the will and the hand of God etching the events of history.

And it is done through a channeled message.

"Can 400 Psychics All Be Wrong?"

Micaiah. 400 Psychics. For three years Syria and Israel continue without war. Pretty good. But Jumping Jehoshaphat, King of Judah, pays a visit to the Ahab, King of Israel, who stirs him to hostilities. Ahab wants to recapture some land, Ramoth-Gilead, which Syria took from them in an earlier battle. Being Ahab's ally, Jehoshaphat, pledges his service and his troops. But it is not his custom to go to war without consulting a psychic. Enter an interesting episode of psychic counseling.

As the host, Ahab, declares a psychic faire, which attracts over four hundred of the nation's best. To a person they give a favorable reply to his query, saying,

"Yes, go up and invade the land; you can wrest it back, for the Lord has given it to you." (1Kg. 22.6)

One flamboyant channeler even goes down in history for his dramatic presentation of that lie. Zedekiah, son of Chenaanah, makes a set of iron horns for himself and, enacting out a gouging, rampaging victory, declares to the two kings,

"With these you shall push the Syrians until they are utterly destroyed." (1Kg. 22.11)

But Jehoshaphat still feels uneasy. After hearing these four-hundred, he asks Ahab if there might be another. To appease him, Ahab sends for Micaiah. But he has the officers and detectives who pick him up let him know what his reply had better be; this aggression is important to Ahab:

"Behold, the words of the prophets with one accord are favorable to the king; let your word be like the word of one of them, and speak favorably." (1Kg. 22.13)

What are the odds? 400 to 1.

Micaiah replies,

"As the Lord lives, what the Lord says to me, *that* will I speak." (1Kg. 22.14)

This is not what they want to hear.

Nevertheless, rushed into royal audience, flanked by sworded soldiers, Micaiah does what he understands he must. He replies to the king's query, "Shall we go to

Ramoth-Gilead to battle, or shall we forbear?" with the commanded words. But you can bet his body language blazons his super-contradiction to the words.

Jehoshaphat calls him on it, and demands he speak the *truth*. Now the psychic frees up, spins around, putting himself in the position of channeling, projects to the cathedral of enchantment, and reveals what sees:

"I see all Israel scattered upon the mountains, as sheep that have no shepherd." (1Kg. 22.17)

But reason prevails. It is 400-to-1, after all. After a riotous round of police brutality on Micaiah, they throw him unconscious into prison.

Would you believe it comes to pass? In the battle of a single day, Ahab is killed, pierced through the heart by an enemy arrow. He has his driver pull him from the fray, and, propped up in the glimmers of dusk, watching the battle, he dies. The blood from his wound is washed out of his chariot the next day, a delight for lapping dogs and a stain on bathing whores. As predicted. A shame.

To Understand The Ways Of Psi
This short story is a rich resource for all who seek to understand the ways of psi.

The True Dilemma? Or, is it false but true? Or truly false? Or truly stated falsely taken? Or false, truly taken? Oh what a riddle! Every one of the four hundred psychics speaks falsely, though they speak truly. They speak what God gives them to speak. God, sporting his trickster suit, fills them with a "lying spirit" (1Kg. 22.23). In accordance with the Lord's designs on them, they do truly lie.

Then, for additional drama, he channels a distinctly different message through Micaiah. A true message also. Micaiah, like the other psychics, can't do anything other than honor the urging of the Spirit.

Or might we reconsider? Micaiah at first, under the clubs of the government's political correctness campaign, actually does speak falsely. Interesting. Then, upon entreaty by Jehoshaphat, he speaks truly.

Don't you imagine God loves it, playing with humanity, confusing them with allegories, riddles, and ambiguities? Causing those who truly practice their art to speak falsely? And those who might lie to speak truly?

The Perverseness Of The People. One stumbling block many people put in front of the messages of true spiritual revelation is their insistence that the message be good. In other words, they don't really come to hear the word of the Universe. They really want to be confirmed in their biases. They literally don't hear it otherwise – it doesn't register. You will find 401 in this world who will do exactly that for you, seeking your approval. The only way to find the truth, however, is to really seek the truth. Jehoshaphat does.

It is a perceptual block. The truth is revealed. But that is not enough. The human individual may have biases that prevent them seeing it or, seeing it, may have biases that prevent them from acting on it to their benefit. As Jesus says,

"Be watchful how you hear." (Lk. 8.18)

They block it with their understanding, even when they are actually *sure* of the message, as Jehoshaphat obviously is. I mean, come on! He has 400 psychics giving him the Cosmic go-ahead. Can 400 psychics all be wrong? Yet he still seeks out another. Somewhere in his heart he knows they are wrong. Even, however, when he receives that honest contrarian reading, he still invades Ramoth-Gilead, at the cost of a king's life. What perversity is this?

The Perverseness Of The Prophets. The independent prophets are prey to the same opportunistic foibles as any other independently employed person. That they are artists – psychic artists – only has tangential significance when it comes to how they represent and fulfill their product. They are sales people for their own wares, and every sales person has a structural bias to their product. The make a profit; they eat. They make a handsome profit; they eat handsomely. Sometimes, to make things happen correctly, coveting that payday on the end of the task, they'll perform according to that end.

There is another angle that's involved here, also. Haven't we all seen a "hanger-onner"? This is someone who, assuming they ever had a passion and a commitment to their profession or interest, has since lost the touch for it. How often do we speak of someone simply "going through the motions?" This phenomenon is also noteworthy in the sales profession. There are certain stresses attendant the need to perform on a daily basis.

Like the salesperson, prophets and psychics are real people. Any psychic who quits courting the source of their power through meditation and purposeful ritual can backslide. God says it:

"If you invoke me and pray to me, I will listen to you: when you seek me, you shall find me; if you search with all your heart, I will let you find me." (Jer. 29.12-13)

We might say, "Stick with it consistently, for salvation and the gift is won daily."

Then there are the people who never really "get it." In this profession, as in all human professions, it only takes "credentials" or an indication you want in to get in. After all, if you want to say you're a salesperson or a psychic, who's to say otherwise? It is something you make/declare yourself. The magic may or may not really be there. It is easy to get in, but few really offer the services of the inspired.

This outcomes of the drama of the lying psychics brilliantly displays the perverseness of populist thinking. Doing what everyone else is doing is seldom right. It is surely neither brave nor creative.

Do you want to be a leader or a follower? An aspiring eagle or a sheep safely tucked in the herd? Baa-a-ah... This crowd of psychics is obviously relying one on the other to come to a consensual reading. Every one of them has lost their individuality.

Only Micaiah stands alone.

Isaiah, First To Last

Not counting the article *the*, the channeling in *Isaiah*, the longest book in the Bible, starts immediately. The first bona fide word that begins the corpus of sixty-six chapters is "vision":

The *vision* of Isaiah which he saw concerning Judah and Jerusalem. (Is. 1.1)

He then transduces the boundaries of the senses, from vision to the words that are a segment of his vision,

"*Hear*, O Heavens, and give ear, O Earth;

for the Lord has *spoken*." (Is. 1.2)

Rebroadcasting, Isaiah then delivers the very words of God.

From this starting point, the book of Isaiah develops in a series of oracles, prophetic statements uttered with the voice of the Divine. Language is an amazing tool. It allows us to see easily when God is himself being either quoted by the medium or has assumed the medium's functions and is speaking directly through the medium, using the medium's body, brain, and vocal apparatus in real time.

The second oracle of Isaiah likewise relates a clairvoyance. With the words that open it, Isaiah strengthens the conflation of the senses of sight (saw) and sound (word), in effect now, instead of referring to them as different yet allied domains, identifying them as one and the same thing.

"The *word* which Isaiah *saw* concerning Judah and Jerusalem." (Is. 2.1)

He drops immediately into relating the vision he saw of latter days. Nowhere in the oracle does God speak directly. Instead, Isaiah rebroadcasts, describing scenes of desolation and restoration for Israel.

Isaiah is practically non-stop channeling. Channeling after channeling, oracle after oracle follow. Let's take a quick touch-and-do on several of the prescient utterances.

For a few samples, he opens chapter 13 with "The oracle concerning Babylon..." He opens chapter 15 with, "An oracle concerning Moab..." He opens chapter 17 announcing, "An oracle concerning Damascus..." He opens chapter 19 announcing, "An oracle concerning Egypt..." He also opens chapters 21, 22, and 23 with "An oracle..."

He offers an oracle inside many of these chapters, also. As he gets going, he quits "announcing" the fact that he is uttering an oracle, and, with the reader and listener attuned to it, just goes straight into multitudinous oracles, speaking the very words of God and describing the psychic visions God gives him.

In chapter 44, speaking through Isaiah, God asks the nation who – other than himself –

"Who has announced from of old the things to come?" (Is. 44.7)

Of course, the way he has done this, since we have no written record of his own, nor record of him ever speaking to any but select psychics, is through the inspired utterances and writings these clairvoyants produce.

Truly, Isaiah is a *major* channeling figure.

"You're Gonna Die!"

Isaiah. One time King *Hezekiah*, king of Judah, gets sick. Isaiah, unsought, brings him the channeled message:

"Thus says the Lord,
'Set your house in order; for you shall die, you shall not recover.'"
(2Kg. 20.1)

And he leaves.

Coming from this renowned soothsayer with a reputation of accuracy, the king is startled into repentance, and he prays. Before Isaiah, winding his way out of the massive federal building, even gets out of palace, things have changed. The word comes to him differently. He journeys back to Hezekiah and channels the new message of God, saying that God's changed his mind and will have him back on his feet and out in public concourse within three days. Further, he will grant a fifteen year extension to his life. Things do unravel in accord with this second message.

He Delivers An Erroneous Message

Here is another instance of a psychic with an erroneous message. True, one of them is right. But, if a psychic is allowed to prognosticate till he hits it, he's not very good, is he? The first prophecy is clearly erroneous. But – the question is apt – erroneous to *whom*? It is erroneous to Hezekiah, Isaiah, and everyone looking at it from the human angle.

Yet, God has a higher purpose. As a superlative artificer, misdirection is one of the communication modalities God employs to accomplish his purposes. Now, how does Isaiah channel an erroneous message?

Involvement Learning

Jeremiah's in the groove and enjoying the pleasures it affords. Chapter 18 tells of his famous visit to the potter's shed. The action of the potter in fashioning a pot, that spoils in his hands, and then refashioning it into another vessel, provides the visual inspiration for Jeremiah's lesson. God will destroy these people and make something else of the remnant. In Jeremiah's physical involvement, what he encounters in the material world illuminates and demonstrates his consciousness.

This device of involvement learning is characteristic of Jeremiah. Chapter 19 not only entails physical involvement and movement, but also offers a visual aid to the people he's delivering the message to. Following God's instructions, he buys an earthen flask. He then gathers some of the elders and congressmen and takes them out to the valley. He opens his discourse with,

"These are the words of the Lord of Israel." (Jer. 19.3)

He then channels. God, at the climax of his discourse, using the bodily apparatus of Jeremiah, breaks the earthen flask, illustrating just how he is going to deal with recalcitrant Israel.

The Chariot Vision

Ezekiel hails from the same broad era as Isaiah and Jeremiah. His book, like those of his compatriots, is foremost and consistently a book of oracles. Scholars classify three broad segments of his output into oracles of warning (chs. 1-24) before the fall of Jerusalem; a middle period of oracles against foreign nations (chs. 25-32); and oracles of hope and restoration (chs. 33-48) after the fall of Jerusalem/Judah.

He is a prolific visionary. Over the course of at least twenty years, he records a number of visions and visitations by God. Much of his channeling is describing and narrating the visions and messages coming to him, but he frequently delivers the actual words of God, too.

Ezekiel identifies himself, the time, and the circumstances in the opening words of his book. After giving the date, he writes for posterity:

> As I was among the exiles by the river Cheber, the Heavens were opened, and I saw visions of God. The word of the Lord came to me, and the hand of the Lord was upon me there. (Ezek. 1.1-3)

He receives a *vision*, and hears the *word* of the Lord. Thus, even with his very opening words, Ezekiel identifies the medium and the nature of the insights and messages he is sharing with us.

In this flagship chapter Ezekiel then shares what is known as the fantastical "chariot" vision. A tempestuous stormfront introduces the four mystical creatures – who have been the subject of intense interest throughout the centuries. In an early literary embodiment of the principles of holography, each of them has four faces, four wings, and the hands of a man. Ezekiel herein appropriates ancient mystical iconography to communicate the highest representation of wholeness. Borrowing from the Sumerian mystical tradition, he identifies the four faces of the angels as the face of a man, a lion, an ox, and an eagle. In this move they become forever part of the Judeo-Christian tradition, also.

The Mystical Tradition

These represent the four cardinal matrices so prevalent throughout all of nature. For instance, there are the four seasons, and the four cardinal directions of north, south, east, and west, images of the totality of the experience.

You can find a more indepth treatment of this subject in my book, *The Grail And The Tarot Correspondence.* The archetypical family consists of two males and two females. Thus, the male and female – father and the mother – pair on one level, and, under their influence, the second duality, we find the children paired, the son and the daughter.

These are the beings and energies associated and identified with the four categories of the Zodiac and the Tarot. They are identified as cardinal *fire, water, air,* and *earth* signs. Tied to the family metaphor, fire is the spiritual father, the fire sign of Leo the Lion. Scorpio is water, the mother, Goddess of emotion. Air is the quick intelligent young man of Aquarius. And the ponderous hefty bull of Taurus is Earth cardinal, the demanding teenage girl.

Astrology, Tarot and the magical, mystical, alchemical, philosophical traditions have their roots in the same tradition. There is a strong Jewish mystery tradition, dating from their days as Sumerians themselves.

Thus Ezekiel conceals and reveals indisputably deeper meaning below the level of the literal images, setting, and story itself. We are moving through the shrouded lands of Mystic Myth. Adventure galore!

These spirits are the escorts and courtiers of the Divine, able to move with ease in any direction or any dimension. Their spoked chariot wheels have, as you will undoubtably notice in the near future in some graphic or sculptural representation, eyes all about the outer edge of the wheel. This mystic omniquad sets the stage even before God himself appears in glory high Heavens, enthroned in a laserly intense light.

The Call To Channel

Having seen the vision of the chariot before God, the awed *Ezekiel* prostrates himself before the mighty majesty. This is no chance encounter. God, traveling with all the majesty of any head of state, comes specifically to raise Ezekiel. His first words to Ezekiel are:

"Son of man, up on your feet! I would speak with you!" (Ezek. 2.1)

He then gives him his charge and commission to serve as a channeler of his words. He briefs him on just what he shall do, and how he shall do it:

"Son of man, all the words that I shall speak to you, receive in your heart, and hear with your ears. And go, get you to the exiles, to your people, and say to them,

'Thus says the Lord God ....'" (Ezek. 3.10-11)

Channeling all the while.

Psychic Considerations

Visiting this site at the moment God is conferring the gift of channeling gives us an especial opportunity to discuss certain topics relating to the receiving of the call as well as to carrying it out.

The Call Is Internal. Those who lack vision demand diplomas and certificates for credentializing. Paramount to the petty, meaningless to the inspired. God gives the visionary true power.

The authorities haven't given Ezekiel an official conferral, allowing him specific powers and scope. Ezekiel's initiation and charge come in the tripping of a paranormal experience.

How meaningful? You decide.

Rebroadcasting. With God's words in this ceremony of investiture we receive illumination on what becomes Ezekiel's signature method. Ezekiel shall introduce his lectures with, "Thus says the Lord God..." God tells him, or at least he believes God tells him, and those who believe in the accuracy of the scriptures must too, that he wants him to receive the visions and the words and rebroadcast them at a later time.

Ezekiel becomes the inspired teacher-minister who works up an effective presentation to communicate his themes, telling the people that it is the Supersensible God who is ultimately responsible for the messages and their meanings.

Oh Son Of Man. Also, note that already the "son of man" is becoming a common feature in the spiritualscape. This is always spoken in direct address from God to Ezekiel. Every single time this is said, it is God speaking directly to Ezekiel. Instead of calling him by name, he calls him "son of man."

By the way, consider this son of man motif. If someone stepped forward today, calling himself the "son of man," claiming he has the very words of God to deliver to us, how would you respond? Wouldn't most of the world (when polite) say, "Is this guy *c-r-a-z-y,* or what?" After all, these visual and auditory hallucinations are not common, except among the people stuffed into our institutions.

Dramatic Channeling

In another signature of his style, *Ezekiel* dons the performer's robes. God contexts Ezekiel's first channeling assignments in dramatic presentations.

God instructs Ezekiel to take a sharp sword and cut off his hair and beard. He's then instructed to weigh the hair into three equal portions. He burns a third part in the town square; walks about the city, striking at a third part with a sword; and scatters the final third to the winds.

This serves as Ezekiel's attention arresting opening to the words of God:

> "A third part of you shall die of pestilence and be consumed with famine in the midst of you; a third part shall fall by the sword round about you; and a third part I will scatter to all the winds." (Ezek. 5.12)

The drama illustrates what God is set to do.

A Riddle, An Allegory

God loves riddles in *Ezekiel*'s time. God, speaking through Ezekiel, reveals his mystical method of teaching, illustrating, and warning: story and allegory – *words* serving as a cover for a deeper level of significance. Noting the similarity between this instance of allegory and Ezekiel's other channeled allegories, we can appreciate the fact that God herein provides in clear language the key to understanding all of Ezekiel, as indeed, many of the apparent babblings of the other psychics, too.

Ezekiel receives explicit instructions:

"Son of man, propound a riddle, and speak an allegory to the house of Israel. Say,
> 'Thus says the Lord God...'" (Ezek. 17.2-3)

With this setup, God launches straight into the story, the story that's come to be known as the "two eagles" riddle:

> "A great eagle with great wings and long pinions, rich in plumage of many colors, came to Lebanon and took the top of the cedar. (Ezek. 17.3)

And he goes on describing the actions of the great eagle.

But he will be contested,

> "But there was another great eagle with great wings and much plumage..." (Ezek. 17.7)

It's not needful to our present purpose to develop just what that story is. Read it in one of your own Bibles. God gives Ezekiel the full riddle to tell. What is germane to the moment, however, is that we notice that God is herein intentionally structuring riddles and allegories to communicate his message. You have it on good word – the instruction of God to Ezekiel.

God knows that when Ezekiel delivers the message, the people won't understand it. Like a good coach, he instructs Ezekiel how to capitalize on this. God reassures him this will provide the perfect opportunity to lay out the correspondence between the story and the nation of Israel. God tells him to ask,

> "Do you not know what these things mean?" (Ezek. 17.12)

When the mystified people reply, "No, we do not," then, of course, he explicates – with great drama.

The Key To See

Ezekiel lays out the deep story signified by the surface story, in the words God gives him to use. He reveals that one eagle is the king of Babylon, and that the other is God himself. In the process of doing this God unveils the significant aspect of his communications through psychics. God is teaching us the method to divine the deeper levels of the events of Biblical drama. He is giving us the key to the ability to *see* and *hear* the story underneath, to solve the riddle, to understand the allegory. *But to see!*

God reveals his sacred gems in story. Thus the blatant secret is concealed from those who, though they have eyes, lack the sight. By extension, all the story the Bible tells, from a single verse to the whole of the panorama spanning the two covers, conceals God's story. At the same time, interdependently and synergistically, every thing – from the paramount theme of the story to the smallest symbolic artifact – communicates. Only those who recognize it as manifold sacred perceive the authentic value therein.

After all, don't a number of people today believe that God gives his lessons in truth in the casual garb of a carpenter's life and his stories?

Dramatic Coaching

Ezekiel. Pathos too, is a weapon in the performer's arsenal. Hey, if you're going to be channeling the Lord, stage it properly! Poor staging can detract from the effect you want to create – good staging can *create* the effect. So, after giving Ezekiel some sharp prophetic words to say, God coaches him:

> "Sigh therefore, son of man, sigh with breaking heart and bitter grief before their eyes. And when they say to you, 'Why do you sigh?' say to them, 'Because of the tidings! When it comes, every heart will melt and all hands will be feeble, every spirit will faint and all knees will be weak as water! Behold, it comes and it will be fulfilled!'" (Ezek. 21.6-7)

Such drama! Ezekiel gives us an insider's view of the channeler's art. Sure, as a channeler you must receive, but you've got to deliver, too. And it's not just letting it all hang out, either – there is an *art* to the presentation component. What will most effectively convey the message? Through his inspiration of the creative artist, God has many mediums at his disposal.

A Potpourri Of Prophets: A Popular Practice

The writers of the final twelve books of the Old Testament form a group of psychics classed together under the rubric "minor prophets." *Hosea, Joel, Amos, Obadiah, Jonah, Micah, Nahum, Habakkuk, Zephaniah, Haggai, Zechariah,* and *Malachi* are minor based on the volume of their output. The body of most of these psychics runs only several chapters. Fully half of them are three or fewer chapters, with the two longest books, Hosea and Zechariah, containing fourteen each. Contrast this with Ezekiel of forty-eight chapters, Jeremiah of fifty-two, or Isaiah of sixty-six.

It has been said that sometimes the people who say the least say what is the most important.

Even if these prophets are not called major prophets, their very inclusion in the Bible speaks volumes, especially when we consider our premise that God is speaking to us through these scriptures. What is God saying? *You who have ears, listen!*

First of all, every one of these writings is the record or result of a channeling experience. Every one of these twelve sequential prophets opens clearly indicating the fact that what follows – the words, statements, images, stories, and quotes, are either directly the very words of God or are inspired by the visions and designs of God.

Our purpose is neither to study these psychics nor their utterances, but to note the language which clearly indicates the channeling experience. Though for the most part we'll work to keep the tour moving smoothly to its purpose, because we're here, however, we will enjoy select delightfuls of their messages. Even knowing how way leads on to way, we'll save some others for another day.

Glamorous But Unfaithful

Hosea follows a formulaic opening. He starts off identifying these words as the channeled words of God:

The word of the Lord that came to Hosea... (Hos. 1.1)

The second verse reiterates the fact that what is about to follow is *channeled* material. In fact, though the Revised Standard Version of the Bible uses the phrase, "spoke through," we know we could see the synonymous term, "channeled through":

When the Lord first spoke through Hosea, the Lord said to him,

"Go, get that babe you've been drooling over, but *marry* her." (Hos. 1.2)
Oh, you bet he does!

How Fortunate For Hosea!

Hosea's message is unusual, don't you think? God gives Hosea permission to have relations with a classy whore. How fortunate!

Stop a moment and think this through. How would this sound if your uncle came by dating a known prostitute – admittedly very attractive – and said he loved her so much he was going to marry her? And not only that, but tried to convince you that God was telling him to do it?

Hosea, however, is but performing at God's word, revealing God in his actions.

Naturally, marriage with a nymphomaniac can't last. Later, God inspires him to play with another lover. True to his tastes, she is someone's beautiful wife who wants some action. Hmm. Hosea has enough ministry money that the affair lasts, not a single night or weekend, but numerous months.

"I Will Pour Out My Spirit"

The entire book of *Joel* is a channeled utterance. It renders, he announces in his first words,

"The word of the Lord which came to Joel son of Pethuel." (Jl. 1.1)

The message God channels through Joel is a message of destruction, surely, but also of restoration. God is about to chastize the nation, but he also wants to inspire the innocent victims who will necessarily suffer through the period of tribulation while he is cleansing the toxic people from the nation. Once the pogrom is executed, the docile people remaining will be restored and honored among the nations.

God is using what communications consultants refer to as *negative incentives* and *positive incentives*. In other words, God is threatening them with evil consequences for their continued disobedience, as well as enticing them with the promise of milk and honey for their Godly behavior. It is an effective strategy, still well-used by governments against their citizens and companies against their employees. God will ensure that people worship him in the manner to which he has become accustomed.

Joel starts his book with the vision of what surely must have been as fearful in the imagination of the people of his day as the nuclear holocaust is to us of this day, a plague of locusts:

> What the cutting locust leaves, the swarming locust will eat. What the swarming locust leaves, the hopping locust will eat. And what the hopping locust leaves, the destroying locust will eat. There will be *nothing*. (Jl. 1.4)

The people may not die from the blast, but they will surely – and more painfully – die from the consequences.

After all the agony, suffering, and death God inflicts, peace and prosperity shall return to those humbled survivors who turn to him with praises from a heart overflowing with gratitude and love. They shall be happy with the blessings he dispenses,

> "You shall eat in plenty and be satisfied, and praise the name of the Lord your God, who has dealt wondrously with you." (Jl. 2.26)

Yeah.

Joel also affirms that the greatest of the gifts God promises his people are the psychic gifts of clairvoyance, through the medium of visions and dreams:

> "And it shall come to pass afterward, that I will pour out my spirit on all flesh; your sons and your daughters shall prophesy, your old men shall dream dreams, and your young men shall see visions." (Jl.2.28)

He makes clear that the gifts are not only to the priests, kings, and princes, but to everyone, including,

> "*Even the menservants and maidservants...* In those days, I will pour out my spirit on *everyone.*"(Jl. 2.29)

We are living in this age. Even a carpenter or a mechanic, a cowhand or a teacher, as well as a business person or one of the stock or landed gentry can channel the voice of God today. Indeed, God has become more accessible to us all.

A Sheep Guy Feels The Spirit

Amos. Speaking of cowboys, how about a sheepguy? It all starts one day when Amos, a normal guy, in a manner less dramatic but similar to Moses, receives the call.

Amos announces the channeled nature of the book, and identifies the fact that it came in visions, in this very first words. He starts the book with,

> The words of Amos, one of the sheep-farmers of Tekoa, which he received in visions concerning Israel..." (Am. 1.1)

After this introduction as to his position and where his words come from, Amos then moves into giving God's channeled words. He introduces God, first saying he "roars from Zion" (Am. 1.2), and then goes into the formulaic, "Thus says the Lord." From this point on, most of the book is God speaking through the channel. The words recorded for posterity are the very words of God, spoken through his selected channel, Amos.

Amos is interesting reading. He gets wound up, like a televangelist, even punctuating his comments. He'll be rocking on, speaking God's very words, and end that string with the phrase he frequently uses, "says the Lord God" (Am. 1.8; 1.15; 2.3; 3.15 *et al.*). *Amen!*

When he concludes with one of these phrase, he catches his breath, and launches again, with the introductory tag, "Thus says the Lord..."

He uses one or the other phrase (or, in a few cases a clear variant of them) a total of forty-two times! Not a bad accomplishment in a book of nine small chapters! And he sums up his entire book, credentializing the words he has rendered as the very channeled words of God in his final words, "says the Lord your God" (Am. 9.15).

Jonah Turns Tail

Jonah is a fantastic story, cited equally by scholars, by preachers, and by little old Sunday school teachers. However, as famous as the story is, few realize that the basic framework of the story is a channeling event. But it is. Every episode in the entire story either involves actual channeling or occurs as a consequence of either channeling or *not* channeling. It is because Jonah resists his channeling mission, in fact, that he gets himself into that tango with the whale. Interesting.

The announcement that this is a channeling event comes with the very first words of the book. It opens with,

The word of the Lord came to Jonah son of Amittai:

"Go to the great city of Nineveh, go now and denounce it, for its wickedness stares me in the face." (Jon. 1.1-2)

Here's where the trouble starts. Jonah gets it all wrong. He does not want to deliver the Lord's message to the probably ungrateful inhabitants of the city. So he turns tail, setting out, instead of into the desert, across the sea. He boards to Tarshish, a far country in the opposite direction.

But it is not that easy to turn your back on the Lord. Especially when he has singled you out for a specific mission. The famous storm on the sea arises while he is fleeing. This storm so frightens the experienced sailors that they invoke the powers of divination to find the person responsible for the storm. It is Jonah. Overboard he goes; and the seas drop into calmness.

No, Jonah doesn't end up in the belly of a whale for three days as a random event, but as a direct result of his running from fulfilling his Divine commission to channel. Even though he changes his physical location, the inner turmoil follows him, so strong that it causes a hurricane on the sea. The three days of dark isolation give Jonah ample time and circumstance to reconsider his position.

Jonah, who sees the futility of ignoring the call of the heart, goes to channel. That also has its own adventures. You can easily enjoy the whale story; it is only four chapters long.

"All But Me... I'm Okay"

Micah, too, opens his book with the unmistakable language of channeling. His very first words are,

This is the word of the Lord which came to Micah... which I received in visions... (Mic. 1.1)

His entire book is channeled material.

In the verses of Micah we again see how close to his heart God holds the psychic arts. He would, for they are his communicative link with humanity. This passage is the antithesis of God's passage in Joel when he promises clairvoyance, dreams, and visions as the highest reward. Instead of promising to *give* visions and divinations through the psychics. God swears he will *cut them off.* A horrible fate! A veritable wasteland! He is again communicating just how deeply he values the psychic arts.

God fosters the psychic arts, but not the lying arts. When you take the mantle to channel, you take the commitment to speak as you are spoken to. But the people don't usually want to hear that. There is a group of sold-out psychics in Micah's Israel. Channeling through his instrument, Micah, God speaks directly to these people. They shall lose their gift:

"It shall be night to you, without vision,

And darkness to you, without divination...

You shall be disgraced, you shall be put to shame,

For I will not speak through you, but will silence you." (Mic. 3.6-7)

Of course, Micah adds, this does not include him. In fact, he tells us, he is empowered and in flow:

"But as for me, I am filled with power, with the Spirit of the Lord, and with justice and might, to declare to Jacob his transgression and to Israel his sin." (Mic. 3.8)

Would you expect anything less?

On another note Micah is laureled with a special fame for his efforts. His is the verse scholars cite to Herod when the wizards pass through his realm looking for the ruler born under the bright new Eastern star:

But you, O Bethlehem Ephrathah, who are little among the clans of Judah, from you shall come forth for me one who is to be ruler in Israel, whose origin is from of old, from ancient days." (Mic. 5.2)

God has an advantage; the prophecy is accurate. In Bethlehem, among the clans of Judah, Jesus is born.

Even today, we who read these channeled words of Micah have the pleasure to,

"Hear now what the Lord is saying..." (Mic. 6.1)

"True Vision Awaits Its Time"

Habakkuk also opens up with words indicating his is an *oracle* which he receives in a *vision.* You should be getting used to it by now. Again, he does it with his very first words:

The oracle of God which Habakkuk the prophet saw. (Hab. 1.1)

The entire book is record of a vision.

Habakkuk also has an exceptionally clear recording of just how the psychic gets the channeling process going. Basically, he prepares the opening for God by the active process of entering into an elevated state (on the tower, metaphor for prayerful expectant state), and then waiting passively for the influx of the Lord, which will surely come. Those who meditate recognize this dynamic.

As God says elsewhere, we ever engage conflict to experience peace. There is a dynamic tension. We climb to enter that sweet spot wherein we are flooded with the Divine afflatus. *Ad rosem per crucem; ad crucem per rosem.*

Habakkuk is somewhat upset. He is being laughed at because some of his predictions have not shown out. It looks like he was wrong. *Some psychic!* He goes to complain to God concerning the time of fulfillment. Habakkuk says,

> I will take my stand to watch, and station myself on the tower, and look forth
> to see what God will say to me concerning my complaint. (Hab. 2.1)

This he does. He enters into deep meditation.

The Lord answers him with words indicating that it is up to the psychic only to channel the prescient words of God and, armed with the foreknowledge that imparts, to prepare himself accordingly. "*I,*" God answers Habakkuk, "*will* fulfill them *exactly* on time":

> "Write the vision;
> > make it plain upon tablets,
> > so you may run who read it.
> True vision awaits its time;
> > it hastens to the end –
> > it does not lie.
> If it seem slow, wait for it;
> > it will surely come,
> > it will not delay." (Hab. 2.2-3)

The vision is to be fulfilled.

The Motivational Speaker

Haggai marks a major political shift in the history of the Jewish people. All the destruction and chastisement God has been threatening the people with... Guess what? It happens!

The city of Jerusalem has been invaded, the Temple has been destroyed, and the people have been taken into a captivity that endures for seventy years. As the wheel of fortune rolls, Babylon herself is conquered by Persia. Cyrus, new governor of Persia, doesn't care where the Jews live. If they'll be happier in Jerusalem, let them return. And so another chapter opens for the Jews, the period of the restoration, running from 538-515 BCE to 72 CE, when the temple is destroyed again.

Haggai opens with the Jews back in Judah. After giving the date and his authority, God, he tells us,

The word of the Lord came by Haggai the prophet to Zerubbabel, governor of Judah.... (Hag. 1.1-2).

How much more clearly can a man tell you he is channeling? And he uses this phrase a number of times in his short two chapter book. His work, the words he writes and speaks, is the word of the Lord to Zerubbabel. Haggai simply identifies himself as the medium, the channeler, the receiver and the broadcaster.

God has brought the people back to their land, but they are troubled and living in lack, making great efforts, but reaping little at harvest.

But there is a solution! It is time for a Temple, God says:

"Go up to the hills and bring wood and build the house, that I may take pleasure in it and that I may appear in my glory." (Hag. 1.8)

History records that Haggai is the motivational speaker who stirs the king and the people to build the Temple. The credit, of course, belongs to God. After all, Haggai is merely a messenger of God, a channel for the Spirit. He is not the power source itself, but only a mouthpiece for the real power, the Spirit of God.

On Reincarnation

Malachi too, opens with an oracle, announcing he speaks the very word of God, and then going right to it:

The oracle of the word of the Lord to Israel by Malachi.:

"I have loved you,"

says the Lord... (Mal. 1.1)

His is a short two chapter book that concludes the Old Testament. Throughout his channeled piece God speaks. All the way to the end. Don't let the size fool you. It is vitally important.

Especially as it relates to *reincarnation.* We will defer moving deeply into the reincarnation discussion. For now, it is sufficient to recognize that *God himself* speaks the words that reveal the fact of reincarnation in our spiritual-material existence. This is not the theory of a crack pot professor, but a statement of God's own:

"Behold, I will send you Elijah the prophet before the great day of the Lord comes." (Mal. 4.5)

Speaking thus, the Old Testament, like the New Testament, ends as it should, in the very words of God. A new age looms. Significant. *O, you with ears, hear!*

Jesus Assures Seekers They Can Channel

Followers. Though the idea of ever being so far afoul of the establishment that it could happen in their own life would make many a person feeling like a good Christian gasp – *this should be a sign – Jesus* is an outlaw. He is constantly at odds with the hierarchy of the church and the state, all that runs the realm of Caesar. From his first public performance at Canaan, all they've ever done is gun for him... him who has no real concern for them anyway. But of course, that's the problem.

And he talks about these things with his followers, who become subsidiary targets along with him. He tells them to ignore the people who proudly stand as the pillars of society, for they are nothing but hypocrisy. "Yeah, these indignant types, whom due obsequiousness would sufficiently flatter, will charge you with crimes. And they'll have you on the spot, and you'll have to answer them. *Don't give in!* When you are before these men who garland themselves, simply open to channel. The right words will be there." He says:

> "And when they bring you before the synagogues and the rulers and the authorities, do not be anxious how or what you are to answer or what you are to say; for the Holy Spirit will give you in that very hour what you ought to say." (Lk. 12.11-12)

"Simply open yourself. The Spirit will channel through you. The right words will be there."

"I Am Jesus, The Channeler"

Jesus. It's not like it's a sudden thing. Jesus has had plenty of premonitions. He's going to die soon. The establishment has been plotting against the troublesome man making himself one with God. He goes invisible for a bit but then decides to walk right into the court and face it. He makes the trip to Jerusalem for the celebration of Passover, a feast celebrated with all the feeling which we associate with our Thanksgiving and Christmas today. These are the man's final days. Talk about *attitude!* Talk about a blaze of glory!

Now is the moment. It is Jesus' final evening. Destiny has arrived. It is Passover. Jesus' every word is charged with the high energy of the Eternal. Judas has slipped out on his venture of ill, and Jesus has but an hour to reflect. He gives his final discourses, the distillation of all he has to say. And he concludes with the heartfelt prayer of a man facing the Divinity of translation. With his Eternal viewpoint, he sums it up; he has accomplished what he came to do, to bring the awareness of God to seekers ready to hear:

> "Father, the hour has come; glorify now thy Son, that glorifies thee. .... I glorified thee on Earth, having accomplished the work which thou gavest me to do.... I have manifested thy name to those seeking knowledge of your ways." (Jn. 17.1-6)

History acknowledges that Jesus does indeed succeed in his mission.

Sometimes I think that all the world knows Jesus speaks of God as *Father.* Sometimes I think that incredibly few know what he means. Even this portentous night – and it seems almost irreverent – Phillip, a surface seer, mistaking the metaphor for the substance, challenges Jesus to "show" him this"father." "*Then*," he says, "I'll believe."

Jesus doesn't buy into the challenge, of course, not this night. But he does respond. He asks Phillip how he can ask such a question. "How can you not know God?... When everything I say is the very word of God?":

"The words that I say to you I do not speak of my own accord, but the Master Within does his works." (Jn. 14.10)

The identification of the channel with the source is complete. Looking at the channel, you are looking at the source:

"When you see me you see the Spirit." (Jn. 14.9)

If you recall, we experience the same phenomenon with Abraham when the men shapeshift into God. If you recall, we encounter the same phenomenon with Moses at the burning bush – sometimes an angel, sometimes a God. If you recall, we experience the same phenomenon with Gideon – he keeps seeing and hearing alternately God and the angel.

The phenomenon is unmistakable. And you have it on Jesus' word. Jesus is a channeler of the Spirit, making visible the glory of God in his person, his actions, his stories and lessons, and his prayers.

One Passage Illuminates Others

This one passage of clarification on this night when Jesus is being both metaphysical and clear above all, gives the light to numerous others. Because we understand channeling, and because we understand the phenomenon of identification which accompanies that enchanted process, we understand Jesus' statements of the Godhead.

This makes understandable Jesus' statement:

"I and the Father are one." (Jn. 10.30)

This makes understandable Jesus' statement:

"I am the Son of God." (Jn. 10.36)

This makes understandable Jesus' statement:

"I am in the Father and the Father is in me." (Jn. 10.38)

We understand the charge, leveled even in this day by those who cannot see against those with expanded consciousness:

"You, being a man, make yourself God." (Jn. 10.33)

Jesus speaks from that grace place of total identification. All done with twinkles of consciousness.

As The Spirit Gives Them Utterance

Apostles. It is Pentecost. One of the most famous, and, amongst the believers who emphasize it, one of the most magnificent instances of channeling is actually a group experience. The apostles, after the execution of Jesus, are huddled together worrying and praying in the upstairs room. Their entire reality matrix has been irrevocably altered, so a period of uncertainty is quite natural.

Acts tells us that the appearance of the Divine Spirit illuminating and empowering their souls comes suddenly:

Suddenly a sound comes from Heaven like the rush of a mighty wind, filling all the house. And they each behold the vision of a spiritual fire, burning like a torch above the spiritual center of their beings. (Acts 2.2-3)

And the afflatus exhibits itself in their behavior immediately:

> And they are all filled with the Holy Spirit and begin speaking in tongues, as the Spirit inspires them. (Acts 2.4)

The Holy Grail visits the round table with the empty throne, reestablishing his connection with them. From this point on, filled with the Holy Spirit, they are wired. They are channelers of the Divine Energy Current flowing through them.

This sudden inspiration of the Spirit has real, tangible effects in their lives. Indeed, the entire interesting book of Acts is really a testament to the power of the Spirit to move human beings.

Of course, to "normal" people, the apostles' sudden excitement appears questionable. Moved by the channeling Spirit, they go out on the street, each speaking a language he does not know. Each speaking a language that reaches a nearby heart.

Peter, in his first act of leadership, taken intuitively, defends their case publically. He gets into a parked chariot to get high, and addresses the fascinated bystanders, assuring them that "These men are not drunk, as you suppose" (Acts 2.15), but that instead, they are men possessed by the Spirit, the destined recipients of the psychic gifts, foreseen by the psychic Joel hundreds of years prior:

> "'And in those days it shall be that I will pour out my Spirit upon all flesh, and your sons and your daughters shall prophesy, and your young men shall see visions, and your old men shall dream dreams.'" (Acts 2.17-18)

The Spirit accomplishes a mighty work that single empowered day. Three thousand receive the word and baptism.

From this point on the apostles and disciples of that early era live a charmed life, which of course, then as today, provokes fear, anger, and aggression in the self-righteous institutionally approved spiritually obtuse:

> And fear descends upon every soul, for these men are different, performing authentic signs and marvels. (Acts 3.43)

Of course, they don't care. When they have the occasion to suffer for their beliefs, suffering that could be relieved by complying with at least the outer adherence to the politically correct position, they count it as a light burden and an honorable opportunity.

"Above All Else, Desire To Prophesy"

Initiates. Impelled by the Pentecostal fire, the psychic arts assure their place as an integral component of the Spirit-centered life. The disciples of Jesus' own century indeed live a deeply spiritual life, closer – in a temporal sense as well as in attunement – to the Spiritual life that Jesus channels to humanity.

The flowering of gifts is well recorded in the writings of Paul. Paul suggests to the practitioners of the Christian faith at Corinth, for instance,

> Follow the way of love, and eagerly desire spiritual gifts, *especially the gift of prophecy.* (1Cor. 14.1)

In the discourse that follows, he makes clear that there are other gifts, tongues, service, and the like. But he raises channeling above all others, for it delivers the Spiritual Presence of the Universe to its widest audience:

He who prophesies speaks to men for their upbuilding and encouragement and consolation. (1Cor. 14.3)

Paul ends this letter with a variant of the same words he opens it with,

My brethren, *earnestly desire to prophesy.* (1Cor. 14.39)

This gives true service to humanity.

Peter's Position On Channeling

Peter, part of the same community as Paul, also states his position on channeling. He, too, acknowledges that channeling is only one of the important and valuable spiritual gifts. He, too, states that *every body receives a gift* and that he or she should employ it in the service of others (1Pet. 4.10). He knows that life is short, and that one way or the other we will be judged. "Simply because we live there will be a valuation and a judgement made. We are but stewards of the variously manifesting Life Force," he says. "Our charge and our greatest high is to share it."

Just as Haggai offers one of the clearest outlays of the process of entering into the meditative state wherein one can reliably receive psychic impressions, Peter offers a clear – make that a blunt – statement on how you acquire ability in the psychic arts. You just *do* it. You assume that, because you do it, you do it with power. *That* you do it is an indication from God that you *are* to do it. So you do it with confidence. Peter states simply,

You who speak, speak as one who utters oracles of God. (1Pet. 4.11)

Also, for what it is worth, remember, this man is the first pope of the Christian era, selected by Jesus himself.

Channeling, Channeling, Channeling God

When discussing Biblical channeling we end with *John.* And here is a fact so gargantuan that it is overlooked by the typical reader: the *entire* book of Revelation is a channeled document. Make no mistake, the very first words John pens state it point blank:

The revelation of Jesus Christ, which God gave him to show to his servants what must soon take place; and he made it known by sending his angel to his servant John, who bore witness to the word of God and to the testimony of Jesus Christ, even to all that he saw. (Rev. 1.1-2)

This is the language of channeling. For our understanding, this reads:

▸ that *Jesus Christ* is the keynote speaker in this address
▸ that *God* gave this oracular revelation to him
  ▸ with the specific intent that he might give it to humanity
▸ that Jesus accomplishes this task by sending an *angel* to John
  ▸ who channels the message to John in a *vision*

▸ that John completes the process by faithfully transmitting the message

Quite a lot for a few little lines, isn't it? There are five links in this chain of sacred transmission: God, Jesus, Angel, John, you. Speaking to you, John is channeling the angel, the angel is channeling Jesus, Jesus is channeling God, God is the ultimate source. Call it what you want, call it what your preacher or your conscience says you must, but the phenomenon of transmission – is it anything other than *channeling*?

Voices of angels, voices of Gods, visions of Heavens, and passions so intense John writes to polished intent... This mystic rapture, this vision, is not this psychic activity?

Naught but channeling, channeling, channeling God.

The End Zone

On this excursion into psychicspace we've noted myriad distinctions played out in lots of different scenes. You never know who might be channeling, how it'll come, what the message may be, or what it is they will be doing.

You can encounter a "normal" channeler, like Moses, Isaiah, or Joel. They receive the message and in turn share it with humanity via spoken or written means.

Then there are Samuel and Solomon who channel the Spirit's intents by implementing them in action. Samuel anoints two kings following his intuitions; Solomon speaks with wisdom and wealth previously unaccessible.

Like Samuel, the channeler may even be one returned from the dead.

Like Bezalel, it may come in through the inspirations of artistic production.

Or, as with Ahijah or Ezekiel, it may be delivered with the costume, voice, and staged interaction of the theatre. Ahijah prefers the inspiration of the moment, revealing the word of the Lord in real time, whereas Ezekiel prefers to craft and rehearse his presentations beforehand, rendering them for maximum effect.

It can manifest in any fashion, as it does in Hosea's fast lifestyle with wild women.

The insignificant may channel, as Amos the sheepboy or Jesus the carpenter.

Channeling is pervasive, an accompaniment of the spirit-filled life. It's not just a statement, it's an adventure.

How about you, are you ready?

Chapter 3

Dreams And Visions:
Windows Of Reality

---••••---

In a dream, in a vision of the night,
when deep sleep falls upon you,
while you slumber on your bed,
then God speaks to your inner ear...
(Job 33.15-16)

Dreams... The subject holds us with a spellbinding fascination. Visions and dreams. One and the same. Ancient literatures of the Egyptians, the Greeks, the Hebrews, and the Romans speak of visions and dreams. The poets and philosophers of the Middle Ages and the Renaissance theorize about them. All peoples of all places weave a dream mystique, from loin-clad natives of the savannahs to Arctic Circle Eskimos. And we, members of the global village, driving the cutting edge of evolution, likewise are fascinated by dreams.

Dreams... The subject is vast, traversing the sweep of humanity. An extensive consideration of the place and substance of dreams even solely in the Bible – but one congruent source with the distributed records of humanity – in one chapter of a single book is a labor even Hercules could not perform. Our purpose holds but to visit the shores of a relevant sampling of the Biblical rendition of the psychic phenomenon of dreaming.

Is It A Dream, Or A Vision, Or What?

Your own common sense informs you of the similarity of the two states of dreaming and visioning. Both impact the consciousness through the autonomic nervous system. It's *when* it occurs that marks the distinction. Does it occur during a trance or a sleep? Where are you during sleep? Where is your consciousness of yourself, that is? Don't you "forget" about yourself and your normal waking concerns during the night, even when, in a dream, you are all too aware of yourself? Isn't this the identical situation when you fall into a trance or, in its lighter forms, a *day-dream?*

Considering *dreams* in the broadest sense, there are three categories, the dream, the vision, and the creative visualization. The "normal" dream, of course, is the most common, as everyone experiences dreams. The meaning of the word used this way needs no consideration or adjustment. It visits during sleep. Dreams are made of the ephemeral.

The vision is akin to a dream. It too is made of the ephemeral and the moment. Here people wide awake, such as Abraham, Balaam, or Mary, Cornelius, Peter, or John see, hear, or feel something from the non-material dimensions. Something slips through. The hard veil of formal consciousness for a brief moment or two dissipates, and a scene and/or a messenger appears. They may be either oblivious to their Earthly surroundings or indeed, the vision may play itself out in the theatre of apparent reality.

The visionary medium may in fact be favored by the already spellbound. As John, in the lengthiest and most detailed of Biblical visions, says, "I was in the Spirit [already] on the Lord's day" (Rev. 1.10), when the spiritual vision of such grandeur and scope took possession of me.

Though we can identify them as distinct psi phenomena, yet simultaneously any distinction we make between *dreams* and *visions* is at best a distinction of the air. In both instances people participate with a higher reality, interacting with the realm of the unincarnate. In both instances they are open to the subtler influences of the spirit realms, channeling through the individual's subconscious. We consider them synonymous for our purposes in this adventure.

Finally, creative visualization is a phenomenon well described by its name. Creative visualization is akin to dreams and visions as well as to magic. It is the active arm of dreaming – instead of only receiving impressions, you transmit them to make something happen. It is the process of envisioning a thing, person, or circumstance until, in some "mysterious" way correlated with the visioning, it comes about.

This process can be invoked with specific intent. Thus, a man strategizing to increase his herds, enjoying it before it happens, seeing it happening before he commences, engages in creative visualization. Where do these psychic urges and impressions that guide his success originate from? Do they originate from the person? Where does *any* thought originate from? And where do they go?

To The Powerful, The Famous, And The Unnamed

Dreaming is the most widely distributed gift. The rolls of the dreamers tally such notable individuals as Abraham, Jacob, Joseph the Dreamer, Samuel, David, Solomon, Jeremiah, Ezekiel, Daniel, and Mary – anointed individuals, dreamers, prophets, visionaries.

Then we have Joseph, a humble non-influential man who is visited numerous times with instructions and strategies to safeguard the treasure that has been concealed with him, the infant Jesus. And Peter the apostle, unknown except amongst those of the net along the beaches of the Jordan before opening to a transformation in his consciousness. The unknown.

But the dream rolls include, as well, the names of many on the "heathen" side of the fence: Abimelech the peaceful ruler; Pharaoh, emperor of a wide realm, the undisputed leader of the undisputed first superpower nation; Nebuchadnezzar, a complex man with extensive sentiments as well as a mighty warrior-commander; and even the wife of the governor-judge who pronounces sentence on Jesus, sealing his fate, Pontius Pilate. Rich, powerful, and famous.

Even the rank-and-file, the otherwise nameless support staff for the drama makers of history, are represented in the record of dreamers of psychic import. Thus we have poor people such as a butler and a baker dreaming dreams of imprisonment, release, and execution. We have two lowly grunt soldiers dreaming and interpreting dreams of psychic import on the fields of battle. Unnamed.

We all dream... Nightly. It is the one time in the day (for most of us) that we let go conscious constriction. The unconscious organisms with their mechanisms working perfectly spread before us the larger metaphysical world. In fact, this process works so well, that if we don't voluntarily release objective consciousness, it will be taken from us. This is a significant point. Hence the very common and so well understood phrase concerning "falling" asleep. We don't think it's strange.

When else can the SuperConscious, the designing Intelligence of the Universe informing every swirling photon of energy in every dimension, communicate freely with us? And how but in dreams, visions, and feelings in the heart, all given to us in our receptive Alpha moments?

We see Daniel and Habakkuk consciously orchestrate passive entry into the Divine Center. Sleep is the normal process we all go through that serves that same purpose – only most of us are unconscious about it.

The High Promise Of Prosperity: Dreams And Visions

Dreams are such an important feature of the Divine theme park that God actually withholds dreams to express his displeasure and dispenses dreams in the fulfillment of prosperity.

People who believe in taking responsibility for their spiritual life, and we have a great many with this understanding during these times, know that God is not a unidimensional event. God responds to us according to our behavior. The threats and times of psychic famine and impotence come in response to our getting heavy and out of tune. As we purify, turning our lifestyles and intentions to the Spirit, we naturally experience more of Divinity. It's always there, but it responds to us according to our beliefs and values, which manifest in our actions, which create the reactions we receive, our consequences.

It is always a bad sign when God does not communicate with humanity in visions and in dreams. We clearly feel God's displeasure with Saul when he will not respond to his inquiries. As Saul tells Samuel, called back from the dead:

> "I am in great distress... for God has turned away from me and answers me no more, either by channelers or by dreams." (1Sam. 28.15)

Samuel confirms this.

The flip side makes us feel better. We've mentioned previously how repetition underscores the meaning or import of a theme or a message. In this regard, there is one passage that is repeated verbatim, hundreds of years apart. God, channeling through Joel, promises better days ahead. He forecasts the ultimate blessing, saying,

> "And in those days I will pour out my Spirit on all flesh; your sons and your daughters shall prophesy, your old men shall dream dreams, and your young men shall see visions." (Joel 2.28)

Good news.

This is the passage we visit in relation to the apostles at Pentecost in the previous chapter, "Channeling." Prophecy, of course, is the *use* made of one of the psychic channels of transmission. Prophesy can come through visions, dreams, and inspirations. These are all vehicles for channeling. Visions and dreams hold an honored court in delivering these Divine missives.

Peter, spokesman for the group gone spiritually mad, compelled by the influx of the Spirit, says, "These are the times spoken of by the channeler." He recognizes this as a great flowering of prosperity, fulfillment in high connection with and service to the Divine Spirit.

Awake! These are the timeless, eternal days that have been, that are, and that always will be, in the seamless HoloCosmic web of eternal life. When we're most fully alive, the Spirit flows freely through us.

"What Does It Mean?"

Even touring the expanses of psychicspace we're still so confined by time and space! We will tour but a few principles of the never ending universe of dreams. From time to time in our adventures, as different principles present themselves, we'll note their particular application. There are three that we will consider now.

First, dreams do indeed have a meaning. They are meaningful. By the way, the Bible does not ever show a dream that does not have meaning. Hmmm... Second, patterns of themes appear in a person's dream. The principles are universal. Third, Biblically directed principles of dream interpretation are available to us today.

Dreams Do Have Meaning

While there is no case for *every* dream, the Bible indisputably teaches that dreams do indeed have meaning. A dream or vision can be readily understood, such as the dreams Joseph receives to shuttle around his infant son. Contrast this with John's vision of Revelation. How many different theories of interpretation do you want? Should we limit the search to a specified number of years? After all, the dream is complex, symbolic, multidimensional, and veiling. Every era proposes its own fifty-two interpretations.

Just in case it is difficult to see it, to hear it, or to believe it, God outright *says* he communicates through his selected channels when he states, through his channel, Moses,

> "Lo, the psychic among you, *I* the Lord make myself known to him in a vision, *I* speak with him in a dream." (Num. 12.6)

The Bible is, after all, we accept as a premise of this tour, the word of God. If the Bible posits such significance to dreams, in its pronouncements as well as in its stories and poems, shouldn't we do as much?

Thus, in the counsel of dreams, God helps humankind avoid evil fates. Ask Abimelech. As with Joseph, God can give us the direction we need to choose and develop a favorable path.

Humanity has long revered dreams as giving counsel. Though Freud seemed to introduce the idea to post-Victorian polite and erudite society, it is not a new phenomenon. David writes in one of his songs,

> "I will bless the Lord who has given me counsel: in the night-time wisdom comes to me in my inward parts." (Ps. 16.7)

Elihu, in the words that open this chapter, reminds Job to listen to his dreams, because that is when God whispers to us.

Dreams and visions come while you are most assuredly in an altered state. Mysts move between the two worlds. In visions of the night, in dreams, the soul embraces its Divinity.

One might charge, "Well, the Bible's only *one* source."

Further, as you know, the Bible, strictly as a book, is powerless. A source unconsulted, a source unconsidered, is a source with no effect. It only gets its meaning from the esteem we living human individuals give it, the influence over our lives we defer to it. We could ignore it, as we do so much other sacred ancient and contemporaneous literature. All things move in cycles. We but evidence our own relative cultural and personal values in the way we esteem the Bible and its stories. Even if the meaning is self-created, however, it *is* meaningful. Though it may be only one source, it is a significant source.

Consider, however, that though it is but one source, it does not disagree with any substantive works on dreams. They all point in the same direction.

It is easy to get carried away on certain issues and even forget to note the blaringly obvious. We keep talking about God and humanity. But a dream visits a sole individual. Though dream researchers as well as the Bible tout limited instances of group dreaming, the dream still comes to one person at a time.

So how do we connect the two, the human individual and humanity? The answer lies in the individual's passion to communicate, either compelled by the excitement of the dream – very understandable – or in the recognition that they are but a channel. As such, they have accepted the commission that complements the privilege of receiving these magnificent dreams and portents. However they do it, they take the individualized dream and in turn communicate it with others. Look at their effects, these thousands years later.

The Themes Of Dreams

When we stop to consider the themes of dreams, we see that every dream or psi event has its unique historical placement, need, powers, lessons, and guidance. This holds true whether you're considering the particular participants and/or us, posterity. Said another way, a dream is always personal. The dream is about *you* – about your own life and affairs.

It's just that what's personal depends upon your position in life. Thus you have an elderly missed-his-chance Abraham, paired with a woman past her time, dreaming about a son and an heir. A number eleven son of twelve dreaming of dominion. A Pharaoh and a caliph dreaming at the level of kingdoms and succession. A butler dreaming about wine, and a baker about cakes. A new father's dreams concern the welfare of his infant son. And the highly intelligent and inspired Daniel dreams complex high dreams of spiritual depth and development.

The Interpretation Of Dreams

The ability to interpret dreams and visions is another aspect of the gift of dreams. Interpretation can be separate from the gift of the dream.

We might compare it to receiving a letter from a person in a country different from our own. What some call the "far country." Let's assume this language is a language of symbols, a universal language. Yet it is a language we are not familiar with.

Now when you receive this letter, it contains a message directed to *you.* Unfortunately, written in a higher key, you don't understand it. It is written in Divinese, which, though you are certain contains a meaning of ponderous import, is meaningless – and therefore effectiveless – to you.

This is exactly the position Pharaoh finds himself in. This is exactly the position Nebuchadnezzar finds himself in.

There are lots of books on dreams and dream interpretation. It is a perennially popular subject. There are a number of good works and babbles of trashy works on dreams. If your interest is anything beyond the superficial, you should definitely read – even if you have to wade through archaic social ideals of a Victorian Europe – Freud's *The Interpretation Of Dreams.* It does a tremendous job of detailing the principles of interpretation. The principles he describes are the principles of the Divine, as revealed in the Biblical stories. Much of Freud's insight, after all, comes from his wide literary reading.

Dreams offer their insight, advice, and direction principally when they are understood. Hence the repetitive dream, trying and trying to get through, as we see with Pharaoh dreaming the same dream twice, cloaked in different messengers, the grain and the kine.

Enter the bilingual person who understands the language of dreams. By examining the message, he or she can reveal the contents of it, translating it to terms you understand. The message is for you, the dreamer. This, we understand, is part of the Divine outworking.

Additionally, because of their insider's insight, the dream translator/interpreter may find themselves in a position to profit personally, as Joseph and Daniel do. They are accolated with prestige and lavished with wealth. These riches and this prestige are the tangible evidence of their metaphysical success. In accordance with the Divine outworking, even the interpreter plays a significant part in the affairs of the dreaming person.

Of course, as Joseph and Daniel illustrate in their rounded characterizations, the dreamer and the interpreter can both be the same person.

Another important point to note regarding the interpretation of dreams is that simply by the fact that certain dreams are remembered they have already established themselves as different. The average person remembers less than a handful of the multitudinous dreams she or he dreams during the course of a single year. Dreams lose their definition and impact upon waking just as stars in the dawning.

Allegory And Metaphor. Freud first publicly postulated in a *scientific sense,* necessary for his era, that dreams are the stage of the unconscious. A dream is a constructed drama to communicate a message. In this situation or story, one thing represents another. Psychology accepts this postulation wholeheartedly. Literature always has. Sacred literature does. There is a deeper meaning. The dream is a metaphor.

The dreamer sees or experiences some reality during the night's sojourn into the mists of the unconscious. But it is not about cows and grain, for themselves, but what they represent to the dreamer. The spiritual reality the dream speaks is embedded beneath a "local habitation and a name." As many have pointed out, it is for this reason that Ezekiel dreams of angels in chariots and not angels on laser powered footstools.

Pharaoh dreams of grain and cattle – sustenance to the land. A similar fate arrives to them both. The seven healthy kine are eaten by the seven gaunt kine, and they are still gaunt. And Pharaoh awakes. The seven plump good ears of grain are eaten by seven thin and blighted ears, and they are still thin and blighted. And Pharaoh wakes.

As Carl Jung consistently teaches, the dream contains both the problem *and* the solution. Seven represents the years. The seven healthy cows that appear first are the good years of plenty of food. The seven knob-kneed cows represent the seven bad years to follow. That's the problem. The way to survive through the coming bad years is to, during the bad years, live off the surplus of the good years. The grain scenario – dreamed in a second dream – repeats the identical theme. Food and food. Cattle and grain. The weak eats the strong and survives.

In one of Isaiah's trances, the Lord sings a song for his beloved, "a love song concerning my vineyard" (Is. 5.1). He looked for grapes, but the vineyard yielded wild grapes. It is useless. God says he will destroy the vineyard, removing the hedge and letting it return to the wildness it is producing. No more special protection. Not much further, God reveals the allegory plainly,

"The vineyard of the Lord of hosts is Israel..." (Is. 5.7)

This gives us a lesson for all interpretation.

How much more clearly can God teach us the way to find meaning in the liminal productions of the psychic realms? God is at his best in the story form, the essence of the unconscious.

Dream Devices. With the next brief excursion of our psychicspace adventure we'll share an array of terms Freud uses to discuss dreams. Our object here is not to become dream experts. That's a different course. Nevertheless, we look at these terms because of their outrageously common sense. People easily understand these erudite principles and intuitively acknowledge them as holding the rank Freud assigns to them.

The *manifest content* is the outer, obvious content of the dream-story. Thus, the manifest content of Pharaoh's dream is cows eating cows, corn eating corn. Ah, but he teaches us to divine for the *latent content*, the story or representations underneath – what the dream is really about, food.

Distortion is a constant accompaniment of the dream state, as when the mystic hears speaking like trumpets, or a Pharaoh dreams of grain eating grain.

A particular theme, event, or omen is emphasized through *compression*, also referred to as *concentration*. Thus, Pharaoh dreams his dream – in variations – twice. Food is embodied in the main characters of both dreams. The importance of food in this dream is underscored by *overdetermination*, which represents a subject in repeated and varied ways. Thus in Pharaoh's dream of food, food not only manifests as food itself, but it does so twice, in the kine and the grain. But multiply this by two, also, for each foodstuff appears in a vigorous form and in a feeble form. Additionally, there are *seven* ears of corn, and *seven* cows of both the good and bad representations. Further, what raises these symbols to even greater prominence is that they do not appear simply as props on the stage with human or divine actors, but as the *actors themselves!*

Throughout his lengthy opus Freud admonishes us to peer deeply. These are some of the devices we use to divine that deeper meaning.

"Is It Real? Or Is It Only Metaphysical?"

No disputing. Though it is certainly a psychical reality, a dream seems like a physical unreality.

But there is more. Physical reality is but the realm of manifestation. All things have their origins in psychical reality, in the subjective realm of the unmanifest. Thus, first God decrees, *"Let there be light."* Then light enters the field of physical reality. In a similar manner, the inventor first envisions a product to fulfill some need. Later it evolves into physical reality.

Therefore, the psychic substance of a dream is a real thing. In its subjective substance of insight and emotion, it is like a powerful seed which, nurtured, has the power to burst the membrane of its confinement.

In actuality, the psychical and physical realms are connected totally from degree to degree. They are but two poles on the continuum of one reality, just as the roots of darkness and leaves of light are two poles of a single event. Though divided in appearance, though divided for ease of discussion, they are unified, connected seamlessly in the matrix of the HoloCosm.

Therefore, certainly some dreams, at least, should have physical world consequences. Some do. Though it's difficult to be certain what John the Revelator prophesies, there are lots of other psychics forecasting. We know precisely what they are dreaming about. Isaiah, Jeremiah, Ezekiel, Hosea, Joel, Amos, and others participate in the unfolding creation of reality by seeing it and by helping others to see it. The dream of Pharaoh does accurately forecast the drought and famine conditions. Implementing the advice encoded in the dream, the throne meets the threat with abundance.

Solomon dreams God gives him the genie's choice, and he picks *wisdom*. Does this dream have any effect or manifestation in reality? After all, the proof of the reality of the dream's clairvoyance is in the outpressing of reality. And yes, Solomon does receive the wisdom he seeks. The stories of his wisdom are legendary. He still enjoys a reputation – 3,000 years later! – as the wisest man on Earth. His Proverbs are relevant, ennobling, and enjoyed yet today. And he dreams he receives more....

The fugitive Elijah eats two helpings of a meal served in a dream. On that psychic nourishment he runs forty days to safety. Surely this is a supernal food that can take a man over a month in desert country. Here again we see clearly demonstrated for our instruction, inspiration, and guidance, the intercommutability of the psychical and the physical realms.

Speaking of such stuff as dreams are made of, yes, Virginia, it is metaphysical. And Virginia, it is physical as well.

****

Dreams And Visions

In your tour through the scape of dreams, it may seem that you have been here before. Of course, this is true. *Déjà vu.* The features of the dreamscape are the same, coterminous with the ESP and channeling scapes we've just traversed. It is as if we are making different passes over the same territory, but we catch different highlights each trip because we have different "lenses" for our vision.

We of the superpower nations and their playing peers, the technologically advanced and alert, could consider it like looking at the map of an area. We see different things with infrared photography, sonagraphy, and computer imaging than we do simply with a 35mm wide lens camera shooting out of an airplane.

However, we know the area more fully when we see it through the different perspectives. We will turn the lens of the psychic arts on a few dreams that reward noting here. The composite picture that arises is the whole, richly interdependent.

"You're A Dead Man!"

Abimelech. Talk about lucky people! Abimelech sure has to be one. It all starts when Abraham, following his nomadic ways, journeys through the territory of the Negeb. In those days the bandits are a little worse and the police and leaders are a little more open than they are today. Abraham reasons that if he says Sara is his *sister*, not his *wife*, then nobody would attempt to kill him for her. They wouldn't have to have him out of the picture to take her, they could just take her.

His relationship is incestuous – she really *is* his sister. So he technically does tell the truth. But he lies by omission in the fact that she *is* also his wife.

Surely, his plan for what he foresees works perfectly. King Abimelech takes her. You know what he plans. But fortune is smiling on Abimelech. He may have touched her in intimate places, but before he gets to the big event, he falls into a doze. He is saved from imminent ruin through the missive of a dream.

God comes to him and says,

> "You're a *dead man!* The woman you've taken is a man's *wife.*" (Gen. 20.3)

Still in the dream, Abimelech, accustomed to discourse with characters of rank, protests his innocence. After all, he adduces,

> "Didn't he himself say to me, 'She is my sister'? And she herself say, 'He is my brother'? I'm innocent of any wrong intent." (Gen. 20.5)

God replies, saying,

> "Well, you're right. But I'm warning you... You'd better not do what you're planning, or you *will* be a dead man! You, your wives, your children, even your kingdom!" (Gen. 20.6-7)

Abimelech goes soft. The dream reveals both the complicity and its simple solution. Abimelech acts on the mystic intelligence, and restores her at the earliest opportunity, the next day.

Who Does God See?

Oh, what does this say to people who believe that God only visits their chosen elite? Doesn't God visit and speak to whom he would wish?

In fact, consider this: would you attempt to confine the workings of God, who creates and sustains all the Universe in all its manifestations and infinite graduations of intermolecular and interstellar complexity? Sounds abysmally arrogant, doesn't it?

A Super-Precognitive Dream

Jacob's mother has an extreme distaste for the women of the country where they are sojourning, Canaan. This is the land, of course, they hold in dreams of dominion one day. That day is many generations in the future, but Abraham sees the vision, and as progenitor of the race, his son, Isaac, carries it on, imparting it to his son in turn, Jacob. The native women weary Rebekah no end.

So Jacob, always compliant in a guileful way, decides it is a good time to journey to Paddan-aram to seek his wife. Both his father and his brother are angry with him. Esau, understandably, wants to kill him. It is a very good time to go.

Shaken, pondering his purpose in this life, he comes to a certain place where he lays down his head to sleep. No motels back then; no soft pillows. He takes a stone and lays down to sleep with it for a pillow.

At this place, at this crucial time, he dreams,

> There is a ladder set up on the earth, and the top of it reaches all the way to Heaven; and behold, the angels of God are ascending and descending on it! And behold, the Lord stands above it... (Gen. 28.12-13)

The God identifies himself as the "God of Abraham." *Whew! It's not another God!* Once that's out of the way – that is Jacob knows exactly which God is speaking – God speaks directly to the befused man, promising him,

> "Behold, I am with you and will keep you wherever you go, and will bring you back to this land; for I will not leave you until I have done that of which I have spoken to you." (Gen. 28.15)

Jacob, aware of the magnitude of the psychic visitation from God, swears aloud: "Wow! *Wow!! WOW!!!* Man! surely *the Lord is in this place*!... And I didn't know it!" (Gen. 28.17)

And he says,

> "This place is *awesome!*... Why, this is the "*house* of God, and the Stairway To Heaven!" (Gen. 28.17)

Armed with this confidence, Jacob has the fortitude to push on. His move is pivotal in the annals of the Jewish race and the Hebrew persuasion.

How awesome is this place! The entire history of the Jewish race is hanging by a single thread... in the person of Jacob.

The powerful precognitive dream is right. The phallic ladder of masculine fertility is raised. Though Jacob certainly has adventures aplenty during his sojourn, it is his character that drives him to find and encounter adventures, anyway. Always has been, always will be. We, heirs of his kinship's blood, see God delivers on his promise.

About The Future We Cannot See

Herein is one of the major dilemmas we've addressed before. As long as we live and move and have our being in this psi-spiri-Universe, we will have questions about the future we cannot see. Hindsight is 20-20. What's important is not the past, but, as chart traders say, the "right edge." In other words, when you're moving forward without any certainty, but with indications only, of what tomorrow will bring, can you be successful then??!

Will you believe what God says?

The Winning Stake

Jacob thrives in Paddan-Aram, marrying two of his cousins, and having a great number of children with them – and with the darker breed on their property. By the time he departs he has two wives, two concubines, twelve sons, a vast herd, great riches, and all that goes with it in terms of family and support people.

You can bet he always knew he'd go back home. He left years earlier with that intention. But *when*?

When it is time, God comes to Jacob in a dream and urges him on.

But First!... Jacob has a major coup to pull off before he disappears, never to be seen again. Doesn't he think like the gunfighter? His father-in-law has agreed to give him – however unlikely it may be that there are any – the striped, spotted. and mottled sheep of his herd.

But Jacob has Divine guidance. He shares with the twosome in bed, the women to whom he's pledged most his love and his trust, Leah, and his preferred, Rachel,

> "I had a dream, and in the dream, in the mating season of the flock I lifted up my eyes, and saw that the he-goats which leaped upon the flock were striped, spotted, and mottled.
>
> "Then the angel of God said to me in the dream, 'Jacob,' and I said, 'Here I am!'
>
> "And he said, 'Lift up your eyes and see, all the goats that leap upon the flock are striped, spotted, and mottled; for I have seen all that Laban is doing to you. All the healthy offspring of this flock – as unlikely as Laban ever imagines it – shall belong to you. You shall steal his entire herd, whether he, his sons, or his daughters like it or not!'" (Gen. 31.10-12)

Which, following the insights and directives of this dream, Jacob does. It takes a round of seasons, because the breeding time must come.

And it comes. Having worked out the details beforehand, ever crafty Jacob packs out on the sudden during a regular business day when Laban is occupied afar. Oh, and does he ever end up with the richest portions of the man's herds and riches! something he considers his just due. He goes wealthy. And his wives, his other squeezes, and the children he's fathered are happy that way.

When Laban hears of it, he gathers his kinsmen to posse after Jacob. He can stand losing the daughters and the grandchildren, but it's tougher in the money game.

It's like when poker players don't want the person with the winning stake to leave. They think he's got their money, and, as long as he's still in the game, they have a chance to win it back.

God is a major player in this adventure laden drama. First he appears to Jacob, telling him to return to his homeland, showing him how to rape the wealth from Laban on his way out, and now he appears to Laban. After seven days on the chase, when they are closing in on the more encumbered Jacob,

God comes to Laban the Aramean in a dream by night, and says to him,

"Take heed that you say not a word to Jacob, either good or bad." (Gen. 31.24)

They catch him. Laban wisely takes heed, and though he makes minor argument, he does not do what he would have. He ends up acknowledging Jacob in his departure. Jacob was exposed and outgunned. It could have been bad, but for Laban's change of heart.

With God even entering the very dreams and hearts of the players, is it any wonder Jacob is successful?

Any God Will Do

Again we see it is not necessary to be a believer to any particular Godform for the one HoloGod to speak in your visions, dreams, or intuitions. Laban has his own Godforms he worships the Divine through, yet the one Divinity speaks to him.

Joseph The Dreamer Dreams

Joseph. A butler. A baker. Pharaoh. The gift of sensitivity brings many blessings. Not only does Joseph dream, and understand his dreams, he possesses a flair in interpreting the dreams of others. Much fortune comes his way with these psychic skills.

On Earth As It Is In Heaven

Joseph – eleventh of the twelve sons of Jacob, first son of his favored wife, Rachel – has a dream. He shares his dream with his brothers, saying,

"We were binding sheaves in the field, and lo, my sheaf arose and stood upright; and behold, your sheaves gathered round it, and bowed down to my sheaf." (Gen. 37.7)

His brothers taunt the green seventeen year old, challenging his prescient vision of dominion over them. And they hate him all the more.

He has another dream, similar to the first... He makes a big mistake. (If such a thing is possible in the outworking of God's plan – remember, *destiny*.) He shares the dream:

"I have dreamed another dream; and behold, the sun, the moon, and eleven stars were bowing down to me." (Gen. 37.9)

They understand the allegory. They understand Divine language is figurative language, and that the dream concerns more than the stars in the sky. They tell their dad, and this time even his father, Israel, chastises him for his delusions of grandeur.

We, of course, know about the fertilizing power of dreams that repeat.

Through a complex concatenation of effects and causes, it happens. The brothers bow to the floor before Joseph, in fear first, and later in gratitude. The father and all the family's families pay Joseph homage. His power is vast. But for now, in fact, this hatred stirred by the youth's dream fulfills the designs of the God. The dream provokes his brothers to take life-threatening actions against him that lead him into Egypt in the hands of Ishmaelite slave traders. Once in Egypt, though he rises somewhat for a time, buffeted by evil fortune again, Joseph finds himself in bondage again, albeit this time, in jail.

Hold this thought, because we develop it further through the next two sections. The fulfillment of Joseph's repeated dream is closely tied to the dreams of three heathen men, a butler, a baker, and a pharaoh. And what a long series of synchronicity it is!

"Inside Of Three Days..."

Potiphar, one of Pharaoh's officers, buys Joseph from the traders. Apparently Joseph has a lot of charisma with the opposite sex. After several years of able service, he is caught in the bedroom with Potiphar's wife. Of course he is innocent... Nevertheless, the evidence convicts him.

He is thrown into prison. Hmm. If you don't consider being in prison such a bad thing, you'll recognize that the Lord loves him still; the Bible tells us,

> The Lord was with Joseph and showed him steadfast love, and gave him favor in the sight of the keeper of the prison." (Gen. 39.21)

He has charisma with the guys, too. The keeper likes him and trusts him so much that he makes him head orderly.

One day Pharaoh's chief butler and baker come tumbling into prison. Something irritated his highness. Joseph, of course, has free commerce with these men, as, though confined to prison, he's not confined to a single cell. One day he encounters the two men with drooping faces. They moan, in reply to Joseph's inquiries, that they've each had a dream, but that "there is no one to interpret them" (Gen. 40.8).

They don't know about Joseph's facility with dreams; they've only seen him in his prison blues. But Joseph does. He immediately asks to hear their dreams (in the same Biblical verse), asseverating that "interpretations belong to God" (Gen. 40.8). The chief butler tells Joseph his dream:

> "In my dream there is a vine before me, and on the vine there were three branches; as soon as it budded, its blossoms shot forth, and the clusters ripened into grapes. Pharaoh's cup was in my hand; and I took the grapes and pressed them into Pharaoh's cup, and placed the cup in Pharaoh's hand." (Gen. 40.9-11)

This is the dream.

This is the interpretation:

> "The three branches are *three days.* Inside of three days Pharaoh will lift up your head and restore you to your office; and you shall place Pharaoh's cup in his hand as again, as when you were his butler." (Gen. 40.12-13)

And Joseph says,

> "Please, remember me when it is going good for you again... Please mention me to Pharaoh, and get me pardoned. I'm not like all these other guys in here. I'm really innocent. Hey! I was stolen, abducted, from

Israel, and even here, I haven't done anything so bad they should *put me in the dungeon*! (Gen. 40.14-15)

At first the baker is scared of Joseph's offer of metaphysical aid, but when he hears the fortunate interpretation of his partner's dream, he opens up. Alas, for his stupidity. He already had, the story communicates, the certain feeling of doom. This is the dream:

> "There were three cake baskets on my head, and in the uppermost basket there were all sorts of baked food for Pharaoh, but the birds were eating it out of the basket on my head and flying away." (Gen. 40.16-17)

Joseph answers,

> "This is its interpretation: The *three* baskets are *three* days... Bubba, inside of three days Pharaoh's gonna lift up your head-- like really! – and leave you dangling on a tree; and the birds will eat your flesh and pick your eyeballs out and fly away." (Gen. 40.18-19)

It comes to pass on the third day hence. It is Pharaoh's birthday, and he throws a party for the servants of the city. During the gala he calls the prison detail up, and entertains everyone by raising the butler and hanging the baker. The poor people love it.

Variations On A Dream

The butler at first does not find the opportunity to speak to Pharaoh about Joseph. He's been humbled. He stuffs it. Soon he forgets about it.

Two years later, however, Pharaoh dreams a dream he – though powerless to divine its meaning – is ponderously certain contains precognitive insights. He searches the court, trying priests of every persuasion and reputation, but finds he does not really have anyone very able in that field. Guess he never thought he might need such an expert. Can you imagine state funding for *Dreamology*? He needs someone to tell him what it means. But no one is able to help Pharaoh.

Then the butler remembers. Pharaoh sends for Joseph immediately.

Joseph answers Pharaoh. He tells him that, though psychic – that is, able to commune with the Spiritual realms – he is but a channeler. The gift of dreams is a psychic gift... God is the giver and the gift.

> "God is the speaker, I but the instrument." (Gen. 41.16)

Pharaoh shares his dream:

> "In my dream I was standing on the banks of the Nile; and seven cows, fat and sleek, came up out of the Nile and fed in the reed grass; and seven other cows came up after them, poor and very gaunt and thin, such as I had never seen in all the land of Egypt.
>
> "And the thin and gaunt cows ate up the first seven fat cows, but when they had eaten them no one would have known that they had eaten them, for they were still as gaunt as at the beginning. Then I awoke." (Gen. 41.17-21)

And he falls asleep and dreams again, a different dream:

"In my next dream, I this time saw seven ears growing on one stalk – full and good! – and seven ears, withered, thin, and blighted by the east wind, sprouted after them, and the thin ears swallowed up the seven good ears.

"To be honest, none of our magicians and prophets can tell me what these dreams mean. I hope you can." (Gen. 41.22-24)

How God favors Pharaoh! God is communicating with him. Pharaoh is open. God comes to him in a dream, giving him the advice that saves, not only Egypt, but the entire world populace, including Israel. Pharaoh is sensitive and intelligent. He, being a spiritual adept himself, *knows* the Divine Spiritual Universe is manifesting to him, speaking to him, and guiding him. Pharaoh is working diligently to understand the dream. With the very next written words in this Biblical passage, Joseph begins his reply to Pharaoh:

"Pharaoh, my lord, your dream is one. God is revealing to you what he is about to do! The seven good cows are seven good years, and the seven good ears are the same seven good years. Yes, Pharaoh, the dream is one. The next scene is the same thing!

"See, the seven lean and gaunt cows are seven years, and the seven empty ears blighted by the east wind are also the same seven years of famine. I say again, God is showing you what he is about to do." (Gen. 41.25-28)

Then, pre-Freud, he says it again, adding the emphasis due God's repeated efforts of communication,

"And the doubling of your dream means that this outcome is destined, a fate that cannot be avoided." (Gen. 41.32)

God communicates directly with Pharaoh. Joseph foresees the future in the dream. God, through Joseph's interpretive abilities, reveals it *explicitly* to Pharaoh. Pharaoh believes.

Because he believes in the message the mystic reveals, *he acts on it.*

God's HoloCosmic will in action, combined with Joseph's innate intelligence, puts him, at the age of thirty, in the number two slot in the entire nation, Secretary of the Treasury over Upper and Lower Egypt. There he will carry out the plan received whole to survive the coming bad years. *It would take a mystic to divine. How hard it is to get the profane to recognize the seeds of destruction in their wanton prosperity!* The rewards attached to psychic sensitivity can be *enormous!*

Joseph is swept up to wealth so unmeasurable that need of any kind becomes meaningless.

Of Psychic Verities

We find here a good point to stop and jot a few notes on dreams and dream interpretation.

Non-Complexificious Dreams. The dreams of these men – Joseph, the butler, the baker, and Pharaoh – are not complex. Compare these with the apocalyptic vision of John the Revelator, to see the contrast. And we have no record of a sequence of dreams with these men, as with Ezekiel, who dreams dream after dream, it seems, on a daily basis. They are simple. But symbolic.

Here is the great news in this fact. A dream need not be strung together with complexities to be indeed a dream of the Divine. God communicates to each individual dreamer – *you* as well – at the level of their comprehension... Or, as these dreams indicate, at a level at which *we can find the answers. Oh, psychic interludes are so meaningful!*

To Be Human Is To Be Connected With The Divine. We see again the folly of believing that God only loves and communicates with "insiders." Pharaoh and his domestic servants are outsiders to the Hebrew philosophy. To be human is to be connected with the Divine. The capacity is hardwired into the human constitution. No more privilege is required.

Psychic, Advertise! Look at Joseph's forwardness in his offer to interpret the prisoners's dreams. He doesn't play coy, giving them the glorious chance of drawing it out of him.

Anyone who has the gift should be forward about it. What if Joseph had only "hinted" that he possessed the gift, and these depressed men – notorious for missing innuendos – did not actually realize that Joseph could assist them? Would Joseph have done them the service that he does? Would Joseph have done Pharaoh and himself the service that he does? Would Joseph have done *us* the service that he does?

"As I See It..." Another notable thing about Joseph is his ability and/or willingness to tell the truth as he sees it. After all, this is what psychic reading is all about. Looking him straight in the eyes, Joseph tells the baker, *"You're gonna die!"* Obviously – there is no way around it – God, through the medium of the Bible, is saying that a psychic can accurately predict death. It *does* happen here – in the Bible – doesn't it? The vision, the dream, the lay of the cards or the stones is accomplished by the querent – or, to be more exact, the querent's unconscious. Or, to be more exact still, in this HoloCosmic Universe, simultaneously the querent's unconscious and the SuperConscious, coupled in synchrony, the SupbraConscious.

The psychic but fulfills the damned blessing of objectifying the truth. Reading is not that difficult if you possess the gift. Telling the truth is.

The Mystical Shining

Moses is a psychic of major proportions, a man who rises to the call of the times. His historical opportunities are akin to those that fell to the founding fathers of the United States of America. They rose by their dedication, lifted by the times. It is not often this conjunction occurs.

One day the mystical shining breaks through to Moses' furrowed consciousness: The angel of the Lord appears to him in a flame of fire out of the midst of a bush. And lo! the mystic bush is burning, yet it does not. (Ex. 3.2)

The omniscient narrator tells us Moses thinks to himself,

"What a *marvel!* I'd better check this out and see why the burning bush isn't burning!" (Gen. 3.3)

Many psi occurrences are of the nature that they can be overlooked or ignored, because they don't obtrude. They subtly invite, with provocative enticement. On the other hand, some are so arresting that they cannot be overlooked. Thus, God, having effectively roped Moses' attention, calls his name two times.

The Lord identifies himself and says,

"I have seen the affliction of my people who are in Egypt, and have heard their cry because of their taskmasters; I know their sufferings, and I've come to deliver them out of the hand of the Egyptians, and to bring them up out of that land to a land flowing with milk and honey....

"Come forward, I am sending you to Pharaoh that you may bring forth my people out of Egypt." (Ex. 3.7-10)

Then, to the unbelief of fundamentalist mis-readers, we see God actually arrange a channeling situation. Responding to Moses' concerns – or is that excuses? – of his own ineloquence, God tells him that instead of channeling his messages straight through him to the people, he will add Aaron in the chain. Thus God will channel to Moses, Moses will channel to Aaron, and Aaron will channel to Pharaoh and the people and you. "You," God tells Moses,

"You shall be to Aaron as God." (Ex. 4.16)

The Ways Of Psi

The stories of Moses hold many a mystical insight of power for us. Here we stop to discuss the phenomenon of identification again, as well as to ask a very transpersonal question.

Identification. We see the phenomenon of *identification* in action here. Moses does not apparently keep in mind the distinction that he is talking to a subordinate officer in God's hierarchy of princes, an angel! The angel is as God to him. Nor does the writer of *Exodus.* Nor does but *seldom* a reader! But he is. Everyone thinks God is speaking in these lines.

The angel amidst the flames of the burning bush is channeling God. The angel *is* God. Moses understands who speaks. This is identification.

Moses may have some doubts he addresses to God, but he never doubts it *is* God, the Supreme Being.

And the same holds true when Aaron is added into the link. Though it will be Moses, and not an angel bringing the message, Aaron shall hear God when Moses speaks.

What Would You Accomplish??! It will not be easy breaking the people out of their lethargy . His people are institutionally entrenched, comfortable in their victimness. As bad as it is – being known – slavery is more comfortable to the average mind than the risks on the road to riches. It takes a big heart – driven. Neither will it be easy prying open the serpentine jaws of the Pharaoh. Yet history unfolds according to the intimations Moses receives.

Think what power that would give to your actions! What would you accomplish moving forward on your dreams if you were performing them with the inner certitude that God has selected you to achieve your task?

"Am I Not Your Ass, Whom You Have Enjoyed At Your Pleasure?"

Balaam. The twelve united tribes of Israel are successfully killing the inhabitants of Canaan, taking the land as their own. A worried king – about to be a target of the Israeli military machine – seeks Balaam's services to resist their aggressions.

Thus Balaam is introduced as a psychic adept. As God interacts with Moses or Ezekiel, he dances with Balaam. Balaam is not a man who simply gets hit with one spontaneous occurrence, on which he builds all his fame, or even a couple of deep times when the Spirit responds to the ornate stimulants of ritual. When we first meet him he is in fact being sought out for divination and directive prayer by King Balak. He has already established his power center.

During Balaam's second trance focused on the issues surrounding Balak's request to mystically fuddle the designs of the Jewish people, he doesn't mean it, but God tells Balaam that he can go and see King Balak.

This is quite a point. This kind of bypassing causes misunderstanding enough in our human relations, but when God does it too?... God *says* he can go, but Balaam is supposed to know he doesn't mean it? Sound familiar?

Then guess what? Balaam gets in trouble. An angry God sends a martial angel down to block his path. Here's the thing, though. At first, probably because of his preoccupations with the king and the nation, admittedly a heavy hand, Balaam does not see the angel with the razor-sharp and shining drawn sword. It's like a policemen with his pointed gun out. But his donkey does!

What follows is an interesting play of push and resistance between the at-this-moment superior brute and the inferior man. The angel suddenly appears in the road and the donkey, frightened, just as suddenly makes an evasive move between a row of vineyards. Like an old west cowboy with a self-willed horse, Balaam starts striking her ass to get her turned around.

Then, moving through the alter-dimensions, the angel now of a sudden appears before the creature in the row. There's not room to turn around, so the donkey compresses herself in fear against the left wall. This catches Balaam's leg and foot, so Balaam amplifies his anger, striking the brute twice harder. The fit and armed young angel is having fun taunting these two. (Just doing his job, of course.) He disappears.

The animal is spooked. But Balaam is too agitated to discern and investigate it.

Then, not too far distant, in a narrowed path between rock outcroppings, where the animal cannot physically turn around or evade him, the armed angel appears again. She does the only thing she can. She crouches to the ground. Now, standing up, Balaam takes his staff to beating the recalcitrant animal.

Then, as interesting as any scene in any comic book, she looks to the outraged Balaam and asks,

"What have I done to you, that you have struck me these three times?" (Num. 22.28)

Outraged, Balaam has an answer:

"Because you have made sport of me! I wish I had a sword in my hand, for then I would kill you!" (Num. 22.29)

And the ass replies with two questions that bring sense back to Balaam, helping him to slow down enough to see the reality of the situation:

"Am I not your ass, upon whom you have ridden all your life long to this day? Was I ever accustomed to do so to you?" (Num. 22.30)

With this the vision comes. Balaam sees the angel threatening with his drawn sword and instantly falls to the ground in fearful submission.

Balaam is penitent. Further, after the sport, God is in a good mood; he changes his mind again, deciding he can utilize the way things have turned out after all. He tells Balaam to go ahead and go to Balak. It will serve his purpose. "But!" he says,

"You shall channel *only* and *exactly* what I tell you to." (Num. 22.35)

Remember, you are but an instrument. Leave your self-will out of it.

Peering up at the ripples of the soldier's developed thighs, chest, and biceps, Balaam agrees. When he gets to Moab, he gives the anxious king the bad news that he cannot curse those whom God does not curse. He says,

"The word that God puts in my mouth, *that* must I speak." (Num. 22.38)

He will channel faithfully.

Of Psychic Verities

We encounter some interesting and significant psychic verities in the psychicspace of Balaam. First, we see that animals have psychic sensitivity, more than some humans. If fact, even the best of humans, attuned to the psychic drama, miss a lot, too. We also see that spiritual direction is *everywhere*, and that it comes when you need it.

Animals And Psychic Sensitivity. Believe it or not, we can get some clues to enhance our psychic life from those who are less constrained by a thought system that favors objective reality, animals. We, with our superior frontal human consciousness have boxed ourselves into a four dimension reality. Animals are closer to the spiritual axis/centre of it all.

The intuitive and instinctive recognize the greater reality more easily. This sensitivity has been traded as the cost of analytic development. We are in the midst of evolving back to the point wherein we are naturally in tune with the intuitive life again. Only this time, we possess the benefits and insights that analysis gives us, too. We are a more whole being. We are learning to integrate our spiritual natures and our material natures in this world wherein we as human spiritual beings recognize the spiritual in material experience. As Balaam attests, it's not happening without its bumps, scrapes, and humbling moments.

Spiritual enlightenment and direction is everywhere for the spiritually aware. It is in the stones and the treetops, as the stories of David demonstrate, and in the behavior of animals, as the story of Balaam tells.

Nobody Gets It All. Balaam is an adept in an uncrowded field. His reputation says that he is powerful, and accomplishes what he will, which is no doubt true. However, you may find it interesting to notice that even Balaam, who talks to the very God, blows it bigtime with the angel! Not once, not twice, but thrice!

This passage illuminates multiple mysteries of psi. Among these, it demonstrates again the multifaceted approach of psi as well as the role of the individual mystic's present and particular level of consciousness.

Balaam, as a professional, receives his communications at night. Usually. But psi won't be constrained by the barriers of the mind. It takes no part in the belittling process. The spiritual world is everything. Then comes an angel in the day. Psi is come, it is there, but Balaam doesn't see it.

Balaam, in addition to having psi appear outside the familiar channels, is under a lot of stress. There he is, minding his own wizardly business when the king and his concerns bust his routines. It's a long way from the books and prayers of the magician's high tower to the anxious brass applauding palace walls. Everyone's receptivity varies according to the things that are going on in their world. There is a rhythm to everything. Psychic or not.

The Universe Knows When You Need Correction. And we think electronic surveillance is powerful! What about psychic surveillance?

Balaam is corrected even in the act of his error. When you have joined the ranks of the spiritual elite, there's no guarantees your own self-will won't flair up from time to time. You still move midst duality. You still are human, with the foibles characteristic of the human animal. Yet, as we see here, God uses the psychic dimensions to correct your way.

Balaam is clarified in his mission and intent because of this vision.

It will do the same for you.

Angel At The Winepress

Gideon. It is a time when judges rule the Earth. It is the time after the patriarchs, the budding of captivity, and Moses. It is the time before the kings and the Babylonian victory. It is a time of transition; a time of uneasy, uneven, and eventful growth for the fledgling nation of Israel.

And trouble plagues the nation again. They are being oppressed and bullied by one of their large neighbors, Midian. Midian feels threatened by their hostile takeover of the land of the Amorites, their erstwhile neighbors who are vanished, exterminated. So, while they still possess sufficient superiority, they depress Israel's ability to prosper. Every year, for a period that endures seven years, they come with their herds of people and oxen and camels and graze the land, utterly destroying all its fruit and sustenance. Israel takes to the hills.

In this state of affairs one virile young Gideon is working. He is beating out wheat in the winepress, hiding his activities from the Midianite intelligencers, when an angel suddenly appears before him, saluting him with the words,

"The Lord is with you, you mighty man of valor!" (Jg. 6.12)

After some give and take, Gideon becomes convinced the Lord has charged him to accomplish the great task – to overthrow the Midianite oppression.

Empowerment in a vision. Gideon does.

Reflections

Looking back over this episode, we discern lessons in the timing of psi, in the awakening to psi, and in the responsibilities of psi, timely taught.

Psi When The Times Demand It. There is a mystical truism that psi comes according to the need. This is usually repeated to anxious neophytes seeking the marvels of psi phenomena in their lives. But what it means is that the Spiritual Universe doesn't just appear and act for the fun of parlor games. Even in the student developing psi abilities, manifestations of psi phenomena may not flood their life and existence to the scope they would prefer.

However, when there is a need, that makes all the difference. The elements of psi always respond to a sincere and meaningful call. And need is by definition a deep call.

The Israelites, driven by adversity, are turning to God with renewed hearts when the story opens. And the HoloCosm, being both the call and the answer, both the answer and its outworking, responds.

God judges their hearts sincere, so he determines to reestablish their dominion. He sends an angel as himself. Gideon gets it.

God sends Gideon, an active man with psychic proclivities, to turn the people's hearts back to God. Thus again, at least some of the time, this sacred text explicitly attests, psychics and channelers are sent by God.

What we see here is that God goes to the length necessary, even to the point of repeating in variations in psi phenomena, to communicate when the times demand it.

The corollary of this is that when there is no call or need for psi activity (except for among the developed, who keep the arts of priestcraft always alive), it may not be particularly active. Here, for instance, in a matter of a few days we experience visions, dreams, intuitions, and empowerments. After this burst of empowered activity which ends the Midianite threat, the land has rest. No more psi activity is recorded during the years of peace.

Awakening To Higher Consciousness: When The Gifts Come. There are no indications Gideon is essentially any different from the other citizens of Israel before the apparition of the angel. Even he, a young man in the fullness of masculine strength and activity, who could and even *should* do something about the oppressive political climate, is whining.

But there is a marked and empowering change in him when things add up to the point of seeing the angel. What is an especially interesting treat for psychic students in this story is that we actually see the process of Gideon opening up.

This all takes off one mythical "one day."

As a result of the mass consciousness of petition among the people, which includes Gideon, the angel appears. Then, look at the opening! Having established communication with the angel, God himself speaks to Gideon!

And Gideon doubts – but when divinations settle those doubts, he is a powerhouse!

God continues to inspire, direct, and assist Gideon in his purposes through dreams and the voice of intuition. When the gifts come, they *come.* Let this inspire, direct, and assist you.

See, and marvel.

This Is No Mere Pleasant Mystical Diversion. Gideon's charge is of significant proportions, requiring great resources to pull off. It is a political task that demands organization, money, and might. It involves significant personal risk. It is no mere pleasant mystical joy. Gideon has a TASK to do. It's akin to the difference between the sublime ecstasies of the poet in the garden and the general's war station command.

You have heard it said you receive no charges you are not capable of carrying out. Gideon does possess ample strength and ability to accomplish the purposes that God puts before him. He has the capacity to develop as he needs. This of course, is *why* he's been chosen, among an army of prospects. Because he *is* up to the charge. This is new ground for him, but driven in the grand vision of service to God and his humanity, indeed, Gideon is capable. Besides, significant parts of the campaign are scheduled for accomplishment in the fifth dimension, a Merlin-like advantage the Midianites lack. *Gideon believes!*

The vision passes, but not the power. Gideon accomplishes what he is inspired to do. Therein is his greatness. Therein is the will of the Lord accomplished. He routs the Midianites and restores peace and prosperity to the land.

Contrast this with another common arena of the psychic mystique. Most of the psychic occurrences we encounter concern the future, as in the case of Samson's momma, whom we visit soon. She is given an intimation and intuition of the future.

But other than keeping her temple holy – significant at that – she is given no great task to perform. Rather she is to watch what happens with her destined son.

And Gideon's reward? What an honor! He is made judge with all its prestige, wealth, and privilege.

"I Had A Dream..."

Gideon. Midianite soldiers. This is the story of a dream and the power of interpretation. The recipients and participants in this dream, too, inspired by the dream's latent content, fulfill the destiny God has decreed.

While Gideon is doing some close call spying on the Midianites, prior to engaging them, he overhears a soldier telling his tent mate,

> "I had a dream; and in it a giant barley muffin comes tumbling into our camp, and levels and dishevels every tent in the camp, including Commander's." (Jg. 7.13)

This is the manifest content.

And his comrade, certain of the fate, perceiving the latent content, answers,

> "This is no other than the sword of the dashing Gideon. Our fate is sealed! God has given Gideon the victory!" (Jg. 7.14)

The Lord had promised Gideon he would hear what he needed to hear to be inspired to action. He flashes back to camp and, in hushed high energy, gets everyone charged for the victory, which they take that night.

They catch the Midianites off guard, lounging in their underwear. The slaughter is swift and certain. It's a banquet of blood! His soldiers catch Oreb and Zeeb, two Midianite princes trying to flee, kill them on the spot, and bring the hideous heads straight to Gideon's roving command. Gideon himself executes sentence on the kings, Zebah and Zalmunna, slaying them ritualistically with his tuned sharp sword.

"And the land rests forty years in the days of Gideon." (Jg. 8.28)

Consider This

There's an array of things we can note in this scenario. Let's touch-and-go on a few highlights.

Psi For Everybody. No way could you call either Pharaoh or Nebuchadnezzar *uncouth* heathens. History leaves the evidence of their royal sensibilities. But in the soldiers we have the spiritually blunt and obtuse.

Nevertheless, to execute his designs, God makes use of all peoples. All are hardwired into the psychic dimensions, accessible by God at God's will.

Through The Psychic Channels. Isn't this amazing synchronicity, that Gideon, of all the tents he could chance upon, strikes upon one with a dreamer in it? Remember how difficult it is for Pharaoh to find an interpreter? And Gideon's tent has both the dreamer and an interpreter!!! This dream illustrates the multi-dimensional HoloCosmic interdependence of all participants in the scape of reality.

Dreamer, interpreter, and brave-hearted man all together. It is not named coincidence, but *synchronicity.*

Check this out! Gideon is neither the dreamer nor the interpreter. He is a third party. Yet he *recognizes* the dream's significance, and *acts* on it! Herein is the great secret. First the seeing, the perceiving, then the *acting,* the high fruit of God-empowered psychic insight. No insights, no powerful action. Action not compelled with powerful insights, insipid ineffective actions. Insights, no actions; perhaps passing good feelings, but no fulfillment. And the message and empowerment may come from the dream of another. Isn't this *wonderful?*

The Bible Is A Living Document. Back to basic principles, and the very basis on which he constructs his Bible, here God teaches us once again that we learn vicariously. Scripture is not dead and dry with the dust of bones. It is a living document, vitally alive in our present. Simply by reading and integrating insights we can activate the capacity we need to drive into the inspired action he would have us perform.

Reading, of course, is but one avenue of empowerment. We surely have our own dreams, visions, and meditations. Much of it can and *does* come from our driving engagement in our lives. Yet Gideon does not dream, he does not interpret. He *recognizes.* As we see, even the issues, dreams, and activities of others in this HoloCosm are the dreams, issues, interpretations, and activities of our own. But he does followup as he should – he *acts.*

Continuity Of The Sacred Moment: The Everlasting Present. Here is a good point to recall. As we read, study, and marvel round these psychic implications, we ought from time to time to simply take a moment to re-center ourselves.

These events and dramas are important events and dramas to the participants. Legends today, once they made their decisions engaged in the adventures of the moment. Don't pass this story – or any Biblical story – off as of no great pith and consequence. If you'll make that shift in consciousness into *being alive in the moment,* recognizing *this is it!* not waiting for anything else, and recognizing that all these stories speak of the present moment in eternal reality, you'll be rewarded beyond today's conceptions of blessings. This is the everlasting present, the mythic moment forever.

Samson's Momma

The circumstances surrounding the birth of *Samson* are uniquely similar to those surrounding the birth of the special child Jesus. An angelic visitor visits each of the soon-to-be mothers, before conception, foretelling the birth of their special sons.

The angel who visits Samson's mother tells the barren woman,

"Behold, you shall conceive and bear a son." (Jg. 13.3)

He then informs her that this child is special:

"The boy shall be a Nazarite dedicated to God from birth; and he shall
begin to deliver Israel from the hand of the Philistines." (Jg. 13.5)

To this end, the angel informs her, she should maintain herself pure and undefiled,
watching what she takes into her body.

Quite naturally, she runs and tells her husband about the supra-terrestrial visitor.
She knows who he is. Upon questioning, she admits she did not ask where he hails
from. Hedging, she uses the non-committal term "a man of God" rather than calling
him an angel. She says to her husband:

"A man of God came to me, and his countenance was like the
countenance of the angel of God, very terrible; I did not ask him where
he was from, and he did not tell me his name; but he said to me,

"'Behold, you shall conceive and bear a son; so then drink no wine or
strong drink, and eat nothing unclean, for the boy shall be a Nazarite to
God from birth to the day of his death.'" (Jg. 13.6-7)

As if this isn't enough, beset with questions as to what they should do in raising
the boy to further God's choices, Manoah, the woman's husband, entreats the Lord.
The Bible tells us,

God listens to the voice of Manoah, and the angel again visits the woman.
(Jg. 13.9)

She runs to her husband, who accompanies her back to the sacred spot. Now he
gets to ask the question burning in his heart:

"Now when your words come true, what is to be the boy's manner of life,
and what is he to do?" (Jg. 13.12)

Then the angel, with mystic obfuscation, replies that solely that which he has
already told his wife is sufficient direction for their part in fulfilling God's plan.

Catching the not subtle hint, Manoah asks no more questions regarding the
destined child. Manoah invites the psychic messenger to dinner. The story runs:

And the angel of the Lord says to Manoah,

"If you detain me, I will not eat of your food; but if you make ready a
burnt offering, then offer it to the Lord."

For Manoah did not know that he was the angel of the Lord. (Jg. 13.16)

So Manoah prepares the altar. When the flames are high, stretching toward
Heaven itself, the angel steps into the fire, and ascends in the flames while Manoah
and his wife look on in amazement. Suddenly gone.

Then Manoah *knows.*

And it happens as the emissary foretells. The woman bears the son and rears
him with Nazarite vows. And he grows to be a tremendous problem to the
Philistines.

God's words are fulfilled.

Reflections

After reading a passage of scripture, it's always rewarding to reflect on some of
the lessons therein encoded for us. Of course, while we do this, aware that this

book is written for us at our level of consciousness, as well as for the more highly evolved, we acknowledge that we are passing over much more than we could ever see and discuss. Nevertheless, without fear or regret we embrace what we do see.

What Destiny Decrees The Moment Performs. Here again we see the question of fate and freewill juggled in sacred literature. Actually, it's not correct to say the question is "juggled." It is only raised during our objective evaluation of what goes on in the story. The Bible takes fate and destiny for granted. The designs of the Omnipotent will unfold.

But we who are still Earthlings wonder. Since Samson is anointed even *before his birth*, is he free to do otherwise than what he has been selected, dedicated, and trained to do?

He grows up driven by impulses to serve the Lord's purpose. In respect that he seems to willingly serve the Lord's purpose, it looks like freewill. But, this is the design all along. Does he really have freewill? Being dedicated to the Nazarite sect from weaning, isn't he *trained* to make the choices he makes?

Meditate on this.

They Never Doubt. We who would be channelers of God's word and God's will ought to take note of a fact of such monumental significance it might be overlooked: Manoah and his wife recognize a high and important psychic significance in the message.

They never doubt that the woman who has been barren these so many years will bear fruit. They jump straight to questions that show they've accepted the message of the Godlike man. They don't question "if" the things the angel says are true and will come to pass; instead, their questions are of the "what then?" variety. Look at the wording. When Manoah addresses the angel, he does not ask by what authority the angel says these things, but asks instead, " *When* these things occur.... *what* do we do?"

Dreams Don't Eat, They Feed. The Bible give us all kinds of information about the spiritual dimensions of reality. This includes angels. We saw in the recent story of Gideon that the angel had magical powers of directing lightning through its staff and of disappearing into thin air. (This isn't to mention that the angels generally appear out of thin air, also.)

In this story we get another explicit distinction and indicator of angelhood. Manoah's angel, like Gideon's angel, does not eat the food it is offered. The parenthetic explanation is written to us as insiders, explaining Manoah's odd behavior. You don't offer an angel a meal, because, angels, being ghosts, don't eat material food:

Manoah offered the angel food because he did not know that he was the angel of the Lord. (Jg. 13.16)

Contrasting this, this same phenomenon, eating, is used to demonstrate that the Jesus come back from the dead is *really* back. In that incident, Jesus *eats* fish to prove that he is not just a spiritual energy or apparition focused for the time being in front of his apostles.

Dreams don't eat. They feed, they nourish, they strengthen, and they embolden.

Fourth Time's A Charm

Samuel is but a youngster when God first starts appearing to him in dreams and visions. Interest and activity in the spiritual life has descended, but when interest in spirituality starts waxing again, spiritual phenomena perks up.

Samuel, young neophyte of the Order keeping midnight vigil before the ark, is sleeping in the presence of the Divine.

Then the Lord calls,

"Samuel! Samuel!"

and he replies,

"Here I am!" (1Sam. 3.4)

We, as readers of the passage, have the benefit of knowing it is God. Samuel does not. He runs to attend to his elderly mentor's needs. Doing so Samuel wakes Eli up; Eli assures him he didn't call for him, and chides the boy in a wizardly way. "Now go back to sleep."

And a second time the vision descends on Samuel and a voice calls his name. Eli, aroused a second time, assures the puzzled boy,

"I did not call. Lie down and go to sleep!" (1Sam. 3.5)

And a third time the vision descends on Samuel and a voice calls. And he thinks it is Eli and rouses him a third time.

Finally Eli perceives what is occurring. He instructs the boy:

"Go, lie down; and if he calls you, you shall say, 'Speak, Lord, for thy servant hears.'" (1Sam. 3.9)

Sure enough,

God comes and stands forth, calling as at other times, "Samuel! Samuel!" (1Sam. 3.10)

This fourth time it takes.

Of Psychic Verities

This passage offers us some special truths related to the persistence of psychic messages and the conflation of the senses in the realms of alter-reality.

It Will Not Be Restrained. The narrator of this passage explains to us that Samuel does not recognize the visitations of the Lord because he hasn't yet been initiated into the psychic arts.

What we see here is an instance of the spontaneous initiation of the prepared soul. Spiritual progress will not be constrained by traditions and practices. The schoolyard sequence of graded initiations, even in this spiritual apprenticeship of

Samuel's, are designed to develop and lead the aspirant upward. They are never intended to be limits to hold the boy down. Thus the Lord comes in mystic communion to Samuel in the borderland light of visions and dreams. Samuel is awakened to psi, the manner of God.

Doubling? Trebling! Quadrupling! We also see in these christening visions of Samuel the principle of repetition all over again. Surely, the Unconscious does communicate with us, as Freud articulated, until we get it.

When it is time for Samuel to get it, being new to the arena, he fumbles three times before catching it. If a doubling in psychic demonstrations evinces an extra significance, as Joseph and Daniel, the Bible's premier dreamgicians, say it does, then what does trebling do?

Then it comes in its fullness – on the *fourth* visit!

Could it indicate that when it's your time, *it* will get *you?*

And Samuel grows, and the Lord is with him, and his deserved reputation in the psychic arts grows apace.

The Mystical Conflation. The song of a springtime Sunday bird catches your attention and you immediately imagine a happy Disney songbird trilling in the fullness of pleasure and joy. You might imagine a bird with a full chest, wings at its side, perched on an interior branch of a tree singing, not for an audience and approval, but in the airy buoyancy of God and creation. And you haven't "seen" the bird. *Ah, but you have.* Our sense awareness sympathetically orchestrates a picture or a vision of any stimuli. The mind supplies the missing parts.

This mystical conflation is a gift that comes with the turf of being born a human being. So it is that in this written passage the emphasis on Samuel's christening visions is on sound. There is only the nariest actual reference to anything of the sight sense. Let's look at the structure of the four visions of what surely is a single dream:

1st: The Lord calls, "Samuel!"
2nd: And the Lord calls again, "Samuel!"
3rd: And the Lord calls Samuel again the third time.
4th: And the Lord comes and stands forth, calling as at other times, "Samuel!"

Following the logic of the story, we find it is only in the fourth segment that we see any hint of the visual domain of sensation. This fourth opening tells us the Lord comes to Samuel, but we're not sure if the Lord really comes forth and stands by Samuel in the first three episodes of this dream. He could have been calling from behind a cloud. It does not say. What it does say is that he *calls* like he calls the previous three times: he calls Samuel with his name.

Yet, these *are visions*, the Bible explicitly says, when it tells us that "Samuel is afraid to tell Eli the visions" the next morning.

And we get the picture, don't we?

There is an important concept imparted in the poet's use of the visual word to reckon the incoming auditory sensations. Of course we know that words create images, as every story ever told is told using words. And oh! the pleasures of a story told! Whether it's a *Cinderella* or a *Joseph*, it is all understood in terms of the visions it evokes. Psi is a multidimensional phenomena.

Samuel is what we refer to in NLP as an "auditory," rather than the more common "visual" person. Yet whatever the channel of preference, it always comes down to some type of conceptual-emotional understanding.

This is clear, even to the chagrin of those afflicted with the myopia of fundamentalized di-vision.

How To Have A Dream

Solomon. Have you ever fantasized what you would ask for if you rubbed a lamp and a wish-granting genie appeared? The story of Solomon's request for wisdom is widely told – preachers infer we are supposed to take it as a measure of the man. And would you be surprised that Solomon, who's learned how it works, calls the genie up again, later in his reign?

"And Solomon Awakes, And Behold, It Was A Dream!"

The drama of Solomon's dream is well known. This is the most widely circulated legend about this amazing man. Even most lip-service-only Christians know the story of the granting of wisdom and riches. Few people know, however, that this event occurs in a dream.

Solomon goes to a great deal of preparation for his time of communion. A young man, he has just risen to the role of kingship in the political arena, and needs confirmation and strength. This visitation is not simply an intuitive flash that visits while Solomon is tending his business. That would be perfectly legitimate, of course. This is much more. Solomon makes specific preparations, journeys to the elevated ground of Gibeon, and there prayerfully and ritually, in Cosmic alignment with the seasons of the day and night, offers a thousand burnt offerings upon the altar.

In this high state Solomon is conducted past the portals of mortality, into the sanctum of the Lord:

At Gibeon the Lord appears to Solomon in a dream by night; and God invites him,

"Ask. What shall I give you?" (1Kg. 3.5)

Who could resist? God, in this illuminated state, invites him. What would you ask for if a wish granting genie made you the same offer? Solomon replies,

"Give thy servant an understanding heart to govern thy people, that I may discern between good and evil; for who is able to govern this thy great people?" (1Kg. 3.9)

Solomon's request so pleases God that he promises him this and something more:

"Because you have asked for wisdom, and not long life, or riches, or the life of your enemies, behold, I now do according to your word. Behold, receive ye now my gift, a wise and discerning mind, so that none like you has been before you and none like you shall arise after you.

"And I give you also what you have not asked, both riches and honor, so that no other king shall compare with you in riches and glory." (1Kg. 3.11-13)

And Solomon awakes, and behold, it was a *dream!* (1Kg. 3.15)

It all comes to pass as the dream foretells. Starting immediately! When Solomon arrives back in Jerusalem the first thing he does is throw a huge party for his servants. Already we see evidence of his wisdom. It is at this party that the two whoring bitches approach him. Ever a man ready with the ceremonial blade of his sword, Solomon solves this case with his newly tempered wisdom.

About the wealth?... What do you think? The man has *666 talents of gold flowing to him EVERY year!* The man builds a magnificent Temple, at a magnificent sum, upon which many mystical organizations – the Knights Templar and the Masons – yet today pattern their own Temples on. In his palaces and summer homes every vessel is golden, for "silver is not considered as anything" (1Kg. 10.21). The man maintains seven hundred high-maintenance wives and three hundred racy concubines. Most men have a challenge managing one.

See you later. I'm going to pray for wisdom.

Mystic Moments Dedicating A Temple

Twenty years later, when Solomon finishes his grand building project, the Temple of the Lord, he receives another mystical dream. In a situation with many similarities Solomon again receives the psychic-spiritual confirmation he is seeking. God affirms that he has accepted the dwelling place Solomon has caused to be built, consecrates it, and promises to keep it hallowed.

All the elders of the tribes of Israel, all the priests of Israel, even all the men of Israel assemble at the new and as yet unchristened Temple, the dwelling place on Earth of God who dwells in Heaven. In a great and solemn ceremony, Solomon prays. And when the priests ceremonially carry the sacred stone, the Ark of the Covenant, the very representation of God on Earth, into the Inner Sanctum of the Temple, a luminous cloud of glory fills the Temple.

And Solomon prays. With a heart-opening prayer he calls. In oratorical incantations before the assembled multitudes, kneeling before the altar with outstretched hands, praising God for his glory, praising God for his great works, supplicating God's understanding for the foibles of every person on the path, and petitioning his gracious remembrance "whenever they turn to you in prayer and meditation" (1Kg. 8.38), Solomon and the nation of Israel dedicate the Temple.

High on reverence, that night when he sleeps,

The Lord appears to Solomon a second time, as he appeared to him at Gibeon." (1Kg. 9.1-2)

This dream isn't so famous. The Lord says simply that he has heard Solomon's prayer, and has indeed consecrated the Temple:

> "I have heard your prayer and your supplication, which you have made before me; I have consecrated this house which you have built, and put my name there for ever; my eyes and my heart will be there for all time." (1Kg. 9.3)

And all is well.

Reflections

On every escapade we miss more than we catch, and this site is so rich! Were we given to complaining, we could complain, *"So many Truths! So little time!"* But we are not! Even knowing how way leads on to way, we revel in joy through the interesting spots we visit. We'll save the others for another day.

Once In A Blue Moon. Perhaps these two dreams are only related because they concern the welfare of the nation. But how could that possibly be the case in the case of a monarch? Rather, the story of Solomon's dreams indicates how seldom God may speak directly to an individual.

Perhaps these two dreams are told to us because only in them does Solomon directly invoke and petition God. Yet surely Solomon prays more often. Surely, most of us pray meaningfully more than twice in our lives.

For us it might be while raising a family or writing a book. Solomon is neither a priest nor a psychic. He is deeply involved in the affairs of the world, governing a rising power. He has a lot of concerns in his life. Prayer is only an element of his life, not the focus of his life. Destiny has thrust different concerns on him. Like most of us at our present stage of evolution, these significant psychic dreams only visit Solomon once in a blue moon.

Now, if you want to have more psychic fruits in your life, your models might be Isaiah, Jeremiah, or Ezekiel. However, these are all, you are of course aware, what we would call "weirdos." *Ah, well.*

Rites Of Passage. Solomon's great breakthroughs come as rites of passage. That is, he is involved in initiatory, dedicatory, prayerful events celebrating an eventful change. The two rituals we see him involved in are his coronation and the dedication of the Temple, the two summits of his reign.

It is appropriate. Both of these events are magnitudinous, pivotal points in the life of Solomon the man and Solomon the king. One involves his ascension into the highest temporal office on Earth, the other involves the completion of the most sacred task of building the Temple of God. The associated rituals are designed – through ornate ritual combined with soulful prayer – to mark clear the distinction between the *before* and *after* states, to conduct the soul through the passage ceremonially and psychically. So the man rises in dominion.

This is ever the purpose of ritual, to construct a participative event that lifts the postulant to a higher degree of consciousness and concomitant power. The prescribed ritual accomplishes this through opening a channel from the Universal, allowing the Universal God Presence to surge in, empowering the individual participant(s) in the ritual. It simultaneously stimulates and signifies an inner change in consciousness. Its root and fruit implant the realization fully in the consciousness.

Ritual is the royal road to the center of the universe.

According To Your Word. Some psychic events and phenomena occur spontaneously. For most people, in fact, all the psychic manifestations that occur during the course of their lives generate spontaneously. Both of Solomon's epic dreams, however, come after a period of dream incubation, a period of preparation, ritual, reverence, fasting, and extended prayer. He falls asleep in this highly charged prayerful state. There is a formula here.

God is demonstrating to us here, as he does well also in Exodus, Daniel, and Haggai, that we can stimulate and generate psychic activity by our own efforts. It speaks of the capacity to *develop* psychic powers. Some have a greater sensitivity by the natural inclinations imprinted through the birthing matrix than others, but all can learn about and develop their psychic powers.

It's like a foreign language. Anyone who makes a sincere and concerted effort, *can* learn the language. They may never become fluent, but it may not be a need of their circumstances or inclinations. They may not need to make public appearances. But anyone can quite easily learn to communicate for the affairs of business and living.

Preparations are made, consciousness is prepared, the solemn dedication is intoned. Herein is the dedicated left-brain effort. Then we let go, and God ascends in our consciousness. Hereof the creative right component of our psyche. Can it be so simple?

Look at Solomon's integrity of heart! In his moment of destiny, before all the Universe he prays for an "understanding heart." In this phrase, eons prior to twentieth century psychology, Solomon encapsulates in figurative language the integration of the left brain and the right brain, *understanding* married to *feeling.* This is the marriage of the king and the queen in Medieval-Renaissance alchemy.

When you want to communicate with the Divine, you can. And in that same state, the Divine communicates to you. Ritual and prayerful meditation are the bricks you lay on the royal road to psychicspace.

You, *frater* and *soror,* are the one these books are written about. You, brother and sister, are the one these books are written for. If you want more psychic activity in your life, *believe* you can have it. *Act* on your faith. And it comes to pass. Can it be so simple? You've heard it said "according to your word." God demonstrates it herein. Yes, you can open the gates of psychic activity in your life.

The Reality Impulse. Some people believe there is a distinction between "reality" – so called *hard* reality – and the psychi-spiritual realms. In fact, as you know, most people. However, these dreams of Solomon, particularly the first one, show how a driving impulse can be *imparted in a dream*, so that the purely psychic, a "mere dream," can function as the guiding energy in an individual's life. Or, in the case of a king, a kingdom's and its allies' lives.

This guiding impulse is surely at first a physical unreality. It is but a psychic reality. *Real indeed!* It is so real, as a matter of fact, that most people don't even know the events related in Solomon's story occur in a dream. The far reaches of their imagination stop at the short barriers of conventionality. *It just happens*, they think.

Yet, as we've discussed, from this dream the highest riches of the *psychical* and *physical* realms manifest. Solomon arises from this dream a man empowered with wisdom and wealth. Spiritual reality, hard reality, it is all *reality*. Who can but admit the effects are dramatic and *real*? Who can admit that the occurrence of this dream embeds in fact a *real occurrence*? What if Solomon had said, as many would do, "Bullshit! It was just a dream!"?

One Mystical Meal

Having just spoken of the physical reality of the psychical domains with Solomon's dream, it seems particularly appropriate to stop in on a dream of *Elijah's*. It comes after Elijah has just made the priestcraft of the kingdom of Israel first, fools, and second, carcasses on the lapping banks of Brook Kishon. The royal lady takes the front on this effort. She swears to own Elijah's life within twenty-four hours. An instant fugitive, he beats the hasty back path out.

One day into his run, Elijah dreams a dream. And in his dream he eats. It is repeated:

And the angel of the Lord comes again a second time, and touches him, and says, "Arise and eat, else the journey will be too great for you." (1Kg. 19.7)

The very next verse tells it all:

And he arises, and eats and drinks, and goes in the strength of that food a full forty days and forty nights to Horeb the mount of God. (1Kg. 19.8)

This is a dream. The guiding impulse is surely a physical unreality. It is a dream, but a psychic reality. But it is so real, as a matter of fact, that Elijah does not need to eat again for forty days! It happens!

The Material Is The Spiritual

Truly, it is as they say. Wouldn't it be *supernormal* if you were to dream a dream and become so possessed, assured, and driven by it that you didn't need bodily nourishment for almost six weeks?!!

We of the spiritual dimensions recognize, attempt to live, and make every effort to awaken others to this intercommutability of the distinctions between the *spiritual* and the *material* realms.

We have the same opportunity challenging us throughout our lives as presented throughout this mythic text, recognizing that the material *is* the spiritual. The spiritual *is* material. Any distinctions we make are only the result of our nearsightedness, which – helpful though it may be for normal commerce – leads us to divide-and-conquer. We set up classifications because certain items share predominant traits, forgetting that the different *genera* are in fact species of the same progenitor, families of the same family.

"He Took Me By A Lock Of My Head"

There is no shortage of engaging visions in *Ezekiel*. The entire book is the record and the message of one vision after another. He has several of high interest, including one in-depth vision that begins in chapter 8 and runs through chapter 11. In this vision, with the elders of Judah sitting before him, Ezekiel trance-channels God. The elders, though frightened in the presence of the paranormal, are not surprised, because that is the very reason they have assembled before him.

This passage indicates just how psychics are esteemed. Unlike our highly rationalistic society these current days, even the *elders* of the nation are gathered before the shaman. Sounds a little like Native American spirituality, doesn't it? Our leaders have to keep it prudently concealed today.

Ezekiel starts off by saying,

> The hand of the Lord God fell upon me. Then I beheld, lo! a form that had the appearance of a man; below what appeared to be his loins it was fire, and above his loins it was like the appearance of brightness, like gleaming bronze. (Ezek. 8.1-2)

This figure whose carriage is a body of radiant fire is indeed an otherworldly creature.

But Ezekiel goes one further. This is not just a vision that he sees, viewing from a disassociated state, like watching a TV screen. No. It's interactive. The original virtual reality, he enters into the action itself:

> The angel put forth the form of a hand, and took me by a lock of my head; and lifted me up between Earth and Heaven, and brought me to the entrance of the gateway of the inner court at Jerusalem... (Ezek. 8.3)

What a consuming trance this is! And here he sees the glory of God, describing it as only Ezekiel does, "like in the vision I saw in the plain" (Ezek. 8.4). Oh, he does use the word *vision* to describe the experience that takes him, doesn't he?

And in this vision the Spirit takes him to several locations, demonstrating to him all the complaints of the Spirit, even all kinds of "vile abominations, creeping things, and loathsome beasts." And, even before the wide-eyed elders of Israel, who have brought Ezekiel prestige with their presence, and money for the practice of his gift, Ezekiel sees God indicting the elders, who commit acts in private that they do not want known.

And he sees the fantastic creature he saw years earlier at the River Chebar, and he is inspired. The inspiration tells him to prophesy directly against Israel and the elders. He does:

> Then the vision that I had seen went up from me and things returned to normal. And I told the exiles all the things that the Lord had showed me. (Ezek. 11.24-25)

And Now We Understand

Again we see God communicating with humanity through psi to effect his ends. We see God communicating no other way. And we see how respected practicing psychics are. And now we understand when we see the same phenomenon in our own day and time. It gets pretty hard to condemn, doesn't it?

The Man's Madness

Embodying the dream in the hearts of the exiles, *Ezekiel* experiences a vision of the Temple restored. He begins,

> One particular day, the hand of the Lord was upon me, and carried me in the visions of God into the land of Israel, and set me down upon a very high mountain, on which was a structure like a city opposite me... (Ezek. 40.1-2)

So Ezekiel, at least now, when he is writing about it, recognizes this as a visionary land. His senses don't fool him into thinking it is of the same vibratory coarseness as material reality. He is keeping the two planes separate. While he shares the message he shares the method. He describes projection.

Once he is fully engaged in his altered state, a ritually clad God or angel appears and speaks to him. He prepares Ezekiel, before he shows him the remainder of the vision. Ezekiel has received the good fortune of being brought into this visionary land for a specific purpose, that he share the vision and the message:

And the man said to me,

> "Son of man, look with your eyes, and hear with your ears, and set your mind upon all that I shall show you, for you were brought here in order that I might show it to you; declare all that you see to the house of Israel." (Ezek. 40.4)

This is not random psi. How few believers have ever questioned the reality of Ezekiel's fantasy? There is a purpose to Ezekiel's madness. A Divine method.

He Chooses Dreams

Daniel is the greatest dreamer of the Bible. By most standards he has no close associates. After all, of no one else does the Bible explicitly say,

> God gave to him a special sensitivity in dreams and visions. (Dan. 1.17)

His writings are, as a matter of fact, a collection of dreams, visions, and interpretations.

Daniel's collection of stories, each involving omens and mysteries in dreams and visions, is, the apologists reluctantly admit, riddled with "problems." Ah, but we know the psychic arts are used for a multitude of purposes, a multitude of ways.

Harper's Bible Dictionary provides a good thumbnail consideration of these dilemmas. It speaks, in sympathy with many committed Bible scholars, of a "series of thorny problems," including the growth of the Book of Daniel by "accretion" over the course of time. As they wrote more stories, in accordance with the practice of the time, touting the authenticity of their story, storytellers would attribute their work not to themselves, but to some great figure of legend; thus Daniel became greater and greater. They admit Daniel "bristles with historical problems," such as the "transformation of Nebuchadnezzar into a beast," a story lifted from an incident in the then current stories of Nabonidus.

In several instances Daniel's version is but one variant of circulating legends. Certainly you're familiar with etymology charts of *words*. When you're looking up a word in any better dictionary you see the word's derivation. The dictionary is terse on this information; scholars go even deeper in their linguistic works. This same principle holds true with the etymology of language on a larger level up, the level of legends. Just as they've traced the story of the Grail through a number of incarnations, they've traced the derivation of several of Daniel's stories to previous legends. They've been hard-pressed facing this "deficiency."

Some of his characters and events are fabricated totally, such as the "wholly unhistorical Darius the Mede." In fact, irony of irony! Daniel himself is a fictional character in a first person fictional tale. Daniel is an old wise-man legend, descending from the character *Dnil* of an Ugaritic legend.

The story is set in the current time (for the author's contemporary audience of course), but it's not historical fact. Isn't this what we do in a lot of our movies? In fact, isn't it rather the movie that holds itself out for historical actuality rather rare? For instance, consider *Ghost*. It takes place in the early 1990's in New York City. It is well vested with the appropriate props – high finance, computers, love, handguns, greed, slums, and warehouses – that make it a *fin de siecle* tale. But doesn't it speak of much more than a series of cause-and-effect occurrences in New York City during a particular period of time? Isn't it about love, and death, and life after death, and letting go? And isn't it about how we make that metaphysical connection, and why? And who does it, and when?

And Daniel's "*accurate*'prophecy' is written after the fact." Others are *incorrect predictions* of the future.

These problems cause major dilemmas – for the dogmatically biased, that is. Since they already know what they must prove.

They are vested in wanting some predetermined result, such as a historical purity, to prove that their God is speaking, when we see so clearly through the story of Daniel the *channeled word of God. He's telling a story, my gosh!* What most scholars and saints call "problems," are the *blatant* indicators of what he's saying. He's a Steven Spielberg. Of course there is a latent level to the story. He leaves events, items, and circumstances – clues, hints, foreshadowings, images – indicators to the deeper level, where the true essence, meaning, and joy resides.

You can see. You can partake of both levels of reality at once. With *awareness.* What a difference! You always *do* partake of both levels, but, lacking the skill, passion, and adventure that can be yours! Then, instead of a plodding brute, you're a skyborne dancer, the nearest thing to an angel on Earth.

Whoever the author of Daniel is, he fashions the book so that himself, as the character Daniel in the drama, participates in dreams and visions *par excellence.* These efforts to present Daniel's metaphysical insight in dramas of mystic import, follow, no doubt, the natural outgrowth of his interests and inclinations.

A Terrifying Nightmare

Daniel lives during the time of Jerusalem's rebellion from and consequent defeat by Babylon. He is among the group of Judah's noble youth hand-picked to serve in the conqueror's palaces. He ages there. He experiences Nebuchadnezzar's power and Babylon's subsequent defeat by Persia. He longs always for the time when he can return home.

There are multiple dreams in the book of Daniel by its two primary protagonists, Daniel, and the great Babylonian king, Nebuchadnezzar.

One day Nebuchadnezzar awakes in trembling and fear. But that's all he has, trembling and fear. He can't remember his dream! The court psychics plead with the king, assuring him that they can *interpret* the dream, if he will but *tell* them what it is. We see here that we are dealing with psychologists, not psychics. These persons, though practicing the mystic arts, are doing it from a psychological level. That's sufficient for most occasions, and it's a good way to get started, but that limits them to interpretation. Without the faculty of second sight, they are but guessing in the dark concerning the king's dream. And he won't even give them any hints!

The king becomes exasperated with their overrated abilities when they can't help him, and, though promising to reward with "many wonderful gifts and honors" (Dan. 2.6) the psychic who reveals the dream and its interpretation, pronounces the sentence of death on every magician in the realm.

Now Daniel hears about it. He's not been consulted previously because he is on the government's list of potentially seditious persons. He is a free thinker. He is psychic. He is a Jew. So the agents of the government show up in the night to take him in "for questioning." He'll never come back, of course. A terrifying nightmare... Except for the fact that he finally hears what the commotion is about and seeks immediate audience to assist the king.

Believe me, the king wants to see Daniel! He remembers the mystic youth of Hebrew blood. Since Daniel's had no time for prayer, mediation, and reflection, having been aggressively coerced on the instant from his home, he's not prepared to give the king his answers, but seeks permission to share a reading on the dream and its meaning on the morrow, securing at the same time a temporary release on the death sentence for all the other psychics, priests, astrologers, magicians, and sensitives, including his beloved companions of Israel's blood.

That night Daniel tunes into the universal ethers where all things always exist, and reads the dream, and understands its message. Here is how it happens:

Daniel goes to his house, and makes the thing known to his companions, that they would desire mercies of the God of Heaven concerning this secret; that they themselves should not perish with the rest of the wise men of Babylon.

Then was the secret revealed unto Daniel in a night vision. Daniel wakes and blesses God, saying,

"Blessed be the name of God forever! For wisdom and might are his; and he changes the times and the seasons; he removes kings and sets up kings; he gives wisdom to the wise, and knowledge to them that know understanding; he reveals the deep and secret things; he knows what is in the darkness; and illumination dwells with him.

"I thank thee, and praise thee, O thou God of my fathers, who hast given me wisdom and its glory, and hast revealed now what we desired of thee: for you have now made known to us the king's matter." (Dan. 2.17-23)

Interesting. *Daniel himself has a dream* – which he requests of God – *to interpret the king's dream*. He has a dream of the dream and understands its meaning. Thus we see the interdependence of persons and graces in this spiritual world of ours.

When Daniel is ushered into the king's presence the next morning, he acknowledges the portentous nature of the dream, saying that,

"God has made known to King Nebuchadnezzar what will be in the latter days." (Dan. 2.28)

He then goes on, feeding into the king's intense interest, revealing the dream to him in these words:

"Your dream and the visions of your head as you lay in bed are these:

"You saw, O king, and beheld, a great image. This image, mighty and of exceeding brightness, stood before you, and its appearance was frightening. The head of this image was of fine gold, its breast and arms of silver, its belly and thighs of bronze, its legs of iron, its feet partly of iron and partly of clay.

"As you looked, a stone was cut out by no human hand, and it smote the image on its feet of iron and clay, and broke them in pieces; then the iron, the clay, the bronze, the silver, and the gold, all together were broken in pieces, and became like the chaff of the summer threshing floors; and the wind carried them away, so that not a trace of them could be found. But the stone that struck the image became a great mountain and filled the whole earth." (Dan. 2.28-35)

"This was the dream," Daniel continues, "now we will tell the king its interpretation":

"You, O king, are the head of gold.

"After you shall arise another kingdom inferior to you, and yet a third kingdom of bronze, which shall rule over all the earth. And there shall be a fourth kingdom, strong as iron, because iron breaks to pieces and shatters all things; and like iron which crushes, it shall break and crush all these.

"And as you saw the feet and toes partly of potter's clay and partly of iron, it shall be a multicultural kingdom, divided amongst itself; so the kingdom shall be partly iron and partly clay, partly strong and partly brittle; they will not hold together, just as iron does not mix with clay.

"And in the days of those kings the God of Heaven will set up a kingdom which shall never be destroyed, nor shall its sovereignty be left to another people. It shall break in pieces all these kingdoms and bring them to an end, and it shall stand for ever; just as you saw that a stone was cut from a mountain by no human hand, and that it broke in pieces the iron, the bronze, the clay, the silver, and the gold." (Dan. 2.38-45)

In other words, Nebuchadnezzar – whom Daniel flatteringly addresses (as politicians and judges *love* to be flattered) as "O King, King of Kings, to whom the God of Heaven has given the kingdom, the power, and the glory, and into whose hand he has given, wherever they dwell, the sons of men, the beasts of the field, and the birds of the air, making you rule over them all" (Dan. 2.37-38) – is the greatest king of his line. From him it all runs downhill, into the fourth generation when it falls apart.

Of Psychic Verities

Our stop in this psychicsite particularly brings up several exciting psychic verities.

The Precognitive Factor. God has given Nebuchadnezzar a look at what we know is often the preoccupation of regals – "Will my sons succeed me? What will happen to my kingdom when I'm gone?" When MacBeth wants to know, the mystic sisters tell him. When Nebuchadnezzar wants to know, the mystic Daniel reveals the shady truth from the particulars of his own dream, given him directly by God. And,

"The dream is certain, and its interpretation sure." (Dan. 2.45)

Fulfilled In The Moment. The mystery comes to Daniel in a trance. He wakes, recognizing that his intention is fulfilled. There is no second-guessing, no doubt. And he praises God and gives thanks. Consciously or unconsciously taken, this is part of the formula, acceptance and acknowledgment born of the certitude the inspiration is Divine. After all, when God speaks, need you need doubt it?

Daniel does not wait to "test" it first. He accepts. And he acts. Not a weak worrying action, "hoping" he's doing the right thing, but a striking action, born of psychical revelation.

Action is the result of the marriage of the intellect and the intuition, cognition and emotion, mind and the heart. Prepare yourself, consciously entering by way of ritual and prayer into the contemplative state, wherein you undergo the emotional experience of bliss in the moment of living. You will recognize it. The timbre of Daniel's action is the offspring of psychic inspiration. Living action flows naturally.

Psychic Interdependence. We see in this story the psychic interdependence that is such a fact of our shared human-spiritual experience. The king, a *non-select* person has the dream, a dream he is certain possesses *psychi-spiritual proportions.* Daniel has powers of clairvoyance and interpretation. Each unique and differently stationed, they symbiotically work together and support one another in the web of humanity.

A dream and psychic ability translate into abundant favor and riches for Daniel. After the reading, Nebuchadnezzar, certain what Daniel says is true, showers position and tremendous wealth on him. This lets us see another angle on the psychic reality issue again. Certainly its effects are real and tangible, aren't they? Riches respond to the psychic dimensions.

"One Like The Son Of Man"
Time passes in captivity. Political leaders of local note come and go. One night during the first year of the reign of Belshazzar, Nebuchadnezzar's son, Daniel dreams:

> I had a dream and visions as I lay in my bed. Then I wrote down the dream, and herewith tell you the sum of the matter. I saw in my vision by night, behold, the four winds of Heaven were stirring up the great sea. And four great beasts came up out of the sea, different from one another. The first was like a lion and had eagles' wings. Then as I looked its wings were plucked off, and it was lifted up from the ground and made to stand upon two feet like a man; and the mind of a man was given to it. The second one was like a bear.... (Dan. 7.1-5)

Daniel continues describing four creatures. We here encounter the four beasts again. We see, again, an alternative treatment of a common literary and spiritual motif. Four powers represented by four creatures.

And from the horns of the fourth beast comes the "Ancient of Days" riding on a flaming chariot-throne. And, with the clouds of Heaven billowing around him, "one like the Son of Man" (Dan. 7.13) approaches the Ancient of Days, and receives from him:

> All dominion, and glory, and kingdom... an everlasting dominion that shall not be destroyed. (Dan. 7.14)

Even within the dream Daniel asks a bystander what the meaning of the dream is. Lucid dreaming. The angel shares what he knows: at the end of four powers shall come the one who will rule forever.

These Psychic Cites

We see several points in this dream worthy of our intense interest.

Daniel Writes His Dream Down. This is an important principle. Mystics and psychologists tell us to pay attention to dreams. The most effective way to empower dreaming is to value your dreams enough to write them down.

This accomplishes several things. First, since you write them down you have a record of them. This way you can go back to them later, mining insight after insight as they occur to you in your meditations and intuitions.

Also, you're far more likely to get the true action and images of the dream if you write them down. Memory fades, and, before long, all you might recall are the salient points of a dream that's not written down. Writing it down, however, your mind is stimulated by associations regarding a still-fresh psychic occurrence. You have the opportunity to recall greater depth of details in mood, colors, events, actions, and meanings. Everything is interdependent; in the act of faithfully recording one sequence or event, you recall and record a greater panorama of detail.

As you move more deeply into psychicspace, the psychic terrain becomes more and more your world. And you see more. This is why the dream is given you.

Model Of Equivalence Between Dreams And Visions. Throughout this text we acknowledge that, though we might fish for distinctions between what we label a *vision* and what we label a *dream*, they are essentially the same. Reread this passage of Daniel and notice how often Daniel himself – fulfilling God's will to our benefit – codes in this equivalence.

Daniel talks of having *dreams and visions* this particular night. He describes what he sees, he tells us, in his *vision by night*, writing the *dream* down. He makes other references throughout the whole of this seventh chapter, identifying his vision as a dream, his dream as a vision. One and the same.

Interpretation. The flavor of Daniel changes in certain respects with this seventh chapter. By this time Daniel is older and more mature. With age he himself starts going to others to receive help interpreting his dreams.

However, there is a uniqueness we must notice herein. Daniel is a lucid dreamer. For instance, after seeing the fourth beast metamorphosize into the Son Of Man's presence, he approaches a bystander and asks him what the dream means. But this is not just any old bystander. This is a bystander who is himself a character within the dream associated with Daniel's consciousness, with Daniel's head lying on the pillow this one night during ancient days.

The angel tells him just what the dream means: there will be a succession of four kingdoms until the one comes whose dominion will last forever. At this early point we begin to see the hopes of the Jewish people for a savior king manifest in their unconscious productions. They want it, so it naturally makes its way into the Bible.

Interpretation goes both ways.

"Seventy Weeks Of Years Are Decreed!"

Another ruler rises in Babylon. Darius the Mede now rules the land known as Chaldea. Seventy years have passed. In Daniel's joyful studies one day he encounters a prophecy of Jeremiah which he interprets as meaning the time of captivity, his major concern, is finished.

Flushed with intimations, he lifts his breast Heavenward in deep and lengthy prayer. With the next verse, having positioned himself into a holy trance, the vision opens to his inner sight:

> At the time of the evening sacrifice, while I was speaking and praying, Gabriel, whom I had seen in the vision at the first, came to me in swift flight.
>
> He came and he said to me,
>
> "O Daniel, I have come to give you wisdom and understanding. Therefore consider my word and understand the vision. Seventy weeks of years are decreed concerning your people and your holy city, to seal both vision and prophet, and to anoint a most holy place.
>
> "Further, know and understand that from the going forth of the word to restore and build Jerusalem to the coming of an anointed one, a prince, there shall be seven weeks. Then for sixty-two weeks it shall be built again with squares and moat, but in a troubled time." (Dan. 9.20-25)

So Daniel tells us, he has his understanding fulfilled by the messenger Gabriel, in the afflatus of a vision. Such in-sight!

Psi Feeds On Psi

"Psi feeds on psi," is an old mystic maxim. Daniel illuminates this verity. This entire dream/vision, as a matter of fact, is triggered by an especially poignant passage in Jeremiah which drives Daniel deeply into devoted prayer. In the transport of this meditation Gabriel comes again, with the vision of adventures upon the upcoming release of the captives.

This is why the mystics of every persuasion advise you to spend time with the sacred truths of humanity. Spend time with the psychics, they say, if you want psychic riches yourself.

Taken In Their Midst

Years later, three years into the reign of another ruler, Cyrus king of Persia, Daniel, as he is wont to do, withdraws from the world of daily commerce, modifying his activities into an abstemious lifestyle, refraining from all meats and wines for three weeks. This purification brings on a heightened sensitivity to the beings of psychicspace. And though he is with members of his Jewish community on the banks of the Tigris River when he sees the great angel glowing in the sky, the others with him do not see it.

He is alone in the vision and its *real* affects, yet others are aware something's going down. They are arrested in a holy dread. Daniel tells the story:

> And I, Daniel, alone saw the vision, for the men who were with me did not see the vision, but a great trembling fell upon them, and they fled to hide themselves. So I was left alone and saw this great vision, and no strength was left in me; my radiant appearance was fearfully changed, and I retained no strength. Then I heard the sound of his words; and when I heard the sound of his words, I fell on my face in a deep sleep with my face to the ground. And behold, a hand touched me and set me trembling on my hands and knees.
>
> And he said to me,
>
> "O Daniel, man greatly beloved, give heed to the words that I speak to you, and stand upright, for I have been sent to you." (Dan. 10.7-11)

This scene foreshadows the scene of psychic possession that occurs with Saul in Acts 9, when he is taken in the midst of others. They cannot see the Godforce either – *but they know it is there.*

The celestial visitor next informs Daniel of various things that shall come to pass in the future.

The Sensitive Sensitive

You may have noticed that some psychics get weak when they are visited by psi. This phenomenon goes back a long ways, at least several thousand years to Daniel. Not just once, but many times he elaborates on his incapacitation. Sometimes it happens in the dream, as we've just seen. At the onset of the apparition, all his companions scatter, leaving him all alone. But he himself needs help, all the strength in him being robbed by the ethereal terror of the moment. He writes:

> I turned pale; my radiant appearance was fearfully changed, and I retained no strength. (Dan. 10.8)

He only recovers when Gabriel touches him.

Sometimes it happens afterwards, so that he's not himself for an extended period of time. For instance, in chapter eight he tell us that after the vision,

> I, Daniel, was overcome and lay sick for some days. Finally I got well enough to rise and tend to the king's business. (Dan. 8.27)

We see in Daniel the archetypical sensitive sensitive.

"How Can It Be? I Am Old And My Wife Is Old And Barren"

The elderly *Zechariah*, husband of the aged and barren Elizabeth, goes one day in his duties as a priest to burn the mystic incense, always pleasing to God. And while the incense is burning, and Zechariah is offering prayers, an angel takes form at the right side of the altar. Zechariah has a normal reaction in those unaccustomed to the liminal – fear and trembling.

But the angel reassures him, and then gives him some unbelievable news:

> "Do not be afraid, Zechariah, for your prayer is heard, and your wife Elizabeth will bear you a son, and you shall call his name John. And he will be great before the Lord, and he will turn many of the sons of Israel to the Lord their God, going before him in his spirit and power of Elijah..." (Lk. 1.13-17)

This prophecy causes further consternation in Zechariah. Oh, he *wants* to believe, but considering the advanced age of both himself and his wife, he expresses doubt. *Mistake!* Lo! he gets a sign alright, though it's surely not what he would have wanted. The angel, who identifies himself as "Gabriel who stands in the presence of God" (Lk. 1.19), lashes him with dumbness.

Zechariah, who has lost all consciousness of time during the altered reality of the angel's visit, finally comes to and exits from the Holy of Holies. The people have been wondering. As if spirituality coincides with the marks on a sundial. When he can't talk, their suspicions are confirmed: *something* happened in there!

He is dumb until the moment he names the newborn infant by writing out, "His name is John."

O Pure Of Heart! Your Pledge Is Accepted In Heaven

Lo, one day, a day similar to today, in the cusp of a New Millennium, a devout and virginal teenager named *Mary* is stopped by a resplendent being that appears suddenly before her.

Eastern tailed, the angel greets her in words pregnant with high renown:

> "Hail, O favored one, the Lord is with you!" (Lk. 1.28)

Elevated words. Why is she troubled? She wonders what these high words portend. Gabriel then renders a similar message as he delivered to Zechariah:

> "Do not be afraid, Mary, for you have found favor with God. And behold, you will conceive in your womb and bear a son, and you shall call his name Jesus.
>
> "He will be great, and will be called the Son of the Most High; and the Lord God will give to him the throne of his father David." (Lk. 1.30-32)

Like Zechariah before her, Mary expresses doubt, saying,

> "How shall this be, since I have no husband?" (Lk. 1.34)

Ah wonder of wonders! Even Gods and angels favor the fair of the race! Mary is a pure young attractive female. Unlike with the old man, Zechariah, the young male angel favors this beautiful breath of spring's flowers. Instead of a curse for doubting, the angel explains that a God shall visit her in the night, impregnating her with the seed of Divinity:

> "The Holy Spirit himself will visit you in the night, and desire will overtake you, and he shall come in you. Therefore the child to be born will be called the Son of God." (Lk. 1.35)

News?... Or, pretty heavy news?

Now think. What would you say if a friend told you an angel – and not just any angel, but Gabriel – visited her daughter, and that she got pregnant by God in a clean dream? And, of course, her child is different!? Her child is destined to be special! And you wonder why Joseph struggles?

How many millions of otherwise normal people, people who wouldn't believe it if someone from their church was claiming such a thing, have believed this story for hundreds and now thousands of years!

"Elderly Elizabeth, your cousin," the angel goes on to inform her, easing the pressure of the moment a little,

> "has conceived a son. And she's already in her sixth month! With God anything's possible." (Lk. 1.36-37)

We here see Gabriel giving her the news he knows she does not know. You see, it took a traveler then to spread the news. There were no phones or postal systems. Commerce was village wide only. Psychic scientists working in the university labs of today term this "remote viewing." Of course, the "With God anything's possible!" coming from the angel's tongue applies to more than one thing.

And Mary, having had those few moments to allow the intuition to fluoresce through her ready womb, replies in those ultimately pure and poetic lines of hers:

> "Behold, I am the lover of the Lord. Let it happen according as you say." (Lk. 1.38)

Readily now she accepts.

Now the angel vanishes before her eyes, with her pledge.

Evolution. As Merlin might say, pulling his cowl to shadow his face, a reflex when he perceives these mighty insights,

> "The future takes root in the present."

The Joseph Saga Of Dreams

Joseph. The words of Matthew are the beginning of that half of the sacred corpus we've compiled and titled the *New Testament*, giving God the credit meanwhile. As students of communication, we understand the significance of beginnings and endings. Beginnings make the first statements, letting the reader or viewer in on what the story is going to concern and how it is to be taken. Is it trivial entertainment meant to please a moment, or is it serious? Take it for what it is, this very book, Matthew, starts off with *five* psychic dreams.

"Who's The Father?"

When an unmarried female gets pregnant, don't we always want to know who the father is? Matthew opens running the genealogy chart, showing how Jesus, main character of the New Testament, is of the lineage of Judah. Joseph is descended from David and from Solomon, son of David on Uriah's wife. Once he establishes that through verses 1-17, he introduces a complication.

Joseph's not Jesus' father after all. Jesus is illegitimate.

Though social mores give Joseph the legal right to make a whoring spectacle out of Mary, being the essentially good man that he is, he decides simply to disappear, letting her go her way alone:

This is the story of the birth of Jesus. Mary his mother was engaged to Joseph; but before their marriage she came up pregnant. Being a man of principle, and at the same time wanting to save her from exposure, Joseph decided to have the marriage contract set aside quietly. (Mt. 1.18-19)

He's made his decision based on the evidence gathered with his rational mind – after all, one thing he does know is that *he hasn't slept with her*. That evening he disperses past the portals of sleep, his heart heaving over the maiden of his vows, and,

An angel of the Lord appears to him in a dream and says, "Don't be afraid to take Mary home as your wife. She is pure, you know. She has conceived a Divine Being in her loins, by a Divine Being winged from Heaven's heights." (Mt. 1.20)

This God, the angel explains, wants Joseph's paternity.

Joseph receives the empowering intuitions he needs to accept her, to love her fully, and to take the child as his own and love him fully. Joseph agrees to legitimize the bastard child with the name and lineage of Judah.

Follow Your Dream

Many are familiar with the story of the *three astrologers* who come seeking Jesus after his birth. They pass through Jerusalem, capital of the land, and openly talk about the purpose of their visit. Ever the same, the government is threatened. King Herod himself invites them to the white house dining room, and, after royal dining (and judicious questioning), sends them officiously well on their way, requesting that they let him know when they've discovered the object of their quest, that he might "go likewise and offer homage to the child king."

And the subterfuge might have worked, but the sorcerers, psychic professionals, after all, receive a dream:

Being warned in a dream not to return to Herod, they depart to their own country by another way. (Mt. 2.12)

When Herod realizes the astrologers have deceived him, and he won't so easily find the child, he hastily makes the decision to assassinate the child nevertheless. Only it will have to be messier.

The government helps the people again. They kill every single male child under two years of age. This, Herod and his cabinet reason, will surely terminate the threat.

Flee On Your Dream

But Joseph has his own dream. Shortly after the three magicians depart, an angel appears to him, directing him:

"Rise, take the child and his mother, and flee to Egypt, and remain there till I tell you; for Herod is about to search for the child, to destroy him." (Mt. 2.13)

He follows the guidance he receives, cloaks the child and his mother under darkness, and steals through the city gates. Once outside the gates, he breaks into a run.

And it's a good thing he does! Again we see how God works out his purposes through the psychic realms. The destined child is saved.

It's Safe Now, The Old Man Is Dead

But, as with all incarnate life, the time comes when Herod himself dies. Joseph, living the constricted life of a laborer in a foreign country, with little outside communication, nevertheless receives word:

When Herod dies, behold, an angel of the Lord appears in a dream to Joseph in Egypt, saying,

"Rise, take the child and his mother, and go to the land of Israel, for those who sought the child's life are dead." (Mt. 2.19-20)

Would you believe a figment of a dreaming imagination? Would you believe it enough to actually *act* on it? Joseph believes the Divine is communicating to him through the psychic channel of dreams, and he believes it with such a conviction that he bases his life's actions on it, including the child's welfare. When he rises that morning he gathers the child and the mother and sets way for the land of Israel.

But You Better Not Go Back Home

As Joseph approaches his home state of Judea in his own country of origin and tradition, he is suddenly frightened when he hears who the latest ruling political figure is. He knows the government and the law are not refuges from unfairness but in fact are the tools of inequity and subjugation. The government, legitimized by posturing in mass delusion, ever aligns itself as the mortal enemy of the creative and spiritual life. Hey, they've already slaughtered an entire generation of males to get to his son!

But, the years have been good to Joseph. He is in tune to the point that, pressed with a concern for the child's welfare, needing to make a decision promptly, as he *is* on the road with a loaded trailer, he dreams a dream. And,

Guided in a dream, he withdraws instead to his wife's hometown in the district of Galilee, in the town called Nazareth. (Mt. 2.22-23)

The gospel next postscripts that Joseph (exercising what he believes is his free will) chooses the destined course:

This was accomplished that what was spoken by the prophets might be fulfilled,

"He shall be called a Nazarene." (Mt. 2.23)

So the child has a new home. Born in Bethlehem, sojourned in Egypt, they call him Jesus of Nazareth, the Galilean, because Joseph follows his heart, pictured in a dream come one night on the road. As readers, we are insiders to another dimension of God's chess game.

Consider These Things

There are several things the tour members have been asking about. Let's hit on a few of them. The first item concerns the perennial fate and/or freewill conundrum. Another regards the timing of psychic phenomena in an individual's life. And a further item of special note is the illustration of the mystic principle, "When you receive psi, *act* on it."

Fate Or Freewill? Here is one to consider. Joseph appreciates the guidance God gives him through the psychic dream channels. Who wouldn't appreciate the guidance of God, the omniscient power and player? But, Matthew tags on to the end of the infancy narratives the statement that these seemingly billiard ball choices that eventually get Joseph and, consequently, his child, in Nazareth are done with a design. Divine design, true, but nevertheless, someone other than Joseph is actually calling the shots.

Does Joseph actually make the choices at the exercise of his free will if he is inspired and directed by God to do as he does? Isn't God, the master chess player, putting things in the minds and hearts of his characters that in effect *cause* them to do what *he* wants them to do? Isn't the cargo, the child who is to become the Christ, of sufficient worth that God would not allow for mistakes?

Or, do you suppose, that God – who sees the weight of every heart   selects a man among men who would naturally *want* to make the choices God would want, who can embrace no higher purpose or joy than aligning his individual will with the will of the Cosmic? *Ad rosem per crucem; ad crucem per rosem.*

As The Need Arises. Every human individual is a character in God's cast. Consciously or unconsciously, we all play a part. Both the knowing and the unknowing are identifiable groups within God's society. They each exist with and for the other, only from radically different viewpoints.

The only time Joseph figures prominently in the Bible is in these stories. And Joseph only has recorded dreams around the period of Jesus' conception, nativity, and infancy. This speaks with major relevance to our particular interests, things of the psychic nature. Surely it teaches us something!

God needs a man's ability to protect and direct the masculine particulars of family life efficiently. He's found such a man. Joseph is a good, industrious, and humble Jewish man.

When the infant destined to play a major role in the ascending regeneration of the world, wave after wave rolling over centuries across time, is in his midst, Joseph is mystic. When Joseph has his deepest involvement with life, doing the things it is a father's place to do, providing for the welfare of his family and his spiritual son, he receives the deepest astral communications to guide him.

When You Receive Psi, Act On It. What distinguishes Joseph from most people is that, first, he is a sincerely good person and, second, *as the dreams come,* pregnant and clear with the answers, Joseph *acts* on them. Each of the decisions and consequent actions he takes involve major life changes and circumstances.

All Joseph's dreams are accomplished quietly within the confines of a quiet family's trials, apparently meaningless to all others in society at that time. Joseph never is an Ezekiel or a Jeremiah, mesmerizing large crowds, nor a John, sending his contraband manuscript out from his prison psychic paradise. Yet Joseph channels God's will through activity.

In Joseph's story we see how unerringly correct inner guidance can be. It is God that directs Joseph regarding the girlfriend pregnant with another's seed, the flight to Egypt, and the decision to settle in Nazareth, Galilee. All in dreams.

Your Turn. Certainly, we can't believe Joseph is but a random selection. As seer-seekers of the psychic arts we want to know how can we induce this state wherein we, by grace and works, serve as receivers and channelers of God's will. If esp is a gift that does not come randomly, what do we do to honor and receive it?

Your opportunities are different, but rest assured, we each have a spiritual role to play, no matter how privately or publically performed it is. We align ourselves with the Joseph consciousness to discover and implement elegantly our own destined portion in God's work. We reach and we receive God ever through the psychic channels.

The willingness and dedication come first. All in magic time.

The Apparition Of Jesus Dazzling

When *Peter, James,* and his brother, *John,* ascend the mountain with *Jesus,* and, enspirited by profound prayer with the Master, see him gloriously shining in his light body, they see, as Jesus himself indicates, a vision.

The passage runs:

And he is transfigured before them, with his face shining like the sun, and his garments gleaming white as light. And behold, there appear to them Moses and Elijah, talking with him.

And Peter says to Jesus,

"Lord, it is well that we are here; if you wish, I will make three booths here, one for you and one for Moses and one for Elijah."

He is still speaking, when lo, a bright cloud overshadows them, and a voice from the cloud says,

"This is my beloved Son, with whom I am well pleased; listen to him."

When the disciples hear this, they fall on their faces, and are filled with awe. But Jesus comes and touches them, saying,

"Rise, and have no fear."

And when they lift up their eyes, they see no one but Jesus only.

And as they are coming down the mountain, Jesus commands them, "Tell no one the vision, until the Son of man is raised from the dead." (Mt. 17.2-9)

Of Psychic Verities

There are a number of psychic verities shining from this brief stop in psychicspace. We see again the altered reality of the visionary and mystic, the exhortation to secrecy, and the reactions of new initiates to their first powerful psychic manifestations.

Psi In Action. Anytime a person sees something that is not visible to objective consciousness, they are seeing past the veil into the psychic realms. They are having a spiritual experience, in every sense of the word. They are seeing entities, actions, and dramas, seeing visions and hearing voices of a different vibratory frequency. They are transcending the quite limited frequency range of the senses of the normal human instrument.

This explains why, though one may see – as in the case of Daniel or Paul – others, even in the very location with the seer, do not. They are not in the same state.

This explains why anybody who speaks of these visionary realms, judged by the limited though surely developing sensibilities of the "public," is put down by the majority of people. After all, they have the benefit of consensual normalcy. (They just don't recognize it is a sliding relative normalcy.)

Another interesting point to re-cognize here pertains to time. Time is irrelevant in the realms of psychic attunement. Thus, Moses and Elijah, themselves from two different eras of national history, both flow together with the presence of Jesus.

Psychic Secrecy. Do you wonder why Jesus enjoins his companions not to tell anyone what they've seen? The psychic arts have always been developed in mystery schools and secret societies. For a good reason. These things are to be kept secret, to prevent stirring the ire of the less evolved types. Their provocation can cause complications. Ask Jesus.

Jesus does not want this additional element of controversy adding to the complications of his already complex public affairs. He is picking his battles. Healing and talk of realizing his Divinity is already doing quite well for his controversial show.

"Some self-righteous triggerman is bound to get him," we'd say today. Any idiot can terminate an earthly incarnation. The system legitimizes it, being the expression of mass consciousness.

First Reactions To Psychic Phenomena. In this story we see Peter, James, and John, Jesus' apprenticeship companions, getting fearful when the spiritual intensity is amped up. When Jesus, in company with two other shamans, Moses and Elijah, transforms into his ghostly glory, they don't embrace the vision. Instead they behave with confusion and fear.

First, they offer to build the three supraenlightened individuals booths. This is not the behavior a spiritual adept would exhibit. The apostles are actually intruding into the vision they have been given to see, interrupting the high summit with meaningless mundane concerns. It's like an orderly whispering to the president that they are running low on ice. It shouldn't happen.

Then the apostles drop to the dirt, impulsively hiding their faces from the phantoms, like a four year old child. Some time later they come to with Jesus shaking them, waking them up. They are safe in the returned objective consciousness. The moment of waking HoloCosm has passed.

Their behavior, crude though it is, is very normal. People learn their way into comfort and ability with demonstrations of the psychic arts. These things are only feared because they are unknown. As they are experienced, and experienced again, and experienced simultaneously with the evolution of spiritual maturity, they become normal and accepted.

The Governor's Lady: A Woman's Intuition

Lady Pilate. At the far end of the story of Jesus, his death, we still see the royal role of dreams in humanity's affairs. Lady Pilate, wife of the Roman prefect of Judea, dreams a dream the fateful midnight of Friday the 13th. It has her stirring in her bed from the stroke of midnight till 4am, so that, when Pontius wakes about six, he does not wake his now peaceful wife. The servants prepare his breakfast, straighten the hang of his toga, and send him on his way.

It is to be a fateful day. Her dreams tell her so.

When she wakes, she sends her courier straight to her husband in the forum, urgently into the proceedings:

"Have nothing to do with that righteous man, for I have suffered much over him today in a dream." (Mt. 27.19)

To Follow, Or Not To Follow? That Is The Question

Destiny in the balance...

Psychic activity reveals itself in measure with the need. The more significant the life events, the more likely they are to be accompanied by dreams, omens, and portents, *trying* to break through and influence our behaviors.

We've been praising the power generated by the right guidance in dreams. Joseph, stepfather of Jesus, is but one example among many. Pilate, however, *does not* follow the plan laid out for his salvation in the psychic impressions of his resonating half, Lady Pilate. Sad fact.

We who study the spiritual disciplines should take note of the fact that Lady Pilate, as well as the governor himself, are nonbelievers from the ethnocentric viewpoint. Yet, the Spirit speaks directly to them. Psi is ever the working of the Gods. It is a human phenomenon, not a tribal trait.

Pontius Pilate, in this pivotal historical/spiritual role is given a chance – before the deed – to pull out from it. He thus makes the choice to cooperate in his destiny of infamy. He commits the act the dream warns him against.

Because Pilate follows his own self will, expedience dictated by his ignorant and manipulated subjects, he makes the wrong choice. Like a twice elected, impeached president, wheels of the circumstances of the time, combined with erroneous judgement on his own part, relegate him forever to infamy.

Who could know? How important is it to follow the clear advice of dreaming!

Stranger In Their Dreams

Ananias. Paul's vision on the road to Damascus hurls him into three days in the belly of the twilight lands. To resuscitate him from the darkness, God visits Ananias in a vision and directs him to Paul's aid.

God also tells Ananias that he has already visited Saul, and that he's expecting him:

> "Though blind, in his psychic sight, even in a vision, he has seen you come and restore his sight." (Acts 9.12)

Ananias questions if there isn't some misunderstanding, saying,

> "I've heard about the evil things this man is doing to the new age movement. With the government at his side, he's hunting us down and hassling us unmercifully." (Acts 9.13)

But the great work is accomplished by the Lord, who sees all. He does not reassure Ananias with rational arguments, but solely with the assurance that it is his intention that Ananias go, to serve God's plan:

> "Go, for he is a chosen instrument of mine, to carry my name before the Gentiles especially." (Acts. 9.15)

Thus, directed solely by the intuitions of the vision, overriding tons of objective evidence giving contrary advice, Ananias seeks out Saul. When he finds him, exactly where the vision said he would, indeed, through solely a magical invocation accompanying the laying of hands on Saul's crusty eyelids, he serves as the channel of God's healing.

Destiny unravels as Ananias foresees. Reflecting the inner change of consciousness, Saul changes his name to Paul and begins preaching. The Jews don't like it and set about to cause him legal problems and actually to murder him. With our historical perspective we see how the Spirit assists humanity in the outworking of its evolutionary plans. Paul thus turns to the more receptive Gentile peoples. Indeed, Paul is destined to be the greatest missionizer the religion forming around the Christ will ever have.

The Destiny Of Symbiotic Dreams

Cornelius. Peter. Peter is about to get the call to preach to outsiders, too. Clairvoyance this time? Guidance? Direction? How *does* one receive the word of the Master, but in the intuitive channeling of visions, dreams, divinations? Peter does not dream alone.

Goodly and concerned for the welfare of the Jewish people, Cornelius, a centurion, meditating at about three one afternoon, sees a vision on the inner screen. The time is noted, offering a testament that the man is neither drunk nor imbrued in a dream of sleeping. It is a *vision*, come to him during the time of normal waking consciousness.

High in contemplative prayer,

> He sees clearly in a vision an angel of God come, enter, call his name, and talk to him. (Acts 10.3)

Even though it is an angel, he is struck with dumbness born of terror. When he finally regains sufficient control of his vocal apparatus to speak, he addresses the angel as the very presence of God himself, saying,

> "What is it, Lord?" (Acts 10.4)

Look how Cornelius recognizes the Lord in the angel. And this is an outsider! Surely the Spirit moves in all points of the Cosmic stage. Cornelius speaks straight through the channel to the Lord.

The mystic messenger compliments him on his prayerfulness and gives him the missive:

> Send men to Joppa, and fetch here one Simon who now calls himself Peter. He is lodging with Simon, a tanner, whose house is by the seaside." (Acts 10.5-6)

Following these explicit psychic behests, Cornelius, coming back to waking reality, calls two of his servants and one of the soldiers who wait on him, and sends them promptly to Joppa.

The next day, even as they are approaching the city, having traveled the better part of twenty-four hours as the clock goes, the Spirit engages in another psychic occurrence. Peter, waiting for the servants to prepare the noon meal, excuses himself, knowing he has an hour of peace for meditation. He ascends to the high place of the rooftop and drops into a meditative trance. Like Cornelius' psychic experience, Peter's, occurring at the noon hour of the day, is a waking *vision*, rather than a sleeping dream.

And in his trance,

> He sees from high in the sky something like a great sheet descending toward the Earth, let down by four corners held by invisible spirits. And teeming on the sheet are all kinds of animals and reptiles and birds of the air.
>
> And Peter hears a voice speaking to him, and it directs him, "Rise, Peter; kill, and eat."
>
> He recognizes the Lord on the instant, yet replies, "No, Lord; for I have never eaten anything that is common or unclean."
>
> But the voice rings in reply, saying, "What God has cleansed, you must not call common." (Acts 10.11-15)

God commands him again, "Rise, kill, and eat."

But Peter, still rigidly in the grasp of his dogmatized ethnocentrism – though we see it surely in the process of breaking up – refuses again. He has been taught, trained, and has uncritically accepted as *fact*, that "outsiders" are unclean filth and, other than essential commercial contacts, are to be revilingly avoided.

Finally, the third time, with a corner of the sheet close enough for Peter to walk onto it from his visionary high place, God directs him, "Rise, kill, and eat," that is, mix with and partake with these "unclean" beings. Then the vision suddenly folds itself back up into Heaven, and in an instant it's over.

Peter, recognizing the dream as the bearer of God's intent, ponders upon the meaning of the dream. Behold, it looks like the vision – and its *effects* – arrived none too soon! Even while he is engaged in prayerful contemplation of the dream's message,

> The Spirit speaks to him again, and says,
>> "Behold, three men are looking for you. Rise and go down, and accompany them without hesitation; for I have sent them." (Acts 10.19-20)

Even as Peter *asks* for the meaning to be revealed it *is* revealed in actions on the stage of reality. Even while he is asking to understand his vision, the circumstances to actuate its intent come *to his very door!* These men at his door are among the profane, unclean men seeking the illumination of God. How can synchronicity work any more preciously than this in the stage of space and time, superbly orchestrated by the SupraConscious, for whom time and circumstance are but elements of intrigue? It is a HoloCosm, you know.

God accomplishes his purposes through the psychic medium of visions, complete with their actions, lines, and symbols. And look how long lasting this vision! Nearly 2,000 years already!

Peter does the thing that God has called him for. He teaches. And,

> The Spirit falls on all who hear Peter's word." (Acts 10.44)

The Jewish companions who accompany him, spiritually sincere guys, after all, are "amazed" when they see that the Spirit enters into the life of the "unclean." They have a hard time accepting those of different races and nations as equals.

Peter, high on holy enthusiasm, vocalizes the question in their hearts,

> "Can any one forbid water for baptizing these people who have received the Holy Spirit just as we have?" (Acts 10.47)

He follows that statement with the only answer he could give, commanding all present to receive the initiation and the extra graces attendant into the spiritual life.

Egalitarian impulses begin to flower. And he stays some days, teaching the marveling spiritually developing beings.

Dancers In The Drama

Peter, the man who becomes Christianity's first pope, is herein instructed to break the law. He dreams this dream of acceptance. Even though his church, his society, and the laws of his people prohibit this behavior, he recognizes the dream's instruction to speak and instruct.

Empowered by the certitude that accompanies psychic phenomena, he executes the intuitions he receives. Recognize what a monumental commitment Peter is making. He's never been a law-breaker and a renegade, but an appropriately docile law abiding citizen. Now, however, he is filled with the Spirit of God!

The Spirit's fullness lifts us beyond the petty conventions of the whiney political "hard" realities. Peter chooses to follow the instructions imparted in the dream. Because he accepts the dream as a psychic messenger, and because he has the fortitude to act on its message, history is changed.

Cornelius is his partner in the dance. Without his complementary vision, come in prayer, and without his own moves to followup on it, this whole story could have emerged stillborn. What if he'd not sent his men for Peter? What if he'd not opened his house, and had a group eagerly awaiting Peter's arrival?

Peter does not dream alone. His dream could have been a fancy and a novel thought, turned in time, to a passing fancy. But even in the moment of his dreaming Cornelius invites him to speak to their group.

The men's dreams, as well as the good from their actions, dance interdependently with other's dreams and good actions, as well as with the other organic components in the living spiritual organism. They both give life to the other, thereby creating something greater.

A person who happens to be born with a different skin color or in a place that professes a different mytho-belief system is no longer automatically unclean. "Where is their heart leading them?" becomes the new meaningful question.

We, too, are invited to work with others in this web of humanity.

Will you act on your heart?

Whisked To The Third Heaven

Paul is defending himself and his philosophy one Middle Eastern day. While he admits that he may not present his new philosophy with the "superlative" skill of some of the proclaimers of competitive philosophies, what he teaches, he says, is very deep and true knowledge, indeed.

To communicate the deepness of the high truths he's encountered, he talks of visions:

> I know a man in Christ who fourteen years ago was caught up to the third Heaven – whether in the body or out of the body I do not know, God knows. And I know that this man was caught up into Paradise – whether in the body or out of the body I do not know, God knows – and in this vision he heard things that cannot be told, which man may not utter. (2Cor. 12.1-4)

These are higher truths than he deals with in a normal day's writing. It *is* meant to impress.

By the way, the repetition of the "whether in the body or out of the body" motif has a message. If it intrigues you, don't go away.

Look what we've found! Many of the psi events we visit in this chapter speak of the power of a dream to shape reality, and now we encounter Paul presenting the vision of a spiritual associate with the unexamined assumption that a vision or a dream can actually take you into Paradise! Let you with eyes not refuse to see!

Revelation: Record Of A Single Vision

I would invite us here to recall our lengthy visit with *John the Revelator* in the chapter on channeling. We're visiting John again to note what serves our specific interest on this part of the tour, visions and dreams.

A single drama – a visionary trip – structures the entire book of Revelation. John starts by setting the scene of dedication, prayer, and meditation, saying,

"I was in the Spirit on the Lord's day..." (Rev. 1.10)

Then he tells his readers that what follows is a vision. First, he says, he hears a voice speaking to him, coming from behind him. When he turns to see who is speaking, sure enough, the visual images are there. He sees, you recall, midst a mystic scenario, "one like a son of man" (Rev. 1.13).

The son of man is his ferryman through the fantastic new psychicspace he has just entered.

As if the mystic apparitions weren't enough to do it, from time to time John reminds us that what he's describing is in fact a vision he's seeing. For instance, in the act of describing the horses he sees released with the four angels charging out to destroy one-third of humankind, he says:

And this was how I saw the horses in my vision: the riders wore breastplates the color of fire and of sapphire and of sulphur, and the heads of the horses were like lions' heads, and fire and smoke and sulphur issued from their mouths. (Rev. 9.17)

The entire widely respected book is the record of a single vision! Surely God knows what he is doing. Surely he communicates with the author and with us this way for a purpose.

The Dream Is Never Over

In this chapter we explore the paranormal through the psychicscape of dreams and visions. Not everyone channels, not everyone does magic, but everyone dreams. The Biblical lineup of dreamers testifies to the uniform distribution of this gift throughout humanity.

A wish-granting genie gives Solomon all his expansive heart desires, an angel visits Mary to announce she will carry Jesus, and an angel carries John on the psychic trip that becomes *Revelation*. These seem like special dreamers in the Earthly drama of the Divine.

Abimelech, Pharaoh, Nebuchadnezzar, and Pilate's wife are all temporal rulers, and therefore privileged. They are not, however, members of the culture that produces the Bible, being, therefore, "outsiders" to God's plan. But they dream the dreams of God, nevertheless.

But many normal people, believers and heathens alike, dream, too. A butler and a baker in Pharaoh's prison dream. Even an ass sees an angel in the road. And a Midianite soldier on the battlefield before Gideon dreams. Joseph dreams the duration of Jesus' infancy. Cornelius dreams of a big Peter, staying with another man, a Peter who can point him in the new age ways. Everyone dreams.

Certain people display a knack for interpreting dreams, too. The two Biblical players most adept in this art are Joseph and Daniel, both dreamers themselves. But they also help others understand their dreams, which they are unable to understand on their own.

If you ever had any doubts, you certainly see now that God communicates with all humanity, about all kinds of things, through dreams. I hope this chapter has stimulated you to honor and stimulate your own dreams and visions. Daniel, who we know studies dreams, provides a good example for those of us who want to develop along the dream axis. Study dreams, set out to dream, record your dreams, interpret your dreams, and act on your dreams. Share your interests and abilities with others.

The dream is never over; the blessing lives. Joseph dreams of dominion that he spends twenty-two years watching blossom to fruition. Solomon starts the next day and retains blessings and favors through the duration of his life. Joseph dreams it's time to leave Bethlehem and the destiny of the entire world is altered. *What is your dream?*

Chapter 4

Divination: Let God Tell Us What God Wants

---·····---

*The lots may be cast into the lap,
but the decision is wholly from God.
(PS. 16.33)*

Divination is another aspect of esp. Just as God speaks through the dreams, visions, and utterances of professional channelers, kings and peons, insiders and outsiders, he speaks through the fall or selection of stones, cards, and straws.

Divination Is...

Divination is the requesting and/or understanding of contrived or naturally occurring material events, circumstances, and the like that reveal the Lord's intentions, desires, or advice in relation to the topic under consideration. It is another of the Universe's ways of speaking to us. The word does not have to come in a story, a vision, or a dream. The Spiritual Universe encompasses everything. The Spiritual Universe is implicate in *all* reality. The Bible indicates it can and does come in the play of materiality. It *is* materiality. This is the domain of divination: the Divine manifesting in the material.

Divination is the method we use to discern God's will and God's word, wherein God *tells* us what he wants.

What makes divination stand identifiably apart from the other forms of esp is that the Universe communicates with we humans through a *physical* instrument, item, or occurrence. This makes it distinctively different from the pure metaphysical constructs of visions and dreams.

When we discard superficiality, we see three allied forms or practices identified as divination. They fall into two classes. First, there is divination by consulting a *chance indicator*. This is a class by itself. Indeed, God speaks through the fall or selection of stones, cards, and straws. The Tarot, a pendulum, runes, the I-Ching, and Urim and Thummim are all of this class. This is the most common and most visible practice of divination.

The second class moves away from the contrivance of a dedicated instrument. It includes two specific applications of divination by outer *signs*. In the first type you, the querent, mystic, or psychic – and by virtue of being human we are all this person, some just access it better than others – request a sign to confirm or guide your understandings and actions in life. For instance, you might say something like, "If she *asks* me specifically if I would like a drink of water *with a twist of lemon in it*, then she's the one." Whether she does or whether she doesn't, you receive the information you need to understand and act on the situation.

In the second type of divination by reading the signs, you interpret a naturally occurring event or condition in accord with mysti-psychi principles. For instance, suppose you're walking in the woods, considering some event of importance in your life. Questions, like perhaps, should you make a spiritual journey or should you marry person *X.* If, on the sudden, you're frightened by the sudden uprush of a covey of birds your wandering presence has put to rout, you might interpret this as a sign you should stay away from the action under consideration. But you didn't *ask* for the sign; you just understood it. "Outside" reality participates in your subjective world.

The distinction that guides us to call this type more *divination* than *synchronicity* relates to the fact that, though it may come coincidentally, it comes not as a thing or event in itself orchestrated in a higher purpose, but as an *indicator.* The Divine's response to a query is an answer.

We discuss all three varieties as our tour marvels through the psychicspace of divination.

To See Beyond

If the Bible challenges people to see beyond appearances on any psychic subject, it does so in relation to divination. There are several entirely sensible reasons why a person's objective consciousness could have trouble accepting divination. Let's look briefly at two of the most common objections. First, on a purely physical/mathematical basis, the act of divination "looks" random. It can be shown, it can be calculated. Second, there is an outright spoken proscription in the Bible, specifying divination as one of the forbidden arts. But people trenching these lines of thinking are judging by appearances, a costly mistake. The true message is clear and unequivocal as ultraviolet light.

Not By Chance. The lay of the cards, the fall of the stones, the rustling of the trees... These do not come at random... A divinatory event is not just a "chance" event, but, as in every situation, a dance between the participants. Divination, and indeed all psi, involves both partners moving point-counterpoint in the rhythm of cause and effect – question and reply – in the all-embracing HoloCosm that is the Energy that is God. What participants put into the matrix, participants receive in complementarity from the matrix. The event is specific and real.

A human can shake and cast two bones marked with dots in their hands. The dots that land upright tell the diviner something. A human can shuffle a deck of cards and select one or a number of them. But it is God that determines what side of the die falls face up, and God who selects the cards for the querent. As we shall see shortly when we visit the Urim and the Thummim, it is God that has instituted the structure for interpretations of these events, and God who gives the intuitions as to how these things should be interpreted in the specific case at hand. Herein is the essence of divination. Understanding what these signs mean.

Old science is classical physics. The new science, itself a product of the current global afflatus, simultaneously a synergizing drive to that same afflatus, is quantum physics. One does not invalidate the other. One fulfills the other. Classical physics does indeed discern the laws of reality at the material level of effects. Herein one calculates the *odds*. However, what we've seen from peering into the infinite inner realms of the subatomic universes scientifically and empirically demonstrates the existence of a different body of law and principle operating that realm that informs the material.

Thus quantum physics, a recent addition to the scientific pantheon re-erected in the Renaissance and fortified in the Age of Enlightenment, is discerning the ultimate spiritual unity of all life and creation at the subatomic levels. It is facing the facts. That *spiritual* realm is the source of the *material. It is the subatomic levels that manifest all that appears as ultimate reality. Especially when called to do so*, implicate reality expresses meaningfully as explicate reality. For the first time, divination, as well as all psi, can be understood by the rational minded as well as the intuitive.

"No, No!" We toured the psychicsite of the supposed Biblical proscriptions against the psychic arts in the introductory essay. Admittedly, yes, it *could* sound like they are being denounced. That is what the words – lifted literally and taken out of context – say. But, surely we are called upon to read this book, widely acclaimed as the greatest book ever written, with sensitivity, don't you think?

Those who understand see these fundamentalist misinterpretations supported solely on the reinforced twigs of bias. Twigs will be twigs.

Curiously enough, speaking of judging by appearances, actually *doing that* for a change, might be what the key is to understanding the Bible's embracing position on divination, another of the favored arts of Godly communication. The meaning of those passages contexted with the action of the moment, reveal quite a different story. The Bible clearly accepts and even *actively promotes* the psychic arts, including divination, in our spiritual life. This is a big difference.

Divination is demonstrated and practiced successfully for us in this Spiritual Guidebook a number of great times. Upon reading the proscriptions with the least sensitivity of historical and racial awareness, they turn out not to be proscriptions at all.

"I'm Not So Sure..."

We've several times mentioned the appeals to specifically mis-presented Biblical passages the anti-divination right uses to assert their case for the evil of psi. Failing to see what is before them – both in terms of their own psychics who are in fact practitioners of the art and in terms of the context in the channeled Biblical passages themselves, taking surface details only – they glory in their naive hypotheses.

Well, here's good news for the right. The psychic left also has a couple of not-so cases they tout to establish their position. When they talk about Laban divining over Jacob and Joseph divining over his brothers as instances which provide Biblical sanction of divination, they are falling into the same trap of uncritical prejudicial reading.

They enter into this error in the same basic way the hard-line right does, by taking a literal reading of the words with no sensitivity to the story's context.

"I Have Learned By Divination..."

Laban, is known to be deceitful and trickerous. By the time we encounter him in the divination scene in Genesis 30.27, we've already seen him sorely seduce the trusting Jacob. He's stolen the best years of Jacob's youthful manhood, enforcing the *assumed* fine print in a marriage contract.

Jacob's just entered this foreign land when he falls in love with Rachel and strikes up a bargain to buy her from her father. According to their agreement, he is to work for Laban for seven years and then receive Rachel in marriage. But, Laban pulls a good one on him. On his wedding night Jacob is bewitched, so that he doesn't know until he wakes the next morning that the woman he entered last night is the elder, plainer daughter, Leah. Laban substituted her in his bed. Now Laban tells him, "I'm sorry, but the custom of this country does not allow that the younger daughter marry first. That's not the way it's, done. But!" he says, "if you will serve me another seven years, you can this day possess my younger, ravishing daughter, also." Horny, Jacob enthusiastically agrees, and because of his love for Rachel the years seem but a few days.

Then Jacob stays on a few years longer still. He doesn't have a job back home; here he does. Plus, there's this thing back home with his elder brother, Esau. Finally, Jacob decides it's time to go, to chance it.

Laban reacts to Jacob's request for leave to return with his wives, his offspring, and his wealth to his own home country. Laban does not want Jacob to go, because Jacob has prospered him greatly. His own sons have not been able or inclined to do as much.

But Laban says the proper thing. He proposes to settle accounts with him. He contexts it with divination:

> "If you will allow me to say so, I have learned by divination that the Lord has blessed me because of you; name your wages, and I will give it." (Gen. 30.27-28)

Jacob is to take the spottled, speckled, and black sheep and lamb from Laban's herd and breed next year. This is a small fee, for such increase as Jacob's management has brought Laban. Laban agrees, but with trickery up his sleeve. That very day he removes all such animals from the herd.

The man is outright dishonest. He does not want Jacob to go, but if Jacob does go, he surely doesn't want him to take any wealth away. Should we trust him now, even in the very midst of another untrustworthy action? When he says he has "found out by divination" we know it also is a lie designed to aid him in seducing Jacob again. This flattery is designed solely to misdirect Jacob, coaxing him to drop his guard, even while Laban is orchestrating the theft of Jacob's sheep. We can't trust anything Laban says. The words are there, but the sense is wrong.

"Is Not This The Cup From Which My Lord Divines?"

Divination by reading the fluid in a cup is called hydromancy. It is similar to crystal gazing, but the psychic looks, instead of into the ball, into the cup. Joseph the dreamer is involved in the only case of hydromancy mentioned in the entire Bible. It is unlikely, however, that the case is anything but bogus.

It all starts some twenty years earlier when the jealous brothers sell him off to slave traders. Then after the series of events that places Joseph in command of the wealth of Egypt, his brothers, driven by famine oppressing the world, end up bowing before him, requesting the sustenance of life.

Joseph recognizes them as his brothers, the ones who separated him from his home, his family, and his Israelite life, that caused him so much pain for so many years. They are not trying to keep their identity secret. They, because of perceptual blinders, are unable to recognize Joseph. They did not expect that they could ever see Joseph again. To their minds and their affairs of *years*, he is dead. They are unable to form any conception of their dead brother in the political position and significance of this man in a foreign nation having any relationship to them.

Joseph, for his part, holds the veil to his identity. And they don't know that Joseph, who is using an interpreter to maintain his disguise, can hear the turmoils of their guilt, which they argue about amongst themselves.

Joseph's playing the enjoyment of some long delayed payback with his unsuspecting brothers. They feel an evil misunderstanding descending around them like a net. Playing the part of the important personage of state which he is, Joseph drops pulls the heavy lever on the machinery of political incriminations, the only ones from which you cannot escape. As the story goes:

> Joseph, remembering the dreams of dominion over them, accuses them saying,
>
> "You are spies, you have come to see the weakness of the land!" (Gen. 42.8-9)

They protest their innocence, pleading that they are but honest men, ten of the twelve brothers, one of whom is dead, of an honest man in Canaan. Simple non-political folks. Hungry people.

But Joseph keeps repeating the charge that they are spies. Finally he relents to try their innocence by testing out their story. The youngest brother they claim they left at home must come to Egypt. They say they left him because his brother, Joseph, was killed some years ago, and their father could not stand the threat of any ill coming to his remaining youngest, Benjamin, sole remaining offspring of his beloved Rachel. Joseph acts like he's thinking it over and says he'll allow one of them to go home and fetch the younger brother whilst the others remain in prison. If he does not show up with the youngest son of Israel, all the brothers in the cell shall be put to death. If he does show up with this younger brother, their story is true and they shall all go free.

These boys are on the spot big time! He's enjoying the payback, and he's paying it back right now with interest!

After holding them all in prison for three days, he tells them he has decided to let nine of the brothers go home, with the food they came after, holding only one of them in the dungeon. They still have to return with their youngest brother to prove their innocence. Being in a jamb, with no choices anyway, and this sounding far better than the alternative, the brothers agree.

The nine brothers journey home with the food, meeting with other nice but incriminating adventures along the way. They find the money they had paid for the grain in their grain sacks. This adds to the level of their fearfulness, because they are afraid they will be accused and convicted of stealing the grainstuffs, the money, or both! Oh, the evils of political incriminations! Can't imagine such injustice, can you? Thus they delay returning. But it's bad times. The food, though it was all they could carry, eventually runs out. Now they must resolve the issue of what to do concerning the fate of the brother imprisoned in Egypt, Benjamin at home, and Joseph, the powerful politician. "It's hard to please an asshole, and a powerful asshole is even harder!" they are thinking. But they cower before the man.

Because they bring their youngest brother, Benjamin, Joseph acts satisfied with their innocence. He sells them more food that day, and on the morrow sends them off for home.

But trouble chases them down. Joseph sends his steward out, who himself prepared the food bags as Joseph instructed, hiding their money again this second time, but additionally hiding a special silver cup in the mouth of Benjamin's load. Following Joseph's instructions, the steward overtakes them and says,

> "Why have you returned good for evil? Why have you stolen the silver cup. Is it not from this that my lord drinks, and by this that he divines?" (Gen. 44.4-5)

The men, secure in their integrity, protest. They would *never* do such a thing! They are condemned by their own words,

> "With whomever of your servants it be found, let him die, and we also will be my lord's slaves!" (Gen. 44.9)

The cup is found in the sack of Benjamin.

Joseph repeats the charge before the prostrate brothers:

> "What deed is this that you have done? Do you not know that such a man as I can indeed divine?" (Gen. 44.15)

He pronounces the sentence: the person in whose bag the cup was found shall be his slave. This, of course, is the big dread the brothers have had all along, that of harming their youngest brother, which would surely take their father's grey hairs straight to the grave. Joseph's still at the carnival, however, strumming the boys' guilt and helplessness.

This cup is the centerpiece in Joseph's ruse on his brothers. It is a plant from start to finish. The entire series of events surrounding the hydromancy, including the events leading up and away from it, are events of subterfuge on Joseph's part. Indeed, Joseph only wants to show them that they are helpless victims under his thumb. In spite of their innocence, they are faced with the ultimate price. To heat the fever of their fear and helplessness, the divination cup is used to lead them to think the mysterious powers of the God of Egypt is arrayed against them... And what mortal can combat the Gods and survive?

You certainly wouldn't want to contradict the Biblical sense here and insist that Joseph does practice divination, and that this cup is his divination cup. It may be so. It wouldn't disturb the story line. These two points are not really crucial to the story's statement. However, to insist that they are true rather than just possible, is underreading the entire sense of the story. We know Joseph experiences and enjoys psychic communion in wisdom and in dreams, but we don't know about divination. This passage does not support it. We do know he's doing everything possible to mislead and frighten his brothers.

We cannot use the drama around Joseph's cup as a structural member in the argument for the Biblical blessing of divination.

However, the psychic left does not need Laban's divination nor Joseph's hydromancy. These cases say something, but nothing to prove that divination either does or does not work or that it is or is not favored by God. There are multitudes of other cases sufficient to that cause.

****

Divination: Listening To God

Everybody has an urge to know the future. *How will things turn out? What should I do to win? Would the action I'm considering be wise?* And, it turns out, the Undifferentiated Cosmos has the answers. Divination reveals these answers.

Let's see how it works!

In The Speaking

When *Abraham's slave*, gone to Mesopotamia to get Isaac a wife, utters the prayerful words looking for a sign to identify the one right woman, he is invoking divination. He invokes it in these words:

"O Lord, God of my master Abraham, grant me success today, I pray thee, and show steadfast love to my master Abraham.

"Behold, I am standing by the spring of water, and the daughters of the men of the city are coming out to draw water. Let the maiden to whom I shall say, 'Pray let down your jar that I may drink,' and who shall say, 'Drink, and I will water your camels' -- let her be the one whom thou hast appointed for thy servant Isaac. By this I shall know that thou hast shown steadfast love to my master." (Gen. 24.12-14)

And God gives it to the first female who approaches to say just these words and to perform these very acts. It unravels just as the slave has requested it happen – *if* this female is the right female. In fact, Rebekah approaches even "before he has done speaking" (Gen. 24.15). After she fills her jar, he asks for a drink. She quickly gives him a drink, and then pours the remainder of her water into the trough for his camels to drink. That's not enough, so she goes and gets more for the camels.

Then the passage goes on, speaking to a common dilemma we have with divination. Though she does *precisely what he sets forth* as the deciding event of this "outward sign" divination, he still wonders if the Lord has indeed prospered his ways. Even in the very midst of the fulfillment of his prayers, fulfilled with the sign he has *just this moment requested*, he wonders. Oh humanity!

The man gazed at her in silence to learn whether the Lord had prospered his journey or not. (Gen. 24.21)

Of course, God did.

This surely shows God at work. The point is, that the slave, surely a commoner – he is but a slave – utters this divination, setting up the requested "sign" as a "sign," and God fulfills it. This is divination. The Book confirms its accuracy.

High Divination: The Urim And The Thummim

Moses. The Urim and the Thummim is the archetypical divinatory device of the Bible. Throughout the Bible, a number of other things are used, such as water gazing, examination of the entrails of animals, divination with arrows, casting lots, wind in the trees, and the undirected actions of a woman or a man, but it is these magical stones – first cousins of the still extant rune stones – that hold top place in the hearts and affairs of these favored people God displays in the Bible.

The Urim and the Thummim is a *chance indicator* divinatory device. That is, a question is held in mind, which may or may not be spoken aloud, and God answers the querent by the apparent random fall of the stones. Ah, but these are enchanted stones! The stones, tuned with the Infinite, respond to the intimations of the Infinite. The reply formed in God's heart influences the selection and the fall of the stones.

Some people make the mistake of undervaluing the significance of the Urim and the Thummim in the Bible. This is understandable, given the consciousness of our current age. We are not an age given to mysteries, the occult, and the Divine. We are heirs of the recent Age of Enlightenment, with rationalism in ascendency. We have nothing to compare it with. The Urim and the Thummim is far more valued and consulted among the Jewish people than any other divination device, even the Tarot cards among the people of our culture and our time.

And well they should be significant! The Urim and Thummim is an institution ordained and established by God. It is, indeed, through this oracle that God answers the queries of the people's hearts and welfare.

Shortly after the Hebrew people make their dazzling escape from the land of their nourishment turned captivity, they set about fashioning many elaborate implements of worship. Though they don't know it at the time, they are destined to be in transit for a long time. They will need many answers during the upcoming years. God gives them explicit instructions on how they are to construct the breastpiece of judgment, the box that holds the sacred lots:

First he tells the people to create a rich and elaborate mantle, called an *ephod*, for the priests. Then he tells them to make a lavishly bejeweled box:

> "And you shall make a breastpiece of judgment, in skilled work; like the work of the ephod you shall make it; of gold, blue and purple and scarlet stuff, and fine twined linen shall you make it. It shall be square and double, a span its length and a span its breadth. And you shall set in it four rows of stones. a row of sardius, topaz, and carbuncle shall be the first row; and the second row an emerald, a sapphire, and a diamond; and the third row a jacinth, an agate, and an amethyst; and the fourth row a beryl, an onyx, and a jasper; they shall be set in gold filigree. There shall be twelve stones..." (Ex. 28 15-21)

Then he instructs them to attach the box of judgment upon the ephod with woven lace bands of blue and, to hold it securely, twisted chains of gold. Then, climaxing this article, he instructs them:

> "And in the breastpiece of judgment you shall put the Urim and the Thummim, and they shall be upon Aaron's heart when he goes in before the Lord..." (Ex. 28.30)

God himself places a high value in these magical stones. He surely has his reasons.

Of Psychic Verities

God's attention to divination surely indicates something, doesn't it? Yet today, as he would have it, there are diviners among us.

Through These Enchanted Stones. We here visit God formalizing a divine link wherein people can inquire of God and hear his reply. Thus God himself legitimizes divination in the establishment of the Urim and the Thummim.

He plants myths around this device, to elaborate its importance to humanity. He wouldn't make such elaborate preparations to establish reverence around the institution of divination if it wasn't indeed, as his book indicates it is, an oracle that reveals his will. Do you think he would encourage his people if divination were, as some hardline rights assert, a practice "of the devil"?

Given God's purpose in composing this book, to eternally guide humanity to blessedness, which includes, of course, the present moment of eternity, what Jesus calls "our daily bread," it is inconceivable that divination would play such a major role in the lives of the esteemed Biblical characters if God didn't want it to. Over the upcoming pages we will visit numerous instances of divination with the Urim and the Thummim.

To This Day. The Urim and the Thummim, alas! are no longer publically accessible. They make it through the Exodus, the Judges, the Kings, and destruction of Jerusalem, being in Babylonia with the exiles. They even make it back to the homeland. Ezra and Nehimiah contain the last mention of the Urim and Thummim, during the early days of the restoration of the people in Judah and the rebuilding of the Temple.

These are tempestuous bandit-ridden times. One half of all the men, in shifts, are assigned to the martial detail. The other half work on the construction of the Temple. Those who carry burdens do so in such a manner that one hand always holds their sword. Even on those impossible tasks that demand both hands, the men keep their sword girded at their belt. Can you imagine such a lawless society in which even construction workers wear guns they are ready to use at all times?

It is no wonder they are hidden. The Urim and the Thummim as physical artifacts, like the stone tablets of the covenant and its elaborate case, the Ark of the covenant, have long since disappeared from general accessibility. The tradition instituted by Moses, however, passed on to the service of Joshua, through the entire period of the judges, the kings, and beyond, endures to this day. This is what the Urim and the Thummin is. Divination has not died out.

"Where There's Smoke Or Fire..."

Moses. This pillar of fire and smoke that directs the pilgrim Israelites into Canaan is a miracle of rare device, spanning the boundaries of the two worlds of God and humanity:

> The Lord goes before them by day in a pillar of cloud to lead them along the way, and by night in a pillar of fire to give them light, that they might travel by day and by night; the pillar of cloud by day and the pillar of fire by night does not depart from before the people. (Ex. 13.21-22)

Imagine how this would be presented in the movies! A column of intense fire stretching straight into the reaches of Heaven, powerful by night embedded midst a moving intense radiance of Spirit. A stormy pillar of clouds billowing with Divine passion by day. Light in the dark, dark in the light.

This rare mystical device serves the function of divination. The tribe correctly understands the word and the will of God speaking through the marvelous interplay of the qualities of fire.

Of Psychic Verities
This site provides us with several interesting psychic verities.

With An Outward Sign. Its meaning is simple. Not complex. The movement of this otherworldly column of smoke and fire indicates a move-on to the wandering Israelites. When the pillar does not move from the camp, neither do the Israelites. When the pillar moves, so do the Israelites. It reveals the will of the Lord with an outward sign. Possessed with the knowledge of God's will, ascertained through divining the meaning of this event, reading and divining the sign and its significance, the Israelites pattern their behavior upon its word.

Is It A Column Of Fire And Smoke... Or Is It God? It is interesting how, though the book identifies the "physical" item/artifact as a pillar of fire and smoke, when speaking of it, identifies it as God. The passage simply says it, like it is the most believable thing in the world. We're familiar with this phenomenon of *identification* with channeling, and now we see it in the allied phenomenon of divination.

Not Just Like An Angel – FLASH! And She's Gone. The column endures. It is not just a magical apparition projected from the hearts of the people during the stresses of escape.
The process continues throughout their wilderness sojourning. Well into their second month of running they pause to recoup and nourish their forces. The pace slows down. It's not nonstop running anymore. The need is gone. One of the things they do is build a portable Tabernacle to house the presence of the Lord in dignity. The column takes up residence above that Tabernacle. A sight to behold!
Sometimes now the cloud does not stir from keeping its watch for months:

> Whether it is two days, or a month, or a longer time, that the cloud continues over the Tabernacle, abiding there, the people of Israel remain in camp and do not set out; but when it is taken up they set out. At the command of the Lord they encamp, and at the command of the Lord they set out; at the command of the Lord by Moses. (Num. 9.22-23)

How're Your Reading Skills? The art of divination includes not only *getting* the signs, but *reading* the signs as well. It's for this reason that psychics are synonymously called *readers*. Certainly, when we review the work of the psychics and prophets of the Bible stories, we see this in action. Look at Joseph, Moses, Ezekiel, and Daniel. Each of these know what to do with what they receive. These individuals can interpret the information, the wishes, and the mandates coming from the Godforce. The diviner just uses a material artifact of some sort instead of the purely metaphysical substance of visions and dreams and impressions. By dedicated agreement and attunement, this device indicates the same things as other types of readings, in a specific way.

The Israelites possess the perception to read and follow God's word expressed in the particular motions of a dancing pillar of fire and smoke.

Who Can Withstand The Awesome Power Of A Quake?

Moses has his troubles keeping control over the young nation on the move. Challenges to his authority come from all sides, from his psychic sister and brother priest down to the peons of the people. The high of escaping from Egypt wears off quickly when the people encounter the threats and hardships of the desert wilderness. They are upset, because at least in slavery they had security. As people rescripting their destiny, traversing the wild lands, they are beset by incertainty at every side.

They hadn't known it was going to be so rigorous. And not everything the self-appointed superstar Moses says or does works out exactly like they think it should. Or like Moses thinks it should! They complain. Moses must persuade them. He uses divination and magic extensively in these efforts. It always makes a good show.

Korah, Dathan, and Abiram voice the typical complaints against Moses. Moses sends officers out to escort the offenders, but they refuse to come. They send word back:

> "Is it a small thing that you have brought us up out of a land flowing with milk and honey, to kill us in the wilderness, that you must also make yourself a prince over us?
>
> "Moreover you have not brought us into a land flowing with milk and honey, nor given us inheritance of fields and vineyards. What? Will you put out our eyes? We will not come up." (Num. 16.13-14)

It's hard to tell what Moses would have done had they come up. But we sure can see that he does better than that now. He *kills* them. "Control by any means," seems to be his motto during this period. He will make all the people more docile by removing the trouble makers, demonstrating for the survivors the severe consequences of non-compliance. Only, since it is *God* doing it, it is divination and magic.

Since the men won't come to Moses, Moses and his yes-men go to them. He tells the people around them to scatter quickly, as his business concerns just these men, "their wives, sons, and little ones" (Num. 16.27). In his fine oratorical style he addresses all those in attendance, promising a sign of his authority:

> "Hereby you shall know that the Lord has sent me to do all these works, and that it has not been of my own accord: if these men die the common death of all men, ...then the Lord has not sent me. But if the Lord creates something new, and the ground opens its mouth, and swallows them up, with all that belongs to them, and they go down alive into Sheol, then you shall know that these men have despised the Lord." (Num. 16.28-30)

The moment he speaks these words the ground quakes, opens its mouth, swallows the protestors, their fright-faced families, and all their possessions. On the instant all trace of the rebels disappears.

God has rendered his verdict. This is not a chance occurrence. And all Israel submits to the indomitable will of this Moses, lest the same thing happen to them.

It could be magic.

Bud And Pretty Blossoms

Moses tells the people that he, his brother, Aaron, and their tribe, the Levites, have been selected by God as the people charged with the cushy duties of the nation's sacred industry.

What a boon! This is a position of luxury and ease, for the people of all the other tribes must tithe. Whoever occupies this post of privilege, God says through Moses, is to be rewarded by the people at large, with,

> "All the best of the oil; all the best of the wine; all the best of the grain; the firstborn of every living female, be it beast, bird, or human; and liberal first gifts of money." (Num. 18.12-13)

God gives this to Moses, Aaron, and the Levites.

The covetousness of the others rises. After all, this is outlandish wealth for an easy responsibility. The others have to really *work*!

So Moses has to do something to convince the people that this is not his own decision, benefitting his family and tribe because of self-interest. This is the way *God* wants it. "They must have a sign," he says. So God directs Moses to call the tribes together. The elder of each tribe, after writing his name on it, gives Moses his walking staff. Moses puts them in the sanctuary of the meeting tent, telling the people they shall know in the morning who is to enjoy the lavish perquisites of the priesthood. God will make his will visible, God will make his will known. The rod of the man whom God chooses shall sprout.

Can you believe it?!

> When Moses enters the tent the next day the rod of Aaron for the house of Levi has sprouted and put forth buds and the pretty blossoms of the almond tree; and it bore ripe almonds, too. (Num. 17.8)

Stunning! Impressive. The process of months compressed into the secrets of a single night... on one man's rod. Meaningful. Moses helps them understand. The sign is certain. The people quit their murmuring.

It could be magic.

The Cornerstone Of Conquest

Joshua. When the Israelites encamp across the Jordan from the land they've selected as their own, they make preparations to occupy it. Moses knows he's not going to make it. He's dying. Joshua is the fitting choice for the tasks immediately ahead. They need a strong military leader. He passes theocratic dominion on to Joshua.

After God instructs Moses to commission Joshua, passing the power in a public ceremony by the laying on of hands, he tells Moses where Joshua shall receive his instructions to lead the nation in their battles of conquest:

> "He shall consult Eleazar the priest, who shall inquire for him by the judgment of the Urim and the Thummim before the Lord. According to what the lots say, at his word they shall go out, and at his word they shall come in, both he and all the soldiers of Israel..." (Num. 27.21)

Thus divination is the cornerstone of God's plan of conquest. It is through the mystic messages of divination that he will make his will known to the Supreme Commander, Joshua.

The Dice Will Tell

Joshua. The fighting men of Israel make their final preparations to enter Canaan. They galvanize their resolve and organize their forces. Their first efforts outside the land of the wilderness they've lived in for so many years are met with astounding success. Their first battle, at Jericho, is a *major conquest.* Only after they gain access to the city by magical means do they put hot blood on their sharpened swords. Victory is complete. Jericho and its inhabitants are no more.

Then they suffer a crushing defeat, a tragedy of espionage, of judgment, and of execution. They are in a very vulnerable position. All that they own and all that they is is rolling beside them into battle. They have no other stronghold. They are surrounded by enemies on every side, and they feel it.

Joshua, in his single recorded moment of incapacitating doubt, cries to the Lord:

> "If only we had been content to settle on the other side of the Jordan! I beseech thee, O Lord; what can I say, now that Israel has been routed by the enemy? When the Canaanites and all the natives of the country hear of this, they will come swarming around us and wipe us off the face of the Earth!" (Jos. 7.7-9)

In defiant exasperation, God scolds Joshua:

> "You pitiable thing! – Stand up! !!! Why are you lying prostrate on your belly and face?
>
> "Israel has sinned!" (Jos. 7.10-11)

Oh! It seems one of the raiders turned marauder. God instructed the Israelites to execute summary *total* justice to the inhabitants and the possessions of Jericho. Only the valuable vessels and items of silver and gold and copper and all the money were to be spared. They were to go into the coffers of the priests.

Joshua, even though he's the leader of the nation, is innocent of any knowledge of such a deed. The betrayal! But, who? He doesn't know who it could be. *Divination will tell!* Joshua decides to call the tribes together on the morrow and settle the issue quickly.

The description of the choosing of the guilty man the next day does not specifically identify the Urim and the Thummim as the instrument of divination. Not by name, that is. Of course, that's how they make their decisions. Of course, that is how they've been making their decisions for the past forty years. Forgive them if they take it so for granted that they simply refer to the lots with the synonymous term of *choosing* or *taking*. In the context of what precedes and succeeds this scene, it can be by no other method than divination that God makes the guilty party known. There is no mention of interrogation, argumentation, and evaluation.

Scholars and sensitives are in agreement on this point. The judicious scholars and editors of the *New Oxford Annotated Bible Revised Standard Version* say in their footnote to Joshua 7.14: "The Lord 'takes' by the *casting of lots.*"

Joshua brings the people together early the next morning,

- ▸ tribe by tribe of the nation of Israel, and the tribe of Judah is chosen
- ▸ clan by clan of the tribe of Judah, and the clan of Zerah is taken
- ▸ family by family of the clan of Zerah, and the family of Zabdi is fingered
- ▸ and man by man of the family of Zabdi until the lot falls to the unfortunate man, Achan

The lengthy concatenation of divination is accurate. The guilty party is informed on, not by spies, police, or informers, but by the mystical stones of the Urim and the Thummim.

And so they carry out the Lord's decree, and remove the abomination from amongst them. Joshua takes everything the man is or owns – himself, the booty, his wife, mother, sons and daughters, and even his oxen and asses and the family's tent and their clothes – and stones them all to death. Full of energy, riled, and bloodthirsty for the Lord, they pile a high pile of stones over the remains, all, which remains as a hill and a reminder to this day.

Sure enough, a time of military superiority and expansion follows... a time of aggressive outrage against the inhabitants of the land... a time of theft, deceit, massacre, slaughter, annihilation, pillage, booty, spoils, and land. This is the Promised Land, the land flowing with milk and honey they take as their own.

The *Prized* Possession

Joshua. The land sums up God's promise to the Israelites. The land – *the Grail* – and its conquest, are matters of the gravest importance to every member of the nation. It is the land Abraham trod with the determination to make it his; it is the land kept alive in the visions of his son, Isaac, and in the heart of Isaac's son, Jacob. It is the land almost mythical the twelve sons of Israel, moving into Egypt with their families dream of. It is the land the Jewish people picture while aliens in Egypt, it is the land they fight the journey and the wilderness for, and the land they've been killing for in Canaan. Nothing stops destiny. This land is their land.

No *man* is politically willing to shoulder making the decisions on such an important issue. Why would Joshua want to make any political enemies – from within? If he were to apportion the parcels it would be inevitable. All pieces are not created equal. The special interest groups would crucify him, thirteen hundred years before Christ. *No thanks! God* will do it, for who can argue with God?

Three tribes have settled on the way into Canaan in the TransJordan area. Now Joshua first gives Caleb, his decorated general, the choice Hebron, promised him by Moses. Then he subjects the remainder of the land and the remainder of the tribes to the lotting process. Eleazar, a psychic by profession, casts the deciding lots:

> Their inheritance is decided by lot, as the Lord had commanded by Moses. (Jos. 14.2)

God himself portions the parcels through the replies of divination. Something so vitally important can neither be left to chance nor to the decision of a human being. Divination tells us what God wants.

"Just Needed To Be Sure, God... It *Could* Have Been a Coincidence"

The *Gideon* episodes contain several interesting divinations. Following the advice of the angel he's been seeing, Gideon has set things in motion to rebel against the Midian oppression. He's put the call out, and fighting men have gathered to rout the marauders.

But Gideon still has his doubts. He asks for a sign that God really will accomplish this great deed of delivering Israel by his hand, as he has promised. This time, however, instead of simply requesting a sign and leaving it up to that, he sets up the parameters with God:

> "If thou wilt deliver Israel by my hand, as thou hast said, behold, I am laying a fleece of wool on the threshing floor; if there is dew on the fleece alone, and it is dry on all the ground, then I shall know that thou wilt deliver Israel by my hand, as thou hast said." (Jg. 6.36-37)

In the morning it is so. In fact, the fleece is so wet that Gideon wrings a whole bowl full of water from it.

"Hmmm... It could have been a coincidence," Gideon is thinking. *O sure! It happens all the time, doesn't it?* But he overlooks this blatant fact in his insecurity. *Oh humanity!* His new robes fit him ill.

So he asks God, "Please don't be upset with me, but I just need to be *sure*. Would you give me another sign?":

> "This time let it be dry only on the fleece, and on all the ground let there be dew." (Jg. 6.39)

And the book informs us,

> And God did so that night; for it was dry on the fleece only, and on all the ground there was dew. (Jg. 6.40)

Even Gideon, one not given to metaphysical speculations, can't deny the authentic evidence of God's will. He goes to battle, and, with many an adventure in the process, redeems Israel.

But To Have You Understand

This scenario touches again on one of the dilemmas surrounding divination. We sometimes doubt the very answers – very clear answers – we receive, even when we receive them *exactly* as we request them. Gideon has already received the sign that he is to lead the Israelites, when the angel first visits him, consuming the food in the fire. But he asks again.

So God shows him again. Playing impossible odds. How could the fleece be wet and all the ground dry? But Gideon continues to doubt. So he asks again.

And God answers as requested. Again. Only then does Gideon really *understand* and move forward.

Even In The Lowly Cattle

At one point in their skirmishes with the *Philistines*, the Israelites foolishly carry the Ark of God into the actual battle. They want its magical influence big time.

But, contrary to what the Philistine victors expect will happen when they possess the ark, all does not go well for them. The hand of God is heavy *against* them. They had thought it a talisman of such influence that it would benefit *whoever* possessed it. This is a talisman with *consciousness*. It causes an outbreak of tumors amongst the people. Some die; all are panic stricken. They shuttle the cursing ark from city to city, but it plagues everywhere it goes.

It's magical, alright, and it's potent. But it's definitely particular in whom it favors. It is making its will known... and who's so foolish to buck a curse?

The story is an interesting story, one that carries us to many considerations. Also, since divination is akin to magic, there is a lot of interpenetration between the two, more visible at times than at others. We will see even more of this interesting episode when we grasp the "Magic" adventure in chapter 5.

Finally, they determine that they must do something about the problem. So they call the psychics, the priests and diviners, to ask them what they should.

The psychics tell them to prepare a guilt offering of small golden sculptures and then,

> "Take and prepare a new cart and two dairy cows upon which there has never come a yoke, and yoke the cows to the cart, but take their calves home, away from them. And take the ark of the Lord and place it on the cart, and put in a box at its side the figures of gold, which you are returning to him as a guilt offering. Then send it off, and let it go its way.
>
> "And watch; if it goes up on the way to its own land, to Bethshemesh, then it is he who has done us this great harm; but if not, then we shall know that it is not his hand that struck us, it happened to us by chance."
> (1Sam. 6.7-9)

The diviners establish what shall be the sign and what it shall indicate. The action of the cows shall indicate the will and the word of the Lord either way. These special instruments, milch cows who have never carried the burden of human commerce, still open to the innocent intuitive whisperings of the Universe, have been selected and dedicated to reveal the Lord's will.

The men readily follow the psychics' advice, and put the clean cows to the cart. And,

The cows go straight in the direction of Bethshemesh along one highway, lowing as they go; turning neither to the right nor to the left ... all the way to the border of Bethshemesh, where the people see them and take them with great rejoicing. (1Sam. 6.12-13)

Here Is The Secret Secret

Again we see, rather than small items that fall by chance to indicate the God's will, we can set up an "outside" event. The cows are not dice or cards. Once they leave the hands of the Philistines they are totally on their own. But, because they are dedicated to the task, they reveal God's intent. God does it...

This is not a chance occurrence. The divination correctly expresses the word of God. Thus the secret stands revealed. You set up a divinatory indicator by the psychic charge you give to it. We as humans are hard-wired with the ability to do this. You learn to do this through training and practice in meditation and the magical dimensions of psi. Instruction is available. The Philistine psychics demonstrate their abilities time immemorial.

The Philistines are outsiders, but the story shows clearly they are receiving their answers from the same power that the Israelites worship. Of course, created by the same sole power they would. Whether it's the fleece of a lamb, marked bones or stones, or queenly cows, instruments tuned to the infinite, dedicated to divination, express the word and the will of God.

"You Shall Have a Sign The Lord Has Anointed You"

Samuel. Saul. Some years later the Israelites get their king. Now they are like the peoples who surround them. And the story of that first king, his initiation, his induction, his reign, and his end, rings with tales of many psychic adventures. It is a magical time, for good and for ill.

In this particular incident, which we visited in depth in "Channeling," there are two major incidents of divination. One involves a revelation to Saul himself, since he has to psychically accept the throne and its grand perks and massive responsibilities. The other plays out before the assembled hundreds of thousands of Israel.

The Divination At Anointing

Saul, having no luck finding any ass, has sought the sight of a seer. This seer, Samuel, anoints him king the next morning. As he is doing this he accompanies the ceremony of investiture with dedicatory words. He takes a flask of oil in his right hand, kisses Saul on both cheeks, and as he ceremonially pours it over Saul's head, he says,

"The Lord anoints you prince over his people Israel. You shall rule the people of the Lord and deliver them from the enemies round about them.

"You shall have a sign that the Lord has anointed you prince to govern his heritage. And this shall be the sign: When you depart from me today you will meet two men by Rachel's tomb in the territory of Benjamin at Zelzah, and they will say to you, 'The asses which you went to seek are found, and now your father has ceased to care about the asses and is anxious about you, saying, "What shall I do about my son?"'

"Then you shall go from there and come to the oak of Tabor. There three men going up to God at Bethel will meet you, one carrying three kids, another carrying three loaves of bread, and another carrying a skin of wine. And they will greet you and give you two loaves of bread, which you shall accept from their hand.

"After that you shall come to Gibeathelohim, where there is a garrison of the Philistines; and there, as you come to the city, you will meet a band of prophets coming down from the high place with harp, tambourine, flute, and lyre before them, prophesying. Then the spirit of the Lord will come mightily upon you, and you shall prophesy with them and become possessed and transformed into another man." (1Sam. 10.1-6)

Thus Samuel is explicit in the divination he sets up. Samuel lays out a whole string of events that will occur to corroborate the sign, removing what he is saying far from the realm of chance. He does not just say, for instance, "You'll meet some men who have meaning to you today," which is vague enough that it would likely be satisfied under any circumstance, like newspaper astrology.

"But," he says, "you will encounter...

- *five* men... but not all at once

First, you will encounter:

- *two* men
  - at a specific place: "by Rachel's tomb"
  - at a specific time: "when you part from here"
  - and they shall say a specific thing: "The ass you went out looking for...."

Then, after that, you will encounter,

- *three* men
  - each carrying something:
    - one carrying three kids
    - another carrying three loaves of bread
    - another carrying a skin of wine
  - at a specific place: the "oak of Tabor"
  - going to a specific place: Bethel
  - for a specific purpose: to worship
  - and they will say and do a specific thing: greet you and give you two loaves of bread

Then, after that, you will,

- see a band of prophets approaching, prophesying

Then, after that,

- ► the spirit will take possession of you and you will prophesy in that Godly rush

Then, after that,
- ► *you will know that God has chosen you*

No kidding! Surely, if events unfold as Samuel says they will, that's a good sign that the Lord has indeed spoken. Consider the odds against these events occurring as Samuel divines. Astronomical!

The Seer Knows, The Divination Goes

This is also a unique divination amongst Biblical literature for another reason than the incredible string of foreseen events.

Samuel is not divining. In a lot of cases, such as when Rebekah consults the psychic to receive information about the offspring in her womb or when the diviners of Philistia set the milch cows loose, the psychic who casts or sets up the divination is actually as in the dark to the real answer as anyone else consulting therewith. However, in this incident Samuel is talking about something he knows will unfold.

But to Saul it is presented as a divination. And it functions with the significance that Samuel programs into it. Indeed, Saul accepts his dignity when the Lord confirms it with these signs.

Then Samuel, in much the same manner as Merlin with Arthur, gives Saul his first lesson in kingship, telling him that what the king wants to do is alright. The king, checked only by God, has the absolute ability to do as he will:

"Now when these signs meet you, do whatever your hand finds to do, for God is with you." (1Sam. 10.8)

You are not surprised,

All these signs come to pass that day. (1Sam 10.9)

Wouldn't you be surprised if Saul *didn't* believe that day?

"God, This Better Work!!!"

With the skeptics aglee, Samuel is on the spot. Impulsed by this sudden, dramatic, and mystical series of events, Saul has undergone a radical transformation of consciousness. He's not acting like the Saul the people know. They are talking about him. Samuel knows that things will blow unless Saul is immediately chosen by the nation. They've got to feel like they've got a voice in this thing. So he immediately calls to assembly all the tribes in all their families and all their men for the purpose of selecting the king they've been calling for. The day they've been clamoring for has sprung upon them. They will divine the Lord's will. But here's Samuel's tricky spot: if the lots fall by chance, the chance of Saul being selected in the divining process is *remote*!

Here is how it goes:

- Samuel brings all the tribes of Israel near, and the tribe of Benjamin is taken by lot.
- He brings the tribe of Benjamin near by its families, and the family of the Matrites is taken by lot;
- Finally he brings the family of the Matrites near man by man, and Saul the son of Kish is taken by lot. (1Sam. 10.20-21.

We, as readers of the intriguing story, have the background knowledge the contemporaries of Samuel and Saul do not. We know Saul has already been anointed by God, in a ceremony channeled through Samuel. These people do not know that. They think the lots are in the process of *selecting* the king. Because of what has transpired, however, we know that the lots are actually in a position of *confirming* a king. The lots *must* fall as they do.

Whew! The odds against this occurring simply by chance are astronomical! Factor in the years involved, from the days of Jacob and his sons in Canaan, through the 430 years of the Egyptian salvation, the days of the desert wanderings, and the entire period of the Judges, a time when decades pass at the stroke of a pen. Count the generations. Multiply by the number of offspring in a family during these expansionist years of the nation. Even the family of a man at that time might include 300-400 males alone! My calculator won't go that high.

And the stones choose Saul. God has spoken. The people, buoyed with emotion, confirm the choice! They see him a span nobly taller than everybody around him, and they fall into: "Long live the king!" (1Sam. 10.24). A band of valorous men immediately assemble themselves around Saul. Destiny has changed course for Saul.

Divination But Reveals God's Design

Of course, this is the very purpose of divination. To determine God's will. God *has* selected Saul; we know that. We've seen the anointing. The dice but let God speak to the assembly in a language that they understand. Devices dedicated to this end become efficacious tools to accomplish God's work, as revealed again in this story.

As insiders to the whole story, we see it well.

The Sign Is The Augur Of Its Fulfillment

Jonathon. The war runs hot and cold between the Israelites and the Philistines. In a state of tension during which both forces are posted for battle, Jonathon, one of Saul's sons, goes out scouting the Philistine posts. He comes upon a guarded pass through two towering crags. It would ordinarily be a good place to avoid, being a strategic spot on the Philistia occupied road.

He tells his armor bearer that they are going to approach the pass, however, affirming,

"The Lord is on our side. Nothing can stop him. He can bring us safely through, whether we are few or many." (1Sam. 14.6)

Having thus dedicated the upcoming encounter to the Lord, Jonathon then, inspired in the moment, lays out the manner of reading the Lord's will in the encounter. Jonathon says to his squire,

> "Behold! We will cross over and let them see us. If they say, 'Stay where you are till we come to you!' then we will stay where we are and not go up and fight them. But if they say, 'Come up to us!' we will go up. This will be the sign that the Lord has put them into our power." (1 Sam. 14.8-10)

Of Things Divinatory

Though it is an absolutely essential component of the power of divination, it is not enough to be able to read the signs. You have got to *act* on them, too. And *believing* with a belief that is *knowing* gives you the power to followup into accomplishment.

"This Will Be The Sign..." Thus Jonathon establishes the divination. He dedicates events as God's answer to a question, even using the phrase, "This will be the sign..."

This is an important component of divination. "What does or *will* the sign mean when it occurs? How will I know what it is saying?" Jonathon provides for both opportunities.

As Jonathon utters the dedication it manifests. They show themselves and the Philistine soldiers call to them to come up. Jonathon at that instant *knows* "the Lord has given them into the hand of Israel" (1 Sam. 14.12).

This is the first engagement of this campaign. Jonathon and his armorbearer slaughter about twenty men. This gives the Israelites the advantage of forward momentum in the campaign that has now burst alive. This swift setback throws panic among all the Philistines and conquers their ability to be effective soldiers.

The Magical Powers Of Faith. All this is accomplished because *Jonathon* enters into this engagement with the confidence to accomplish it by relying on the behest of the Lord. He believes completely God can accomplish what God wants to accomplish, no matter what the odds or disadvantages may be. So he's therefore naturally willing to move forward, his welfare and very life on the line.

It works! Sure in the reply, we assume the magic mantle of power and protection, and express the energy to accomplish what God would have us do. It is up to us to do the thing wholeheartedly, even "risking" our welfare if it is called for. We can't escape risk anyway. Jonathon, as a soldier, will fight battles, after all. In the same way, we will continue to encounter the challenges of life.

The difference lies in whether we are in attunement with God or not. Jonathon evinces his attunement in the magical domain in the very asking to know his answer in the soldiers' reply.

God answers when we ask for a sign, and he will even answer according to how we ask the events to witness.

Do it like Jonathon. Jonathon is about his Father's business, doing the job of the Cosmic, as such. Even in the act he remembers God, knowing nothing can outdo God, not numbers, not positions, not advantages. When he asks for guidance by divination, accordingly, he *acts* on the answer he receives. *Only ask, believing.*

"Jonathon, What Have You Done?!"

Jonathon. Saul is wearied and cannot see that victory comes battle by battle. He loses a skirmish and thinks it's the war. Now at the point of abusing his royal power, he lays an oath on the people not to eat anything until he is avenged on his enemies. Jonathon, out killing Philistines – the *only* one out killing Philistines – does not hear the ban and the curse. He then joins up with them.

And the warring continues. When they enter a forest with golden sweet honey dripping from the trees, Jonathon tastes some of it and is immediately refreshed, his eyes and his disposition perking brightly. But the fatigued Israelites around him will not touch a taste to their lips. They tell Jonathon he has done the cursed deed. *Uh oh.*

Late in that day Saul is trying to decide whether or not to mount a night offensive against the Philistines, so he "inquires of the Lord" (1Sam. 14.37). As has been the tradition for hundreds of years, from the time of Moses when God gives humanity the lottery to discern his will, an Israelite commander is consulting the lots for battle. But he receives no answer.

Saul recognizes there is a problem... No answer *is* an answer. But not a good answer.

He calls the warriors to council and rages, "Where is the fault?!! That man shall *die*!" All the men look down and are silent. So he consults the lots to discover where the fault lies. He separates the royal house from all the Israelites. Then he invokes the Lord and says,

"If this guilt lie in me or in my son Jonathon, O Lord, let the lot be Urim;
if it lie in thy people Israel, let it be Thummim." (1Sam. 14.41)

The lot pulled from the wizard's hat is Urim. The people are cleared. Jonathon and Saul are taken.

Stunned, Saul shivers, then looks at the priest and says in a lowered tone:

"This time cast between me and my son, Jonathon." (1Sam. 14.42)

And Jonathon is taken.

Saul turns to Jonathon and says,

"Son, tell me, what have you done?" (1Sam. 14.43)

Jonathon admits to the crime, also stating it was but a minor infraction. "Also, I didn't know about your prohibition, I was out killing Philistines when you pronounced it!" But he submits to the penalty of death. And Saul, in his royal see, confirms it:

"You shall surely die, Jonathon." (1Sam. 14.44)

But the people are not so bad off as Saul. They will not hear of it. "Kill the only champion we have?" They ransom his life and he lives. We are observers as the house crumbles from within.

Of Psychic Verities

It is not our purpose on this tour to thoroughly investigate and teach exactly how the different instruments of divination work. Rather, we are here to recognize the indisputable word in the Bible that they *do* work, that the *process* of divination reveals the word of the Universal. Nevertheless, we can't help noting a few things.

Surely we don't see the whole picture in this divination episode with Jonathon. But nowhere else do we see the whole picture, either. Everywhere we pick up some part or awareness that combines in synergistic fusing with others to create the picture we see. As such, the picture is always partial, always evolving, always suggesting.

"If It Stands On End We're In Trouble!" The lots here are identified as separate and distinct stones. Thus, the process of divination can select one or the other, and these stones indicate God's will according to the way they have been dedicated. Essentially, dual application of the stones is no more complex than flipping a coin: "Heads, we'll go out to eat; tails, we'll eat in," or "Urim, it's out; Thummim it's in." Or, "If Urim comes up, the fault's in us. If it's Thummim, the fault's in them."

But there is more to it than that. It's as if we were saying, "Heads, we'll go out to eat; tails, we'll eat in; and if it stands on end, we're in trouble." In Saul's first divination, about whether he should attack or not, this third option is figuratively the reply he receives. He is not told to attack, he is not told to refrain from attacking. He knows there is trouble.

This indicates that the lots also have different faces, like dice, or at the minimum, a frontside and a backside. Thus, even when a stone comes up, different sides or combinations can indicate different things.

Through A Progressive Series Of Answers. We also see that the final answer to a question may come at the end of a string of different casts or selections. Thus we see Saul, working in accord with the way the Urim and the Thummim work, receiving his answer through a progressive series of answers that finally indicates the fault is in his son. We've seen this process in action before, as it is the progressive refinement of God's choice of a king that finally announces it is Saul himself.

Evolution In The Divine Realm. Because of what you see here, some people have criticized the Urim and the Thummim as being too simplistic. They say the divinations of Joshua, Saul, and David are too simple. But it's not about simplicity, it's a question of whether the reputed replies really do or do not originate from the

Spiritual realm. These same skeptics, by the way, call the dreams of Joseph and Pharaoh simple.

Yet everywhere in the universe we recognize an economy of effort. After all, it is but the wind that scatters seed. It is the water, falling in the same kind of rain it has always fallen in, that nurtures the seed to fruit. In infinite variations the process is repeated time after time, year after year, generation after generation like clockwork. We understand it easily. Surely this is too simple.

And there is another thing. Just as a Darwin perceived connections that were there all along, but overlooked by the mass of humanity, sensitives and psychic scientists see the tracks of evolution revealed in these early passages of the psychic arts.

From the dawn of time, increasing complexification has been the rule of evolution. The history of humanity affirms this. Humanity and its extensions have grown more complex with the upward spiral of the ages. Methodologies complexify over time. Our *relationship* with the realm of Divinity is surely an extension of our individual, group, and collective consciousnesses. Look in the annals of archeology. All peoples express and develop this relationship in their own unique ways. We have developed.

In this light, divination is presented in the Bible as a *type*, as something that reveals and affirms a process. One example that metaphorically illustrates this process of the co-evolution of the extensions of humanity with humanity is humankind's manner of locomotion. In the beginning we were forced to move on foot. Then we discovered – not invented – the wheel. Today we pilot starcraft from planet to planet and beyond. Yet the earlier modes of transportation have not been eliminated in the process of evolution. We usually make the decision based upon our need. Are you going to take a bus to get upstairs? Sometimes we still walk.

The tribal peoples of Biblical times were simpler, and they had less leisure and less ability to comprehend the complexity that is now natural to us, citizens of an advanced society.

Still, in today's society, the ways of the Urim and the Thummim are sufficient for many applications. It is surely exact enough for much insight. While coin-tossing is seldom a dedicated event, but is usually left in the chance realm, how many times in your life have you seen the situation in personal affairs, sports, business, and government when a simple coin toss is used to decide an issue?

A King And His Rune

David. Abiathar. As you might expect, the Philistine influence is a major facet of David's life, too, since he rises to power in Saul's reign. Their power and influence overlap. We see in the story of David's rise the story of the rise of a charismatic leader and a successful political faction. He's kind of a Robin Hood – enemy to the throne, champion to the people.

All his days David relies on divination to hear the Lord's word. In fact it is interesting, having the perspective of David's entire life before us, to recognize just where his obviously Spirit-inspired individual strengths and reliances lie. David is very good at praising, praying, loving, and being inspired by God. But God seldom talks back to him directly. David is not a bonafide channeler in the traditional sense of being a trance-channeler who opens up and allows the Spirit to speak through him or her. David, a musician and a poet, channels the Spirit through his art: his lyre and his lyrics.

But when it comes time to *hear* the Lord, rather than talk to or about the Lord, David seeks a psychic. We drop in on some of these seers at various points throughout this book, seers such as Ahimelech, Abiathar, Nathan, and Gad.

And in this exclusive David jaunt we're embarking on right now, you'll enjoy a number of novel and exciting things, ideas that few people ever grasp – ever even have the chance to see – being already programmed to blind allegiances.

The reliance that David, Israel's perfected man, places on psychics and their divining tools speaks in strong accents to us. For instance, we see David, who has consistently relied on psychics, suddenly finding himself with restricted access to them. As a serious outlaw, the police, the dick force, the army, and the national guard are all out looking for him. Most of the time he stays hidden far away. When he does venture a reading, he risks his life – and, the lives of hundreds of others. In spite of all events, Spirit makes sure David has a way to divine with the Infinite.

We also receive a good accounting of the way David asks his questions. This is not accidental. We are receiving instructions for our own benefit and guidance. Pay attention.

The stories clearly say that a reliance on psychics is a good and favored thing. Just the same, in the story of Saul the Bible shows us how disrespect toward psychics is an evil that recoils back on your own head.

There is a universal field of consciousness that can be connected with. David divines, asking questions of the yet unborn linear future, asking questions of which he can have no objective knowledge. These answers from the sanctified psychic realm are not imaginations or things to "consider" with David. They are palpably real psychic verities. He *believes* in the answers he receives. He executes the directions he receives with regal accomplishment.

We see in the story of David's "unsought" anointing to the kingship that when you are in sync with Spirit, Spirit will find you out. The Spirit will bring to you ongoing opportunities for your progressive benefit and direction. And why not? Your progress is the progress of the Spirit.

And there is so much more for you to marvel over!

It's A Bad Time To Be A Psychic

By this time Saul has acknowledged David as his mortal enemy. He now has legions out hunting him down. One day he receives whispered intelligence of David moving through the vicinity.

He turns to his troops and followers, giving them his speech of the promise of wealth, assuring them that David cannot give it to them. Then he roars, "Why are you then betraying me? You knew about David, and have kept it hidden from me."

Doeg the Edomite speaks up and tells Saul what he's learned about David. He says he's seen David going in to get psychic readings and metaphysical supplies from one of the psychics at the compound, Ahimelech.

Saul then summons all the priests of the compound, and they come running.

Saul calls Ahimelech to the carpet, and charges him,

> "Why have you conspired against me, you and David, in that you have given him bread and a sword, and have inquired of God for him, so that he has risen against me, to lie in wait, as at this day?" (1Sam. 22.13)

Ahimelech's defense, spoken truly, is twofold. He first attests that, contrary to Saul's opinions, David, the king's son-in-law, is his most faithful servant. Second, he tells Saul that this is not some new thing he's done just to help David against Saul, saying,

> "Is today the first time that I have inquired of God for him? No!" (1Sam. 22.15)

It takes no deliberation on Saul's part. Hard to believe the justice system could so pervert the word and the facts to serve its own interests, isn't it? He hurls the execution order, commanding the throne guards at that moment,

> "Turn and kill all the priests and psychics. Kill *all* of them! They knew what was going on; they are conspirators!" (1Sam. 22.17)

But the guards, conditioned to respect the psychic school, are powerless to move against the representatives of God.

So then Saul turns to the curring Doeg and says,

> "*You* turn and fall upon the priests." (1Sam. 22.18)

Fawning for political favor, "Doeg kills eighty-five who wore the linen ephod that day." Then he goes with a police team to the compound and kills every living being there, man, woman, child, infant, ox, ass, and sheep. Ah, the governmental answer.

The Warrior And The Wizard

But it seems there is a survivor. One of Ahimelech's sons, Abiathar, escapes, and runs to the only safe place there is, straight to the camp of the "most wanted." Saul bands them together. *Now the warrior has a wizard in his house!*

When Abiathar flees, he takes the magical lots with him. As the sole remaining incarnation of the Keepers Of The Lots, he's the only one who can make them work. Nevertheless, invoking its powers of taxation, the government declares the lots they covet stolen goods.

If they are stolen, still they divine aright.

With Abiathar in camp, David relies distinctly on his guidance.

Word comes to David that the Philistines are fighting against Keilah, and are taking the harvested grain. David jumps up. He and his outlaw band, pledged as the Arthurian knights to David, make preparations to right this wrong. But, there are some cautious voices in the mix. Since they will be exposing themselves to government spies, agents, and informants, they will be risking their own well-being when they go to do it. David puts Abiathar to work. He asks him for a reading.

Abiathar casts the hot lots and they come up saying that he should attack the Philistines and save Keilah. David happily announces the divination's reply. But some of those same cautious voices are insistent. They speak the debilitating language of doubt.

So Abiathar throws the Urim and the Thummim again. Again, the Lord speaks through the way they fall:

"Yes, David, go to Keilah; I will give the Philistines into your hand." (1Sam. 23.4)

This time the divination says, instead of simply you shall be victorious, "*I,* even *God myself, I* will do the fighting. *I* will defeat them. *I* will put them into your hands."

Sure enough, when David and his band of merry murderers go to Keilah they turn the tables on the Philistines, capturing all their supplies and equipment, slaughtering all but a few escapees, strategically enough to take back the evil report of utter defeat to Philistia. David enters the city amidst high celebration, and quickly moves to re-establish order.

The wizard comes through for the warrior.

Insider Information

The fear of the cautious voices comes true. Report of the marauders' escapades reaches Saul. Saul rejoices, because he now even has David trapped inside a walled city. Saul sees David as already imprisoned, but awaiting the executioner's sword. David saves the city from the enemy, the Philistines, and now Saul, in the pursuit of his personal enemy, moves to destroy the city, his own city as king, to rout out and kill the man, David.

This weighs heavily on David. He calls Abiathar to counsel in his tent, and has him throw the lots. He wants to know if indeed Saul is coming to Keilah.

Abiathar reads the Urim and the Thummim he's cast on the rug lying between him and David, looks up, and says,

"Yes, he will come down." (1Sam. 23.11)

Now David needs some more information for his strategizing. Remember... Saul is the "sanctioned" and sanctioning government. David, though he's just done the men of Keilah a good deed, is the outlaw. David will only help them, Saul, being the government, if they resist, will crush them.

David asks God,

"Will the men of Keilah surrender me and my men into the hand of Saul?" (1Sam. 23.12)

And the psychic throws in the runes a second time, looks at them, looks up, and says,

"Yes, they will surrender you." (1Sam. 23.12)

Armed with this psychically gathered insider information, David and his men quickly quit the town. When Saul hears David has gone, he quits the expedition.

Of Psychic Verities

How about a little de-deconstruction? We see in these passages at least two violations of generally accepted psychical principles. One of these is that David divines a second time, immediately, on the same question. The other one is that a divination does *not* come true.

Divining A Second Time. A second divination, asking exactly the same question, is generally discouraged. It evinces doubt and disbelief. Skeptics don't get the paranormal rewards of God. They self-position themselves as the profane, unbelieving, unseeing. Nothing can help them, because their own consciousness blocks any good they might receive from divination, channeling, and esp generally. The lay of the cards a second time, even revealing identically the same answer, benefits them no more than the first reading.

This is not to be confused with God revealing his wisdom progressively through a series of divinations. That is the way the lots work. Subsequent divinations develop the initial reply. The distinction is that you are making a second divination because you need additional information, not because you are filled with doubt. Thus, we see David in the second episode asking the rune stones if Saul will come to Keilah seeking his life. When they answer affirmatively, okay, he has that answer. But that situation begets another question: will the citizens stand behind him or will they turncoat on the hero outlaw? Refinement is a different issue, asking the same question is redundant.

Yet in the first divination episode at this psychicsite we see David approach the Lord through Abiathar and re-ask identically the same question. What gives?

There is a noteworthy distinction here. David does not ask again because of *his* doubt. He asks because some of the men with him are fearful; they express doubt. So the reality is that, though the words of the question are the same the second time, we have a different divination. David undertakes this second divination *not to discover the Lord's will.* David already knows what God's will is. What he does in this second divination is part of the scheme to accomplish that design. His repeat visit to the tent of cards is *to publically display the Lord's will* and instructions. He's suckering them in. And it works; aware that Spirit speaks through the cards, the men rally to the cause.

But Saul Doesn't Come Up. The diviner tells David that Saul will come to Keilah, and that the citizens of the walled city will surrender David to him. David slips out of town when he gets this intelligence. Losing his motive, Saul cancels the Keilah campaign. So what happens here? Do the lots divine aright or not?

Obviously, things do not occur as God has indicated. Saul does not come to Keilah; the frightened citizens do not give David up.

The key to this conundrum is openly hidden in the purpose for which David shakes the bones. David does not approach the divination with a question of fate, but seeking immediate psychic counsel about what to do next. Can the Lord be wrong? No. Then why doesn't Saul come to Keilah and capture David, as the lots say he will. Because everything is interdependent on everything else. Something in the mix changes, so the outworking likewise changes. David departs from Keilah; Saul cancels his campaign. David is not captured and taken into custody. Once in police custody, just like with a J. Harvey Oswald, it would be a simple thing to silence the threat he poses forever, even in full public view, with no trial and no reprisals.

God, like the government, spreads misinformation and lies when he thinks it will accomplish an adjudged higher good.

This reading simultaneously points the light on another of the truths of divination. In this regard we assume that *had* David stayed, Saul *would* have come to Keilah, and David would indeed have been turned over to him. The fruit of the psychic arts do not always speak of the inexorable wheels of fate. They reveal a possible, probable future, one that we may, catalyzed by the horror foreseen, differently direct. This is the purpose for which David consults the mystery-speaking stones this day.

Sir David Rescues A Town And, Most Of All, Two Dazzling Ladies

Sir David and the brigand knights gathered around him enjoy a string of wild adventures. One of their more outrageous exploits involves their subterfuge conversion to the Philistine cause. Once the only safe place for the mystic Abiathar was the enemy camp of David; now, the only safe place for the enemy camp of David is in enemy land. David and all who are with him feign conversion to Philistia. Thus, in the palace and in the company of the vital enemy of Israel, David takes his ease. He performs for the new crown admirably well, biding his time.

David is clever, but he is eventually forced into a potential battle situation against the homeland. He does not know what he's going to do, but he has to play along to maintain the charade. David marches against Saul in battle, the very battle foretold by Samuel brought back from the land of spooks and goblins.

At the last minute, before the engagement begins, David and his cowboy team of commandos are sent home. The Lords of the Philistines fear that, though certainly functioning as a loyal subject and captain over the recent years in Philistia, David could turn to his blood in the battle.

Come to find out, while David and his brigand band were out, tribes from Amalek came and raided their unguarded camp. They took the booty of cash and collectibles, the booty of their wives and marriageable daughters, and their children, leaving nothing but smouldering tent poles. Even the two prettiest wives David brought with him into Philistia, Ahinoam and Abigail, are amongst the plunder.

This is too much! Some of the men openly call for rebellion. They start talk of stoning David. The cost of following David is just too great.

And David, now even an outlaw amongst his outlaws, turns to divination for guidance and strength. David calls for the ephod; Abiathar hastens:

"Shall I pursue after this band?"

And God says,

"Pursue."

And David wants to know,

"Will I overtake them?"

And God reassures him,

"You *will* overtake them *and* you *will* rescue your families and your goods." (1Sam. 30.8)

You can call this nothing but divination. God speaks in the "random" fall of the stones. Guided by God, high on hatred, roaring with revenge, the victory is consummate. David and his noble knights perform as God answers. And – *Oh women! closer to his heart than anything!* – he *personally* rescues at the red point of his sword the two beautiful ladies, his wives. They kill Amalekites from twilight one day straight through until twilight *the following day*. Out of a whole city of men, women, and children, only a small disarray of young men escape David's sword. Though they will never restore the race, they will tell the story. The others are dispatched on the spot. While the Amalekites didn't kill anyone, the Israelites kill *everyone!* Total and complete! The people are no more. And the victorious David and his army reclaim everything the Amalekites had taken and, as further rewards, everything – the money, jewelry, silverware, cattle, and other valuable goods – the Amalekites had ever owned.

Respect for David flowers afresh amongst his jubilant enriched men.

The Way Is Cleared

Destiny clicks another thunderous notch... All obstacles to the throne are cleared. A wearied runner, witness to the battle between Philistia and Saul, brings the news. The battle has gone against the Hebrews, the man says:

"The people have fled from the battle, and many of the people also have fallen and are dead; and *Saul and his son Jonathon are also dead.*" (2Sam. 1.4)

What Samuel has seen comes to pass.

David is amazed. But this man has brought the crown from Saul's head and the armlet from his arm to David, whom he addresses in hope of favor, "My Lord." David and his brigand band wail and fast and make loud grieving until evening. Then David calls one of his officers over and sends him to finish the vile messenger in their midst.

The crown jewels, emblem and spirit of royal power, are in David's hands now. Is there another leader such as him in all of Israel? What is he to do?

With the threat of Saul gone, David inquires of Lord as to whether he should now re-enter Judah. He receives the affirmative word, "Yes."

"That's settled," he tells Abiathar, "now shake them again. I need to know what city I should go to."

And the lots say, "Hebron."

With the will and the fortune of the Lord, revealed in divination, he follows up on this instruction.

And the inhabitants there anoint him king of Judah. And he takes the crown on his head and the armlet on his arm. Hmm... That doesn't take long. Like the widow who grieves a day and marries at the end of the week.

Dual Divinations

The Philistines find Saul's body and rejoice. But it's not going to get any better for the victors, conquerors of the nation of Israel, benefactors of David. David is king in Israel now. David, king now in his homeland, shows his true colors.

Another opportunity presents itself, so David inquires of the Lord. He calls for the Urim and the Thummim and asks,

"Shall I go up against the Philistines?"

And the lots say *no*. So David, in the lotting process of refinement, asks again,

"Should I go around to their rear?"

And the lots say *yes*.

"Should I march right in, or should I amass my forces and then, at a moment swoop upon them?"

And the lots say *wait for a sign*. With this the lots themself have set up further divination to be accomplished by a natural sign. And Abiathar receives the message from God: the sure sign of attack and victory is when the winds pick up and stir noisily the tops of the balsam trees.

A sound of nature shall take on the character, even *becoming* as it is spoken in the psychic revelation, the thing that is proposed. In this case, to indicate it is time to *march*, David will hear *marching* in the trees.

"When you hear the sound of marching in the tops of the balsam trees, then bestir yourself; for then the Lord has gone out before you to smite the army of the Philistines." (2Sam. 5.24)

God does. David does. Together they chase the Philistines mightily from Geba to Gezer.

How paranormal!

Of Psychic Verities

David, model of humanity, relies on the Spirit to speak through divination, and in that same heart, he follows up on the truths revealed to him therein. Oh, but we have so much to learn from him!

The Sign Of The Trees. The Sign Of The Trees is the story of two divinations combined in one event. Here we have both the divination of inquiry by a dedicated device, lots, and the divination of an outward sign, marching.

This story belies the facades of separateness. Commonly the two manifestations of the art are separately practiced. Nevertheless, because of the actuality of the holocosmic distributed nonlocal Spirit, the two are the same psychic aspect of the greater art of esp. Both reveal Spirit's answer or direction to the querent.

However, even while maintaining to the unity of the two types of divination, we still can hold to their separateness. David has a pronounced predisposition toward divination by lots. We've seen his long association with them. And even in this event the answers of strategy and positioning come from the way the stones fall. The trigger, the sign of the trees, comes as a *field* event. It is better to be maximally focused, alert, and present in the battle to come. *Now* is the moment for consultation. *Then* is the moment for execution. *Now* is the time of the lots; the now moment *then* will be revealed in an outward environmental sign.

A Living Testament. David's life offers a living testament to grace in a Godly man of passion, action, love, and fidelity. David relies extensively on divination. We've dropped in on just a few of these psychicspace incidents, noting at the same time the ongoing use David makes of this fascinating art.

What is it David embodies that we might use in our own quests to become more spiritual and psychic? David approaches divination in a prayerful state, mindful that he is linking with the Power of the Universe. David approaches God with the childlike certainty that God does reveal his will through divination. This is the very specific purpose David approaches the lots with.

David's level of trust in the effectiveness of divination is so great that he acts promptly and decisively on the indications he receives. And he does it consistently. This confidence is always bolstered by the fact that God simply *does* speak through the stones... He always has before. It's not even a thing David questions.

And David *acts*!

We spiritual observers – heirs of this story ages old meant specifically for us – see that indeed God speaks through divination. We see it confirmed in the events of David's life. David rises to the throne of all Israel; Israel receives the charmed king it deserves; and David is innocent of any wrongdoing. At step after step in his ascent David first seeks the answer in the stones and then embodies those designs in action. The outcomes always come as God affirms they will.

Arrows And Entrails

In this doubly interesting episode God channels through *Ezekiel*, prophesying even another psychic event, divinations of the *King of Babylon*. Evil is in store for Israel. Ezekiel sees the future in the present, telling the people:

"For the king of Babylon stands at the parting of the way, at the head of the two ways, to use divination; he shakes the arrows, he prays to God, he looks at the liver." (Ezek. 21.21)

Speaking of communication! Ezekiel here tell us that Nebuchadnezzar *will* divine, *what instruments* of divination he'll use, and even what *question* the royal man will ask and what answer he will receive.

Nebuchadnezzar stands connected with the powers of the Universe and asks, "Who shall I invade? Two rebel colonies – Rabbah of the Ammonites or Jerusalem of the Jews?" God replies:

"Into his right hand comes the lot for Jerusalem, to open the mouth with a cry, to lift up the voice with shouting, to set battering rams against the gates, to cast up mounds, to build siege towers." (Ezek. 21.22)

What Ezekiel sees is accomplished.

Of Psychic Interest

As brief as this passage is, it shares some mighty riches of insight on divination. It features different divinatory instruments than the Hebrews use, affirming, simultaneously, their identicalness.

Divination That The Hebrews Don't Do. As an item of interest we see in this psychicstop two methods of divination that the Hebrews never use. Those are pulling arrows from a quiver and inspecting the entrails of animals offered in sacrifice. The process and function of their divinations, of course, are identical. Being invoked, God replies in the nonrandom arrangement of material reality, be it the sign conveyed through an outer life event, the fall of stones, the pull of the differently marked arrows, or the messages coded in the organs of a sacrificial victim.

Divination Is Divination Is Divination. We also see these counterparts of David and the Israelites phrasing their questions in the same way, which, as we've seen, is a feature of specific divining practices. The question is phrased as a closed end, either/or question: "Should I destroy Jerusalem or Rabbah?" God can answer this simple question quite easily. Judging from the passage it looks like there may have been two arrows, similar to the two stones of Urim and Thummim. The selection process is made by Nebuchadnezzar by some method of "chance." Thus the SupbraConscious speaks, and the one that is taken in the right hand is the one for positive forward motion. In this manner God communicates with and guides the people who can now understand him:

"Into his right hand comes the lot for Jerusalem..." (Ezek. 21.22)

Too bad the people don't listen to Ezekiel. They denounce him as a mad mystic. Eccentric and bizarre. They do not do anything to prepare for the upcoming evil. They don't think it can happen to them. After all, they do have alliances.

Too bad for them Nebuchadnezzar doesn't second-guess God. Like David before him, Nebuchadnezzar lets God decide the issues; it is to him but to follow directions. Which he does. He destroys Jerusalem. Thus begins the fruitful period of the Babylonian captivity.

To Catch A Crook

Jonah is a fugitive, running to Tarshish on a Mediterranean ship. He's not a political crook, but a spiritual slider. The inner voice of God is urging him to launch one of the negative tirades, accusations, and threats that so many of the Jewish psychic-prophets are famous for.

But the ship meets an evil power. The seas surge in such a tempest that hardcast sailors are crying like babies in fear of their lives. And in fear of their lives, they pray. And they divine to find the cause of this wrath. Jonah is fingered:

> "Come and let us cast lots," the sailors affirm, "to find out who is to blame for this bad luck." So they cast lots and the lot falls upon Jonah. (Jon. 1.7)

Only at that point does Jonah confess why this massive power of the sea is raging against them. Even so, the sailors do not want to throw him overboard. They fight amore the swelling tempest, but finally they give up. It's too big for them. They cry:

> "We beseech thee, O Lord, let us not perish for this man's life, and lay not on us innocent blood; for thou, O Lord, hast done as it pleased thee." (Jon. 1.14)

They make Jonah hurriedly walk the gangplank. Poor guy. When he hits the water the winds and the seas encalm. The men offer thanks and swear vows to the powerful God of Jonah.

We relish the story of Jonah as the whale's delight in another place. Our purpose now holds to the ways of divination manifest in the story.

Anyone Can Do It!

Once again the Bible displays the lots working for our insight – that is, our *inner sight.* This divination is performed by a multicultural group of heathen persons with a variety of different primary Gods. Certainly these sailors are *ordinary* people; they are not a priested elite. You know how down to earth sailors are, of any clime of any time.

In a way, the men are never really important to God, either. They are just supporting characters, forming the setting across which God chases Jonah, the man with awakening psychic powers, charged to deliver the message of God. But the lots divine rightly for them, don't they?

This certain working of God through the lots openly displays another important piece of divination and psi. *Why do so few see it?* The reason the lots work is that God, by the electromagnetic energy of being, directs both the operator/diviner and the lots. The "chosen people," the people who write this history we study in the

Bible, are not the exclusive heirs to this ability. Any people who invoke God, even under the unique particular Godforms of their own times and locales, may establish a connection. The One Spirit Universal and its power breathes through the human heart turned to it in sincerity, not through some body of codified encrusted dogma.

Jesus On Divination

You sometimes hear nonstudied, biased Christians claim that divination is "of the devil," based on the fact that nowhere in the Bible does *Jesus* speak of it. It is true we find no reference to divination in the Biblically recorded statements of Jesus. It does not take much discernment to recognize that when Jesus makes no reference at all to divination, however, he makes no reference either good *or* bad.

So, by the same logic, Jesus supports divination. True? If you can say Jesus is against it because of the absence of referrals to it, isn't it just as valid to say that Jesus is for it because he never speaks of it?

More to the point, he never speaks evilly about it. Surely, he knows how to cast the evil tongue, as he does against attorneys and church hypocrites. Had he wanted to, he had ample opportunity.

You deserve so much more.

We are intelligent sensitive readers. We are, as God clearly intends we be – since he puts his knowledge and Spirit in a book to guide us – *contextual* readers.

If Jesus never speaks against divination, it is simply because, being steeped in Biblical ethos, he takes it for granted.

Plus, we have more evidence in the acts of the apostles.

To Pick An Apostle

Acts of the Apostles, more commonly shortened to *Acts*, tells the story of the early days of the new Christian cult after Jesus is gone. One other of their band also dies during those tumultuous final days of Jesus, Judas. The remaining apostles feel the need to select a replacement for Judas.

So that's what they do. They put forward two companions who have associated with them since the beginning of Jesus' ministry, Justus and Matthias. But, what's the best way to pick an apostle? *Let God Do It!* So they pray, dedicating the lots to reveal God's voice and God's will in this decisive decision:

> "Lord, you know the hearts of all men. Show us which one of these two you have chosen to take the place in this ministry and apostleship from which Judas turned aside.."

And they cast lots for them, and the lot falls on Matthias; and he is enrolled with the eleven apostles. (Acts 1.24-26)

What fate dangles before Justus it gives to Matthias.

Heirs to a long, venerable, and proven tradition of divination, the apostles cast lots to divine God's will. They bring themselves, the serious question of their hearts, the Spirit of God, and the lots into alignment by a true invocation. Then, as God speaks, the apostles act. They do not second guess his decisions. And even

Peter, the very first pope, is involved in this instance of divination, recorded for our enlightenment these ages later.

Of Psychic Verities
Watch, and you learn many amazing things.

Nothing But Divination. Some of the hardline defenders, people tripping over evidence they refuse to acknowledge, are frankly nonplussed when they come to this passage. They make the typical, standard, general, dogmatized inane apologies, excuses, and convoluted explanations... But how can you call this anything but divination? Can you claim this choice, Matthias, as eons of Christian adherents hold, is any other than the very choice of God?

They Would Have Known. The apostles live, breath, sleep, eat, and serve the beloved master with intimate devotion. *What colossal conceit could assume the apostles wouldn't understand Jesus' feeling toward divination?*
The apostles would have known if Jesus was opposed to divination. They, as followers more in the rush of Jesus than ever before, would never have used divination to determine the course of action on such a momentous concern if Jesus were opposed to it. No.

Wait, Watch, And Listen

We've seen many interesting things on this leg of our psychicspace tour. Divination is prayer with a visible response. The Bible supports, blesses, and encourages divination:
"Ask, and you receive." (Mt. 7.7)
Perhaps Jesus has divination in mind when he utters these portentous words. Funny thing is most people don't believe him (though they profess to worship him and his words). We've seen that the fall of stones, the draw of straws, or the action of a friend or of a foe can be a sign from God. It is the psychic charge you give to the instrument or event that determines how it will unfold.

The great leaders of the Biblical heritage practice divination. Abraham, first man of the new race, finds a wife for his son Isaac with it. Moses rules with it. Joshua and David conquer with it. Even Philistines discover the will of God with yoked cows, and conquering Nebuchadnezzar, fulfilling the will of God, with arrows drawn from a quiver. The apostles, final men in the saga gathered as the current Bible, choose successors with it.

Divination is alive and well.

Now, having become psychic experts after a fashion, we see that it goes even further than God offering us a means and inviting us to use it. We see that God establishes divination as an essential component of the spiritual life, even commanding it, as with Moses and Joshua, as one of the ways we are to understand his will in our lives.

So the next consideration is yours. What are *you* doing about what you're learning? Ask for a sign. Like David or Abiathar, place your intentions and your efforts according to your interests, occupations, and purposes, and ask for the direction of the Lord. Communing with the Great Spiritual Divine in divination focuses everything into the present moment of Eternity. In that magic space Eternity responds to you. Are you willing to pray, ask, release, pay attention, receive, read, and, most importantly, *act?*

Chapter 5

PK, Magic, Enchantment

————————•••••————————

Allmagic is psychic activity. Psychokinesis, termed *PK*, is the generation of an effect on "outside" objects by directed mental or spiritual forces. Magic is psychokinesis. It could be enchantment, which is magic, too. We're now on the campus of the *mind over matter* school. Modern government-sponsored research calls this aspect of the paranormal *anomalous perturbation*.

And there are some amazing things about magic...

Beyond Normal Paranormal

Psychic means of the mind/soul. Both esp and PK are that. Most psychic gifts, the esp arts of clairvoyance, intuition, and telepathy, for instance, may simply "see" a future occurrence or condition. These psychic events originate and have their completion in the nonmaterial realm of the heart and soul. They stay in the realm – a very real and substantive place, with prodigious effects – with dreams and visions, thoughts, and words.

PK, like all the arts of ESP, is communicative. But it goes beyond mere communication. And while it is truly a form of channeling, it extends in a different direction than what we normally consider and call *channeling*. It goes beyond words, thoughts, visions, and dreams into a stimulus that visibly affects some item or circumstance in what is commonly considered the objective world. The adept with developed PK abilities commands unseen forces, powers, and entities to his or her bidding. They are directing forces from subtler dimensions to affect dense matter and events. Things like this aren't supposed to happen – aren't supposed to be possible – in the objective world. Like walking on fire or water, or parting waters with the wave of a wand. Like transforming meager foodstuffs into a banquet for a monastery, or eating a meal in a dream and running forty days on metaphysical fuel. Like creating a fortune in a year's time, or manifesting in the moment coin sufficient to the need.

The very essence of magic, however, is that a psychically impelled event occurs on the stageway of the physical realm. Magic is the phenomenal domain of psi that encompasses most specifically both the physical realm as well as the metaphysical. From the metaphysical into the physical – anything which fits within this rubric is magic.

"It Ain't Me, Babe."

Magic is the exercise of *creative will power.* Nevertheless, the magician is in an intermediary position, performing these fantastic deeds, not of his or her own power, but by directing the power of God to a specific purpose. As in all the ways of psi, the channeler of the power likewise experiences the gift and its ethereal power while performing/using the gift. It is not his or her power. Magicians are but individuals who have developed the facility to volitionally access and implement some of psi's higher points. They learn to facilitate the flow of power through them to accomplish unusual, great, and magical events. Simply, as the high adept Jesus says,

> "It's not *me* that does these amazing things, but the *Master Within*." (Jn. 14.10)

"I, as a particularization of the One Spirit, am but a conscious and developed channeler of the Supreme Power."

"Do You Have To Call It Magic?"

Sure, it is not considered polite by some to so bluntly label PK and anomalous perturbation "magic." We've evolved these clinical terms in respect for social niceness and political politeness. But magic, miracle, wizardry, sorcery, PK, anomalous perturbation, call it what you will, it is what it is. Charge it with negative connotations, if you will, it is what it is: the creating or effecting of an event or circumstance by directing one's mental-spiritual intent.

It is magic when an individual volitionally commands the awesome powers of the Universe. It is magic when these powers, acquired by combinations of inclination, training, discipline, and grace, are exercised with intent.

It is not always necessary to be an adept to manifest sporadic or uncontrolled manifestations of this psychic energy, by the way. The poltergeist phenomena is a good and currently well-documented witness to this fact. An adept, however – a tuned, practiced, and powerful magician – is a *conscious* and *intentful* wielder of the powers that create and sustain the phenomenal world. There is a world of difference. The Bible contains action paintings of many of the highest magical adepts of the ancient stage, the best of the best being Moses, Elijah, Elisha, and Jesus.

Magic And Creative Visualization

Magic involves vision, as, by definition, you form an image in your mind, and then project it from your heart, commanding the Cosmic to fulfill it in form. Yet when discussing magical effects, we generally consider two general domains. First there is what we term regular magic. This is the magic we see when Elijah calls down lightening to kill the fifty-one government dorks come to arrest him. The magician creates a specific *immediate* result or manifestation of the metaphysical power.

The other type of magic is *creative visualization*. (We save a deeper exploration of this aspect for another book.) A person or a group deeply tunes into some thought or dream, and over time, the thing visualized and affirmed is brought into objective reality. Creative visualization can be conceptualized as differing from regular magic in that the result manifests over a duration of time. At some point, it is realized fully.

Abraham with the homeland, Moses with the return, Jesus with love as the highest order, Paul seeing all humanity united in Jesus' Spirit – to name a few – are adepts in this arena too. They each in their time embrace, nurture, and act on grand visions of a new humanity.

"Is It ESP Or Is It Magic?

In our tour several times we'll notice major indistinctions in the classifications of the modus operandi of the phenomena at hand. We will visit several points that beg us to grapple with the issue. What else is new? This is the old interpenetration issue again. The big question of the issue concerns whether, since it begins with visualization, we are simply experiencing esp or whether we are in fact manifesting by magic. That is, do we *see* the end event or do we *create* it? We touched on the skirts of this conundrum with Samuel and Saul in the last chapter, "Divination." For instance, when Elisha sees a woman locked in marriage to an elderly man giving birth to a child, is he simply seeing with clairvoyance and experiencing precognition, or is he actually the *causative agent*, the one who causes the event?

As our discussions throughout this coterminous domain of psychicspace reveal, the answer has to do with *intent*. It is magic when Elisha, speaking with a hard clairvoyant appendage, puts a child in her womb.

Start With Something

An insider look at several of the magical performances you are treated to in the Bible illustrates a principle that it is easier to start with something than with nothing when projecting a substance or event. For instance, we see that Elisha fills many jars of oil from the widow's single one, and Jesus feeds the multitudes with the bread and fishes saved for a single man. As metaphysicians affirm, what we bless multiplies.

Likewise illustrating the same principle, we encounter Elijah struggling through seven trials before he manifests "a tiny cloud." Easily, however, from that tiniest substance, the boomers clap, growl, and deliver on their threat.

Faith, A Critical Element

The magician is a master; he knows, *whatever is held in mind manifests after its kind.* This is, after all, how he does it all. First, it takes *knowing* that you can, and, second, operating from *that* state. Psychical congruence manifests as physical event, condition, situation, and substance.

In the story of Peter walking on water, the teacher cites *faith* as the only variable. He walks when he thinks he can, or rather, as long as he does not "think" about it at all, but just *accepts* it. When he starts doubting, he still has faith – but it is turned inside out into a faith that he *cannot* do the phenomenon. Sure enough, in both instances, what he truly *believes* with the quality of unquestioning *knowing,* he creates.

Magic, which we accept in this chapter as the conscious creation of a predetermined effect, requires *faith.* As Jesus says invoking the magic of the Universal to raise Lazarus from the grave,

"God, I know that you hear me always." (Jn. 11.42)

Why does Jesus know this? Directed effort and experience.

Test it, and build your faith.

Suppressing The Ability To See

An attitude of skepticism, intolerance, and antagonism completely eliminates any chance of adeptship and magic. This is not honest inquiry. The skeptical approach, according to natural law, first suppresses the ability to see and to perceive these magical and psychic things, and therefore prohibits the ability to perform these things with intent and grace. Skepticism is the opposite of faith. It is knowing that you *can't.* Alas, as skeptics, we rob ourselves!

To Accomplish A Purpose

Something prompts the magicians highlighted in the Bible to perform their effects. There seems to be a specific need, circumstance, or purpose beyond mere entertainment.

Moses does not go around zapping rocks and opening springs all the time. Only when the children of Israel are desperately thirsty and flagging of their life. He does not command earthquakes all the time, either. Only when he wants to kill the Israelites who question his authority.

Jesus saves the centurion's dying child upon direct request. Without that, all indications are that he is perfectly willing to let the young girl die. He is in fact *doing just that.* Indeed, the world then is much as now. A certain number of the population at any time is ill or ailing. The specific event which triggers him is the centurion's request. He receives a direct request and responds with love in the particular.

The purpose need not be so heavy as to revive life. It can certainly be but to teach and to inspire, as what other purpose can the brief time Peter spends walking on water serve? The whole thing's very paranormal. There is no indication that either he or Jesus ever adopts this as a mode of travel.

Take a seat and strap in for an amazing journey to a realm of fantastic new magical discoveries in psychicspace!

****

"It's Magic!"

A number of accomplished magicians perform their spellbinding magic throughout the years compassed in the Bible's storying. We visit a goodly share of them, from Jacob, the cool, to Jesus, renegade fruit of the Jewish spiritual tradition. Though we only have reservations at a few of the more notable events, there is more. We shan't exhaust ourselves visiting every enchanted site, but we will see enough to grasp the extent of magical eventry in the spiritual tradition.

Though Shalt Be A Fool Who Trieth The Tricky And The Slick

The feat of the spotted cows is surely *Jacob*'s most outrageous performance. It is so big that, with the riches he scoops in from this one exploit, he lives the life of a prosperous independent man all the days of his life.

Again we get a vivid demonstration of the interpenetrating psychic boundaries of psi. We visited the events that lead up to this magical trick in the previous chapter on dreams. Jacob works for the father-in-law of his two best wives, Rachael and Leah. After twenty years he decides he wants to retire and move back to his homeland. Jacob, you recall, was tricked into that service in the first place, and Laban has intentions of tricking him on the way out, too.

Jacob informs Laban of his desire to leave, and names a "fair" wage for the years of his service. Laban agrees to Jacob's request for the,

> "Speckled and spotted sheep, the black lambs, and the spotted and speckled among the goats." (Gen. 30 32)

Thus Jacob's proposal is that he will take only the less desirable and *less likely* breed of Laban's herd next year when he departs.

Laban pronounces the deal good. But he has no intentions of doing the right thing. His actions post the lie to his words:

> That very day Laban removes the he-goats that are striped and spotted, and all the she-goats that are speckled and spotted, every one that has white on it, and every lamb that is black, and puts them in charge of his sons; and he sets a distance of three days' journey between himself and Jacob. And Jacob feeds the rest of Laban's flock. (Gen. 30.35-36)

But Jacob has psi. In enemy territory, with enemy kids in his beds and in the fields of commerce, ever-crafty Jacob does not complain. He has learned how to play with Laban. This is no stage show entertainment. Jacob steals Laban blind right before his very eyes!

We are grateful for the uncharacteristic explicitness of Genesis regarding what happens. Jacob ponders over the obstacles. *How to resolve these obstacles?* that is the question. Jacob's ponderings seep into his subconscious. And the

SupbraConscious - interpenetrating with the subconscious – reveals the answer. Celestial insight visits Jacob in a creative idea couched in a dream. As he later tells his wives,

> "I had a dream, and in the mating season of the flock I lifted up my eyes, and saw in a dream that the he-goats which leaped upon the flock were striped, spotted, and mottled. Then the angel of God said to me in the dream, `Jacob,' and I said, `Here I am!' And he said, `Lift up your eyes and see, all the goats that leap upon the flock are striped, spotted, and mottled; for I have seen all that Laban is doing to you.'" (Gen. 31.10-12)

The angel herein reveals to Jacob the key to manifesting the striped, spotted, and mottled calves. *All the lusty goats are striped, spotted, and mottled.* Knowing the outcome in advance, It is only up to him to ensure that what he sees, occurs. Then, the herd is his. Very magical.

Now, so far as we can tell, Jacob's solution to the "duly noted" phenomenon, cannot manifest in actuality, because the existing herd is not of that nature. Yet the end, seen in the dream, opens Jacob's own ingenuity and creative spirit. Jacob *acts* to implement it according to the psychical revelations.

He takes fresh rods of poplar and almond and plane, and peels white streaks in them, exposing the white of the rods behind the bark. Then he sets the rods in front of the watering troughs, where the herds come to drink. In case you don't know, once they start drinking heavily, watch out! It lowers their inhibitions. Thus, guided through the intuitions of a dream, Jacob orchestrates a situation wherein when the herd is copulating – empowered with the high emotions of love and sex – they are seeing stripes and spots of alternating white and darkness. As with humanity, so with the sheep and goats. What is held in mind manifests after its kind. *Voilà!* the flocks bear striped, spotted, and speckled calves!

In this demonstration of magic accomplished along the principles of similarity God reveals a *mighty* truth of the powers and the consequences of our minds and emotions. *You with ears, hear!*

Within the craft they say, "Magic is how you do it." You can do it bumblingly or you can accomplish it with finesse. Jacob has class. Guess what? He does not impregnate the entire herd with these images and impressions of spottling, speckling, and stripling. *Oh no,* he only puts the striped rods in the water troughs when the "strong of the flock are breeding" (Gen. 30.41). He creates no influence over the feeble, sick, and weakly. Ha! So he breeds the strong and leaves Laban the feeble.

Thus the man grows exceedingly rich through the exercise of magic. It is accomplished as he intends. Within the space of a year the man receives, executes, and reaps his idea. How about you?

Not With A Sword, But With A Wand

Without question, *Moses* is enshrined in the Wizards and Magicians' Hall of Fame as one of the most powerful magicians ever working the face of Earth. The entire victory over Egypt, every single battle and calamity, is accomplished by means of magic. If the books of his works reveal anything they surely teach that we should never engage in war with a competent wizard! *Talk about stupidity!*

Certainly, as a magician, Moses is head and shoulders above every character in the Bible, including Jesus. Just take note of the relative amount of space dedicated to Moses' magic versus anyone else's. But that's not a put down. Jesus' mission manifests on a higher, wider rung in the evolutionary spiral of humanity. Jesus teaches love; Moses uses magic to kill. The changes Jesus seeks to stimulate are mystical transformations. Jesus only heals the body as a guide or facilitator to the soul. He never directly involves himself in the political machinery.

Moses, on the other hand, *is* the political machinery. Moses' life is therefore more visibly oriented to the material domain. Moses *needs* to be more concerned with the physical world. He has a people to extricate, to transport, and to fashion into an independent nation. He does it superbly, accomplishing it with the grandeur, amazement, and power of persuasive magical acts on the grand stage of ancient Egypt and the Sinai. Solely by the forces of his magic he forces the Emperor of Egypt into an unconditional acceptance of his absolute terms. And you wonder why Hitler sought so assiduously for Moses' power? The Jewish people are exposed and could be swiped from the face of the Earth. Other peoples have disappeared entirely. Magic serves Moses' ends. And the Jews are with us yet.

Deception And Misdirection

This book is not meant to be a treatise on magic. Much of what we talk about we simply accept as natural in the domain of magic. We're all humans, we've all been entertained and entranced by magic many times before we progress to the point where we are reading these words. As such, we don't seek to establish or to justify that deception and misdirection are vital components of magical performance. Most say this *is* magic.

First you decide what effect you want to create, then you plan a way to accomplish it. Finally, you *do* it. Few realize just how early these qualities enter the domain of a major magical effect.

For instance, we see after Moses has decided to save the people of his true blood, he needs to persuade cooperation from all parties. Moses' most dramatic effects bear witness to this end. And this deception begins early. In fact Moses receives instruction in dissimilation in the same afflatus in which he receives the intuition to accomplish the mighty deed of the Exodus. The idea and the method manifest to his consciousness in the same gestalt. *The dream contains the answer.*

God tells Moses to return to Egypt, since the people who would hold grudges from his crimes of wilder days are all dead after forty years. Then he is to lie to the political authorities, specifically Pharaoh, saying,

> "The Lord, the God of the Hebrews, has met with us; and now, we pray you, let us go a three days' journey into the wilderness, that we may sacrifice to the Lord our God." (Gen. 3.18)

Thus Moses misleads Pharaoh. He is actually planing the heinous political crimes of rebellion and desertion. The kinds of things politicos kill for.

This has got to go good! *God is the one directing this subterfuge!*

It will be accomplished by magic, God assures Moses.

"I will stretch out my hand and smite Egypt with many marvels and wonders of evil portent... He *will* let you go." (Gen. 3.20)

That's why Moses has the gahunzas to walk into Pharaoh and war with the mighty man face-to-face.

And it gets better! Not only is Moses going to wrest the people from their place in the sun of the Egyptian infrastructure, he's going to foist another huge one on Egypt. He's going to rob them on the way out!

"And I will give you preference in the sight of the Egyptians; and when you go, you shall not go empty, but each woman shall ask of her neighbor, and of her who sojourns in her house, jewelry of silver and of gold, and clothing, and you shall put them on your sons and on your daughters. Thus you shall absolutely despoil the Egyptians!" (Ex. 3.21-22)

Look at this! Even while Moses robs the Egyptians of their wealth and riches, they *want* to give their money to the Hebrews. *This is enchantment!* Moses and God cast a *mighty* spell over the people. Call it how you want, the fact is a fact is a fact. The finesse is extra!

First, A Demand

Moses seeks audience of Pharaoh. He has plans, before he ever leaves Midian, for a long string of evil magic, ending with the death of all the Egyptians' first-born, the cherished of their hearts. So his first approach, even if following the form of diplomatic protocol, is anything but subservient or requesting. It is not the approach a subject makes to his king. Why should Moses be so different?

He issues his command in the name of the tribal God:

"Thus says the Lord, the God of Israel,

'Let my people go, that they may hold a feast to me in the wilderness.'" (Gen. 5.1)

Not only is Pharaoh not impressed by the reference to the God of an ethnic subculture, but the very effrontery with which Moses and Aaron present it provokes him. It turns into a battle of wills. Pharaoh issues the command that, instead of enjoying a couple weeks of leisure, since they have so much spare time, they shall henceforth make bricks with no straw, maintaining their present output. God, for his own purposes, has put it in Pharaoh's heart to harden. Pharaoh too is acting out his assigned role.

Who is superior? Moses has hatched a plan.

Parlor Tricks With A Magic Wand

Moses' first trick is not too spectacular. He doesn't prove anything with it. He should have known better. In artifice by similarity, he throws down his cane and it becomes a snake. This is an early trick every budding magician learns. Pharaoh,
> then summons the wizards and the sorcerers, and they also, the magicians of
> Egypt, do the same thing by their secret arts. (Ex. 7.11)

No big deal.

They are surprised, however, when Aaron's snake eats up theirs. They don't know how to do that one yet.

Perhaps The Words Are Different...

It is interesting to note how the Bible reveals and instructs us on the essential equivalence of *magician, wizard,* and *sorcerer.* In response to Moses' parlor level tricks Pharaoh summons what they in Egypt call *wizards* and *sorcerers.* It is simply a different language. The Bible, so as not to have us confused, thinking these are different things, identifies them as the *magicians* of Egypt.

It does not matter what name you use, at what time or what place you perform it, when you look at and describe the function, the process, and the results, it is all the same: magic is sorcery is wizardry. Through biased perceptual training, many people have themselves been enspelled to believe that when *we* do it, it is a *miracle* – good, wholesome, and of God – but when *they* do it, it is *magic* – evil, the work of dark power. Presto! it is magic all the same.

Turning Water Into Blood

Aware of his flop, even though he pulls off some kind of "save" by having his rod eat the others, Moses performs his next feat the following morning. He again takes his sorcerer's wand, and meets Pharaoh when he goes out for his morning walk along the Nile.

Moses desperately wants to prove his God is mighty. He approaches Pharaoh with taunts and threats:
> "The Lord, the God of the Hebrews, sent me to you, saying, 'Let my
> people go, that they may serve me in the wilderness'; and behold, you
> have not yet obeyed. Therefore, thus says the Lord,
>> 'By this you shall know that I am the Lord, behold, I will strike the
>> water that is in the Nile with the rod that is in my hand, and it shall be
>> turned to blood, and the fish in the Nile shall die, and the Nile shall
>> become foul, and the Egyptians will loathe to drink water from the
>> Nile.'" (Ex. 7.16-18)

And he does. Through his instructions to Aaron, saying some magical words, he passes his magic wand three times over the Nile, strikes it, and it is accomplished. And it's worse even than he announced. Not only is the Nile turned blood red, but all the water throughout the kingdom in every river, pond, and pool in the land, including the drawn water in the pottery jars of the Egyptians' homes and businesses becomes polluted likewise. Moses' magic is indeed mighty. There is no water left fit for human consumption.

But, the Bible says, the Egyptian magicians perform the same trick. Guess we should overlook the fact that, had Moses really transformed *all* the water into blood, there would have been no water remaining for the other tricksters to demonstrate with. Ah well! He fails to impress Pharaoh with this sleight, too.

Frogs, Frogs, Everywhere!

Seven days pass, and Pharaoh pays little mind to the large demands of Moses. Like Martin Luther King, Jr before Alabama, he's still just a political irritant. So Moses, inspired by God of course, decides his next performance shall be to gross the people out with an invasion of frogs. He seeks audience with Pharaoh again, and to prove his might, forecasts that he will be the one responsible for the invasion of the frogs:

> "I will plague all your country with frogs. Behold, the Nile shall swarm with frogs which shall come up into your houses, and into your bedchambers and on your beds, and into the houses of your servants and of your people, and into your ovens and your kneading bowls. The frogs shall come up on you and on your people and on all your servants." (Ex. 8.2-4)

And, in full view of the assembled and anticipating audience, Moses commands Aaron,

> "Stretch out your hand with your rod over the rivers, over the canals, and over the pools, and cause frogs to come upon the land of Egypt!" (Ex. 8.5)

And Aaron passes his magic wand over the Nile as before, and the frogs come up and cover the land of Egypt.

Again the magicians of Egypt match the performance of Moses.

But the slime is offensive to Pharaoh, so for the first time he calls Moses in and agrees to let the Hebrews go do as they wish, that is, to go celebrate their God.

But when Moses removes the frogs from the land, Pharaoh changes his mind. Still, even in his temporary capitulation we see progress. Moses is chipping away at the balance of power.

Similarity: The Small And The Numerous

The progress that we've begun to see in the last feat grows even greater in Moses' next trick. Moses strikes the dust with his magic wand, stirring up a dense, giant cloud of gnats. We see the similarity between multitudinous small grains of sand and numberful small gnats. And they annoy every human and every animal in the kingdom. But this time when the Egyptian magicians try to do the same, they can't. This is Moses' exclusive. They simply do not know how it is done.

Think for a moment. Pharaoh is surrounded by the finest magicians in all the vast reaches of his kingdom's influence. These are initiates! Surely they are of a lesser degree of attainment than Moses, yet they are insider's to the "secret arts" of bidding hidden powers. These are initiates disciplined to command unseen elementals to perform amazing and mystifying things. They are insiders to the trade. And they fall into fear and doubt! They buckle, believing there is real power in the magic Moses is hurling at them.

Only Among The Egyptians

When Moses sees how uncomfortable the gnats make the Egyptians, he receives a brilliant inspiration. Gnats are bothersome; flies are loathsome!

We find in this mojo Moses implementing another distinction in his magical effects, too. His own people complain sorely about the gnats and Moses, realizing his error, corrects it simply in the command. From this point onward the plagues and evil things he calls forth affect only the Egyptians.

Flies only on the Egyptians! Flies attack every Egyptian, human and beast, so numerous even that the steps they take are on fly-covered ground.

Again, in a matter of weeks, Egypt is ruined.

Pharaoh is willing to talk now. He gives Moses and the Israelites time off to hold the worship ceremonies they are asking for. But he wants them to do it within the broad borders of Egypt. Moses says this is unacceptable, that they must have three days space. Finally, utterly revolted by the flies landing even in his mouth when he opens it to speak, and in his ears, listening or not, he relents. Moses calls off the flies. "But don't go too far into the wilderness," he tells him.

Saddam Moses' Chemical Warfare

Moses next kills all the herds of Egypt, but this doesn't affect Pharaoh.

It's time to escalate further. Moses decides to attack the very bodies of the Egyptians. Herein Moses, savant of the Hebrew people, enjoys the dubious distinction of waging one of the earliest campaigns of chemical warfare. Like a lot of even today's chemical warfare, the intent and effect is not always to kill, but to break the spirit through hideously afflicting the body and its health. And he employs the secret arts to accomplish it.

In a ceremony of similarity – ashes to ashes – Moses takes a handful of ashes from the communal kiln and, in a ritualistic ceremony with words of high incantation, throws them Heavenward.

It works very well. It hideously attacks the Egyptians. Boils break out on all flesh. Picture it. Boils and sores and a defeated spirit.

But Moses is dealing with a Master himself, and though he can't match it, Pharaoh refuses to let the Israelites go.

In Pharaoh and Moses both we see lessons of persistence. In Pharaoh's case: how long does one hold on? In Moses' case: the willingness to do whatever it takes, for as long as it takes.

Sport With The People

Moses hurls hailstones from the skies, totally destroying the Egyptian's food supply. No cattle; no grain. He also kills many Egyptians and even more cattle (though he killed them all in a previous trick) – all that were caught outside.

"Actually," the confident Moses thinks, seeing his victory unfolding, "this is getting to be *fun!*" He decides, like Joseph bringing the people *into* Egypt, to play with his brothers. *It will take even more.*

We really see the evidence of movement in the negotiations here. This time, at only the *threat* of another plague, the open-pused, hungry, still-living reeling Egyptians plead with Pharaoh to let the Jews go worship their God. "After all," they say, "what's a few days worth of bricks compared to the destruction of Egypt?"

So Pharaoh relents. It is at this time that he get his first inkling of Moses' true designs, as Moses now says,

> "Great, and we will go with our young and our old; we will go with our sons and daughters and with our flocks and herds, for we must hold a feast to the Lord." (Ex. 10.9)

Would you load a moving van to go to a high mass? Pharaoh unmasks the deception and refuses to let them *all* go. It is only the men of the Hebrew society that have any status, position, influence, or connection with God, anyway. The women have always been accouterments for the adornment and comfort of men. They have no place in the worship of Israel. Moses is here demanding something that is totally outside of their cultural patterns. It's not hard to see this alerts Pharaoh that something's up.

It is revealed for us, too, that had Moses' desires not been falsely projected, Pharaoh *would* have let him go earlier than actually occurs in the final telling of the story. In fact, we herein see that Pharaoh *does* give Moses exactly what he has been demanding at the sword point of his mighty magic. But Moses, pushing his advantage, asks for more – which is what he intended one way or the other to accomplish anyway. So for a little fun, he orders flogging for the mighty giant tottering on her knees before the Jews.

He commands the air with the casting of his magic wand and locusts come to life on the east wind and consume the land. They eat everything; not a green thing remains. Except in Goshen, of course.

Moses is thinking, "Whereas Egypt freely offered Israel food when we entered, Israel shall destroy all sustenance from Egypt when we depart."

By now the more enterprising Jews are profiting twicely on this turn of events. Not only are their lands uninjured and still fruitful, they are selling the Egyptians goods at jacked-up prices, another way of robbing Egypt's wealth as they go.

Power Play

Amused in the meditations of his sanctum, Moses comes up with a new curse to cast upon the Egyptians. This one will mirror in the physical dimensions the plight they are feeling in the psychological dimensions. Moses will enspell the land to three days of compelling and confusing darkness. Except for Goshen, of course.

Moses doesn't even do his usual shtick and showmanship. He doesn't make a show of ridiculing and demanding with threats and promises of signs and destruction. He just waves his magic wand and the land is engulfed in enchantment.

We see progress. Persuaded by the unutterable intensity of the darkness, Pharaoh relents again. He does it with no prodding or whining by anyone. This time he agrees to let Moses lead all the people, the women and children with him, leaving only their livestock. But Moses, well aware of who has the upper hand now, refuses anything but absolute compliance with his demands:

> "Our cattle also must go with us; not a hoof shall be left behind." (Ex. 10.26)

Pharaoh is trying to negotiate. He has twice offered Moses what he still claims it is he wants – a chance to worship. He refuses to let Moses go, and breaks all diplomatic ties with him. He tells him henceforth, should he come to the court, he will die.

Moses, flushed with joy, dissimulating anger, says simply – and oh so presciently! – "As you wish."

He has an A-bomb planned, that he wants to drop anyway, even if they are already beaten. It's actually better this way. If they surrender, what he wants to do will look bad – *but they haven't!*

Some Angel, Huh?

"They treasure their children the most," Moses is thinking, especially their firstborn males. Imagine what sorrow I will wreak on them if I kill their children!!! They'll *never* forget me!"

Moses does not broadcast this evil event prior to implementing it, either. But first, certain that the atrocity of this magical mass murder will indeed cause Pharaoh not only to let them go, but to actually *drive them hastily out,* he sends his people to ask the Egyptian populace for their wealth, which they freely give. This rich nation gives all their silver and gold as a kind of propitiation, wanting to be spared the results of any further mojo Moses may throw over the land. Pharaoh may not be convinced, but the people are.

Little do they know that the master of deception is even now planning to cause them greater grief than has ever been in the land before or since. He is going to kill every firstborn in the nation, the firstborn of the kitchen girl and the captive in the cell, the firstborn of every breed of cattle, the firstborn of the innocent noble husbands and wives, and even the firstborn of Pharaoh himself, excepting, of course, no murders in Goshen.

Moses commands a legion of angels, and at the stroke of the bewitching hour they enter every house of every Egyptian, sucking the breath from every firstborn, the treasured prime of every family.

It is effective. This time Pharaoh hastens them on – their wives, their children, their herds, and even their recently acquired riches.

This section ends with the story of 600,000 men alone, plus women, children, and cattle – *the entire race* – set hurriedly to the journey, recounting the 430 years of the Egyptian experience.

"Blood Red, Red Sea, Flow Red!"

After all his intuitions, Pharaoh still is incensed to discover some weeks later that the Jews have actually pulled off an *escape*. He receives intelligence reports of them camping in the wilderness and determines to overtake them and bring them back. After all, they do the work that the citizens themselves aren't willing to do! "We need aliens among us."

So Pharaoh chases out with the best of the best. Six hundred warriors, officers all.

The Jews, men alone, outnumber the Egyptians 1,000-to-1. However, right now they are feeling very weak-hearted. The rigors and uncertainties of a hasty dislocation and the road with their goods has got them. They are not in any form, but that they have swords, to be likened to warriors. They start running. No problem, Moses prefers wizardry to outright warfare anyway.

He enters the silence to seek an answer. God, for his part, tells him to get right up and get into *action* doing what he knows is his to do. Moses – like only David and Jesus otherwise so well exemplify – is in flow!

He tells him,

> "Lift up your rod, stretch out your hand over the sea and divide it, that the people of Israel may go on dry ground through the sea. And *I* will harden the hearts of the Egyptians so that they shall go in after them, and *I* will get glory over Pharaoh and all his host, his chariots, and his horsemen." (Ex. 14.16)

You are undoubtedly familiar with this popular story at this point. Moses does as his bulging heart guides him to do: stands over the water, focuses the action of the Spirit in mystical motions with his magical wand, and commands the forces of Nature. A strong dry east wind arises, dividing the waters of the sea, and even drying the muddy bottom, so that it is easy for the hosts of Israel to pass through.

Meanwhile, just hours away now, Pharaoh and his swat team is pursuing. And as the last of Israel is stepping out of the sea bed, on the other side the first hooves of the Egyptians fly headlong into it. And all appears mystically well for the pursuers, too.

But after they are all well into the basin, God furrows his brow. Moses commands; Nature obeys. The waters snap their jaws shut on the host of Egypt.

These bright, young, trained hounds are mastered by Moses' magic.

Their bodies, food for scavenger birds, wash up on the beaches the following morning. It's a real beach.

God Needs To Be Directed

We encounter this repeatedly in this magical mystery tour: God's power is a power of volition. God needs to be directed. It comes especially clear in these Red Sea passages. Note God's concern. It seems that he is impelled by a greater urgency than Moses is, but that he's unable to act without Moses' permission and direction. The implications of the passage indicate that God needs Moses or he couldn't, for instance, either *part* or *rejoin* the sea.

When Moses is being pressed by the army behind him and the sea before him, he prays. God raises his voice to him, asking,

"Why do you cry to me?!" (Ex. 14.15)

He herewith states that the power of execution is not in his own hands, but in Moses'. In other words, he is saying, "I can't, of my own volition, act, though I know what needs to be done. I can accomplish great things, however, directed by you."

He tells Moses,

"Lift up your rod!" stretch out your hand over the sea! and *divide* it!"

It's like he sees the imminent danger and is shouting at Moses, "*Do* it! *Do* it!!!"

After they've crossed the sea, and after the troops of Pharaoh are *inside the wizard's trick* – talk about a house of illusions! – God again, though he knows what needs to be done, does not just do it. He cries out to Moses,

"Quick! Cast your spell over the sea! Command the water to surge back upon the Egyptians, their chariots, and their horsemen!" (Ex. 14.26)

Intent, focus, and invocation are *crucial* magical qualities. He needs Moses to *take* the power and to *use* it. Directed, the power is mighty, something we should all take to heart as we cast the future of our own lives.

God's power, then, is a power of volition. God's power is latent until it is directed to specified ends. Then it accomplishes magical things. God reveals to us this secret of magic in this "if/then" drama. Not before, but *if*, "*you* will lift up your hand, deciding and moving for exactly what you want, *then I* will accomplish it."

The Water At Marah: God The Healer

Moses. With a great distance between the two groups now, Israel is finally and totally free from its oppressors. That does not, however, mean all threat and adventure is over. Indeed, adventure never ends. That surely is the lesson of history.

And so they come to the place they christen Marah, which means *bitter*, because the water is unfit to sooth their parched souls. And they cry against Moses.

Moses, like every astute political leader before and since, knows that, whatever the appearances, he only enjoys his position of power, prestige, and prominence at the whim of the people. He must pull something off.

In a sudden vision of a moment he sees a tree, and knows what to do. He reins the people's attention, and, in psychic unison with Moses' performance, they cast it into the pool. And the water tastes sweet.

Thus it appears Moses has added a transformative agent – hey, he *is* the shaman! – and the people are duly impressed. Moses, not one to let a political advantage pass unharvested, then channels God, who indicates that if they obey Moses they will be cared for. If they behave, Moses will not hurl the hexes on them that he cast upon their Egyptian brethren:

> "If you will diligently hearken to me, and do that which is right in my eyes, and give heed to all the commandments and statutes I lay on you, then I will put none of the afflictions and diseases upon you which I cast upon the Egyptians; for I am the Lord your God, your healer." (Exod 15.26)

See Moses' persuasion at work? It is mighty effective to control a people through the voices of their Gods. They internalize Moses' precepts so that control is established through their very own consciences. How very effective to rule by fear. But I don't think any other governments would rule this way, do you?

Hypnosis: Face Of The Magician's Arsenal

This entire performance may be simply a demonstration of hypnosis, a major weapon in the magician's arsenal. This kind of event is an ordinary magical effect. Nearly everybody has actually seen, or at least heard the marvelous tales about a similar trick the traveling magicians perform even today. He or she can hypnotize a person so that, while *actually* eating a potato, they *think* they are eating an apple, *experiencing* the texture, juice, and satisfaction of a luscious apple.

Don't have to change the actual circumstances of the environment, just change the neural processing of the stimulus. Thus Moses could have performed this trick, not by changing anything at all about the water, but by hypnotizing the people to believe he has. *Hey, he* is *the shaman!* Either way, they *experience* it differently – and therein is magic.

Channeling The Power

Moses. Joshua. Suddenly the sword approaches. Amalek, aboriginal inhabitants of the land, sees the threat the Israelites present in the TransJordan. This is the first time the soldiers of Israel ever engage in any actual fighting. This is also the first mention of Joshua, the man who rises to the position of Supreme Military Commander. Joshua is the one who will wrest the land from the native Canaanites when they cross over the Jordan in years to come. But there are battles for well-being to be fought before then, like right now. Though this battle is fought with the brutal blood and bludgeon of actual contact, yet Moses still wins it by magic.

Moses sends Joshua and his troops to tally their fears and differences with the Amalekites by the edge of the sword. Then he, along with Aaron and Hur, perches himself well out of harm's way on a mountaintop overlooking the field. In this eyrie he stands with his rod lifted to the Heavens, and the battle goes well.

Yet when he tires, and lowers his hands, the action on the field reverses:

Whenever Moses holds up his hand, Israel prevails; and whenever he lowers his hand, Amalek prevails. (Ex. 17.11)

Good thing he brought his assistants. He had to grow weary. They use their ingenuity. Aaron and Hur roll a big stone over for Moses' behind. They then stand on either side of him, each holding one arm up.

Joshua and his swords spew the bloody remnants of the Amalekite women's men like cut grass from the blade of a lawnmower.

The Enemy's Not Pharaoh Now

Moses. The Israelites color their memories of Egypt sweeter than ever contrasted with the rigorous realities of life on the road. They whine. They complain.

The enemy is not Pharaoh now. The people must be controlled, and magic, for a master like Moses, is still the most effective way to accomplish it.

A Good Example

Moses finds himself enchanted by Black beauty. He married Zipporah, a refined specimen, years earlier, but he had left her with her father when he journeyed with military intent to Egypt. Now the people are free. In the wilderness her father brings her back to him – and do the tongues wag! You know how ethnocentric the Hebrews are. Even Moses' own sister and brother, Miriam and Aaron, talk behind his back. As if the preference for women of a darker breed should be a disqualifying concern! What bearing do Moses' sexual preferences have on his ability to exercise spiritual and political leadership?

Miriam and Aaron begin exaggerating their own worth saying,

"Does the Lord indeed speak only through Moses? Doesn't he speak through us as well?" (Num. 12.2)

Oh they say it! And Moses hears it.

Now look at this! Moses calls Aaron and Miriam, saying God has summoned them to a meeting. Moses has prepared in advance. Suddenly the Lord himself enters the tent in a great billow arising from the stage. God commands Aaron and Miriam to come before him. He's already judged, it is time to pronounce. He puffs himself and, sounding a lot like the ventriloquist's throw, pontificates:

"Hear my words: If there is a prophet among you, I the Lord make myself known to him in a vision, I speak with him in a dream. Not so, however, with my man Moses. He is entrusted with all my house. With him I speak mouth to mouth, clearly, and not in the dark and ambiguous speech of visions and dreams; and he beholds the form of the Lord. You can't match him. Why then are you not afraid to speak against him?" (Num. 12.6-8)

The cloud dissipates, and behold, when the three come back to normal consciousness Miriam is leprous, white as snow.

And Aaron cries to Moses to stay his power,

"Moses, forgive us! How could we ever have questioned your authority? We have behaved foolishly; we have sinned!" (Num. 12.11)

Moses needs Miriam, but he wants to make certain she remembers the lesson. He's not about to change her back immediately. Instead, he commands the time of transformation for seven days hence. She must be shamed in front of the entire nation of Israel, "untouchable," "unclean."

And though she lives a number of years, Miriam never speaks against Moses again.

Sexism? Or Power?

It is interesting to note that Moses never does call any curses down on Aaron, though the passage clearly says *both* Aaron and Miriam are questioning his authority. Indeed, Aaron is Moses' right-hand man! Aaron *is* doing magic! In fact, God *is* speaking through Aaron.

We can speculate that Moses is aware of just how much power Aaron has, power that Aaron himself, not being enlightened to the degree of Moses, does not know is his. He believes it is Moses' power. However, Aaron could easily express this power – if he only knew he could. An angry act of an argument could be the trigger to awaken his awareness, a thing Moses can't risk.

"Woe To You Who Question Authority!"

Moses' troubles with the people are not just a one time affair. It does not end with the members of his cabinet, Aaron and Miriam. It runs top down, from the cabinet to the rabble. The people surrounding Moses lack the vision and the capacity for endurance in pursuit of a longterm goal that Moses is obsessed with. He eventually ends up having to kill 15,000 citizens within the space of 24 hours to maintain his control. And, as always with this massive man, his preferred modus operandi is magic.

Magic is much cheaper and – because the people believe it is *God* – even more effective than soldiers and suited agents.

Magic silences Miriam, but her example does not, as Moses had hoped it would, silence the people. A band of the socially privileged visit Moses, demanding some share in leadership and its rewards. In their eyes, they are all equally qualified:

"You have gone too far! For all the congregation are holy, every one of them, and the Lord is among them; why then do you and Aaron exalt yourselves above the assembly of the Lord?" (Num. 16.3)

Moses thunders with theatrics, falling on his face and swearing God will show them in the morning who is holy and who is not. How can they *dare* to question the great God who has blessed them??!

"And would you seek the priesthood too?!!" (Num. 16.10)

Naturally, he frames their actions to maintain his power:

"It's not against me and against Aaron that you complain; it is against the
Lord that you and all your company have gathered together." (Num.
16.11)

Having worked late several nights earlier, Moses is ready. He pronounces the
dreaded curse. Moses commands an earthquake, and an earthquake comes:

Precisely as he finishes speaking these words, the ground under them splits
asunder; and the earth opens its mouth and swallows them up, with their
households – cousins and kindred of every kind – and all their goods. (Num.
16.31-32)

Thus Moses proves his power through his murderous magic. Effective. Yes, he
does have more power than them. Even to this day people read these stories and
swear to Moses' divine commissioning and feel that Moses, unlike the other
fanatical religious rulers they see in the Middle East, is justified in such stiff
political repression.

The people understand they can count on Moses to see them safely through.

Their work done for the day, Moses and Aaron retire into the entitlements of
their positions.

To Cross The Jordan

When Moses dies, God starts speaking to *Joshua*. The mission he gives Joshua
is clear. It is time:

"Arise, go over this Jordan, you and all this people, into the land which
I am giving to you, the people of Israel." (Jos. 1.2)

And, he reassures him, quite natural with a divine charge,

"No man shall be able to stand before you all the days of your life; as I
was with Moses, so I will be with you; I will not fail you or forsake you.
Be strong and of good courage; for you shall cause this people to inherit
the land which I swore to their fathers to give them. I am with you,
directing your every action... Only be strong and very courageous..." (Jos.
1.5-7)

Joshua rises from his meditation and issues the orders. He calls his officer cadre
in and directs them to prepare all the people,

"For within three days you are to pass over this Jordan, to go in to take
possession of the land which the Lord your God gives you to possess."
(Jos. 1.11)

Joshua has the inner conviction that indeed he is the anointed of the Lord. But
he needs to provide the people with an outward sign. He thinks of what his mentor,
Moses, did in the past. The miraculous is always effective. Moses' most acclaimed
trick was parting the Red Sea and crossing on dry ground, forty years earlier. It is
a legend enshrined in the heart of every Jew, all of whose parents or grandparents
were of that generation. Joshua receives the idea couched in the words of the Lord:

"Behold, the ark of the covenant of the Lord of all the Earth is to pass
over before you into the Jordan.... When the priests carrying the Ark of

the Lord of all the Earth set foot in the waters of the Jordan, then the waters of the Jordan will be cut off; the water coming down from upstream will stand piled up like a bank." (Jos. 3.11-13)

Joshua does it again! When the priests step into the Jordan, the waters stop and pile up "like a bank for a long way back" (Jos. 3.16). The priests proceed to the center of the river bottom and wait there in service while all the nation crosses around them. When the priests bearing the ark themselves move toward the mythically promised Canaan, when the final foot of the final man touches the far shore, the pent waters of the Jordan rage forward, so that it even overflows its banks. The nation is in Canaan.

Destiny is fulfilling itself in the decisive grip of a man of courageous action, a man sound of body, strong of will, spiritually inspired, Joshua.

The Tall Wall Falls

Joshua's training in ceremonial magic is obvious in his second major magical feat, the breaching of the walls of Jericho, his first Promised Land battle, his first Promised Land victory.

Not only does his high magic inspirit a bold heart in the Israelites, it also intimidates the citizens, officials, and soldiers of Jericho. As well it should. They become fearful and unable to act manfully on their own. They are in the midst of a powerful enchantment, they feel it, – they are going down. The center of power of the Israelites' God, the Ark, is marching around their city amping up for its destruction.

Note the numbers. Joshua has his troops march seven days around the walled city of Jericho. He has them led by seven priests bearing seven trumpets of ram's horns. Once each day for the first six days Joshua and his train march around the city of Jericho. And on the seventh day, the ritual is consummated!

On the seventh pass of the seventh march of seven days around Jericho, the seven priests bearing seven trumpets of ram's horns blow them off and the people shout mightily. And, with no other effort than this metaphysical mastery, the walls come tumbling down. Resistance is nil.

Thus, inspired by God, enthusiastic and decisive in his new command, less than two weeks after taking command, Joshua has the people engaged in the carnage of wresting Canaan from its owners at the bloody blade of the sword:

They utterly destroy all in the city, both men and women, young and old, oxen, sheep, and asses, with the edge of the sword. (Jos. 6.21)

They burn the city and salt the ground so that it will be infertile forever. And all these *sevens* show it is of Heaven.

To Awaken The Soul

Ritual and its accouterments of formality, movement, rhythm, numerology, repetition, candles, incense, and music enjoy a high place in the halls of enchantment. The ritual ceremonies lift the human consciousness to the state of

God. God consciousness accesses the power of performance. As a magician matures into an adept he or she has less need for the boost a ritual can provide. By this time they've taken residence in the Cosmic and they demonstrate the power naturally. We see Joshua early in his independence, relying heavily on ritual.

The Time Of The Hex

In a ritual of thanksgiving celebrating the successful battle, *Joshua* declaims a magical oath:

> "Cursed before God be the man that rises up and rebuilds this city, Jericho. At the cost of his first-born shall he lay its foundation, at the cost of his youngest son shall he set up its gates." (Jos. 6.26)

And Joshua's fame for magic waxes full throughout the land of Canaan.

Hundreds of years later the time of completion comes for Joshua's hex. During the reign of Ahab, one Hiel of Bethel does rebuild Jericho. Alas,

> he lays its foundation at the cost of Abiram his first-born, and sets up its gates at the cost of his youngest son Segub, according to the curse God put on the ground, channeled in the words spoken by Joshua the son of Nun. (1Kg. 16.34)

Poor boys.

It Does Not Decay

In the fulfillment of these words God illustrates another principle of magic. As we've found out digging among the magical mentors of the Jewish race, the ancient Egyptians, a magical invocation – blessing or curse – does not lose its efficacy with the passage of time. Belonging to a different dimension, it does not decay, but retains its full force. When it is spoken it is spoken to the time of fulfillment.

Commanding The Sun And The Moon

Joshua. The Amorites occupy the land destined for the tribe of Judah, including the cities of Jerusalem and Hebron. Five kings of the Amorites band together against the Joshuan aggressive.

But Joshua surprises the enemy troops, having marched all night to battle. At Joshua's appearance they are thrown into confusion. Slaughtering the Amorites in their underwear is an easy job.

Nevertheless, as easy as it is, it takes some engagement, some time, and some effort to kill a soldier. There are just more people to kill than the span of a single day allows! Ancient battle was pitifully unwieldy and ineffective at night, when candles and torches were the only lights, so Joshua enters meditation, returns, and commands:

> "Stand still, O Sun, in Gibeon! Stand, Moon, in the Vale of Aijalon!"
> The sun stood still and the moon halted until a nation had taken vengeance on its enemies. (Jos. 10.12-13)

Time Distortion

Some scholars peering into this passage see not a *literal* stopping of the sun and the moon in the skies, but a sense distortion, wherein in an altered consciousness it *seems* like these heavenly bodies stand still. Like the accident victim who says she saw it all happening in slow motion. There is, if not an actual time slowing, because accidents don't happen that way, a *perceived* time alteration.

Either way, it is magic, induced at Joshua's magical command.

Gods, Troubles, Rats, And Tumors

The Philistines see the power of Israel's God, paraded powerfully around in the Ark. They see the magic it performs, so when they capture it in war, they believe the power is theirs.

Wrong! The ark is magical, alright, but it uses its magic *against* the Philistines, in favor of the Israelites. Possession of the ritual coffin is not enough. *Consecration* is necessary, and that requires the true heart tuned. This is a *psychic charge*. This the Philistines overlooked. This the Philistines, as the profane, can not possess.

This is an artifact that possesses *conscious* mystical powers. In a true demonstration of the efficacy of this loyal talisman the hand of God strikes the Philistines. He throws a plague of tumors onto the bodies of every Philistine. It is such a serious attack that great numbers of the infidels die within days. They shuttle the ark from city to city, leaving pus, slime, filth, and human agony in its trail.

The only people capable of discerning this mystery – the sorcerers and magicians – are consulted. They reveal what the lords already know: they must give the ark back. They send along, as the psychics suggest,

> "Five golden tumors and five golden mice, according to the number of the lords of the Philistines; for the same plague was upon all of you and upon your lords.
>
> "Yes, you must make images of your tumors and images of your mice that ravage the land. Thereby give glory to the God of Israel that he will lighten his hand from off you and your God and your land." (1Sam. 6.5)

This is all done in accordance with the principles of sympathetic magic. The ritual incorporates the images of the tumors and the mice because they are *similar* to the effect they wish to exorcise. They make a material representation of the magical curse the ark brought on them and are herewith respectfully offering the tumors and mice back to God *with* the Ark.

However, the tumors and rats they send back reek with none of the filth the actual curse calls onto the nation. These images are sculpted in gold. Again we recognize the principle of similarity. They are magically invoking a transformation by the quantum fire of this valued metal made more precious by the craft.

The Unrain Dance

Elijah. We often hear of people resorting to a rain dance to entice the clouds to share their abundance with the parched Earth. But seldom do we consider that drought may actually be the result of a powerful incantation earlier spread across the land.

Thus we see Elijah dance the *unrain dance* upon Ahab and his subjects. Elijah commands the dryness:

"As the Lord the God of Israel lives, before whom I stand, there shall be neither dew nor rain these years, except by my word." (1Kg. 17.1)

Consider These Things

Ah, who can call the forces of Nature? Who can command a fruitful land fall into waste?

What Faith Does. Magic ever demands confidence in the man or woman commanding. Faith is the quality that connects the human with the Unseen. Note Elijah's confidence. He speaks the word with the intent and confidence that it will be fulfilled. This level of congruity is yet hard for the average human to even conceive. And what a person can do who does!

He Is That Force. Elijah herein places himself in the tradition of many of the great magical masters. They demonstrate control of nature. The living spirits of the elements, the forces manifesting as fire, water, wind, and earth – the living conscious souls of their beings – are called *elementals*. Like all beings, they each have their different characteristics, traits, weak points, and strengths.

Magic is accomplished by putting oneself into *alignment* with certain paranormal forces. What Moses, Joshua, Samuel, and Jesus, as well as Elijah are doing with the natural elements is not normal. These men are obviously making and manipulating a connection that the masses of humanity do not access. Although all the masters say we can, few act on the challenge of the profound nonconformity concomitant with that change. *Ah, but the rewards!*

The magician alters the weather by entering in spirit into a working relationship with these higher living forces. It's a top down job, inner direction to outer manifestation. *How big is the human will when used to its potentials!* He "becomes" the force, and, in keeping with that force's powers, chooses to act out as he will.

Thus, in lingering Renaissance terminology, it is said that the elementals perform at the bidding of the magician. A modern firewalker says, "The fire and I are one." Elijah says, "The water does my bidding." It's how the interdependent HoloCosmic Consciousness is.

"You Shall Be Provided For During These Wasteland Years"

Elijah. A Poor Widow. Manipulation is the magician's stock in trade. Misdirection is a base from which he works in every performance. The next trick has a twist to this twist, however. It turns out that the bigger misdirection dupes the magician himself.

Since Elijah has stopped the waters, the land has become a wasteland. He is what the Latin speaking Romans call a *persona non grata*. So he has to hide out. He follows his inspirations and sets camp along one of the major tributaries to the Jordan. As a magician, he is not going to spend his time working in the manner of ordinary men, so for sustenance he drinks from the brook and has the ravens serve him meat every morning and evening. Thus he continues in the development of his craft.

But after a while the brook dries up. Unlike Moses, who, in his early days learned to enspell the entire land *excepting the Jews*, Elijah, living in the land, is affected by the curse of his own mouth.

It is time for another inspiration, which, moving in the schedule of flow, he receives:

> "Arise, go to Zarephath, and dwell there. Behold, I have commanded a widow there to feed you." (1Kg. 17.9)

When the parched Elijah approaches the gates of the city he sees a widow gathering her sticks and asks her for a sip of the water of life. Like a goodly Samaritan woman, she prepares the stranger a drink. And Elijah asks her,

> "Also, please bring me a morsel of bread. I haven't eaten in several days." (1Kg. 17.11)

This touches a chord with her. She begs the case of her own extremity, politely telling Elijah she can't afford to share her last morsel of the sustenance of flesh. Even after eating what she has to eat, she explains, it is so little she will die nevertheless:

> "As the Lord your God lives, I have nothing baked, only a handful of meal in a jar, and a little oil in a cruse; and now, I am gathering a couple of sticks, that I may go in and prepare it for myself and my son, that we may eat it, and die." (1Kg. 17.12)

Elijah looks like just another public park bum. She doesn't know that he speaks the words of life with his tongue. But there is something in his eyes that tells her not to worry. He says he'll wait:

> "After serving me," he tells her, "then make some for yourself and your son." (1Kg. 17.13)

Then, spoken with the confidence of a true and knowing channel of the magic, he makes it so, speaking:

> "For thus says the Lord the God of Israel, 'The jar of meal shall not be spent, and the cruse of oil shall not fail, until the day that the Lord sends rain upon the earth.'" (1Kg. 17.14)

She does as Elijah bids. And according to the magic Elijah directs:

> The jar of meal is not spent, neither does the cruse of oil fail. (1Kg. 17.16)

Elijah eats. And in the drama Elijah accomplishes the good he is sent to accomplish. He provides for the widow and her son.

Consider These Things
This act of the Cosmic drama offers us some special delights. Trickery and subterfuge are daily attributes of the magician's life. But we usually think of the magician pulling one over on an audience, target, or mark. When Elijah gets hungry, he receives directions to the widow's house, who he thinks will feed him – but God, working on Elijah, hooks Elijah with misdirection. *Don't you just love it?* We also see the principle of *start with something* in action again.

The MisDirection Decrypted. Elijah understands the intuitions he is receiving to be directing him to Sidon, where he will meet a certain widow, whose identity will be revealed later, who will feed him. As a man, and then a *magician* on top of that, his interests are elsewhere. He's not very adept at feeding himself. He's hungry and thirsty. So he goes.

But he is misdirected by the promise of a subordinate result/purpose to the act he will actually accomplish. His real purpose and assignment is to provide for the Godly widow and her son. His own self will be cared for *en passant*, in the resulting riches from the performance of his greater good.

This is an interesting illustration of the way the inner voice of intuition works. It will guide us in the direction we need to be led to fulfill its purposes, in the way we need to be reached.

Creative Substance. In this miraculous effect of multiplying the oil and the grain we see demonstrated for us an elemental truth of substance magic. It concerns the fact that it is easier to multiply *something* than it is to create out of *nothing*. This explains Jesus' preference to *multiply* fishes and loaves rather than simply command and have them magically appear.

Raising The Widow's Son
But the food *Elijah* blesses the *widow* with comes too late... for her son, that is. According to her word, though he eats, he dies. He is too far for the food to do anything other than provide him with a moment of respite.

But... complication! The widow now knows Elijah is no ordinary tramp. He has magic. She does not understand the occult and sees the death of her son as connected with the appearance of the sorcerer. She accuses Elijah of being the cause of her son's death. In her grief, any mother might. But when the concerned Elijah asks for the boy's body, she releases him from her heaving bosom. Not only that, but she trusts the visitor enough that she does not follow him when he carries her son into his own bedroom in the upper chambers.

There alone, he lifts his eyes, his arms, and his voice to God, asking in a ritually intoned prayer why he would slay this lonesome widow's only son.

Then, transferring the energies of breath in the ultimate form of hands-on healing, he stretches himself upon the child mouth-to-mouth the three important times of divinity, each time decrying,

"O Lord, let this child's soul come into him again!" (1Kg. 17.21)
And, as Elijah speaks it, so it is:
And the soul of the child comes into him again, and he revives. (1Kg. 17.22)
Elijah lifts the child, descends from the heights, and delivers him to his mother with the words,
"Woman, your son lives." (1Kg. 17.23)
Yes, the appearance of the sorcerer *is* connected with the death of her son. Think about this. A number of people, like Moses and Joshua, for instance, and even Elijah at other times, use magic to destroy life. But to restore life, to raise a person who has passed the portals of death... that is a feat of magical proportions accomplished by the few!

There Will Be A Contest On Carmel

Elijah is lead man on the king's "Most Wanted" list. With the hex he pronounced he transformed the once fertile Israel into a wasteland. People and cattle are only eking out a thread of a barren existence. Cherish the thought of prosperity!

Three years into the enspellment, one day Elijah appears in front of Obadiah, King Ahab's imperial officer.

Recognizing the powerful sorcerer, Obadiah falls on his face. Elijah tells him to rise, that he is to be his messenger. But Obadiah is now as fearstruck about seeing King Ahab as he is about seeing Elijah, for, as he says,

"What have I done that you would kill me for?

"As the Lord lives, there isn't a nation or kingdom where my lord has not searched to find you, and when they would say, 'He is not here,' he would take an oath from them, that they had not found you.

"And now you say, 'Go, tell your lord, "Behold, Elijah is here."'

"What will you do? As soon as I have gone from you, you will disappear to who knows where and I will be left with the king's anger. When he can't find you he will kill me!" (1Kg. 18.9-12)

Taking an oath himself, Elijah swears he will not disappear, that he will indeed show himself. So Obadiah goes and tells the king.

Ahab is *amazed* that Elijah will show himself. Nevertheless, he is a personage of sufficient state that he can't be seized immediately. Ahab, rubbing his eyes, says,

"Is it you, you troubler of Israel?" (1Kg. 18.17)

But the years and the solitude haven't mellowed Elijah any. He barks back:

"*I* have not troubled Israel; but *you* have, and your father's house, because you have forsaken the commandments of the Lord and followed the Baals!" (1Kg. 18.18)

And this early-day Gandhi has something up his ample wizard's sleeve, but the obtuse Ahab can't see it coming. Elijah goes on,

"Now therefore send and gather all Israel to me at Mount Carmel, and the four hundred and fifty prophets of Baal and the four hundred prophets of Astarte..." (1Kg. 18.19)

Here he is face-to-face with the sorcerer who cast such a powerful spell over Israel that all the priests, priestesses, psychics, prophets, and diviners in the land, working three years on it, could not unenspell it. Neither could the various foreign mystery workers they sought unenspell the land. Yet Ahab agrees to stage a royal show with fanfare and all of Israel in witness and every priest and psychic throughout the land on the stage. *Dumb!*

Elijah is the undisputed magician in the kingdom. And oh, he has flair! He gathers the people near, quiets them, and in his prelude asks with a fireside demeanor,

"How long will you go limping with two different opinions?" (1Kg. 18.21)

Once warmed up, he gets more testy:

"If the Lord is God, follow him; but if Baal, then follow him."

And the people do not answer him a word. (1Kg. 18.21)

And then he fires up, the sole remaining practitioner of Yahweh, to face the practitioners of Baal and beautiful Astarte. He sets these prophets against himself, 850 to 1. Herein is the challenge:

"And you call on the name of your God and I will call on the name of mine, and the God who answers by fire, *he* is God." (1Kg. 18.24)

It just so happens that Elijah, who has a high ability with fire, establishes the contest with that element. Not only that, but he establishes it that the Baalians go first. This way they do not get the opportunity to figure out how to do the trick by watching Elijah. He knows no one else possesses these tricks, as he's developed and refined them himself during his years of hiding and has never shown them publically before. He's playing his strong suit.

Both parties get a bull, the Baalians getting first choice. Both parties prepare their altar, but neither lights their fire. And now it's time to call on their God, but the Baalians don't know the trick. What can they say? They hope they can figure it out, relying on their insight and expertise. But it is not to be.

They call on God all morning, until noon, praying for an answer. And Elijah starts throwing jeers and taunts at them, saying Baal must be away on a trip, or asleep, for not hearing their pitiful cries and lamentations. The while they continue trying, whipping themselves into a frenzy, but,

There is no voice, no one answers, no one heeds. (1Kg. 18.29)

Now, at the better time of day for fire magic, when it can be seen easily in contrast with the shadows of twilight, Elijah ritually prepares his altar with twelve stones, one for each tribe of Israel. He cuts a trench, puts the wood in order, cuts the bull in pieces, and lays it on the wood. Then, invoking the twelve again with his numerical metaphor, $4 \times 3 = 12$, he takes four great water jars and, making a show of it every time, has confidants pour them on the bull and the wood – one, two, three times! Not only is the wood of the altar drenched, but it is now even *standing in water*! Boy, he's *really* making this difficult!

When they see what happens next, the king and the unfortunate magicians of Baal are thinking, "He must have been to China during his absence. He certainly has returned in power!" He detonates an explosion:

> Fire suddenly consumes the burnt offering, and the wood, and even the *stones* and the *dust*, and licks up the water that was in the trench. (1Kg. 18.38)

Nothing's left at all – everything in the vicinity is vaporized. This amazing display convinces the people, so when he routs them to seize the other magicians, they do it. They march the priests and priestesses – restrained, tied hand and foot one to the other – down to the Brook Kishon. There, in a holy celebration of blood lasting several hours, neck after neck, man after man, every nubile virgin, and every priestess, takes the sharp edge of the dagger.

The Lord is proven by the magic of Elijah, and satisfied by his blade.

Fire Magic

Elijah develops particular expertise along the fire lane. As in modern times, we see that magicians develop a special competence and ability in an area of the craft. Houdini is an escape artist, Gil Boyne is a hypnotist. Magicians, as artists of any craft, develop their flairs in lines in which they particularly excel, both by interest and inclination.

One of the characteristics of fire magic that we see so superbly demonstrated here is the sudden, deep, and lasting change it impels in people's consciousness. It empowers one to take immediate, decisive action. Not only do the people immediately accept Elijah's God as the true God, but they act on that with a commitment that could prove costly to them. When they massacre the magicians of Baal and Astarte, they are acting as a mob. The sanctioned religion is still the religion of the God and Goddess. Ahab and his wife, Jezebel, as rulers, can't support such outrageous lawlessness. And who should provoke a monarch?

The Rainmaker

Now that *Elijah* has the people's attention, it's time to restore fertility. He didn't want to just do it, because the people would not accept that he had anything to do with it. They would say it was just chance or coincidence. But now that he has demonstrated the awful power of God, and got himself associated with it, they will hold it to heart.

He forecasts his next event in suggestive language. He tells Ahab,

> "Go up, eat and drink; for there is a sound of the rushing of rain." (1Kg. 18.41)

It is time to restore fertility.

And now that the show, the furor, and the slaughter are over, and everyone has gone to their homes, Elijah climbs back up to the top of Mt. Carmel, makes some reverent and directed oblations, and bows so fully he puts his face between his knees. Rising from this meditative trance, he sends his assistant to the other edge of the mountain, to look toward the sea.

He goes, comes back, and reports, "I saw nothing."

Perhaps surprisingly he finds it very difficult to reverse the spell he uttered with such incisive intent those years previously. He has a challenge even for a magician of his calibre. He knows what to do, it just takes more of it than he can easily access. The purpose of that experimentation is ever the working of the will of God.

So Elijah reenters the magical state and again commands God and the elements. Again he sends his assistant, and again the assistant brings the same report, "I saw nothing."

This same scenario is played four more times, each time Elijah entering deeper into mystical communion, marshaling a more powerful intent.

Finally, on the seventh trial the servant reports the first evidence of success,

"Behold, a little cloud like a man's hand is rising out of the sea!" (Kg. 18.44)

That's all he needs. In a little while the heavens grow turbulent with clouds and wind and a great rain rages. The enchantment is lifted; the waters flow again.

The Working Of Adepts

We won't belabor the point of numbers in ritual again, though we can note that it is on the seventh effort that Elijah meets success. Two interesting magical principles we can note in Elijah's performance involve alchemy and multiplication.

He Has Not Failed, But Has Succeeded. The very persistence that we see here is revelatory, certainly worth discussion. We see faith, concentration, and repetitive experimental effort. When his servant brings word that there is no success – repeatedly – he does not take it as indications of failure and lack of ability, but that he needs to do something else to manifest the effect he is after. He has not "failed," but has succeeded in finding he needs to adjust his efforts. And he keeps at it, trying different invocations, different depths of trance until he does hit upon the combination that works.

He is adept in the alchemical art. Though he has never publically performed this magical event before, his intuition ensures him that he can. It is up to him to discover how that will come to pass. He never doubts, though he does need the feedback on the progress of his efforts. The *sine qua non* of alchemy is *experim*entation. When he finally hits upon the combination that works, he sends his servant to town to warn Ahab, and sets about in further concentration to bring the rains down in torrents.

Such is the way an adept works. God speaks to the adept in intuition. The adept does not doubt the effect is to be accomplished, though he may have to experiment to discover how to do it. Having that foreknowledge gives the adept the energy for the persistent effort and experimentation that allows it to actually happen.

It Is Easier To Multiply Than To Manifest. For all the effort, testing, and experimentation it takes to make the first manifestation, with that the remainder flows easily. From a tiny cloud come torrents of rain. It is easier to multiply even a very small substance into a vast amount than it is to pull the first minute particles across the great Cosmic divide between the metaphysical and the physical. Yet it can be done; Elijah does it.

He Firebombs Them

Elijah. After his outrageous display of religious intolerance, killing 850 productive citizens, he goes on the run again. We don't hear too much from him for a number of years.

Elijah sees how Ahab and his wife will die, and tells Ahab the evil fate that awaits them. It comes to pass just as his precognitions prophesy. Ahab's son, Ahaziah, comes to the throne. Ahaziah will tolerate him, so Elijah returns. But he still hasn't gotten any better.

One day Ahaziah falls through the lattice of a second-story window, and is seriously wounded. He sends messengers to inquire of God through Baal whether he will get well or whether he will die. But the feared wizard Elijah intercepts them and sends them back to the king with his own message. He assures Ahaziah, because he is seeking Gods other than the native God of olden times,

"You will surely die." (2Kg. 1.4)

The king has never had any love for Elijah, anyway. Sick, he throws a royal fit and sends fifty government agents to bring him in. They find him meditating on the crest of a nearby hill. This is their first approach, so, but for the intimidation of numbers with swords and daggers, they speak politely to him. The captain addresses him respectfully,

"Oh man of God, the king says, 'Come down.'" (2Kg. 1.9)

But, too bad for them. Elijah's reply is twofold, the statement and the act:

"If I am a man of God, let fire come down from Heaven and consume you and your fifty." (1Kg. 1.10)

He firebombs them. Scripture says in understatement:

Fire comes down from Heaven, and consumes him and his fifty. (1Kg. 1.10)

The king's second force approaches him with more force. He has just killed fifty-one uniformed policemen. The command this time is phrased as a direct order:

"O man of God, this is the king's order, 'Come down quickly!'" (2Kg. 1.11)

Elijah answers this proudly decorated captain,

"If I am a man of God, let fire come down from Heaven and consume you and your fifty."

Then the fire of God came down from Heaven and consumed him and his fifty. (2Kg. 1.12)

Too bad for them Elijah is so good with fire.

The king dies as Elijah's prescience foretells.

Of Psychic Verities
Magic is real; you learn to direct it by getting high.

The Real Effects Of Magic. You occasionally hear a person laughing about the subject of magic, expressing an opinion that it's just something of the fairy-airy dimensions. Why don't you ask the mothers, wives, and daughters of the hundred-and-two men Elijah cinders?

No, though the connection between cause and effect, invocation and accomplishment is seldom so rapid or so direct as Elijah demonstrates it, magic involves very *real* effects in material reality.

This is psychokinesis, the effect in the material dimensions of intentions fostered or directed from the metaphysical inner chambers.

The Position Of Power. Most people would think the balance of power was in favor of the trained and equipped government squads; you have fifty-one of them arrayed against a single man. But the agents come upon Elijah during a time when he is supercharged. When they find him he is deep in the bliss of meditation, high atop the hill. Many of the greatest accomplishments of the spiritual life come from high places, as Moses ascends the mountain Sinai to commune with God, the transfiguration happens praying on a mountain, the last supper is celebrated in an upper chamber, and Jesus raises himself on a cross on Mt. Golgotha.

This is unfortunate for the king's soldiers. You can't outwit a magician in his own theater.

Parting The Waters
Elisha. With his efforts accomplished, in a true spiritual initiation, *Elijah* is raised into power. Nobody ascends to Heaven in a more dramatic way – not Enoch, not Moses, not Jesus. Heaven opens and a chariot of fire drawn by four wild-eyed horses whisks into the scene, as quickly ascending the spiral pathway away with Elijah. It is over in an instant.

Elisha receives what he has earned in his heart. He picks up the magical cape fallen from Elijah's shoulders, and clasps it around his neck. Now he is the sorcerer.

For his first feat he crosses back over the Jordan the same way his master took them earlier. He calls on the power of Elijah, strikes the water with the rolled up cape, the waters part, and he crosses:

"Oh Lord, God of Elijah!"

And he strikes the water, and the water parts to the one side and to the other; and Elisha crosses over. (2Kg. 2.14)

A half-hour ago Elisha was waterboy to a magician, the sorcerer's apprentice.

Few People Do It

Elisha, by the way, is one of only four magicians in the entire span of the Bible to perform this marvel. Interestingly, the four break down into two groups of two.

As we've just seen, Elisha follows the lead of his master; Elijah. Moses and his student-initiate, Joshua, are the other two who perform this marvel. Whereas there are moments between the two performances of Elijah and Elisha, there are decades between Moses' and Joshua's. Whereas Elijah and Elisha take themselves only across, both Moses and Joshua lead a nation. Moses parts the Red Sea, Joshua, Elijah, and Elisha part the River Jordan. Not until the teacher/mentor disappears do either of the younger magicians perform their parting phenomena. It is good to learn from mentors. This is a very early effect for both students, performing it shortly after the death of their mentors. Moses, on the other hand, performs this wizardry well after he has begun his public magical career. It is part of Elijah's final performance.

The Bearclaws End Of The Needling Boys

When we read about the fertility magic *Elisha* first performs we think he's risen straight to a position of positive contribution to society. He restores the polluted waters of Jericho, so that they have been wholesome even to this day! But he still has some growing to do.

From Jericho Elisha retraces his steps. Outside Bethel a small crowd of young boys taunt him about his baldness. Elisha loses his temper,

> curses them in the name of the Lord, and two she-bears come out of the
> woods and tear apart forty-two of the boys. (2Kg. 2.24)

Of Psychic Verities

Ever wonder how they slide this one by? I've heard a lot of preachers, but I've never heard anyone laying any condemnation on Elisha.

Gunning Down School Kids. Essentially it is uncaused... I mean, the only thing the youngsters do is act like youngsters. He could have just passed on with understanding. But no! Instead he loses his temper and pulls off the largest single schoolyard mass murder I'm aware of. (Government jobs don't count, since they are legitimate.) Each of the boys' final breaths comes at the blood-dripping claws of an enraged she-bear.

Think! *Think!!* *THINK!!!* It still happens. What you see here is a lone crazy gone to the school yard, gunning down numbers of innocent victims. In today's world this is a crime of international infamy, even if the criminal *is* acting in the name of God. It's just that Elisha, who of course doesn't have guns, since they aren't invented yet, uses a different instrument, bears. And he is honored for the same. He does it all with magic.

Black Magic By Any Other Name. Since this Biblical passage clearly says Elisha throws the curse at them "in the name of the Lord," we've got some serious considering to do. Is this force that can be directed to cause anomalous events to occur really God, or is it just often identified as God?

Is it a force that can be conjured up and used for good or ill, as directed, or is God wholly a beneficent force? If you hold that God is wholly a beneficent force, you've got some hard explaining to do. What lesson could God want to communicate that justifies the savagery Elisha perpetuates on these grade school youngsters?

The only sensible conclusion is that the psi power exists, and it can be used for good or for evil. It is like electricity in the mundane world. The power is. It can be used to heal or kill. It can run the tools that help a surgeon remove an otherwise fatal brain tumor or it can fry a man straight into the afterlife. Once you learn how to use it, like any power, you use it in accordance with the potentialities of your personality, that is, your level of consciousness.

This is a controversial point. Some people – already more open-minded than most, just in recognizing a part of the magical panoply – deny the efficacy of black magic. But God clearly lays it out for us here again. A black call – a curse – affects the world. The power directed, the event occurs.

The Progressive Development Of Psi. Elisha shows us that, though he may have dominion in magic, he surely has a long way to go with his psychological demons. We also see through the stories of Elisha that he does indeed develop beyond this petulant point, illustrating that the progressive pathway of psychic development involves more than one dimension.

The Mystical Transformation Of Water Into Blood

Elisha. Jehoshaphat. Jehoshaphat. Israel. Moab. Moab quits paying tribute to Israel when Ahab dies. The new king, Jehoram, has to prove his manhood. Plus, the money's outrageous! Moab's been paying "a hundred thousand lambs, and the wool of a hundred thousand rams" (2Kg. 3.4).

So Israel cohorts with its ally chieftains to resubjugate the rebellious colony. Jehoshaphat, king of Judah, with his army accompanies Jehoram to the borders of the war. But before they launch the offensive, a matter of serious undertaking, he suggests they consult a psychic. They are seven days from home, on a march that has tried their supplies of water harshly. The desert is brutal in its unremitting oppression. A local tells them that a man named Elisha lives nearby, and they can seek him out.

Elisha, of course, is just about as apolitically concerned as they come. He, who himself earns little money and is taxed heavily on that little sum, feels no inclination to suddenly enroll in these men's cause. Besides that, he really doesn't like Israel, apostates to Baal. In fact, he throws that in Jehoram's face, asking why he would come to see a follower of the Lord God when he has a God of his own.

But finally Elisha, because he has, as he says, a "high regard" for Jehoshaphat, agrees.

But he must get in state. When he arrives there, in the vales of Avalon, he can communicate with God. And in Avalon of Alpha he can understand God's communications to him. The state of power comes first. In state, the actions the magician takes are powerful. He calls a minstrel in, a maker of beautiful melodies,

> And when the minstrel plays, he enters in the power of the Spirit" (2Kg. 3.15)

He places himself in this borderline mystic state, midway between the mundane and the Divine. Here, the worlds interact, the mundane is empowered by the Divine. Here Elisha channels the Lord:

> "Thus says the Lord, 'I will make this dry stream-bed full of pools. You shall not see wind or rain, but that stream-bed shall be filled with water, so that you shall drink, you, your cattle, and your beasts.'" (2Kg. 3.16-17)

Thus God assures them directly that he will tend to their most pressing need, water. But after that, of course, lies the battle for which they journeyed here.

This fulfillment, accomplished with no outward signs that would announce it – will then serve a military purpose. Elisha continues, not quoting or channeling God now, but speaking what his clairvoyance has revealed to him:

> "He will also give the Moabites into your hand, and help you destroy all that they have and hold dear. Your victory shall be complete: you shall conquer every fortified city, and every choice city, and shall fell every good tree, and stop up all springs of water, and absolutely ruin every good piece of land with stones." (2Kg. 3.18)

Because of the paranormal approval of their intents, and the promised paranormal participation in their battles, they are restored to confidence. *Boy it's good to have a psychic around when you need one!*

And God performs as he says he will. Early the next morning, while it is still totally dark, water flows, and the whole country is filled with water. Meantime, Moabite scouts have discovered the kingdoms camped just beyond the ridge of their city. They rush back, sound the alarm, and quickly assemble every able male from fourteen to sixty-four on the frontier. Then the Moabites encounter a paranormal experience. In the first glints of the morning sun upon the water, the Moabites see that water opposite them as red as blood.

Lifted in sudden joy they cry:

> "This is blood! The kings have surely fought together, and slain one another! Now then, *Moab, to the spoil!*"(2Kg. 3.23)

So they run in with high anticipation of easy booty, but when they enter the camp, the Israelites rise and put them to rout. The organized and disciplined warriors of Israel catch every single fleeing helter-skelter Moabite to the edge of the sword, so that blood does indeed run deeply in the land.

And it unfolds as Elisha sees and foretells in his psychic trance,

They overthrow the cities, and on every good piece of land every man throws a stone, until it is covered; they stop every spring of water, and fell all the good trees; they absolutely ruin the land. (2Kg. 3.25)

With the magic of the Lord on their side, the kings disembowel and sufficiently humble the nation so she pays her just taxes.

The Things Of Magic

This event causes sensitive students to reflect on at least two elements of its uniqueness. The first answers the question, "When is the paranormal magic?" The second issue regards the methods of enchantment.

"How Do You Call This Magic?" How do we call what Elisha does *magic*? Shouldn't we just recognize it as channeling? After all, Elisha simply enters the alpha state and lets God speak through him in words and visions.

But look at the larger picture. Elisha enters this meditation with a specific purpose. He is a psychic, sitting for others. These kings do not come to him simply wanting to know something about the future, but wanting specific assistance. They seek out a magician for magic. They have two massive concerns, drinking water and the Moabites. These are what the shaman carries with him as he passes the portals of the inner dimensions.

And God responds to his intentions. God does not talk about some far off good, or even offer correction or censure, which he is wont to do in general and abstract readings. No, he focuses specifically on the concerns of the kings.

How Elisha accomplishes the magic is secondary to *that* he accomplishes magic.

This does not say that commanding is invalidated, but it shows another way. Once you enter into that magical mystery state with intention, the intention alone is a command. God responds either by a spoken command or an intention held in heart.

The dedicated invocation plays a large role in most conscious magic, and that is just what Elisha's entry into meditation is. He enters the paranormal position with a general intention of war. Knowing that God is far more capable than man, in creativity as well as ability to perform, Elisha does not limit the workings of God, but rather stays open to what the God space wishes to perform.

There is no indication that God is going to perform these magical effects before Elisha enters into his company with this intent. Therefore, Elisha as a magician performs this magic deed.

All true magic, after all, is accomplished by God. Does the gardener make the garden grow?

Victory By Enchantment. This event combines two different types of magical effects. The first involves a material effect, the second is clearly stated to be mystical only. The appearance of the water is a magical event, especially since there are no clouds nor is there any rain.

Then, though the Moabites are hoo-dooed, nothing in actuality changes. There is no need for altering actuality when a reality can be framed in the mind of your marks that causes them to act as you desire. They undergo a paranormal experience. It *is* water, the Bible clearly states; it does not change. Yet it is *seen* or *perceived* otherwise. Because of the magical preparations and invocation of Elisha, it presents itself to Elisha's mark as *blood.* Pure enchantment. Hypnosis. Elisha and God work their nefarious magic in the paranormal domains, not in the realm of material reality.

As it ever is with human things – even if they are *mis*-perceptions – our perceptions and beliefs form the basis of our actions.

What power the magicians possess!

"You Shall Bear A Son"

Being that roads are the sign of the wizard, it's not surprising to find *Elisha* cares little about the "family" scene. He spends a lot of his time traveling around and sharing the company of adventure in the coterminous psychic domains.

He frequently leads study groups and workshops, gives lectures and psychic readings in Shunem. One metaphysical lady of the group, a wealthy lady, befriends him and cooks him nourishing, loving meals when he passes through. Then she even has her husband build him an upstairs addition, a gabled chamber, and furnishes it simply with a bed, a table, a chair, and an oil lamp.

One day he is resting there and tells his servant and companion to go call her. When she comes Elisha tells her he wants to return her kindnesses,

> "What, kind lady, can I do for you? Would you have a word spoken on your behalf to the king or to the commander of the army?"

She answers,

> "My lord, you are a psychic. You live the glamorous life of fame and travel to distant places. It is enough for me that I dwell among my own people." (2Kg. 4.13)

In other words, she says, *nothing.*

Elisha sends her away.

But Gehazi and Elisha talk further about her. Elisha hasn't noticed because of the attentions of meditation and public position, but Gehazi reveals,

> "Well, she has no son, her time is passing, and her husband is old..." (2Kg. 4.14)

"Woo! Go get her again, now," he tells his servant. When she comes he tells boy Friday to take a vacation for a couple of hours. He needs to be alone with her to get her pregnant. Lying close after the passion crests, he tells the lovely woman,

> "Spring time is beautiful, my dear. When the fertile time comes round next year, you shall embrace your *own* infant son."

And she says,

> "No! my lord, O man of God; do not lie to your maidservant!" (2Kg. 4.16)

She quickly gathers herself and withdraws, troubled.

But the woman gets pregnant, and she does bear a son, just as Elisha plants it. And she tells her husband it was magic.

Master Magic? Or Simple Precognition?

This story certainly has elements of precognition in it. The overlap is strong enough not to contest it in any way but to acknowledge it and even celebrate it.

But the sense of the story identifies this as much more than simple precognition. Elisha *causes* this to happen. He is, remember, *searching* for some way to return the favor to the lady.

Though it is the dearest dream in her heart, by dint of the circumstances she finds herself in, she holds no longer the dream nor desire for its actual fulfillment. It is too big an idea for her to accept when Elisha whispers it manfully in her ear. She melts. Because Elisha wills it – and it is a blessing to all concerned – the Universe willingly responds. This is clearly magic.

Elisha speaks it simply as a channeled message, but it is what he does that fertilizes the seed she carries. In the shadows of his mirrored bedroom Elisha wields his wand, and the woman conceives. He fathers her blessing.

News that we receive from a psychic is always portentous, and cause for deep reflection, nourishment, and gratitude. In this manner we get more out of the event. When it occurs as foretold, we know it has a special significance.

Quite a magical event, rich in complexities of blessings.

Who Can Raise The Living From The Dead?

There are a number of similarities between *Elisha* and Jesus. One of the truly magical feats they both perform is raising people from the dead.

Elisha doesn't get out much these days. He spends most of his time in the retreat at Carmel, guarded and tended to as a personage of high spiritual dominion. Though he doesn't get back to see her, he recognizes the Shunammite woman when he sees her urgency on the pathway before the retreat. He sends orders to the guards to let her through.

She tells the story... As it turns out, the young boy Elisha fathered on her twelve years ago accompanies his father out to the harvest fields, where he is being initiated into the man's world of work, commerce, and care. He is working beside his father when he suddenly rises up screaming, holding his head, "Oh my head! My head!" How quickly life can pass, even when one enjoys the apparent blessings of full health. His lies in his mother's lap until noon, when his final shallow breath departs.

Now we see what comes to the virtuous. Watch carefully the woman's actions after her son dies. She takes him up and lays him supine on the bed of the psychic, Elisha. She shuts the door upon him, and tells her husband to have the servants carry her quickly to Elisha's domain. The husband tries to restrain his delusional wife. *"The boy is dead!"* he argues. He sees her impelled by grief, but she is so powerful in her insistence that he complies.

She rushes the jockey along at a reckless pace. Upon seeing Elisha she falls with heaves and tears clasping his feet.

Gehazi jumps to remove her, but Elisha stops him, saying,

> "Let her alone, for she is in bitter distress; and the Lord has hidden it from me, and has not told me." (2Kg. 4.27)

Elisha accompanies her back to Shunem. He enters, shuts the door upon him only and the corpse, and then reinspires life into the boy:

> He climbs into the bed and lays point to point upon the boy, hands on hands, eyes on eyes, and mouth upon mouth. He then gives the blue boy what looks like a penetrating French kiss, with the sound of legions screaming in the room. (2Kg. 4.33.34)

And the mother, in the hallway outside, falls backwards against the wall and drops to the floor.

Inside the room, the flesh becomes warm, the body sneezes seven times, adjusting itself to Earthly reality, light stirs inside the eyes, and the boy regains consciousness. The boy has just enjoyed one of the earliest recorded out-of-body (OBE) experiences.

And the shaman gives the woman back her son with the words,

> "Take up your son, he lives." (2Kg. 4.36)

She bows at the wizard's feet, takes her son, and leaves.

"The Lord Has Hidden It."

There is a selectiveness to the psychic power. The psychic power always manifests in the particular. Just as, though the blade of grass has all the Universal Energy behind it as its life force, it only knows and experiences according to the level of its allotted awareness. So it is with the psychic powers of humanity.

Here is the answer to those smartmouths who say to you, "You're psychic, you should know everything."

The truth is, you don't. You only receive and demonstrate in manners natural for you. Thus, for instance, the chemicals Moses causes to eat away the Egyptians are not sprayed from an airplane, but are airborne with a toss of the hand.

Also, you receive what you either specifically tune into or what the Implicate reality specifically wants you to know. Some things enter randomly, most don't.

Some things are concealed, as the powerful Elisha recognizes.

Feeding The Multitudes

Elisha. Famine ravages the land. Elisha visits the monastery, and finds conditions extreme for its one hundred inmates. Food, even a meager setting, is highly coveted.

It is harvest season, and a traveler stocked from another place arrives with some barley loaves and a few fresh ears of corn. Elisha commands the man,

"Give to the men, that they may eat." (2Kg. 4.42)

But the servant, charged with the discharge of this function, protests,

"How am I to set this before a *hundred* men?" (2Kg. 4.43)

Elisha repeats his command, assuring him,

"Thus says the Lord, 'They shall eat and have some left.'" (2Kg. 4.43)

As spoken by Elisha, when the meal is over they gather up an abundance of leftover food.

"According To Its Kind"

Magic does never violate natural law. What seems like magic is but the utilization of a natural law at a higher or more skillful level than the masses are currently able to accomplish. Magic comes coupled with the attractive fact that we instinctively know, somewhere down there, we *are* capable of operating at the same level.

Elisha arrives at the institute, but at first he cannot help the devotees, though he tries. He tells his trusty servant to boil them up some pottage. But the wild gourds that he can find have no life in them but rather death. So they throw the pottage out. Elisha searches and finds some meal, which they fix an amount of sufficient to slow the approach of death, not to deter it. Why does Elisha not make these foods fruitful and abundant?

This magical event of Elisha's demonstrates an inviolable principle. Elisha could do no magic there, because of their unsupportive substance.

But give him a little something to work with – enter a wayfarer with barley corn – and "Wham!" "Presto!" he feeds them all and has to gather the leftovers up in *baskets*!

The magical powers of leverage and multiplication obtain to the substance they are applied to. Famine, lack, dearth, and death are poisoning the system of the land. But introduce a wholesome element, and Elisha can multiply the blessing, according to its kind.

Firewalking One Day

Shadrach. Meshach. Abednego. One day Daniel's companions have a skirmish with the local religious authorities. Nebuchadnezzar makes a new sculpture of the popular Godform, and makes public proclamation:

> "You are commanded, O peoples, nations, and languages, that when you hear the sound of the horn, pipe, lyre, trigon, harp, bagpipe, and every kind of music, you are to fall down and worship before the golden sculpture that King Nebuchadnezzar has set up; and whoever does not fall down and worship shall immediately be cast into a burning fiery furnace." (Dan. 3.4-6)

The truth is that the Babylonians and Nebuchadnezzar are generally tolerant of the religious practices of the Jews. Over all they are productive taxpayers. But there are always little minds, perfect establishment mouses. And the law provides the perfect opportunity for these types to attack what they fear. Following due process in the legal system, the petty power figures of the desert kingdom, the satraps, the prefects, the governors, and the king's counselors get the three Jewish men sentenced to burn in that furnace.

These boys, Shadrach, Meshach, and Abednego, are even given the due legal option of retraining, but refuse. Real rebels. Their smart attitude infuriates the king. They will rely on their God to save them, they reply to Nebuchadnezzar's threats. So they are laced at the wrists and feet, and, fully dressed in their tunics and all, are thrown into the pit, which Nebuchadnezzar has ordered heated seven times hotter than customary.

Even the police pricks who carry them to the edge of the pit lose their lives to the flames. The book tells us,

> Because the king's order is strict and the furnace very hot, the flame of the fire slays those men who take up Shadrach, Meshach, and Abednego. And these three men, Shadrach, Meshach, and Abednego, fall bound into the burning fiery furnace. (Dan. 3.23)

But the next thing the king sees is *four* firewalkers hopping about! Even at the door of the furnace cold beads of sweat burst on his forehead. The cold of the paranormal. He grasps to the minionettes surrounding his majesty,

> "Who is this fourth man, dazzling like the son of a God?!" (Dan. 3.25)

Even as he speaks he knows. He himself first "hears" it when he hears himself say it. Nebuchadnezzar immediately calls the young men out. The *three* come out. And the satraps, the prefects, the governors, and the king's counselors all gather around the boys, unable to deny that this *brutal* fire did not touch the boys. Not a hair is singed; no chars even of the frays of their mantles; not even the smell of smoke lingers on the boys.

Nebuchadnezzar is so moved that he forthwith proclaims a new decree. How characteristic of the times. Such severe sentences for statements of personal religious preference:

> "Blessed be the God of Shadrach, Meshach, and Abednego, who has sent his angel and delivered his own who trusted in him, – his own who staked their very lives in commitment and confidence rather than serve any God other than their own.
>
> "Therefore I make a decree: Any people, nation, or language that speaks anything against the God of Shadrach, Meshach, and Abednego shall be torn limb from limb, and their houses laid in ruins; for none of the other Gods are able to deliver in this way." (Dan. 3.28-29)

No one is ever executed under this law. Nevertheless, though the Jewish God is not the God of choice, at least it is now a state-sanctioned God. Nebuchadnezzar *legislates* para-equality into the system. This should sound familiar.

These young men living by their convictions bring awe and honor to their God. In their commitment to God, God opens the higher dimensions to empower their experience and to dazzle the world.

Yesterday and today, the firewalk is magic.

By The Thought Held In Heart
The king is no scoffer, but people who *won't see* miss the very thing they charge... And we see the magic of magic – consciousness alone affects reality.

Psychic Scoffers. The king is a superior specimen of manhood. He has every advantage given by blood, education and training, counsel, and reflection. He sees the paranormal. There is no record nor indication that anyone else sees past the veil of material sensation into the etherworld. But what they *all* see are the *results* of the event. The fire is *scorching* hot, even killing the six cops who throw Shadrach, Meshach, and Abednego in. Three men walk out of the still raging inferno, exhibiting not the least evidence of even having stood close to a fire – a fire that they were thrown into bound.

Magic is in the air. Nebuchadnezzar sees the paranormal in action.

All are witnesses to the reality of a magical event. There are puzzled people and there are dazzled people. But of those who see it, there is no one doubting what has happened. The young men exhibit fire immunity. Magical. Miraculous.

But with the passage of time, self-styled "saner" minds invade the turf. Now there are skeptics and doubters. So the skeptics attempt to discount the entire event, charging that these three spiritually dedicated men just know something most of us don't.

Wake up! That's just what we're saying!

The Power Of Consciousness. Fortunately for us, success leaves clues. That powerful secret of transformation is none other than what the mystics tell us, the power of consciousness. We *do* have a role in creating events and in determining how they affect us. Our heart, above all – which but expresses in our thoughts, words, and actions – in certain instances activates this power to accomplish things in such a way and of such a magnitude that we call them metaphysical, paranormal, miraculous, magical events.

This is the essence of PK, anomalous perturbation, miracle, or magic. The "normal" working of reality is altered, affected by the quality of the thought held in heart.

Commitment, independence, confidence, serenity are qualities of the magical state. The intriguing paradox is that these same qualities are the requisites to enter through the portals of enchantment. It takes faith born of knowledge to do it. Magic *is* in what you know. Being most fully human, you become most Divine.

Further, it sometimes takes what appears to be great courage to maintain that confidence. But if you really *know* it, could you do anything else? Do you see? You can grasp where these men are coming from. These firewalkers are not Daniel, a gifted initiate by all standards, but his ordinary, devoted companions. These young men, with their wealth, their relationships, and their lives on the line are unswervingly committed to the magical domain of the Infinite. Aren't wizards all? This is the secret of consciousness which causes all things.

"Good Little Lion! Purr Sweetly, Little Lion."

Daniel. With Belshazzar's assassination, in which Daniel plays a small role, Darius the Mede takes power. This new potentate also recognizes Daniel's exceptional abilities and appoints him satrap over a portion of the realm.

Daniel's land is the most productive in art, mysticism, agriculture, and commerce. Daniel is stealing all the glory from the natural-born Babylonians, so – political creatures ever – they collude against him. But, even under the scrutinizing eyes of high paid attorneys and the prying eyes of undercover agents, Daniel is clean. So they decide to change the law on a point that they know will get him, the law of his inner life.

They seduce the king with flattery:

"O King Darius, live for ever! All the presidents of the kingdom, the prefects and the satraps, the counselors and the governors are agreed that the king should establish an ordinance and enforce an interdict, that whoever makes petition to any God or man for thirty days, except to you, O king, shall be cast into the den of lions. Now, O king, establish the interdict and sign the document, so that it cannot be changed, according to the law of the Medes and the Persians, which cannot be revoked."

Therefore King Darius signs the document and the interdict. (Dan. 6.6-9)

It doesn't make any difference to Daniel. In full awareness that the law has been decreed, he continues his practices of work and worship. The conspirators, of course, are lying in wait. They press charges, demanding the full force of the law be brought to bear on this flagrant lawbreaker.

The king is beside himself, and tries to release Daniel, but the satraps vulture over him reminding him he has signed a law that cannot be altered. Daniel must die, and he must die today. Forced by the custom of the Medes and Persians, the plotting of his advisors and governors, and his own hand, the king complies. He himself seals the giant rock rolled over the opening of the lion's den. It is over for Daniel, he knows. The king moves quietly to his chambers without wine, company, or entertainment and fasts the whole night. He cannot sleep.

And just as day is breaking he goes to the rock to mourn, and calls out rhetorically to Daniel, who *answers* him! He hails the king with dignity:

"O king, live for ever!" (Dan. 6.21),

and then goes on to tell him he is perfectly fine, because he has done no wrong.

The king joyfully commands Daniel's hasty removal from the lion's den, and they find no hurt at all on him. Truly the magic of his God has intervened! The writer of this story makes sure we see this with unmistakable impact, as the lions are indeed hungry.

Like a trader playing the commodities markets, since the market has *obviously* revealed its direction, the king changes his order and commands Daniel's accusers, their children, and their wives be cast into the den of lions. Though there are ever so many,

> before they reach the bottom of the den the lions overpower them and break all their bones in pieces. (Dan. 6.24)

Daniel's small-minded accusers are gone all at once. Magic has suitably established Daniel and his God as workers of great signs and wonders. Daniel continues to prosper under the Persian reign.

Consciousness Is Everything

Congruency of command, combined with the pleasures of enchantment, works magic. Consciousness *is* everything.

Unshakeable Congruency. Unshakeable congruency is a characteristic that distinguishes wizards from the masses who live lives of quiet desperation. Wizards command and persuade the finite through the infinite channels of the paranormal. From the uninitiate's point of view, they command things that are not as though they are.

And their congruency is sometimes demonstrated at the risk of bodily harm. But if they are not willing to engage in the effects they claim are most real and possible, can they be called true magicians? Not to worry, Daniel is a true magician.

So Daniel finds himself before the most gruesomely uncomfortable form of fear and punishment the kingdom offers: the den of hungry lions.

But he knows the secret. All the world responds to the magician's consciousness. He knows God will protect him because that's the way the universe works. The magician knows it is the same for every person. All the HoloCosmic world corresponds to every person's consciousness.

Then what distinguishes the magician from the masses? The magician *knows* how it works, which indeed very few people do, and then, empowered with that awareness, makes conscious decisions about what he or she wants, expecting it with congruency. That manifests it.

With the insights we receive from our understanding of the HoloCosmic Universe, we can surmise Daniel's approach in this illusion. Daniel "sees" the lean lions as cats, whom he gets along well with. (Psychics, sensitives, and mystics generally do.) Daniel treats them as cats. They believe. They are willing, if unconscious, participants in the pleasures of enchantment.

It is not *where* you are, amongst whom or what, but *how* you are. Consciousness is everything. Consciousness is the prime device of the magician.

Most people manifest what they don't want, holding, as they do, those odious thoughts in mind. The petty band of attorneys promoted to satraps don't have the heart or wisdom of Daniel. They would like to have Daniel eaten alive. Like Daniel they receive what they hold in their hearts. Nature responds appropriately.

The Pleasures Of Enchantment. These are the same young, mean, and *hungry* lions that maul and tear humans carnally apart in the blood and meat of a meal. We see them with the group that is thrown to them just minutes after Daniel is removed from their den. How do you figure the difference?

Daniel's life is saved by enchantment, but here is another pleasure we don't want to overlook. There is no indication from the passages that Daniel ever experiences or exhibits any hatred or stress. Throughout the ordeal, and even after it is over he never speaks judgmental words of anyone. He has no hand in the extermination of his accusers. Big government does that. Daniel just goes on living a peaceful life in love. And that's a high pleasure of enchantment by itself. Daniel lives a charmed life, taken by his heart. What can be better than a path which brings joy to your heart and the heart of the Cosmic every day?

The Guy's Sure Taking A Risk!

Some of *Jesus'* most spectacular stories concern him employing his PK abilities. John records his first public event as a demonstration of PK. Jesus lays an *abracadabra* on a group of water jugs and prestos them into a batch of *killer* wine for free distribution to already wine-animated guests at a wedding. People get drunk and do stupid things, but nobody brings a multi-million dollar suit against him for forcing them to drink the supra-laced wine. Today he'd probably be more careful. Oh how magical!

Mary *knows* Jesus' abilities, because of her maturity, likely more surely than even Jesus himself does. She has been mothering him, watching him develop over the years, weighing all things deeply in her heart. For all we know Jesus may provide all the wine their household drinks. When she is involved in this embarrassing situation at her sister's wedding – *We are running out of wine, Oh my! Oh my!* – she asks her son to do what he does.

She knows.... It is time. Blessed Mother.

Like everyone, Jesus has to break the circles of womblike comfort around the status quo. He replies curtly,

"So what, Mom? You know I'm not ready!" (Jn. 2.4)

But he is subdued by the command in her silent eyes. She breaks eye contact and instructs the servants,

"Do whatever he tells you." (Jn. 2.5)

He obeys. Mary nudges him this one last time, and he's flying. He soars.

The story goes on telling us how he transforms – with no discernable show of hocus-pocus, ritual, or command – six stone jars of water into a marvelously fine wine.

Thus begins his public career, which he decidedly *is* ready for. He's grown, he's cleansed, he's dedicated. He's got himself together, just back from his forty day vision quest, here to express incredible ambition, focus, and fortitude.

Destiny In The Balance

This is not Jesus' first psi event by any means. But this is his first *public* psi event. No longer is he an enclaved student at the Temple in Egypt nor at the ashram in India. No longer is he operating within the boundaries of his family or with his circle of confederates.

Jesus begins his public career with the magical performance of transforming ordinary water into whamo wine. In this guidebook for humanity, surely this deserves some consideration. There has to be a purpose. What do you suppose God is saying to us with this?

And news of his magical phenomena and the reputation of the man jumps like wildfire amongst tumbleweed. And many believe.

With this single act, Jesus becomes "somebody." Also with this event springs up the envy crowd. Don't believe anyone sued him, that's just our way of thinking today. They do start the plotting, however. The chain of events Jesus sets in motion with this public demonstration of his psychic abilities leads to his death on the cross.

Guess he *does* take a pretty big risk.

Commanding The Elementals

Although Jesus' main brand of magic is spiritual and bodily alchemy, he also has a proclivity to what we call *elemental* magic. This has to with the control of natural phenomena. In the gospel narratives we have several clips of him commanding fishes, winds, and waves... and *of them responding.*

Of course, such a man is judged mad by normal people. Nevertheless, what he is teaching, however mad normal people think him, however much a threat to the established power structure, however much an embarrassment to his mother and brothers, attracts a large following amongst the new age crowd. The time is right.

Threatened, he will not, cannot, stop.

So many people show up on the banks of the Jordan to hear Jesus that his conversational gathering grows into a large lecture. So that everyone can see and hear him fully, he teaches from a boat rowed slightly out from shore.

Amongst the discourses of the day, Jesus renders the parable of the sower and the seed; the parable of the shining lamp; and his instruction on commitment and success, which he concludes with the famous line expressing Natural Law,

"The rich get richer, the poor get poorer." (Mk. 4.25)

What enchantment! He holds the people spellbound until he tires in the early evening.

So they depart. He's really put himself out today in the hot sun. He reclines and falls into a deep sleep immediately. Even the winds and the waves of a rising tempest don't stir him.

But his companions are very much aware and fighting in fear for their very lives. Finally, they wake him with crying in their voices. He rubs his eyes, stands up, stretches, shakes himself once, rebukes the wind, and shouts at the sea,

"Peace!... Be *still*." (Mk. 4.39)

It works.

Even his companions are scared in the presence of his paranormal powers:

They are filled with awe, and marvel to one another,

"Who is this man, that even the wind and the sea obey him?" (Mk. 4.41)

He is odd. Who can do such magical things but the magician?

He Shows His True Colors

When Jesus stills the storm he does it with no advance publicity, no theatrical showmanship, no lessoning preceding it. He does it quickly in response to the exigencies of the moment. Unlike the magic of raising Lazarus from the dead, for instance, there is no planning, strategizing, publicizing, or staging.

This is an incident of what we call *occasional magic*. Though it has shades of "once in a while," what occasional magic means is "when the situation demands."

This event offers true testimony to Jesus' powers. The absence of props, lights, collusions, and confederates shows Jesus' power does not rely on them. He really has it. Jesus lives, breathes, teaches, sleeps, wakes, and responds in the Alpha frequency. Constantly in state, he responds paranormally in a situation he treats simply as a vicissitude of travel, brought by the moment.

The props of ritual and stage are but to accomplish his designs, *marvel them with magic so they will believe to the glory of God.* But he doesn't have to have them to perform.

5,000 Guests For Lunch

It's like a blow to the stomach when Jesus hears about John. For entertainment's exploits at a high dollar banquet for politicians, they behead John the Baptist. They serve his head – eyes turned upward, drooling with blood swashing around his unkempt beard – before the intimates of the upper council, garnished with pineapple and parsley on an expensive silver platter.

Jesus withdraws to Bethsaida, but the people hungry for spiritual nourishment won't leave him alone. Being called, he speaks. And he teaches with them all the day until evening, when he and everyone else is in need of nourishment, recreation, and rest.

What to do? The apostles advise him to send the people on and themselves exit post haste out the back door *sans check*. He could, you know, they didn't agree to feed five thousand people. It's not included in the price of the seminar. But Jesus never concerns himself too greatly regarding financial matters. They are huddled together; Jesus looks upward brief moments, looks at them with penetrating eyes, and directs,

"*You* give them something to eat." (Lk. 9.13)

They counter with excuses. *So little food, so many people!* Five loaves, two fishes, five thousand!

But Jesus is in state. He directs his confederates to stage the people in groups of fifty each. And then, in the dedicatory position, with the food in his hands,
"He looks up to Heaven..." (Lk. 9.16)
Then he says the magic words, blessing the bread.
The people eat to satisfaction, and when they clean up, they gather twelve baskets of broken pieces and leftovers!

To Tell The Psychic Tale

Jesus does not choose his words and his actions lightly. Nor do the men who tell the tales.

"You Give Them Something To Eat." Jesus is coaxing and coaching the disciples that he has. He's helping them to understand it is not just himself, but that they can do magic, too. And he shows *you* how.

First he dedicates the moment with sacred intent. Next, directing his attention to God, he pronounces a blessing. Then, even in the absence of objective feedback, he moves on the faith of the magic.

Why does it work when Jesus does it? To have the same connection and conviction behind your intentions, actions, and words, you have to *be* like him, too. That's a tall order, but only for our present state of evolution. Jesus shows you what is near, drawing you upward the while.

Of Course Jesus Outdoes Elisha. The Biblical story tellers conform their character to the theme they are developing. Elisha feeds a hundred hungry monks. Jesus feeds thousands, not once, but *twice!* With grace he first feeds five loaves to five thousand and picks up twelve baskets of leftovers. Shortly thereafter he feeds four thousand with seven loaves of barley and picks up seven baskets of crummy bread when they are satisfied.

All to impress you.

Wavewalking

Jesus. Peter. North Americans Neil Armstrong and Michael Jackson have made moonwalking popular. Jesus is the one who popularizes wavewalking. Very few people get either of these down right, but don't we love star-gazing?!

Most of the magical miraculous deeds Jesus performs, he does several times, at the least. He even feeds the multitudes twice. Some he does a great number of times, such as the healings. However, only once does he do any wavewalking.

After teaching all day, and then, at evening, manifesting food sufficient to satisfy masses, Jesus goes up on the mountain to pray. He's been teaching all day, he's relaxed with a meal, and he's been meditating on the mountain. It has been a good day. He is in a supra-elevated state.

But after his hour of solitude he moves to join up with the apostles, who earlier set out to sea. Actually, the wind is against them, so it is hard rowing. They haven't gotten very far.

Jesus is elevated to such a degree that the water supports him. In the ethereal state water can be as solid as earth. Jesus, enjoying a spiritual high, wants to delay profaning himself with intercourse with the apostles. In his paranormal suit he is going right past them like a ghost. Which is just who the frightened apostles think he is. But he feels their fright and speaks to them:

"Take heart! It is I; have no fear!" (Mk. 6.50)

Mark, the earlier writer on this subject, makes no mention of the episode that follows with Peter walking on the waves. Matthew, writing later, caught up in the legends of the man, makes him greater.

Peter challenges the ghost, saying,

"Lord, if it is you, bid me come to you on the water." (Mt. 14.28)

Jesus replies, "Come."

Peter instantly finds himself climbed over the gunwale and walking toward Jesus. *Pretty paranormal.*

Then, however, he re-cognizes what he is doing. *As his heart embraces fear he starts to sink.*

So he calls out for Jesus to save him, which Jesus does. What Jesus says is so revealing:

"O man of little faith, *why* did you doubt?" (Mt. 14.31)

Anyone Can Do It

Not only is Jesus teaching in his discussions and lectures, he teaches in what he does. Of course, his teachings on magic are timelessly accurate.

It's no big deal that Jesus walks on water. You don't have to be a religious expert – even people with the most rudimentary form of knowledge know that Gods possess special powers. And many people think of Jesus as a God. Peter, however, a *man,* walks! This is an incredible event!

Jesus herein demonstrates that anybody can walk on water, a metaphor for doing things of the Spirit, which are non-sense. They are nonsense to people imbued with the mass sense consciousness of the material/political pole of reality. And he again identifies the single element that facilitates or prohibits spiritual/psychic powers: *faith.*

Jesus, in his multidimensional teaching style, shows the way. He instructs, coaches, corrects, admonishes, and points the way, the way of *faith.* It is not by dint of study, training, or experience that Peter walks. It is not due to sex, race, or legislated equality that Peter walks. He does not utter any magical commanding words nor practice any martial technique of concentration and grace. Peter walks only by virtue of, and only as long as he holds to, *faith.*

This is both our blessing and our curse. It takes only faith to access these powers and live with the license of a higher order of beings – the blessing. It demands faith to access and maintain the privileges empowerment gives us – the curse.

The Lazarus Performance

One day news comes to *Jesus* that Lazarus is very ill. Some believe Jesus can save him, so that is the implication behind the news they give him. He should hurry. But he acts unconcerned, even tarrying two days before he sets out to the house of his good friend... almost family.

He could heal Lazarus simply with a metaphysical willing or assent. By this point in his career we've seen him heal many others this way, among these the centurion's daughter. But he does not.

Why not? Jesus is an opportunist. What is the reason? We have it on good authority, Jesus himself, that it is to be recorded and bruited to the "glory of God." Good for his career.

He confidently acts on the intuition that, though Lazarus will indeed die without healing at his bedside, this will give him an opportunity to do another major magical event. He knows he'll get a lot of coverage. He sees in this situation, like Elisha with Naaman, the perfect setting to make a spiritual statement. He acts on it accordingly.

Jesus then receives the psychic impression that Lazarus is dead. Perhaps Lazarus visits him on his way to the Nether Worlds. Out of the blue Jesus rises and announces that they are going to Judea to "awaken" Lazarus. But the apostles are experiencing temporary brain cloud. Finally Jesus speaks it bluntly:

"Lazarus is dead!" (Jn. 11.14)

Ugh! Indeed, Lazarus has been in the grave four days when Jesus finally arrives in Bethany. There is a great crowd of Jews comforting Martha and Mary, Lazarus' sisters, when Jesus arrives. He has his audience.

He is staging the event. Before he does the actual healing, he makes certain that the people are prepared to get out of the magical event what he wants them to get out of it. Martha is the first to see the master. He is elevated, always elevated. He says some cryptic words to her, which she is sure to not understand. She does not. It is to Martha, the example of the sincere but undiscerning person, to whom he says the much quoted sentence:

"I am the resurrection and the life..." (Jn. 11.25)

Indeed, she is blessed by the Master's hand.

When the grieving Mary comes, the one he is spiritually closer to, being a soul of like sensitivities, she falls at his feet sobbing,

"Oh, Master, If only you would have been here, Lazarus would not have died." (Jn. 11.32)

Jesus is moved. He weeps. And all the great crowd sees him. Believers and skeptics alike. Such staging. He looks Mary in the eyes and says only,

"Take me to where you have lain him." (Jn. 11.34)

She does, but she still does not know what he intends to do. When Jesus commands that the body be exhumed, she protests. "He's been dead four days, he'll smell!" Jesus then calls attention to the power of belief. He says,

> "Didn't I tell you that *if you believe* you will see the glory of God?" (Jn. 11.40)

She is silent. The appearances to sense consciousness shout. Yet, underneath, she knows that Jesus is in connection with Divinity. She's seen it too many times. She commands the men as Jesus directs. They roll the stone from the cave's gaping mouth.

Anticipation is building. Jesus is at the ultimate moment. *Will he be able to do it?* Suspense is high. He augments it even more with his preamble performance. He stands before the open cave, lifts his eyes up to Heaven, and intones a prayer in an elegant voice,

> "Great Spirit, I thank you. I know you hear me and that Lazarus is returning to life. I know you *always* hear me. I'm not saying this prayer for myself, but for these who look on. Then, when it happens they will believe I did it. And they will believe in you." (Jn. 11.41-42)

Every face in the crowd is riveted on him. He takes the sorcerer's stance before the gaping blackness and commands in his theater-trained voice,

> "Lazarus, come out!" (Jn. 11.43)

After about thirty seconds, which seem like forever to everyone there, including Jesus, but not Lazarus, they hear a stirring inside. Antique seconds later a mummy stands in the doorway. Awe rolls palpably through the crowd.

Jesus commands, and they remove the wrappings.

Jesus gives Lazarus borrowed time. He lives for an indeterminate period after the restoration. He goes back to his normal life, even inviting Jesus to his house for dinner, which Jesus accepts.

Oh, it works alright! But the event is *too* big. Jesus' public display of his magical abilities gets too much media play. Many believe in him, as he anticipates, but the skeptics and the religious right cry to the government bureaucrats, baby-sitters of the dependent victims, for satisfaction. This day is a day of destiny. For from this day the attorneys and officials plot his death. They can't afford to have a wizard of such magnificence – the people will surely start to listen to him. This might threaten their own entitlements. He is but days away from dying.

Money From The Fish's Mouth

When *Jesus* enters Jerusalem for what are destined to be his final days, the tax officiary comes seeking his "due." Jesus is aware of the legislation, but, of course, being a citizen of Universal dominion, feels it doesn't apply to him. Nevertheless, he chooses his battles. He has important issues.

But, ho! does he pull a good one on the stupid tax collector! (Jesus' mood won't stay so mischievous... So let's enjoy this one with him.) The self-aggrandized subofficiary comes thinking he is getting the money from Jesus. But Jesus, right before his very eyes, "finds" the money to pay him. He tells Peter,

"Go to the sea and toss a line in. Take the first snag you get, and when you open its mouth you'll find a shekel. Take that and lay it in that bad boy's hand for our tax." (Mt. 17.27)

The collector can do nothing. He is paid. But he is buffaloed. He leaves silently, partially unsatisfied, thinking somehow Jesus has gotten over on him. Today Jesus would – with appropriate ah's of amazement and sexual titillation – pull a fold of $100's from the bra of a buxom twenty-one year old. They didn't do that back then in this culture. This is an interesting occasion of Jesus using magic, while for a purpose, for entertainment.

It also shows how easy it can be to manifest money.

Interdimensionality

Answer this question. Do you believe Jesus sends Peter fishing because it is the logical thing to do? It might be. The Bible could be telling us Peter catches a fish, sells it, and pays the tax – in figurative language. Perhaps he receives a telepathic impression that's where he will find the money. Note his precision with the *first* fish. Only if this were worth noting would Jesus note it.

Or does Jesus magically manufacture the event, even putting the shekel in the fish's mouth? The facts of the event can support any choice. *Yes,* or *yes?* Be sensitlve to the context. *Psi* is *psi*

The Case Of The Unfortunate Fig Tree

Jesus, too – though in a minor way compared with Elisha who has she-bears tear boys to pieces – demonstrates the efficacy of a curse.

Jesus, like all unconventional people who reach fame, runs crossways with the law. His very being represents a threat. Remember the times when he had thousands of open hearts following him? Now he's got word-dicing-slicing huddles of attorneys calculating against him. What gives? He's having a rough day.

So that evening, finally out and away from the anxiety of church and state, Jesus sees a fig tree and recognizes he is hungry. But, though the tree has leaf, "it is not the season for figs" (Mk. 11.13).

Jesus is irritated. He may not know the figs are out of season. He utters the curse:

"May no one ever eat fruit from you again." (Mk. 11.14)

When they pass by on the way into Jerusalem the following morning, Peter sees the tree withered to its roots and exclaims:

"Look! Everybody! *Look!* Look, Jesus! The fig tree you hexed has withered to its roots!" (Mk. 11.21)

Voilà! Black magic! *Okay, okay...* grey *magic.* But *still!*

There Is No Other Conclusion

Surely zapping a fig tree is not a serious crime. Jesus did not, would not, could not direct that energy to a person, but he lets a little ray of irritated power blast an innocent fig tree. Kinda like kicking the dog, no? Of course, it's not a consistent manifestation of his character, either, but an aberrant behavior.

This is the same day, by the way, that he loses it in the Temple, also clearly an aberration in Jesus' behavior patterns. Nevertheless, Jesus never makes any apology for the wrong or heedless thing he does.

Here during the time he senses are his final moments on Earth – cometh the night "wherein no one can work" (Jn. 9.4) – he has vastly more important things he needs to talk about.

Thought experiment: *This is a lesson from an adept, given in response to the fulfillment of a curse. What lessons does it hold, what special points may we have overlooked until now?*

Jesus takes the opportunity to explicate a lesson on power and congruency to the insiders... With the same urgency that drove him to curse the tree, Jesus tells Peter we all have that power. and, this is how you get it!: *Only believe...*

"Have faith in God!" (Mk. 11.22)

Ask and command with "no doubt in your heart," believing in the power of your commands. *Belief* is the access key – the catalytic element that causes your commands to manifest in sensate form:

> "Truly, I say to you, whoever says to this mountain, 'Be taken up and cast into the sea!' and *does not doubt* in his heart, but *believes* that what he says will come to pass, it will be done for him. Therefore I tell you, *whatever* you ask in prayer, believe that you have received it, and it will be yours." (Mk. 11.23-24)

There you have it. The master in his final days again reveals the secret to all magic – not just white, healing, wholistic magic; not just to kill, but to heal. Know. Believe. Cosmic forces move when you command with that congruency.

Chapter 6

Psychic Potpourri:
Astrology, Necromancy, Teleportation,
Synchronicity

————————··•··————————

As we wind down our tour and start thinking of home again, we take this
quick and cursory look at a few affiliated psychic arts we haven't visited
yet. This is a hodge-podge chapter, one that takes us through the subject
of psi from numerous angles.

Even though throughout this book we've acknowledged that one instance is
sufficient to establish a point, we've adduced a multitude of instances for each of
the topic areas introduced so far. In this chapter the pace changes. Here two of the
phenomena we discuss do indeed only have one significant witness to their
existence, validity, uses, and position: astrology and necromancy. There are other
points which we'll visit, and we'll enjoy our discoveries there, but picking is slim.

The other two stops in our tour of this chapter, teleportation and synchronicity,
we visit for different, if associated, reasons. There are plenty of instances.

Depending on how far you want to stretch the meanings of words and the
replicability of the acts of a God, there may be little basis for teleportation. The
teleportations of Ezekiel and John the Revelator may, and in fact probably do,
occur in the context of a dream-vision. That is, though the soul may travel, the body
never moves. Also significant is the fact that most of Jesus' teleportations occur
after his death. Then he would surely be a spirit, naturally possessed of the ability
to move through the doorways of perception. It may not be entirely convincing to
peg an argument for the living onto a person or a God clearly of the Spiritual realm.
Nevertheless, we do have the phenomenon. Our visit is germane, entertaining, and
edifying.

The final subject, synchronicity, is a valid and fully associated component of the
Spirit-centred life. The reason we discuss it in this chapter is quite the opposite,
however, of the reasons for discussing the other phenomena. The sheer mass of
instances is overwhelming! In sacred mythology, *everything occurs in*
synchronicity. For newbies in psychi-spiritual awareness, synchronicity seems like
a novel and grand occurrence. Initiates, with the sight developed only slightly, see
all events as the fulfillment of purposes, decrees, and destinies, interdependently
co-orchestrated by the HoloCosm, the individual dancing with the dancing partners
that are God.

****

Astrology

"There are messages in the stars."

Astrology has a checkered past, sometimes venerated, sometimes reviled. Though a good many people today believe there may be something to astrology, most of the Christian ruling hierarchy would vehemently deny the fact. You will enjoy your adventure here.

This excursion on astrology is short. Yet, don't mistake brevity as belying the validity of what we uncover. Rather, let's examine the incidents and the position in the spiritual firmament these things occupy, letting a spiritually discerned understanding guide us into a right valuation of the Bible's true word on astrology.

We don't need a labyrinthine definition of astrology. Astrology can be defined simply in its twofold premise: 1) the stars demonstrate some influence on our lives, 2) they have this influence coded into their positions and actions. A third vital item extends from these premises: we can read the messages in the stars.

Indeed the Bible indicates the stars are given humanity – in the spiritualscape as well as the Earthscape – as a device whose function is that of simultaneous influence and comment.

The idea that there is a meaning in the stars beyond the mere meaning of existence is an ancient belief. The Eurocentric sciences trace the belief easily into the first eras of the United Kingdom of Egypt. Of course, it had to precede that, or it wouldn't have shown up then. The literature, traditions, and artifacts of less prominent Earthly cultures, indeed antedates it several thousand years. We have indications that, from the earliest times people developed to the point where they practiced the arts of art and architecture, however crudely, they practiced astrology.

And we've just talked about the earliest beliefs of humanity in the dimensions of the Common Era of time. Outside of time, outside of the blinders our own culture fits to our eyes, we've discovered numerous civilizations with respect for the workings of astrology. There is an innate human attunement with the stars. A biologist can tell you why.

Only an astrologer, or a society who believes in astrology, would attribute any subjective significance to a star, a star formation, or the movement of a star.

We moderns of the Western paradigm don't have the benefit of the relative "ignorance" to structure our understandings and attributions to the stars. We are materialists, creators of and created by the scientific tradition. We know that the stars are only so much physical matter in process, millions of light years from our own Earth, likewise existing somewhere in this vast interstellar universe. There is no magic.

It would be inconsistent to look for anything other than *physical* causes, precedents, and physical results, consequences in the stars. Not *metaphysical*. Make no mistake. A giant star neither announces nor proves the birth of a God. That's "naive."

Counterpoint. On the other hand, accepting the known forces and interplays of the universe as it is, moderns know that electromagnetic forces of energy, gravity, and the like *do* have an effect on reality.

Everything does, of course. Even the unnoted feather falling from the tie bow on an Indian maiden's dress before her brave, simply because it happens, affects the world. Certainly something as tremendously large as a big bang can be responsible for innumerable lives and dramas of every conceivable level and scale. It is a being of microscopic proportions, a virus, not an army under imperial sway, that stops Alexander the Great. From the innately unnoticed to the perceptualized giants, every event and energy affects the sum total of reality.

Yet the harbingers of a new age are among us rediscovering the indissoluble unity of the spiritual and the physical worlds. The physical is not a world separate from and opposed to the immaterial; the physical world is but one component of the levels of expressiveness of the spiritual totality.

But that's not what we're talking about here. Here, our quest is but to discern the Bible's position on astrology. In the context of the Bible we *must* accept that the stars participate with Earthly events.

God Creates The Stars For Influence And For Signs

The Bible begins with beginnings. It opens with the words,

In the beginning God created Heaven and the Earth. (Gen. 1.1)

This is the Bible tradition's 2200 BCE way of saying, God manifests Self in multitudinous forms and dimensions.

On the fourth day of creation, after manifesting light, heavens with clouds, and earth and vegetation, God says the word and lights appear in Heaven. Some of them only come out at night; some of them only come out during the day. Two of the lights he commands into existence, the "greater lights," are, of course, the sun and the moon. The light beings of the Zodiac belt arrive and depart regularly according to the seasons of the years. Thus God fulfills one of his multi-holo purposes, a way for humanity to distinguish the clear separation between day and night, the seasons and the years.

Thus humanity's destinies are, as he wishes it, controlled from the heavens, as it is these lights in Heaven that give life to Earth. Love springs forth when the human individual experiences the unity of self with the Creative Intelligence that is God, the rhythm of microcosmos with macrocosmos. God creates a top down world, in astro alignment. Further, not only do the lights *do* the actual ruling, they also *inform* humanity of their deeds, presently, as well as, once their silent order is perceived, futurely.

As above, so below. As God structures it, we have the stars to help us countermove or consort with the things that are and the things that will be.

"It Is Written In The Stars"

The stars are given *Joseph* as a hope and a dream during his years of oblivion, underemployment, and incarceration. Simultaneously, the stars were also for his brothers and his father, to confirm Joseph's destiny. Additionally simultaneously, the stars are for us, heirs ages distant, that we may see and believe.

The astrological heritage of Joseph has a coruscating richness. It concerns the young Joseph's dream of greatness and dominion over his older brothers.

Joseph tells his brothers, "I saw it written in the stars.... You shall serve me," and describes the drama of the dream:

> "Behold, I have dreamed ... the sun, the moon, and eleven stars were bowing down to me." (Gen. 37.9)

Joseph reads them right.

Consider that this is a sacred text. What is the Spirit saying to humanity? The veracity of this accepted instance of the stars foretelling the future attests to the archetypical energies and powers accorded the stars.

Psychic Verities

It is amazing the different ways the stars speak. *Listen.*

Signs, Portents, Omens. The message to Joseph, his family, *and to us,* is twofold. First, the stars speak rightly of weighty matters. And secondly, the stars can speak in various ways.

In this episode the stars reveal the future that will come to pass, however distant it may seem on the pathway to fulfillment. And isn't this what the stars speak of? The grander sweeps of an individual's or a nation's life and meaning?

The stars speak not by physical alignments in this instance, as is the more common way, but through mystical drama. And Joseph recognizes elements of destiny in the drama of the dream. It is a lot like the "moral of the story" fairytales we feed to our children. The story cloaks a message eager to be out.

"Oh, If It's Only Mystical..." The special uniqueness and potency of this astrological event, however, is that, until it unfolds on the stage of time, it is wholly a mystical event.

You can always find one with active psychisclerosis who says, "Oh, if it's only mystical, then that means it's not real." Though it is often assumed and projected, rather than spoken, the attending complement to that sentence is, "And since it's not real, I don't have to believe it."

But think again of just what the Bible is. By its very inclusion in this book this episode of astrology *is intended for our benefit.* We can't rightly discount it because it is mystical when the entire essence of the Bible story is that the mystical forces of God are at work in our lives.

Though the stars unveil Joseph's destiny, informing, encouraging, and guiding him to his future, the stars shine not in hard reality, but within the eternal expansiveness of a dream.

Moses Receives The Ten Commandments According To Astrological Timing

Moses is associated with two major achievements: 1) leading the Jewish race from Egypt; and 2) giving the Jewish race (and humanity) the decalogue, or *ten commandments*. It is, in fact, commenced from the events occurring in a ritual on the *third new moon* (Ex. 19.1), on a sojourn that ends up spanning forty years, that Moses channels the ten commandments.

Moses ascends the peak of Mountain Sinai. As is his ritual custom of power, he is alone. Having actively placed himself in the passive powerful position of prayer, on this psychically propitious day, his attention solely on God, God enters his consciousness:

The Lord calls to him out of the mountain. (Ex. 19.3)

The mere fact that the event is not just mentioned, making it a randomly occurring event, but is tied to the lunar cycle, is prima facie evidence that the people perceive the energies of God and are indeed using the moon for a sign to participate when the Heavens' influences are propitiously positioned for human engagement in the atemporal ritual moment.

Jesus' Birth Heralded In The Stars: The Ultimate Instance

Three Astrologers. Early in its history, the dominant cult that evolves around Jesus as a God squares off against astrology. It wasn't always the case, however. Matthew tells the story of the marvelous astrologers come from an Eastern land of spirituality to find and worship the infant incarnation of God. He tells this with the obvious intent to establish credibility to Jesus. In so doing he attributes value, significance, and veracity to the art of astrology.

Conventional Christianity still trumpets this example. Of course, Lord knows what, but they consider it something other than *astrology*. You tell me how calling it by some other name changes what it is.

Jesus has trouble with the law from his earliest days. It starts when the three wizards enter Jerusalem with a question:

"Where is he who has been born king of the Jews? For we have seen his star in the East, and have come to worship him." (Mt. 2.1-2)

There Is A Meaning In The Stars

Here again the Bible teaches us there is a meaning in the stars!

And who hunts him up? Is it the government intruders or the church leaders? Is it their destiny that they always miss it? Those mired in misleading reality, even believing that it is the *real thing* cannot perceive the *real*.

"Following The Magnificent Stars." The three wizards are practicing nothing other than astrology. Clearly it is these astrologers, even identified as such in the *New English Bible*, who are the possessors of the highest knowledge and insight on Earth. Only the astrologers, philosophers who discern in the sun and the moon and the planets and the stars arcane whisperings, perceive the event. Little noted, but of Cosmic proportions.

But they do. This is astrology.

Only An Astrologer Would See. And even today, these thousands years later, truly, they are given the due credit for the fruit of their wisdom, having seen it first. But of course, they can read the stars.

Unlike today, when precise electromagnetic instruments trained in portions of the sky can paint things otherwise unseen to the human eye, the astrologers of antiquity had but their eyes, their hearts, and the body of esoteric insight they built over time. Presumably, other people *saw* the same sky the mystic masters saw.

A normal person might pay it no mind, or might even marvel over it a while before passing on. A scientist would occupy himself with physical causes, precedents, and projections, not metaphysical. Only an astrologer would attribute any subjective attachment to a star.

Now ask yourself. Does the Bible tell us that moments of high import are written in the stars? Does the Bible tell us there are wizards among us who, discerning the starry passages, can see things in advance of the populace?

Necromancy

Necromancy involves calling a previously living person, now a *spirit or ghost*, to one's service. Though at first glance it can appear that the psi phenomenon of necromancy is similar to the numerous Biblically recorded cases involving the dead returning to life, it is distinct.

It is not reincarnation, which entails a person/spirit being reborn into a different lifetime. Jesus identifies John the Baptist as Elijah returned.

It is not raising someone from the dead, of which there are numerous examples. When the shaman raises a person from the dead, restoring the lifeforce to their body, that person in fact *has* a body they can *reinhabit.* Thus Elisha raises the widow's son, and Jesus the centurion's daughter. Death has not been too long present. The person's spirit is still accustomed to the body and, upon command, slips back through the doorway and reenters it. In necromancy there is no body; there is no reembodiment. We have a ghost.

It is not resurrection, in which the dead person themself reenters, and raises, and glorifies their body. This is the domain of only the highest initiates. There is only one recorded case in the Bible.

An additional distinction marks necromancy from raising and resurrection. Necromancy's specific intent, visible in the suffix -ancy, involves inquiry into the future course of events. No one inquires about their fortunes from the widow's son. No one asks the girl anything about their future. No one pays special attention to the people the apostles raise from the dead. Saul, however, asks the Samuel he has conjured up what he sees in the future.

Our purpose in this book is not to suggest that necromancy is all that beneficial, in fact, the "consequences" of the case we discuss, when Saul calls the dead Samuel, are lethal. Samuel is not happy about having his eternal rest disturbed. Our effort here is but to suggest a new way of looking at things. It is up to the reader to evaluate their significance.

Here's our nut on this case. According to what the Bible teaches, even if it does not recommend it, the psychic phenomenon of necromancy is certainly *real*. If the scene proves anything it proves that *necromancy does work.* Formerly embodied people can be called from their slumbers; some people do posses the ability to call them.

Our stop at necromancy is brief, but not without its special delights. We find, after all the associated phenomena are cleared away, we only have one true instance of necromancy. But one is enough to establish it and its character. Wouldn't you say? After all, the cornerstone of the Jesus mythos is but a single instance, too; there is only one resurrection.

"It's A Goddamned Day To Die"

Samuel. Sister. One day King *Saul* consults his usual psychics – the channelers, diviners, and sorcerers of the Lord. *Boy, he should be a-trembling!* God has quit speaking; the oracles are silent.

So he seeks out a medium at Endor and travels there, disguised in different robes, cloaked by the darkness.

He tells the mystic woman,
> "Divine for me by a spirit, and bring up for me whomever I shall name to you." (1Sam. 28.8)

When the witch asks,
> "Whom shall I bring up for you?"

He asks for the most powerful psychic he knows.

There is silence, made weird and reverent by the aromatic candlelight flickering....

And then she sees Samuel rising from the Earth. This Saul cannot see. As she describes the elder man in robes Saul falls to the floor and makes oriental obeisance to him.

Eerie communication through the entranced channel.

Bad vibes!!!

Trailing odors from the soil of the Earth, Samuel complains about Saul's disturbing him, commanding him suddenly from the activities of the dead.

Saul replies,

"I am *scared!* Things have been going really bad for me, the Philistines are arrayed against us now, and we have to fight tomorrow, and I need help and no one else can help me. The other psychics can't get anything." (1Sam. 28.15)

Samuel notes the noticeable. After all, he *is* a prophet of that same God refusing to speak to Saul.

"What do you expect me to do, since it is the *Lord* who refuses to speak to you? It is not Aliazar, the other psychics, or myself. We can but speak as God speaks through us.

"But! these misfortunes are the very ills God pronounced through me some time ago. You have brought them to fulfillment through your disloyalty." (1Sam. 28.16-18)

Then he lays the big one on him, "You are *doomed!*"

He shares his foreknowledge of events yet to occur:

"Tomorrow Israel shall fall to the hand of the Philistines. Tomorrow you and both your sons shall lie with me." (1Sam. 28.19)

I don't think these words were meant to encourage Saul, do you?

The next day all unfolds as the psychic called up from the deeps of the dead divines.

"I Wouldn't Call That Necromancy"

Jesus. Moses. Elijah. All three synoptics – Matthew, Mark, and Luke – record the scene Biblical scholars label the *transfiguration.* In this scene Jesus, who frequently goes up on the mountain and prays alone – that is where he had been, for instance, when the apostles loaded up and journeyed out on the "wavewalking" expedition – has taken three of his companions with him, Peter, John, and James.

As Luke retells it:

As he was praying, the appearance of his countenance was mystically altered, and his clothing became dazzling white. (Lk. 9.29)

Moses and Elijah appear, also beaming resplendent glory. Together they discuss Jesus' great work, the work he is setting in motion in Jerusalem.

But just because these two beings – former prophets and psychics of Israel – appear with Jesus, this is not necromancy. Just because two men who have passed the portals of death appear with Jesus, this is not necromancy. This is no more necromancy than the ritual meal in a religious rite – though the act is the same, eating – is gluttony.

This is evidence of the depth of connection Jesus makes with the Cosmic Soul. Saul is a desperate man, out of sync with the Universe. Jesus is totally congruent. There is nothing in the passages preceding it or coming later that can cast any consideration that Jesus calls these powerful men from the dead. Rather, in the timeless spaceless planes in which Jesus operates, these are his peers.

The difference is not in space. It is in consciousness. Jesus prays. It is more appropriate to understand in this passage that Jesus goes *there*. The difference is everything.

Further indicators for this as the proper perspective comes from yet another psi event in this scenario:

> Then a low cloud suddenly overshadows them, and all around the atmosphere bristles with psychic energy. The apostles suddenly are afraid. And then a voice speaks from the cloud, saying,
>
> "This is my Son, my Chosen... Listen to him!" (Lk. 9.35)

This is not what happens in the "normal" prayer of a "normal" person.

When Jesus prays, the Eternal opens around him.

Very paranormal.

Teleportation

Teleportation can be simply defined as a human being moving with no intervening physical travel through space. In other words, the person does not walk, drive, chariot, trot, ride, or otherwise participate in some physical method of movement to another location. There are no helicopters or airplanes. He or she simply *appears* there. It has specific application to the psychic arts. Differing spiritual traditions refer to this phenomenon as *astral travel* or as *soul travel*.

Many of us are familiar with teleportation through technology from watching *Star Trek*. The Biblical instances of teleportation are of the spiritual realms. There is no aid other than consciousness, angels, and God.

Though there are some subcategories, we broadly consider teleportation as breaking down into two forms. These two forms are called *teleportation* and *projection*.

Teleportation and projection enjoy the same type of notoriety we noted when we discussed the *ESP* and *PK* unity and dichotomy. Teleportation is the inclusive term that includes both the phenomena of teleportation, proper, and projection. Another way of saying it is that both teleportation and projection are teleportation.

It is appropriate. It is often hard to distinguish which one is which. In teleportation the *body* goes with you. The distinction that makes projection is that the *spirit* goes while the body remains on the couch or reclining on the river bank, so to speak. In this type of teleportation, you go somewhere in spirit; rather than being an active "real" participant. Some call this an out-of-body (OBE) experience. Some refer to this as *associated* daydreaming, though you certainly can have a duality of consciousness, that is, recognizing both the vision and the material condition.

What is relevant is that the dream-vision, travel, fantasy is *experienced* rather than just cogitated. The experience is real.

Paul speaks to this fuzzy overlap – twice – when he says, "whether in the body or out of the body, I do not know." He writes of a man he knows who,

> Fourteen years ago was caught up to the third Heaven – whether in the body or out of the body I do not know, God knows. And I know that this man was caught up into Paradise – whether in the body or out of the body I do not know, God knows – and he heard things that cannot be told, which man may not utter. (2Cor. 12.2-4)

This is a *real* spiritual experience.

Sometimes identical language is used to describe experiences of both teleportation and projection. This can lead you to wondering whether, even when it seems something different is described, if it is a different phenomenon at all, or rather an alternative description of the same phenomenon. This indicates that, despite the distinctions, essentially teleportation and projection are the same thing.

Most "balanced" researchers today feel they there is no conclusive evidence for true teleportation, i.e., where the *body* of a person is transported to another physical place. Even when witnesses claim to have seen a teleporter, perception does come through the mind and the heart. They could be reading and translating spiritually focused vibrations. The material minded psychiatrists label the reality of projection nicely as an altered state. Only the spiritually open recognize solely spiritual experiences as in fact *real* experiences.

People engaging deeply in NLP, hypnosis, meditation, and the various arts, all *experience* their imagination. They enter into mental-spiritual experiences with such intensity and abandon that they are like the actor who assumes the role and for the magical time of the drama forgets who she "really" is, *being* the character she set out to portray. Within this mystic enchantment, every scene, every person, every event, every emotional thought, every angel is *real*, being *experienced* fully.

The psychical world is not constrained by the linear components of hard reality. The teleporter doesn't comply with the general boundaries separating subjective and objective reality. The teleporter enters so fully into the experience of the subjective-psychical-spiritual perceptions that objective reality bends. Sensory inputs from the environment that get through become active agents in the spinning of the alter-reality. The reality the teleporter experiences assumes all the qualities, characteristics, and effects of actuality. For these moments of embodiment, the transport is the sum of reality.

We're on the cutting edge of the two worlds with *psi.* The evidence is not all in. However, researchers, adventurers, and writers of the HoloCosmic paradigm affirm that spiritual events are indeed real. In the HoloCosm, lightform is as real as any other form. It don't get no realer. After all, all is but energy and vibration. Can one energy configuration be *more* real than another?

You know the answer to the question, "Is a thought real?"

Angels Seize Them

Lot & His Family. You usually think of angels as blessed do-gooders. Well, it is angels that are dispatched to cinder the cities of Sodom and Gomorrah. But, since it is on the way, they stop by and visit Abraham and Sarah. It is in this visit that God, channeling through the angels, informs Abraham and Sarah they shall have a son of their own blood. Then God decides to let Abraham in on his upcoming venture, the destruction of the twin population centers. God in his multidimensional fullness decides that Abraham and his descendants – *us* – can learn from this horrific Cosmic adjustment.

The angels reach Sodom at evening when – amazing coincidence! – Lot, Abraham's brother, just happens to be at the city gates. He does not know it, but he's the one they came to see. He greets them and invites them into his house for dinner and a night's lodging.

But the men of the city reveal their hards even that night. They come to Lot's house asking for the pretty men who are visiting, anxious to know them, in a Biblical sense. Determined to protect his two guests, he instead offers the virginal flowers of his two daughters to what has now become a rabble. But they don't want women, they want the gentle *men.* Uh huh... The angels are convinced that the city does indeed reek with the unbridled profanity of lusts they have heard about.

They toss a magic web of blindness on the men and defuse the immediate danger, leaving the men groping about at ground level. The angels make the final decision. They *will* destroy the cities of sodomy.

They tell Lot to gather his immediate family and scram,

"For we are about to destroy this place..." (Gen. 19.13)

Lot rushes about at first. He tells his sons-in-law to roust themselves immediately from the city, but they think he is jesting. He then starts to wondering himself. As the first streaks of rosy-fingered dawn reach out, the angels wake Lot and urge him to take his wife and two daughters and rush from the city *NOW!* But he yawns and tarries.

This forces the angels – who *are* going to destroy the city, and who *don't* want to harm this good man – into action.

They seize him, his wife, and his two daughters by the hand and set them down outside the city. (Gen 19.16)

Thus they are taken.

Thus they are suddenly homeless, their sole possessions being the small nuclear family of four and the clothes they are wearing.

But it gets worse. A few minutes later Lot loses his wife when she, disobeying the angel's directives, looks to see the magical process of destruction. Sshe is magically tragically transformed into a pillar of salt. Now Lot has no woman. His two pristine daughters have no men, either. The girls, being raised in Sodom, think like Sodomites. The solution is easy. *Their father!* It is easy for him, too, hard as heck, once he has a few drinks. Interesting story.

Consider These Things

Psi will get you, coming unsought, and working *until* it gets your attention. Psi will protect you.

It Reaches Out And Gets You. We most commonly think of teleportation as occurring when a person enters a trance state. Then they are "transported" somewhere, only to come back some time later. Artists, writers, and musicians speak often of this magical mystery tour.

This story, however, shows another beam on the processes of teleportation. This event seemingly is imposed on the man and his family. (For their own good, of course.) It's kind of like the difference between walking out of town and being taken out in a tornado. Walking is easy, and your world pretty much remains the same. The tornado *happens to you.* You can't control it, and you may suffer some heavy and permanent losses in the tumult. But after all, you're extremely grateful that you're alive at all.

God has written this story to show us that teleportation can happen by unsought influence... Apparently higher exigencies may impel it.

This "it happens to you" aspect seems odd... As it relates to teleportation. But recognizing teleportation as another face of psi makes it seem more common. As we know, you don't always have to will clairvoyance, for instance. It can come as, the result of entering trance intentfully, or it can come cloaked in the images of a dream, a hunch, or an outside event.

Guided When You Would Misstep. Just look what your accumulated good can do for you! In spite of Lot's dallying doubt when destruction is imminent, he is saved. This is good news, as it indicates that it's okay to still be human. Lot does not understand the signals and the clear command, but he is cared for.

Left to the actions of his own understanding, he and his family would have surely perished.

Angels watching over him. Angels protecting him. *Now those are angels!*

"Lifted! Is It Real?... Or Is It?..."

Ezekiel. What, in the decidedly psychic experience of teleportation, is *visionary* and what is *hard reality?*

Ezekiel sitting in his house, enters the alpha meditative state, preparing to channel to a small group of seekers and elders gathered before him. Right away, he recalls in the writing of it,

> A form that had the appearance of a man.... put forth the form of a hand, and took me by a lock of my head. Then the Spirit lifted me up between Earth and Heaven, and brought me in visions of God to Jerusalem... (Ezek. 8.2-3)

Jerusalem, of course, symbolizes the virgin city. Ezekiel runs four chapters describing the marvels he encounters.

He winds down his splendid apocalyptic journey of angels and of lights and jewels and secret meanings and Gods and spiritual friends, and describes the end of the vision, personifying the force that is God:

> And the glory of the Lord went up from the midst of the city, and stood upon the mountain which is on the east side of the city. (Ezek. 11.23)

And God departs for home, but he stops to bless Jerusalem before he goes. Seldom does God himself appear in the scriptures, and this description of him as a glorious light force being is a statement ringing with high mystical reverb.

Then, *while still in the vision*, the Spirit lifts Ezekiel up and takes him into Chaldea, to his companion Jews, the exiles. He finds himself there when the trance lifts. There he shares the details of the amazing psychic experience he has had:

> And the Spirit lifted me up and brought me in the vision by the Spirit of God into Chaldea, to the exiles. Then the vision that I had seen went up from me. And I told the exiles all the things that the Lord had showed me. (Ezek. 11.24-25)

Ezekiel writes the book on teleportation.

The Workings Of Psi

Thus we have both the language of projection and teleportation conflating this one psychic phenomenon. Truly the synthesis. The visionary world is intercommutable with harder styled reality.

First we have the physically oriented word *lifted* describing both his entry into and his exit from the enchantment. Ezekiel is so involved that these spiritual visions become physical realities. He enters a vision. In that vision he is lifted up and delivered into an apparently new place, the Celestial City. When the spell breaks, however, he is no longer in Jerusalem, no longer in the presence of angels. He comes to, finding himself physically in beautiful Chaldea! *Some powerful stuff, no?!*

Thus this metaphysical manual gives us a new look into the workings of psi in teleportation. In this glimpse into the mystic's world we see the weave of intercommutability between the two domains of the material and the spiritual. Is it solely a spiritual experience? An imagination that is somehow unreal? An imagination mistaken for reality? An imagination real? Or does his mystic trip encompass physical reality? And its effects in reality? Why is this compelling, enchanted storied state so elusive?

There Ezekiel begins to talk impetuously about his spiritual experience.

A Boat Slips Through The Portals Of Time

Jesus. The Apostles. This is an unusual case of teleportation. Throughout the mythology of the ages, there are a limited number of occurrences of teleportation, not just of a person, but of a *group* of persons. To further distinguish it, this teleportation includes a rather large physical object, a boat. It happens on the same day that Jesus prays, feeds the multitudes, and gets high up on the mountain alone and prays again.

He sends the apostles across to Capernaum. He'll catch up with them, he says. The seas are tough, and, despite their great efforts, they make minimal progress. He does indeed catch up with them. He comes walking over the water.

This is the wavewalking sequence wherein Peter walks on water. We've visited aspects of this rich story elsewhere. You don't hear this often, as, I guess, most preachers don't understand how it fits in with their party platform. But when they get Jesus aboard the boat,

>Immediately the boat is at the land to which they were headed. (Jn. 6.21)

How paranormal! Check this out! Jesus, the apostles, and the entire boat are magically transported through the intervening space and time so that in the twinkling of an eye they are there.

If we could patent the technology we'd be billionaires!

A Series Of Sightings

Once *Jesus* appears to one person – kind of like Elvis sightings – others start seeing him, too. The sightings start on the day we now call Easter Sunday.

The First Sighting

It is Sunday. In the version of the story as John tells it – details in the four stories vary outrageously – Mary of Magdalena goes alone to Jesus' grave, to anoint and perfume his body. She discovers he has been taken away. She runs to share the shattering news of the theft with Peter and John, and then returns with them to the grave. The apostles run into the grave. Mary holds back, and only peers in. The apostles don't see the two angels, Mary does. When the angels ask, she replies that she is weeping because,

>"They have moved my lord and I don't know where they have taken him."
>(Jn. 20.13)

As she speaks, behind her she feels the presence of a man. She turns to him and he asks the same question the angels had asked,

>"Woman, why are you weeping?" (Jn. 20.15)

Supposing him to be the gardener, who might have assisted in the government's appropriation of the body, she asks as a soror in the depths of love,

>"Sir, if you have carried him away, tell me where you have laid him, and I will take him away." (Jn. 20.15)

She is about to go on, when Jesus interrupts her with a single word that fells her:
>*"Mary!"*

It is Jesus! The men don't see him, either. But emotional Mary does.

Presto! And He's Inside The Locked Room!

Jesus appears magically inside a locked room twice. He's a good study of magic.

The Easter Appearance. In Jesus's second Easter appearance he teleports inside a locked and barred room, appearing to the cowering companions he left behind (Jn. 20.19-23). They have been together, fearing and praying. Today's news that they secretly took the body didn't help any. Who's going to disappear next?

Jesus comes to offer solace and encouragement. First, of course, he must do something that will surely convince them it is him. After all, this is a paranormal experience. He shows them his hands, marred with the recent wounds of large iron nails. He pulls his robe up and shows them his side, open from the spear of Longinious. They believe.

He blesses them in the name of the Great Spirit and leaves the same way he came in.

The Later Appearance. Jesus appears the same way to the same group eight days later (Jn. 20.26-29). The difference this time is that Thomas, who was not with them previously, is there now. Jesus upbraids the men – these men, spiritual forefathers of the Christian faith – for their unbelief. None of them believed Mary's story. Doubting Thomas would not believe the apostles' story.

If they take such convincing, requiring sign after sign, how blest will be the people coming after them who will only have their *words* to believe on!

Poof! And He's Vanished!

In another Easter appearance two brethren are walking to Emmaus, in lively discussion of the events of the last several days. Luke doesn't pull any punches It is "Jesus himself" he writes:

Jesus himself draws near and joins along with them. (Lk. 24.15)

Jesus, of course, becomes involved in the conversation, not, however, revealing he has any real knowledge of or connection with the events. They talk for hours on the road.

And, it turning evening in Emmaus, they decide to lodge there. When they sit to table,

Jesus takes the bread and blesses it, breaks it, and gives it to them.

And their eyes are opened, and they see Jesus. And he vanishes into thin air. (Lk. 24.30-31)

As Sir Thomas Mallory would write it, "astonied, they gasp to one another!":

"Weren't our hearts *burning* within us when he talked to us on the road, while he opened to us the scriptures?!!" (Lk. 24.32)

And they are believers. And they rush back to Jerusalem that selfsame hour and share the good news with the other apostles.

The Magnificent Ways Of Psi

Our visit to this psychicsite holds many jewels of insight and action for us. Significantly, it reveals, not that the events of the world is the Divine in expression, but that the awakening of the second sight is what allows us to see it.

Seen By The Second *Sight.* The problem is not the Otherworld's presence in our lives, but in recognizing it. Even these two spiritual initiates do not perceive the very presence of God in their midst. They do not see Jesus because,

Their eyes are kept from recognizing him. (Lk. 24.16)

The problem is perception, which is what Jesus is always saying. *"Seeing is not enough! You must see with a new sight!"*

It truly takes the focus of a different awareness to see the other world speaking. Our human systems are hardwired, and our cultural conditioning furthers the illusion, to believe only what is within the normal realm of the physical senses. Believing that limited range is the entire band is the problem. So much occurs *beyond* the *physical* senses.

But fortunately we are evolving. And every time an individual opens to a psi sight, not only do they progress up the spiritual pathway, but they lift the consciousness of all humanity.

It's hard for humans to see rightly, but, *oh, when you do!*

The Afflatus. You are changed permanently to the core. Your life is never the same, and, though many of your daily bread actions may only change slowly, if at all, the very reason for your life and being, the reason why you wake in the morning, grows from some unplaceable familiarity to a solid knowingness.

As I wrote in *The Grail And The Tarot Correspondence,*

The vision of the Grail amends and redirects Percival's vision and direction. From this point *he will never be happy in anything other than the spiritual quest and work.* Percival's close encounter with the Grail sets him to his life's task.

Angels, spirits, and Gods, they show themselves in a flash and they are gone. At the moment that you see, all the good that entire psi experience holds swooshes in at once.

That is all that is required. All is accomplished in the moment of recognition.

Metaphor For The Bible. For those who have the sight to see it, this event contains the whole of the Biblical method of teaching, too. This single incident contains, demonstrates, and illustrates the process of the Bible itself. Of course, it is easy to recognize this story is a teaching story... It *is* in the Bible. Of course, since the Bible teaches with it, this *is* the method of the Bible!

Do you see? Even as the companions could not recognize the Spirit incarnate before them until the recognition moment of grace visits them, we, looking straight at the scriptures, may miss all the real substance that is there.

The Bible is not so inscrutable it can only be interpreted by your preacher or priest. He or she doesn't know, either, if they will be truthful. *Life is* personal *and particular.* One size spirituality, just as one size clothes, tools, and meals, does not fit all. The Bible is so coded that in its final application it can only be interpreted to you by you. But here's the catch... with inspired vision.

This is the truth of the HoloCosmos. Everything devolves to the same universal truth: the Divine is in our midst. And the Divine keeps teaching. It is so right that our hearts are burning within us. *But to see!*

The Spirit Of The Lord Takes Up Philip

In the days after Jesus' ministry, *Philip*, who is introduced to psi the day he meets Jesus, does a little magic of his own.

He teaches a man he meets on the road all about Jesus and salvation. The man is in marvels. When they come upon water along the road the man whose heart is pulsing asks Philip to baptize him. He does. They go down into the water together. But after the initiatic words of baptism, the neophyte arises alone,

> The Spirit of the Lord takes up Philip. The eunuch sees him no more. (Acts 8.39)

Philip teleports to Azotus where witnesses see him teaching.

"And, Lo! An Open Door!"

John The Revelator is another great visionary. He opens his magnum opus by identifying the work that is to follow as the channeled experience of a vision.

At first, it seems like the angel enchants John right where he is and he sees into the Spiritual world of symbols, Heavens, Gods, and mythologies. He duly notes the drama, the scenes, and the discourse of the vision, as instructed to do. He scribes the letters dictated to the seven churches, as dictated to him.

That segment being completed,

> After this I looked, and lo, in Heaven, an open door! And the first voice, which I had heard speaking to me like a trumpet, said,
> "Come up hither, and I will show you what must take place after this." (Rev. 4.1)

Then he clearly shares what happens next. Even while within the enchantment of the vision, he passes through the open door. In an instant's flash he finds himself there, unaware of having traveled there. Projection: even while going nowhere from his prison cell, his are the Halls of Heaven.

> At once I was in the Spirit, and lo, a throne stood in Heaven, with one seated on the throne! (Rev. 4.2)

From that point on he's in a fantastic virtual reality.

Synchronicity

Is it coincidental that on our final jaunt through psychicspace we find synchronicity? It is a holistic summation of what the greater world is and what it does.

Carl Jung coined the term *synchronicity* in *Structure And Dynamics Of The Psyche*, calling it a *"meaningful coincidence"* between two or more patently unconnected events "where something other than the probability of chance is involved." Jung, a clinical psychiatrist, led to deep spirituality by his inclinations and the psyches of his patients, of course saw that truth. These are not unconnected events; synchronicities are operating evidence of the underlying spiritual structure of creation.

In *flow*, stuff happens. Chance is transcended. Synchronicity occurs easily because all phenomena are but aspects of a single larger whole. In the HoloCosmic Universe all is one. Desire and fulfillment share a common destiny. They are attracted to one another, being one and the same of the larger body of the whole. Response is natural law.

Space, time, and causality, as commonly conceptualized by the human ego-system, simply do not exist. They are not the reality. All things are an outpressing of the one eternal essence. Always, *all* things work together in seamless harmony for good. We simply term it synchronicity when we notice it. Now we can discuss it.

These are the very discoveries the rigorous research of quantum physics has recently uncovered. Every level of creation interdependently flows in the give and take of expansion and contraction. The fate of galaxies is interdependent with the fate of atoms.

All eternity is webbed at every point to all eternity. Synchronicity is when we see it.

An Angel Will Arrange It

Abraham. Isaac. A Slave. We tour this scene in chapter 4, "Divination"; here we marvel over another facet of its richness. When it comes time for Abraham, seed of all the Jewish race, to go the way of the flesh, the miracle child of his old age is yet unmarried. If Abraham is indeed to become the father of a nation more numerous than the stars gleaming in the desert sky, it is to be through Isaac. Abraham is concerned. This is a pivotal time in the destiny of the nation, yet but this man and his son.

And it is not just about grandkids. He does not want Isaac to marry a Canaanite woman amidst whom he dwells. This would dilute the ethnic sanctity of his line, diluting to nothingness the fulfillment of the promise God has made. And Isaac himself *must not* go to the land of his blood. He has kinfolk there. He would be welcomed, delighted, and easily prospered. He would loose touch with this land they sojourn in now, forgetting the promise that it shall be his.

The solution? Bring in a woman from home. Then the insularity that Isaac, his wife, and family – as aliens in the land – would experience would build the Jewish line.

So he calls his trustworthy majordomo and charges him:

"Take my sack in your right hand, and make a vow that you mean.

"Swear by the Lord, the God of Heaven and of Earth, that you will not take a wife for my son from the daughters of the Canaanites, among whom I dwell, but will go to my country and to my kin, and take a wife for my son Isaac." (Gen. 24.2-4)

Whooh! Whooh!! Whooh!!! Whooh!!!! The servant asks some questions before he swears such a powerful oath!

Abraham answers his objections. If no one will consent to marry Isaac, sight unseen, then he has discharged the duty of his oath. But under no circumstance is he to allow Isaac to enter the lands of Mesopotamia. His job is but to make the effort.

Abraham abides in confident assurance, knowing God will fulfill his promise, assuring his servant,

"The Lord ... will send his angel before you, and you shall take a wife for my son from there." (Gen. 24.7)

Now the man holds his balls and swears the solemn oath. He prepares and departs for Nahor, in Mesopotamia.

The hand of the Cosmic arranges all thing. He journeys to the city, arriving at evening, when the women go out to draw water. He turns inward to God:

"O Great God, ... grant me success today, I pray, and show steadfast love to my master, Abraham." (Gen. 24.12)

And in this contact he prays for a divinatory sign of success:

"Behold, I am standing by the spring of water, and the fair daughters of the men of the city are coming out to draw water. Let the maiden to whom I shall say, 'Pray let down your jar that I may drink,' and who shall say, 'Drink, and I will water your camels,' let her be the one whom thou hast appointed for thy servant Isaac." (Gen. 24.13-14)

Before he is done whispering the prayer in his heart, behold, beautiful Rebekah appears, a flower fair to look upon, a virgin, had by no man. She approaches the spring, and all goes into fulfillment *exactly* as the man utters it.

And Rebekah ends up going home with him. Or do you think this is all coincidence?

From The Pit To The Palace

In spite of the dominating dream action, the story of *Joseph*, is above all a story celebrating synchronicity. Mercy, how God works!

The chain of events that places Joseph in command of all the riches of the opulent kingdom of Egypt – at a crucial juncture in history – begins in the land of Canaan, with an insular family of aliens. Coincidence through coincidence, from the dastardly effects of petty evil though the competent abilities of Joseph's work, leads him over the course of twenty-two years from the pit to the palace.

Joseph ends up as the true savior of the Jewish race, but it had to be arranged. His route is marked with outrageous episodes and periods of both good and ill fortune, all seemingly spinning in and spinning out on the circumstances of hap.

But once you get the big picture, you see it all happens for a purpose. How marvelous the mysterious ways of God!

Joseph is the favored son of the favored wife of the four wives of Jacob. Joseph is Rachel's fair son, pretty, intelligent, and sensitive. And Jacob rewards his pretty son, so much like himself, with a coat of many colors. The less cultured brothers despise him.

In this setting Joseph dreams of lordship. He shares his dream:

"The sun, the moon, and eleven stars were bowing down to me." (Gen. 37.9)

This infuriates them. They will *not* bow down to Joseph!

Thus Joseph's not too innocent manhood is fired off with the mystical messages of dominion and lordship when he is but a seventeen year old youth. Goaded by this dream, the brothers plot his death at swordpoint. And they would have accomplished it, had not two things intervened.

Number one, Reuben, sissified guy #2, would hear none of it. So, in the finest style of rationalization, instead of the direct and messy evil of bloodshed, they structure things where Joseph's death will occur by default. They strip him of his clothes in the hot desert sun and throw him into a deep pit. He will die soon enough. Then they sit down to enjoy their beer and bread.

Number two, another bout of rationalization sets in. They realize they have an asset. What if they can accomplish their *true* purpose, getting rid of Joseph, yet profit on it after all? As an added benefit, then they will have no guilt at all for his blood, since they aren't killing him. So they sell him to Ishmaelite slave buccaneers. Nevertheless, since they can't tell Jacob they've sold the son closest to his heart, they deceive him by telling him he was killed in a boar attack. They bring the cherished coat of many colors, which they themselves have ripped and stained with goat's blood, back home as proof. Thus they crush their father with the affliction of losing the son whom he loved the most.

Meanwhile, it just so happens that one Potiphar, an officer in Pharaoh's army, is out shopping for a slave that day, and, seeing the goodly youth, picks him up. Joseph's natural genius quickly shows up, and he rises to the position of overseer of Potiphar's entire estate. It is thus he has privilege to the chambers of Potiphar's house.

Then a phenomenon not too uncommon against the truly beautiful – desire, envy, and fear attack. Potiphar's wife, dripping with fantasies of the playboy Joseph, is making amorous passes at him. One fateful day when they are alone, she throws herself passionately all over him, rubbing furiously and begging for it. The upright and intelligent Joseph will have absolutely none of it. He exits posthaste.

You've heard it said, "Hell knows no fury like a woman scorned"? She is *humiliated!* and schemes retaliation. She calls her husband and rails off in an award performance that Joseph was trying to seduce her when they found themselves alone. Joseph is picked right up, roughed up, and thrown down into the dark abyss of Egypt's prison. What bad luck! What injustice! What an unfortunate turn of events! All for a purpose.

And that purpose is so that some years later, Joseph will be there when two dreaming slaves of Pharaoh are tossed in. And because he's risen in the ranks of prison life to chief orderly, he sees their sad faces. And he interprets their dreams. All for a purpose.

So that he will be available and chosen when, two years later, Pharaoh is scouring the kingdom in search of an interpreter. Thirteen years have passed since Joseph was carted cuffed and chained out of Canaan. All for a purpose.

And, given his opportunity, Joseph's brilliance, not only in interpreting the dream of the seven years of good fortune followed by seven years of bad, but in making the crafty suggestion that Pharaoh choose a man "discreet and wise" (Gen. 41.33) to accomplish the plan the dream suggests will ensure Egypt's prosperity during the coming evil years, lifts him in one day from the dirt of the prison floors to the polished halls of the palace. Joseph is immediately given the job, royal riches, and the privilege that goes with such a position. All for a purpose.

During the oppressive famine all the peoples of the world journey to Egypt for food. There they see Joseph, who is in charge of the foodstuffs. And this includes the families of Canaan, including his very own family, the brothers who sold him into slavery those decades long ago and their father, Jacob. So that Joseph can refuge the still small, fragile, and exposed line of Abraham.

Joseph saw it. Nine years after being lifted by Pharaoh's dream, twenty-two years after his brothers sell him away, his brothers are bowing before this mighty Egyptian like unto Pharaoh in petition and fear. They are even more dismayed when Joseph reveals his identity. Reckoning is at hand... They think.

But Joseph does not have that heart. Instead he calls them gently near and assures them,

> "Do not be distressed, or angry with yourselves, because you sold me here; *for God sent me before you to preserve life.* For the famine has been in the land these two years; and there are yet five years in which there will be neither plowing nor harvest. *God sent me before you* to preserve for you a remnant on Earth, and to keep alive for you many survivors." (Gen. 45.5-7)

Joseph says it,

> "So it was not *you* who sent me here, but *God.*" (Gen. 45.8)

Amazing, isn't it? In their effort to take life, Joseph is given to preserving life. Joseph sees the purpose. Through a treacherous route filled with intrigue, jealously, and hatred, alternately with times of prestige and prosperity, Joseph is in a position to provide for the survival of the Jewish race. History is at a critical juncture. It could have gone the other way, but the race survives.

Cocooned in the lap of Egypt, breeding in her choicest fields, they thrive. They enter Egypt – a family... They leave – a nation.

The Dimensions Of Psi

This is a dazzling story. The glitter of its obvious points allows people to generally miss some more subtle points of depth. We will enjoy ourselves here a little longer.

Romance In Tel el Amarna. Ostensibly Joseph is sent ahead to Egypt to ensure the survival of the Jewish race. However, the reality of the matter is that, though there may have been a famine, all the world but Egypt was not destroyed. Had the Jewish family not moved to Egypt during this period, they may or may not have actually died out. In fact, the famine may not be historical, either. Not that it matters.

We're not dealing with history here, but with myth, epic, romance. In the hearts of the Jewish race Joseph does provide for their survival during this crucial life-threatening juncture. They come through hard times and endure. Their mythology would idealize this trait – they've needed it so often – and it has indeed worked. The facts of history offer ample evidence they are survivors. This is the story. That's the way it was – that's how important it was – like a story told on a movie screen today. It is certainly not "real," but that's neither the point nor the effect.

Oh, the dimensions of psi!

The Workings Of Magic. It's amazing how it works out, isn't it? Joseph could never have planned it so well.

It is not about taking advantage of others... Nor of ensuring "justice," which is just a legitimized cover for revenge, for there is no unjustice in God's world. Joseph never expresses bitter or resentful feelings over the injustices that are perpetrated on him. In fact, in case you haven't noticed, Potiphar and his wife are never mentioned again in the story. Though Joseph has just spent several years in the pen from their unjust envy, they have no meaning to him.

He loves his brothers and provides for all eleven of their families with the wealth that he's found. There is never a single hint of retaliation, but from his first encounters, opulent blessings.

It is not about the blessing and the curse, or its manifestations as good and evil, love and hate, plenty and penury, freedom and servitude, discretion and naivete... though Joseph surely encounters these along his way.

Check this out. Joseph's fortunes continue to accelerate during the hard times of the great depression. The time all the world buckles under the famine is the time of Joseph's greatest dominion.

The story of Joseph is about dreaming... and *knowing* it is God.

It is about walking through the opposing columns of experience, centred all the while. Joseph is young, rich, and successful. But he has his times of struggle. He keeps everlastingly at it, and it comes to him. There is justice in this world. Even beyond what man can do.

It is about doing what is before you to do, and doing it well. Joseph assiduously employs the gifts he has, exerting himself with cheerful productive efforts in every case in which he finds himself. And he therefore rises above his brothers at home. He rises to the top in Potiphar's enterprise. He rises to the top of the prisoners' ranks. And then he is translated in a minute to the stratosphere at the right hand of Pharaoh's wealth.

It is about readiness. At his time Joseph has been years in the dank of the prison. He's so filthy and only partially kempt they have to bath and shave him before he's fit to stand in the presence of Pharaoh. But, though he may have been in prison, he didn't take the easy or the hopeless way out. He's not been rotting away. He's ready in the instant he's summoned. He interprets Pharaoh's dreams.

It is about management. Joseph has incredible foresight, seeing what others do not see – essential quality number one. He sees the bad years coming. But he also *acts* on what he learns – essential quality number two. Superior knowledge by itself may be a blessing, but it serves no greater good unless it evolves into superior action. When you get right down to it, action tells the tale – you reveal your consciousness in the actions you take. Joseph plans to make advantageous service of what he knows, and he follows his plans. We see the results. He prospers continuously in good times and in bad.

It is about *following your dream*, knowing it is given you by God. Action can be counted on – "For every action there is an opposite and equal reaction." Our own attitudes and actions determine our destiny. Synchronicity works it out. The future lurks indiscernible to the profane. The seer, however, who *acts* on the dream, waits with good humor and consistent application for its appearance into reality.

It is about allowing God to handle the details, simply accomplishing what is needful to accomplish his plan. It's a HoloCosm, after all. This is synchronicity.

In The Very Lap Of Pharaoh

Pharaoh's Daughter. The connections and the problems between the titans *Pharaoh* and *Moses* start early. So does the deception. In the beginning, however, only Pharaoh is a titan. Moses is charmed.

The Israelite people may have started out with one man and his son; they may have entered Egypt as one man, his sons, and their families; but they breed prolifically. Over the course of years they swell to such numbers that Pharaoh perceives them as a threat. So he commands that all male children born to Hebrew women be cast into the Nile. Over time, this should provide a final solution.

But Moses' mother breaks the law. She conceals her pregnancy and conceals her newborn son. But at three months the boy can no longer be hidden. So she lovingly makes a watery carriage of bulrushes for the baby, places it among the reeds, and does all she can do – and the greatest thing she can do – she trusts to Providence.

And then, amazing synchronicity! Moses, of all the babies – and great numbers are killed – not only survives the Nile, but is found and taken home *by Pharaoh's very daughter!* Pharaoh's not thinking. Men will alter their steel strong decrees and destinies swayed by the wishes of the women they love. Of course they know it is one of the Hebrew babies, but, conveniently, royal decrees don't apply to the royal house. "Moses" is the name his Egyptian mother-princess, chooses for the boy. We have no record of his Hebrew name.

Another synchronicity. As you know, wealthy women have assistance with their children. Who do you think she chooses to nurse and love the child? A lady of the Hebrew class... *His very mother!*

How could Pharaoh know? It is the very training in the mysteries and familiarity in the face of royalty that Moses receives in the lap of Pharaoh which equips him to master the monarch some 80 years down the web of time.

Do you think God is purposeful when he writes this orchestration of synchronicities into the Bible? Isn't God saying he is in all things with this passage? Or do you think the drama of synchronicities is just coincidental?

Psi Sets It Up

Philip. A Man Of State. This is a particularly revealing story regarding synchronicity because it reveals its inner workings. We see in this story just how God arranges the events of our lives.

This whole event commences with psi. Arranging the synchronicity behind the scenes, an angel whispers to Philip one day,

"Get up and head south, to the road that goes down from Jerusalem to Gaza." (Acts 8.26)

He does as he is inspired to do, and, lo! he meets someone there. And how does Philip recognize the man? By another psi event. He sees a wealthy man riding by in a chariot, but, that's not significant. He's seeing plenty of people on the road. But now,

The Spirit says to Philip,

"Go up and join this chariot." (Acts. 8.29)

He does as he is inspired to do. Philip opens the conversation with a relevant question, asking the man if he understands the passages of Isaiah that he is reading. The man frankly admits he does not.

Amazing synchronicity! The Spirit has put Philip, who just happens to have the insight the man needs, in the same chariot at the same time! Philip opens up the scriptures. The man is enthused.

This is when they come to a pool of water where Philip baptizes him and teleports away.

Pretty paranormal.

Peter And The Profane

In the early days of the apostles' ministry *Peter* stays for a while with his friend in a seaside estate. One day, while he's waiting for dinner, he slides up to the rooftop and slips into prayer. His prayer is now powerful in its own right. He drifts into trance.

We visit his dream in more detail in the chapter on dreams. Here our purpose holds only to work with his dream in conjunction with synchronicity.

The heavens open up, and a cloud much like a giant white sheet mysteriously descends onto Earth with its cargo, a teeming populace of animals, reptiles, and birds.

Then the unembodied magnificent voice of God commands the hungry Peter:
"Peter, rise, kill, and eat." (Acts 10.13)

But Peter – Ah, don't we have difficulty breaking the barriers of childhood programming? *Even when inspired by God!* – argues against the injunction, *even though he knows it is God* issuing it!

"No, Lord; for I have never eaten anything that is common or unclean!" (Acts 10.14)

Peter and the Lord go back and forth three times like this.

Then the sheet suddenly folds back up into the high heavens and Peter snaps out of the trance. Peter wakes estranged, perplexing the significance of the dream. And even at this moment, strangers come asking for him.

Peter is alerted about the men by the prompting of the spirit. Amazing timing!

Cornelius is hungry for the spiritual food Peter can dispense. He comes asking. In the very moments Peter is struggling with the dream's meaning, the Spirit tells him to go down, meet the men, and accompany them as they wish.

God does not tell him they are gentiles. He sees that when he meets them. But he has already been told to accompany them. Peter now understands the meaning of the dream. The next day Peter sets out on the road with them.

But is this synchronicity?

As insiders to the full drama, it's impossible to say that the dream timed just with the arrival of the three strangers is coincidental. Behind the scenes we see Providence arranging and causing the chain of physical and metaphysical events, meshing them with consummate timing, to further Spirit's own end, in this case the spread of the Good News of Jesus' teachings.

And so Peter and Cornelius meet. As the Lord purposes, events unfold. Peter opens his mouth and teaches. Tradition tells that indeed Peter accomplishes mighty work for the Lord in the expanded role he is led to believe is his.

Do you believe this is coincidental?

How about this?... Can you believe when it happens in your life?

Amazing Things

Our final jaunt through psychicspace has brought us some amazing things. Who would have thought it?... Astrology, necromancy, and teleportation are psychic gifts confirmed in the Bible! *Everything psi is synchronicity!* We recognize this by calling it *psichronicity*.

The multitudes Jesus comes to don't know it. They don't believe in astrology. No one but the wise wizards discerns the starry message broadcast in the skies.

Necromancy, or communication/visitation with the dead, is excellently presented in the movie *Ghost,* starring Whoopi Goldberg, Demi Moore, and Patrick Swayze. But it isn't a new thing, either. Samuel, also, has something to say to one of the still living. And like Swayze in the movie, the process is initiated through a medium.

Bodily teleportation, such as Daniel, Jesus, and Philip practice is evidence of adepthood. Then there is the teleportation of projection, which anyone familiar with what went down in the 1960's understands. This is the teleportation that Ezekiel and John favor.

Synchronicity is the most common first manifestation of psi in a person's life. They begin to notice *coincidences which are not coincidental.* These are the first real feelings that psi is active in your life. It makes for exciting times, early on the path and late. Sometimes it all unravels in the course of a small episode, like with Philip and the eunuch. Sometimes it is far far grander, as in the case of Joseph the Magical Dreamer. Every psi occurrence, in the Bible and out, has an attribute of synchronicity to it.

Going Places

———··•··———

O h, we've marveled over many a psychicspace adventure of Biblical lore. We've seen things we never even dreamed existed, and poked fun at the coverup collusion we've uncovered. We've developed spiritually along the way, for what we learn to recognize, we become. We've had a good time, and we're all ready to get back home. But while I've still got your attention, I'd like to say I really enjoyed being your host on this adventure.

Each of the various excursions through the psychic domains of esp, channeling, dreams, divination, magic, astrology, necromancy, teleportation, and synchronicity were chosen to present the information in the Bible to you in an entertaining environment. We'd love to hear your comments.

You can correspond with us by email, phone, fax, snailmail, and any other technology not now invented but which will be on line during our lifetime. We especially invite you to leave us your email address, and we'll periodically send you free articles, announcements, and news. Also, there's an open-minded psychic discussion group meeting at our web site; check in there.

Ted Martin

psychicspace.com*pany*

7051 Hwy 70S #145

Nashville TN 37221

615-662-4987, 888-*psi-is-it* / fax: 615-662-9152

info@psychicspace.com

http://www.psychicspace.com

When you contact us, let us know you liked *Psychic & Paranormal Phenomena In The Bible: The True* Story! and we'll send you back a *FREE* special goodie!

As a companion to this book, we also offer courses with workbooks, videos, and audios. You can learn to develop your own psychic abilities according to the wisdom discerned It's safe, sound, and vividly exciting! Request *your* free details.

Also, if you liked the poetry of the dedication, "I Will Love One Woman Only," and the benediction, "1311," let us know. We'd love to share some others with you.

We also offer spiritually-oriented adventure tours to many of the world's ancient and modern mystic sites, such as the American Southwest, Cancún, Oaxaca, México, Machu Picchu, the Andes, Peru, the pyramids and beyond in Egypt, Celtic Stonehenge in Britain, sites of the Arthurian and Grail romances of Glastonbury,

England, Wales, Scotland, Germany, France and more, the Holy Land, Tibet, India, and beyond! *Talk about a boost to your spiritual life!* Contact us and we'll rush you *free* a current calendar with full descriptions. *Hope you can join us!*

So the tour is over, we're on our way home, and we're about to land....

There is a question I must ask. Now that you have engaged yourself in this exotic escapade of psychic and paranormal phenomena, what are you going to do when you get back home? Are you going back only with perhaps a bit more knowledge and insight filed into some drawer in your mind, with no impact on your life and affairs? That might be missing the point.

"Today – You Can Do Magic"

Let's reflect a moment, bringing again to our conscious awareness what most Spiritually inclined folks, and even most religiously inclined folks, hold unquestioned: the Bible is an eternal living document, written for our spiritual guidance and inspiration. At every age... It *is* for us *today.*

The division commences. Some people believe these books contain the whole of God's message to humanity, pure, his final visitations to Earth.

But it is what it purports to be, a teaching about the spiritual mystical life. The Bible is a textbook to the sublime portals. We are still as essentially human and divine as we were over the duration of the 1300 individual years of authorship it took to create the book in its present form. It is offered as a sure font to nourish, instruct, guide, and inspire every human who comes within the compass of its effect.

That being the case, this book says *you can do magic today.* There is no other conclusion possible. We believe Jesus knows what he's talking about when he says:

> "The things that I do, you can do also. Hey, even *greater* things!" (Jn. 1.50)

Are we to believe him or not? What do you think?

Jesus says, "*You* feed them," indicating that you also possess the seemingly magical ability to feed vast needs at magic's touch.

Jesus coaxes Peter to demonstrate the absolute power of *faith.* A lesson the firewalker or the wavewalker can never evade again.

Spiritual life is eternal.

God does not disappear from Earth 2,000 years ago. God's seeker-adepts do not lift from the plains, valleys, and mountains of Earth 2,000 years ago. If anything, these evolutionary humans are becoming more common. To say that the Bible is working in imparting spiritual poise to succeeding generations in greater numbers is but to affirm the ongoing natural process of evolution we see around us, the purpose for which it is created.

Welcome To Your Mystical Nature

Here is a more challenging question, though. *Can you believe psi when it happens in* your *life?*

You can learn. It starts with belief and desire. Belief should no longer be a problem. You have seen too many people of different persuasions, in too many psi experiences to believe either that psi comes only to special people or that it is somehow inherently wrong. It can come to you.

Read more, associate with others of like heart – pray together and apart. It starts with synchronicities in your life.

We are all involved in this awakening... What we learn to see we open to demonstrate in our own spiritual adventures. It happens one person at a time – person-to-person. Share your enthusiasm with others. Talk passionately about these vitally important revolutionary ideas. You are one of the select chosen to reveal the great work... Speak as Spirit commands. Accept your charge!

At your time, God will commission you. Your task is but to ready yourself, developing with devoted study, exercise, and application along your intuitively perceived path of contribution. When you come to acceptance of your divine commissioning, *what power your actions will express!* Power that is not yours.

There is a way to get that certitude and that accomplishment. God commissions Moses in meditation; God commissions Isaiah in meditation; God commissions Jeremiah in meditation; God commissions Jesus in meditation. Meditation is the site of the paranormal. Meditate and know what yours is.

Even with the synchronicity that gets Moses the finest education and magical training the world offers, grooming him for the mission he is to assume, God has all things arranged to serve your purpose. But waken to the burning bush within. Even while you enjoy every moment of the process, you are developing into something greater, all the while accomplishing God's purpose. This is the glory of the Lord!

We've taken ourselves over the high ground and the low ground, the common and the exotic, of psychic and paranormal phenomena in the Bible and find that it's all magic. And though the title of the book is about that, the substance of the book is about *you*. The Eternal never changes, but only when we awaken ourselves to the second sight do we *see* it. Welcome to your mystical nature.

It shows up first in synchronicity. Pray. Amazing things happen. Watch. And though the tour is over, you are going places.

Unending

1311

Faire Ladie, aye, we shal meete another dai,

Farre, farre frome this merrie olde Inglande,

Some thousands moones times XXVIII sonnes awai;

In a newe worlde I shal offer ye myne hande.

No falcone shal I flie for playe and sporte,

Tho ye shal stil your loue for horses shew.

And chiluarie may not so common bee in that dai's court,

Or sweete language — these counted may bee that ages' woe.

Some things changeth, and some things neuer,

And some there bee better groweth — lyke your beautie muche!

And Wisedome telleth true loue's foreuer...

So, departing embraced in thine sweete armes, I sayeth suche:

  Ye shal recognize mee, the wai I seeketh to win

  Your loue that dai with poesie agayne.

Ted Martin

Appendix

Books Of The Bible

Books of the Old Testament

Book	Abbreviation	No. Chapters
1.Genesis	Gen.	50
2.Exodus	Ex.	40
3.Leviticus	Lev.	27
4.Numbers	Num.	36
5.Deuteronomy	Dt.	34
6.Joshua	Jos.	24
7.Judges	Jg.	21
8.Ruth	Ru.	4
9.1 Samuel	1 Sam.	31
10.2 Samuel	2 Sam.	24
11.1 Kings	1 Kg.	22
12.2 Kings	2 Kg.	25
13.1 Chronicles	1 Chr	29
14.2 Chronicles	2 Chr.	36
15.Ezra	Ezra	10
16.Nehemiah	Neh.	13
17.Esther	Est.	10
18.Job	Job	42
19.Psalms	Ps.	150
20.Proverbs	Pro.	31
21.Ecclesiastes	Ec.	12
22.Song of Solomon	S. of S.	8
23.Isaiah	Is.	66
24.Jeremiah	Jer.	52
25.Lamentations	Lam.	5
26.Ezekiel	Ezek.	48
27.Daniel	Dan.	12
28.Hosea	Hos.	14
29.Joel	Jl.	3
30.Amos	Am.	9
31.Obadiah	Ob.	1
32.Jonah	Jon.	4
33.Micah	Mic.	7
34.Nahum	Nah.	3

35.Habakkuk	Hab.	3
36.Zephaniah	Zeph.	3
37.Haggai	Hag.	2
38.Zechariah	Zech.	14
39.Malachi	Mal.	4

Books of the New Testament

Book	Abbreviation	No. Chapters
1.Matthew	Mt.	28
2.Mark	Mk.	16
3.Luke	Lk.	24
4.John	Jn.	21
5.Acts	Acts	28
6.Romans	Rom.	16
7.1 Corinthians	1 Cor.	16
8.2 Corinthians	2 Cor.	13
9.Galatians	Gal.	6
10.Ephesians	Eph.	6
11.Philippians	Phil.	4
12.Colossians	Col.	4
13.1 Thessalonians	1 Th.	5
14.2 Thessalonians	2 Th.	3
15.1 Timothy	1 Tim.	6
16.2 Timothy	2 Tim.	4
17.Titus	Tit.	3
18.Philemon	Philem.	1
19.Hebrews	Heb.	13
20.James	Jas.	5
21.1 Peter	1 Pet.	5
22.2 Peter	2 Pet.	3
23.1 John	1 Jn.	5
24.2 John	2 Jn.	1
25.3 John	3 Jn.	1
26.Jude	Jude	1
27.Revelation	Rev.	22

Total Number of Books in the Bible

Old Testament 39
New Testament 27
   Total 66

Index

sensitive, 5, 14, 17, 30, 46, 57, 68, 69, 110, 138, 188, 225, 241, 262
sensitives, 133, 167, 177, 233
sensitivity, 40, 107, 110, 114, 127, 130, 138, 155, 156
seven, 45, 101, 102, 106, 109, 110, 116, 125, 137, 156, 193, 200, 208, 210, 223, 228, 230, 237, 259, 263
seventh, 136, 210, 219
sex, 39, 59, 108, 196, 238
sexism, 208
Shadrach, 229-231
shaman, 129, 206, 225, 228, 248
Shemaiah, 72
showmanship, 203, 236
sight, 14, 21, 31, 37, 45, 46, 56, 76, 81, 108, 123, 132, 137, 147, 163, 170, 187, 198, 243, 257, 258, 261, 271
sign, 14, 20, 40, 43, 78, 88, 97, 139, 154, 159, 160, 163-165, 168-175, 184-186, 189, 190, 209, 226, 232, 247, 257, 261
signs, 15, 17, 30, 58, 78, 91, 153-155, 163, 172, 174, 203, 224, 232, 233, 245, 246
silver, 62, 64, 133, 134, 158, 166, 198, 203, 236
similarity, 80, 95, 196, 199-201, 212
simulcognition, 16, 38, 46
Sinai, 62, 197, 221, 247
sixth sense, 16-18, 37, 38
skeptical, 194
sleep, 58, 71, 95-97, 105, 122, 138, 141, 189, 232, 235
solitude, 216, 238
Solomon, 34, 43, 44, 70-72, 93, 96, 103, 124-128, 140, 151, 152, 277
song, 58, 59, 64, 101, 123, 277
soothsayer, 19-21, 77
sorcerer, 19-21, 199, 215-217, 221
sorcery, 20, 192, 199
soul, 13, 15, 17, 32, 33, 39, 49, 72, 91, 99, 122, 126, 191, 197, 210, 216, 239, 243, 250, 251
soul travel, 251
sower, 235
spell, 25, 44, 198, 205, 217, 219, 255
spells, 68

spiral, 177, 197, 221
Spirit, 15, 18, 21, 23, 24, 27-29, 31, 35, 42, 44, 45, 49-51, 54-58, 62, 65, 74, 82, 84, 86, 88-91, 93, 96-98, 113, 129, 139, 146-151, 162, 171, 172, 178, 181, 183-185, 188, 192, 193, 196, 201, 204, 213, 238, 240, 243, 246, 248, 249, 251, 254, 255, 257-259, 266, 267, 271
spiritual, 1, 5, 13-15, 17, 18, 23, 24, 26, 29-31, 34, 38, 39, 41, 43, 46, 49-52, 54, 57, 68, 69, 71, 74, 78, 88, 90-92, 96, 97, 100, 101, 109, 110, 114-116, 121, 122, 125, 128, 129, 133, 135, 142-147, 149-151, 153-155, 177, 185, 187, 189-192, 195, 207, 221, 227, 235, 236, 238, 239, 243-245, 251, 252, 255, 257-260, 267, 270, 271
spirituality, 13, 15, 122, 129, 139, 247, 258, 260
spoil, 67, 224
stage, 28, 31, 61, 67, 79, 82, 101, 102, 126, 148, 149, 192, 195, 197, 207, 217, 236, 237, 246
star, 86, 237, 244, 245, 247, 248, 251
stars, 16, 101, 107, 244-248, 260, 262
stimulus, 191, 206
stones, 14, 16, 48, 62, 111, 115, 153, 154, 160, 161, 167, 170, 173, 176, 181-183, 185, 186, 189, 217, 218, 224
stories, 13-16, 23, 25, 27, 32, 46, 48, 55, 81, 82, 90, 99, 100, 103, 112, 115, 119, 131, 143, 163, 178, 209, 223, 234, 256
storm, 85, 236
story, 1, 2, 9, 11, 15, 18, 25, 27, 28, 39, 40, 42, 45-47, 50, 53, 54, 58-61, 63, 68, 69, 74, 79-81, 85, 101, 102, 109, 115-121, 123, 124, 126, 128, 131, 135, 138, 140, 141, 144-146, 150, 153, 155, 157-159, 169, 170, 173, 177, 178, 183, 185, 187, 188, 194, 202, 204, 220, 227, 232, 234, 237, 246, 247, 253, 254, 256-258, 261, 264, 266, 269
subconscious, 29, 55, 96, 195, 196

Resources

This is not intended to be a comprehensive resource directory. This section just offers a few hints and a few addresses. Our main source is the Bible, in its various editions.

Above all, follow your own interests. If you read different versions of the Bible, along with a variety of study aids, your understanding will expand exponentially. If you research into psychic phenomena, your understanding will mushroom. Together... WOW!

Look into the Religious, Spirituality, and New Age sections of your conventional bookstores for current books. Examine the indices and shelves of your larger libraries for unbelievably available materials. Antiquarian bookstores can source the little known or limited distribution books your reading and interests encounter. Become friends with metaphysical bookstores to stay abreast of late breaking spirituality flavored psi.

psychicspace.com*pany* offers a variety of spirit-centered books, including a wide array of Bibles in a variety of languages. Please contact us, we'd love to send you free information.

Become friends with spiritual pursuits, and – since your consciousness manifests – the spirituality you seek will flower in your life amidst your companions and your activities.

****

Books

Chopra, Deepak. *The Way Of The Wizard: Twenty Spiritual Lessons In Creating The Life You Want.* New York: Harmony Books, 1995.

Harper's Bible Dictionary. Eds. Paul J. Achtemeier et al. with the Society of Biblical Literature. San Francisco: Harper & Row, 1985.

Martin, Ted. *The Grail And The Tarot Correspondence.*

Sky, Michael. *Dancing With The Fire: Transforming Limitation Through Firewalking.* Santa Fe NM: Bear: 1989.

Talbot, Michael. *The Holographic Universe.* New York: Harper Perennial: 1991.

Psychical Organizations

Contact these organizations for information on psi, their research, their activities, journals, publications, and other materials available for your information and development.

Anomalous Cognition Program
University of Amsterdam
Roetersstraat 15
1018 WB Amsterdam
The Netherlands
    http://info.psy.uva.nl/Psychonomie/research/anomal.html

Association for Research & Enlightenment (ARE)
Sixty-Eighth & Atlantic Avenue
POB 656
Virginia Beach Virginia 23451-0656
    800-723-1112

Centre for Parapsychological Studies
Valeriani 39
40134 Bologna
Italy
    +39(0)51.549410
    http://www.sextant.it/city/gate/sextant/csp.html

Cognitive Sciences Laboratory
330 Cowper Street #200
Palo Alto California 94301
USA
    415.327.2007

Consciousness Research Laboratory
University of Nevada, Las Vegas
4505 Maryland Parkway, Box 454009
Las Vegas Nevada 89154-4009
USA

psychicspace.com*pany*
7051 Hwy 70S #145
Nashville TN 37221
USA
 615-662-4987, 888-*psi-is-it* / fax: 615-646-9152
 http://www.psychicspace.com

Institute Of Noetic Sciences
475 Gate Five Road #300
Sausalito California 94965
USA
 415-331-5650

Koestler Parapsychology Unit
University of Edinburgh
7 George Square
Edinburgh, Scotland
EH8 9JZ
UK

Mind-Matter Unification Project
Cambridge University
Madingley Road
Cambridge CB3 0HE
UK
 http://www.phy.cam.ac.uk/www/physics.html

Parapsychological Association, Inc.
PO Box 797
Fairhaven MA 02719-0700
USA
 parapsyc@world.std.com

Princeton Engineering Anomalies Research (PEAR) Lab
C-131, Engineering Quadrangle
Princeton University
Princeton, NJ 08544
USA
   (609) 258-5950
   http://www.princeton.edu/~rdnelson/pear.html

Rhine Research Center Institute For Parapsychology
402 North Buchanan Boulevard
Durham, North Carolina 27701
USA
   919-688-8241

Rosicrucian Order, AMORC – Worldwide
Château d'Omonville
Scribe I.N.T.
27110 - LE TREMBLAY
FRANCE

Rosicrucian Order, AMORC – United States & Canada
1342 Naglee Ave
San Jose California 95191
USA
   408-947-3600
   http://www.rosicrucian.org

Rosicrucian Fellowship
2222 Mission Avenue
Oceanside, California 92054
USA
   619-757-6600 / fax: 619-721-3806
   http://www.cts.com:80/~rosfshp/index.html

Scientific & Medical Network
Lesser Halings Tilehouse Lane
 Denham Nr. Uxbridge
Middlesex UB9 5DG
England
    +44(0)1895-835818
    100114.1637@compuserve.com

Silva International
1407 Calle Del Norte
P.O. Box 2249
Laredo, TX 78044-2249
USA
    (210) 722-6391, (800) 545-6463
    silvaintl@border.net

Society for Psychical Research
49 Marloes Road
Kensington
London
W8 6lA
England
    Phone: 0171-937-8984

About The Author

"Who Is This 'Minister-At-Large^{tm}' Guy Anyway?"

He is Ted Martin, maverick mystic-scholar. He's a fortyish spiritual seeker, writer, adventurer, and minister, who currently writes his primary return address in Nashville Tennessee. He hails from a large Polish family, and loves four children of his own.

He has a *magna cum laude* Bachelor's in English Literature, a Master's in English Literature; and a Master's with *distinction* in Speech Communication. He was ordained a nondenominational minister in 1987, and has practiced at-large since. Initiated more frequently.

Before the ministry supported his renegade style, he shared parts of this current incarnation first with a career in sales and then as a Communications instructor in the California State University system.

Ted says his greatest influences come from the Arthurian era. He strives to live his life as impeccably honest and in love as Lancelot and Percival.

His passionate purpose is to make successful efforts to enlighten, inspire, and motivate you, the aspiring person, to understand, accept, and engage the spiritual life, with its attendant psychic activity, in your life.

Martin admits: "Many people think I'm way out in my spiritual views. I don't think so. From my studies, experiments, and experience, I find it is through the psychic dimensions that God communicates with humanity. With earnest desire and effort, anyone can open to their own innate psychic gifts. Watching, reading, or talking about ESP, clairvoyance, intuition, telepathy, and the other psychic arts is just the beginning. With a proper understanding, as Jesus says, you can *do* 'great things.' You can experience them in your daily life. This is a spiritual universe.

"I won't deny it. Some seem to have a special knack for it. However, though not everyone can do it equally well, like any art or skill, it is clear that anyone can do it. The most effective aid you'll ever have is meditation, another spiritual skill that can easily be acquired by the hungry heart."

FREE Spiritual Information Request Form

Yes! Ted, please send exciting *FREE* information:

[ ] Books, videos, cassettes, programs you recommend for developing the spiritual and psychical life
[ ] Bibles available in _____ language(s)
[ ] Trips, tours, adventures to the spiritual spots of the world
[ ] Ted, I liked your poetry. Send free info.
[ ] Please include me and _____ in your daily affirming prayer circle
[ ] Other _____

Please PRINT clearly:

Name _____ Phone _____

Address Line #1 _____

Address Line #2 _____

City _____ State _____ Postal Code _____

_____
Country _____

Comments
Phone, mail, fax, or email request to:

psychicspace.company * 7051 Hwy 70S #145 * Nashville TN 37221
615-662-4987, **888**-*psi-is-it* / fax: 615-646-9152
http://www.**psychicspace.com** * info@psychicspace.com

Phone, fax, mail, or email request to:
615-662-4987, 888-*psi-is-it* / fax: 615-646-9152
http://www.psychicspace.com * info@psychicspace.com

Ted Martin
psychicspace.com*pany*
7051 Hwy 70S #145
Nashville TN 37221
USA

FREE Spiritual Information Request Form

Yes! Ted, please send exciting *FREE* information:

[ ] Books, videos, cassettes, programs you recommend for developing the spiritual and psychical life
[ ] Bibles available in _____ language(s)
[ ] Trips, tours, adventures to the spiritual spots of the world
[ ] Ted, I liked your poetry. Send free info.
[ ] Please include me and _____ in your daily affirming prayer circle
[ ] Other _____

Please PRINT clearly:

Name _____

Address Line #1 _____

Address Line #2 _____

City _____ State _____ Postal Code _____

Phone _____

Country _____

Comments _____

Phone, mail, fax, or email request to:

psychicspace.com*pany* * 7351 Hwy 70S #145 * Nashville TN 37221
615-662-4987, **888-***psi-is-it* / fax: 615-646-9152
http://www.psychicspace.com * info@psychicspace.com

Phone, fax, mail, or email request to:
   615-662-4987, 888-*psi-is-it* / fax: 615-646-9152
   http://www.psychicspace.com * info@psychicspace.com

Ted Martin
psychicspace.com*pany*
7051 Hwy 70S #145
Nashville TN 37221
USA